Animal Life
in
Jewish Tradition:
Attitudes and Relationships

Animal Life
in
Jewish Tradition:
Attitudes and Relationships

by
ELIJAH JUDAH SCHOCHET

KTAV PUBLISHING HOUSE, INC.
NEW YORK

Library of Congress Cataloging in Publication Data

Schochet, Elijah Judah.
   Animal life in Jewish tradition.
   Bibliography: p.
   Includes index.
   1. Animals in the Bible. 2. Animals in the Talmud.
3. Animals—Religious aspects—Judaism. I. Title.
BS1199.A57S36   1984   220.8′59   83-12015
ISBN 0-88125-019-8

Blessed are the children
whose parents have taught them
love, reverence,
and deeds of loving-kindness

Abraham Springer	אברהם יעקב בן יוסף
Sarah Springer	שרה בת משה ליב
Harry Greenspan	צבי הירש בן מאיר
Dora Greenspan	דבורה בת אברהם וגיטל ז״ל

Honored by their children
Dr. Sheldon and Judith Springer

In appreciation and affection to our friend
Elijah J. Schochet

TABLE OF CONTENTS

PREFACE

In a great sense, the origin of this volume goes back well over forty years to the West Side of Chicago, where the author, as a child, first fell in love with the world of nature in general, and the world of fauna in particular. Its publication represents the fulfillment of that child's dream to someday author a book about the animal kingdom.

Assisting in both dream-matter interpretation and dream-fulfillment were several formidable scholars whose friendship I treasure—in particular, Rabbi Ephraim Rottenberg, who selflessly shared with me both his formidable scholarship and his gentle wisdom, and professor Amos Funkenstein of UCLA, whose encyclopedic and critical scholarship were of invaluable benefit.

I am likewise grateful to Dr. Moses Goodstine and Professor Moses Tendler of Yeshiva University for making time available from their busy schedules to review portions of the manuscript and for graciously sharing with me both approbations and critiques.

Finally, my thanks to my cousin, Etty Rich, for a thoughtful reading and editing of the manuscript, to my dear wife, Penina, for her careful proofreading, and to Mr. Bernard Scharfstein of KTAV for his special touches of love to this volume.

Three additional debts of gratitude are to be acknowledged:

To the leadership and membership of Congregation Beth Kodesh, whom it has been my privilege to lead and to serve for twenty-three years, since the day of my ordination, for their constant support, encouragement, and respect for scholarship as a rabbinic endeavor. Many themes and insights in this and my other works are the product of their probing questions and thirst for knowledge.

To my own dear family—my wife, Penina, and my children, Daniel Chaim, Joel, and Lisa—for bearing so lovingly and patiently the solitude stemming from my leisure-time scholarly endeavors. They have also frequently opened my eyes and sensitized me to the depth of bonding inherent in living relationships among people, and those between people and animals.

To Almighty God, for having granted to me the privilege of laboring in His vineyard and enjoying both the fruit of His Torah and the pleasant companionship of those "disciples of the wise" in whose lives are reflected the values and ideals of Torah.

For all these blessings I am humbly grateful.

INTRODUCTION

A word is in order concerning the contents of this volume. In discussing and analyzing the place of the animal kingdom in biblical and postbiblical thought, we have chosen not to deal critically with the identification of individual fauna and their species. Although much scholarly work has been contributed in this area, confusion and doubt still exist on many points. Some names of animals appear only once or twice in the entire Bible, bearing no accompanying physical or behavioral characteristics and without any clues as to habitat. In such cases identification is understandably difficult. What, for example, is the *kipoz*,[1] the *zemer*,[2] the *dishon*,[3] or the *eiyim*?[4] What precisely are *achashteranim*?[5]

Confusion surrounds other animals appearing more frequently in Scripture whose identification, long taken for granted, has recently been brought into question. Is the *nesher* an eagle or a griffin-vulture? Were the *barburim avusim* of Solomon's table swans or geese? Is *tzevi* a deer or a gazelle? Were Samson's *shualim* foxes or jackals? Is the *shafan* a rabbit or a coney? In each of these pairs of alternatives the latter choice would seem to be preferable, even though accepted usage is according to the former, although the *shafan*, designated as an animal which chews its cud, may, in reality, be a representative of the *camelida* family.[6]

Difficulties also arise when modern Hebrew incorrectly designates certain contemporary fauna with biblical nomenclature. In many cases etymology is a valuable though not an infallible tool, as is the art of drawing inferences from related languages and comparative studies of ancient and modern translations. Illustrations from ancient carvings also serve as helpful, though not necessarily conclusive, means of identification.

Some fauna which thrived within the geographic borders of Israel during the biblical and mishnaic era are no longer extant in the area, and their true identification may therefore be in doubt. Linnaeus's student, Frederick Hasselquist of Uppsala, who visited

1

the land of the Bible in 1752, was under the impression that no such changes in animal population had taken place. He therefore denied the veracity of scriptural accounts of fauna upon discovering that certain species, notably the lion, were nowhere to be found in eighteenth-century Palestine!

Without becoming involved in technical, zoological, and linguistic speculations, we have relied upon several scholarly works for the identification of fauna, notably F. S. Bodenheimer's *HaHai be-Artsot ha-Mikrah* (2 vols., 1951, 1956) and *Animal and Man in Bible Lands* (1960), and J. Feliks's *The Animal World of the Bible* (1962).

Proper identification of, and familiarity with, biblical fauna enhances one's appreciation of many a scriptural passage.

> Without understanding the agility and fleetness of a Mediterranean fallow deer, who could fully understand this version of the day of redemption: "Then shall the lame man leap like a deer."
>
> Without viewing the regal, prancing gait of the Arabian oryx, who could comprehend: "he has as it were the strength of a wild ox."
>
> And who, having never seen the majestic griffon which dwarfs even the American bald eagle, could truly appreciate: "As an eagle stirs up her nest, broods over her young, spreads abroad her wings, takes them, bears them on her pinions: So the Lord alone did lead him (Jacob) and there is no strange god with him."[7]

But whether or not all of our identifications prove to be accurate is of quite secondary concern. It is the *attitude* toward animals, rather than the animal per se, that we seek to describe. Our principal theme and purpose is to portray the traditional Jewish perceptions of the animal kingdom, to discern the significance of the world of fauna in the religious literature of Israel, and to analyze the distinctive biblical, rabbinic, and postrabbinic attitudes that existed toward animals.

One must be cautious in such a venture. It is tempting to project our own attitudes into ancient writings and to discern therein patterns and philosophies that may be totally nonexistent! Biblical phraseology which seems to convey a specific meaning to modern ears may have meant something quite different to the contemporary audience for which it was intended. The books of Scripture span well over a millennium, embracing prose and poetry, history and law, theology and folklore. One would hardly expect the inspiring paeans to nature in the Psalms and Job to be consistent in mood with the legislation of Exodus and Deuteronomy vis-à-vis a neighbor's straying ox and ass. Yet we submit that there is an underlying unity of thought that pervades Scripture as pertains to the world of fauna.

It is essential to discern the nature of that unity. Much confusion exists concerning biblical and rabbinic perspectives of the animal kingdom. On the one hand, a powerful charge has been leveled against the ancient Hebrews, maintaining that they actually encouraged cruelty to animals! Schopenhauer, in lamenting what he considers to be the barbaric Western attitude of denying the animal its rights, fixes the blame for this injustice squarely upon Judaism:

It is pretended that the beasts have no rights . . . that our conduct in regard to them has nothing to do with morals, or (to speak in the language of their morality) that we have no duties towards "animals": a doctrine revolting, gross, and barbarous, peculiar to the West, and which has its roots in Judaism.[8]

On the other hand, however, popular works by certain Jewish authors attribute to Scripture and rabbinic literature an overwhelming concern and compassion for the world of fauna, some seeing in the dietary laws of Israel a form of semi-vegetarianism, or a "half-way house to vegetarianism."[9]

The truth, as would be expected, lies well between these two extremes. But it is difficult to discern the precise nature of this truth, as there is room for legitimate differences of opinion and interpretation. In order to more fairly present both sides, we have therefore resorted at times to "to and fro" argumentations. In other words, we have offered alternative presentations, trying to show how certain scriptural passages might be deemed highly laudatory or compassionate toward the animal—but then again might *not* be. For this reason we have quoted extensively from biblical literature, and excerpted in toto several poetic selections concerning the animal kingdom, while presenting our own interpretations and conclusions. By the same token, the varying trends and patterns of rabbinic thought vis-à-vis animals have been presented, we trust, fairly, and often with direct quotations, so that the sages may speak directly to the reader.

The following basic conclusion would seem to be warranted: that the world of fauna, although the authentic handiwork of God, is, in reality, far removed from its Maker's hand or concern. Man, on the other hand, emerges as a distinct entity, far superior to the animal, and standing within a special relationship to his Creator. True, man has specific obligations toward animals; he is not to abuse or mistreat them. But these obligations are relatively few, and they bespeak more accurately the relationship of a master toward his servant, or even an artisan toward his tool, than that of a living being toward his fellow living being, also fashioned by the hand of God.

In contemporary terminology, the world of nature may be legitimately viewed as God's ecological system, which must be neither exploited nor violated. Every being within this system—certainly the living beings of the animal kingdom—is entitled to certain natural rights. Man is forbidden to disturb the divine ecological balance. It is only with God's permission that man may partake of the animal kingdom for his comforts and convenience, and man is severely limited as to the extent to which he may disturb the divine ecology. He is limited as to what he may sacrifice or consume. Such limitations are appropriate and easily understandable. Since man did not "make" nature, he has no right to "break" nature, or violate its integrity.

One might even equate the animal to a delicate artifact or tool, employed by man with his Master's permission, albeit with certain limitations placed upon him by the Divine Master, for the animal is His creation as well as man's tool.

Analogies are always imperfect, but one might suggest that the Bible reflects the following pattern of society: At the apex stands God, the Lord of the earth. Beneath Him are His servants, the human beings, who till the soil and herd cattle. The lowest rung is occupied by the animal kingdom. Domesticated animals are to be sacrificed to the Lord, and by virtue of the Lord's kindness, may occasionally be consumed by man at the Lord's table. Wild animals, on the other hand, stand beyond man's solicitude, and are, on occasion, even the agency by which the Lord punishes disobedient human subjects. Most often, however, wild animals are of no real concern to man, and he, in turn, has no obligations toward their well-being.

This portrait holds true for most of rabbinic and postrabbinic Judaism as well. The quest for "perfection of soul and intellect" which characterized rabbinic scholars and medieval philosophers clearly had no place for the animal. With the exception of certain mystics, the saints and pietists who strove for moral perfection had but ancillary use for the animal. It is man who occupies center-stage, always, in traditional Jewish thought. He is judged in part on how he behaves toward subhuman species, but the central arena of his salvation is occupied by God and his fellow humans. Therein lie his principal obligations.

PART

I

A BIBLICAL PORTRAIT

EMPHASIS AND UTILITY

Selectivity of Emphasis

It is characteristic of the Bible to portray its subject matter selectively, for it is a book dealing with special encounters and extraordinary events transpiring within a localized setting. Scripture does not choose to deal objectively with either the world or mankind. It is the Children of Israel who play the central role in the biblical drama, not the children of other nations. It is only certain selected biblical heroes and personalities whose lives are highlighted in the scriptural narratives. This is only to be expected, for the central purpose of Scripture is an *instructional* one, and the thrust of the biblical lessons precludes the granting of equal time and equal emphasis to all historical personages and events.

Therefore it comes as no surprise to discover that the Bible does not attempt to portray the animal kingdom with any degree of thoroughness. No comprehensive portrait of the world of fauna appears in Scripture. The approximately one hundred and twenty different species of fauna that make their appearance are scattered through the pages of the Bible in varying contexts. It would appear that on the majority of occasions it is purely by chance that they are even mentioned at all! The animal generally serves merely as a backdrop or natural background behind the stage upon which man, the principal player, performs his role.

The creation narrative of Genesis hardly attempts to present a thorough or balanced picture of the animal kingdom. Quite the contrary. The crucial factor is an animal's relationship to man; more specifically, its usefulness to man. "Let the earth bring forth

9

living creatures after its kind, cattle and creeping things and beasts of the earth after its kind."[1] It is the creatures of value to man, i.e., the cattle, the domesticated beasts, who merit first mention. Later, when Adam bestows names upon the fauna of the earth, again it is the cattle who are the first to be mentioned.[2]

Furthermore, there appears to be little precision in the biblical nomenclature of animals. *Behema,* the usual term for domestic animals,[3] may also include wild animals,[4] and at times is used to designate larger beasts, in contradistinction to flocks of sheep or goats.[5] Similarly, *hayah,* normally the term for wild creatures,[6] can be applicable to any animal,[7] and at times refers specifically to domestic animals.[8] Except for the general divisions in the first chapter of Genesis, which are based on mode of locomotion and propagation, and site of origin and habitat, no systematic classification of the varieties of fauna appears in Scripture. When animals are referred to as part of God's creation along with man, they are designated as "all flesh"[9] or "all flesh in which there is a breath of life"[10] or "all in whose nostrils was the breath of the spirit of life."[11] Otherwise an animal is described as a "living soul"[12] or simply "living,"[13] in contrast to plant life or inanimate objects.

Man over Animal

Although man, like the animal, is an artifact of God's and not a direct descendant of the deity, and although he too is formed of the same basic substance from which animals sprang forth, the earth,[14] it is man who clearly occupies the superior station. To man, alone is vouchsafed the privilege of having been created by God "in His own image."[15] The precise meaning of this phrase may be subject to differences of opinion (one must also emphasize that man's superiority is "in image" but not "in substance," for man, too, emanates from the earth and returns to the earth),[16] but it clearly denotes a special quality, unique to humankind, and missing in any of the lower creatures. This quality bespeaks God's special interest in, and concern for, man, as well as man's capacity for entering into a special relationship with his Creator. Even the terminology employed by Scripture in describing God's intent to create man is significant. Whereas the animal kingdom comes into being as a result of statements such as "let the waters swarm" or "let the earth bring forth," man's advent is heralded by the phrase "let *us* make man," as if man alone is worthy of God's personal deliberation and special attention.[17]

Man's inherent superiority over fauna is manifest in his right of "dominion" over them (or, to use a gentler phrase, "stewardship"). Scripture clearly proclaims this dominance: "Let him have dominion over the fish of the sea, and over the fowl of the air, and over the cattle, and over all the earth, and over every creeping thing that creepeth upon the earth."[18] This dominion is later reaffirmed in even stronger language to Noah and his descendants: "And the fear of you and the dread of you shall be upon every beast of the earth, and upon every fowl of the air, and upon all wherewith the ground teemeth, and upon all the fishes of the sea: into your hand are they delivered."[19]

In an early chapter in Genesis, God presents the members of the animal kingdom to Adam, "to see what name he would call them; and whatsoever the man would call every living creature, that was to be the name thereof."[20] There is more involved here than a quaint, ritualistic naming ceremony. To bestow a name upon an entity, a name that would endure as its permanent designation, denotes a mastery of the nature of that entity, possibly even one's lordship and dominance over that entity.[21] God, as the Lord of the universe, bestows names upon the structures of the universe and the dimensions of time,[22] while man, designated by God to be the lord of the animals, is here granted similar power to bestow names upon his own animal subjects.

Scripture reaffirms man's superiority over animals in more subtle ways. Beasts are by their very nature deemed stupid and inferior to man in understanding.[23] People who "do not know their right hand from their left" are compared to cattle.[24] The phrase *behema* in Arabic denotes the use of ambiguous and uncertain terms of speech, or speaking in an unknown tongue. In contradistinction to man, who is clearly able to communicate by means of speech, the *behema* is clearly incapable of intelligible communication. The psalmist refers to the "dumbness" of the *behema*, unable to make itself understood.[25] As to man's right of dominion over fauna, the psalmist leaves little doubt: "Thou hast put all things under his feet: sheep and oxen, all of them, yea, and the beasts of the field; the fowl of the air, and the fish of the sea; whatsoever passeth through the paths of the sea."[26]

The Animal as Useful Property

The economic realities of life dictated that the ancient Hebrews establish dominion over animals, for animals comprised the essence of a man's property and wealth, and were counted as an integral part of his household possessions.[27] Indeed, one's social status in a community was determined by the amount of livestock which one possesssed.[28] It is significant that animals probably constituted the earliest form of currency! Cattle were used as a means of making payment in the form of barter long before metal was employed for monetary value.[29] The Latin *pecunia,* i.e., "money," is derived from *pecus,* "a sheep," and the Greek *polyboutes,* denoting a rich man, means literally, "rich in oxen." Needless to say, the domestication of animals proved to be a decisive advance in world history. Beasts of draft made possible agricultural development, horses revolutionized modes of warfare, and camels facilitated the development of extensive caravan routes across desert areas.

Scripture records in a variety of ways the practical importance to man of specific species of animals, both in their living state and after death. Agricultural pursuits necessitated draft animals for plowing the soil. Oxen, the most powerful of all domestic animals, commonly pulled plows,[30] as well as wagons[31] and threshing sleds;[32] there is also reference to asses performing these tasks.[33]

In addition to its field chores as a beast of burden,[34] the ass seems to have been the riding animal par excellence. Important personages as well as common folk,[35] men, women, and small children are all depicted as riding upon asses.[36] It is significant that the prophet Zechariah envisions Israel's king of the future riding upon an ass rather than a horse.[37] Ass-ownership was an economic necessity for the average Israelite. During the biblical period, asses were among the most popularly used animals, and in the early years of the Second Commonwealth they appear to have been the most numerous of all species of domestic beasts in Judea.[38]

Sheep, on the other hand, the first animals to be singled out by name in the Bible, are numbered among the basic possessions of men of substance.[39] Their wool was prized for clothing and fabrics,[40] and sheep-shearing was an occasion for rejoicing and revelry.[41] The skin of sheep was used as a tent-covering,[42] while ram's horns were hollowed out and sounded as musical instruments and alarms.[43] Goat's hair was also used as a fabric for tent-coverings,[44] as well as a stuffing for cushions and quilts,[45] while goat-hides were made into skin pouches to serve as receptacles for preserving and transporting liquid nourishment in the desert.[46] Wearing apparel, notably girdles and sandals, was frequently made from animal hides; the prophet Zechariah wore a "hairy mantle,"[47] as presumably did Elijah and Elisha.[48] Animal skins were also made into parchment, while the tendons and sinews of bulls and the horns of wild goats were used in the preparation of bows for hunting and warfare.[49]

Even the esoteric invertebrates of the sea had their uses, for articles of clothing, along with ornamental cloth and tapestries, were dyed with the blue and purple dyes extracted from certain mollusks of the Mediterranean.[50]

From the earliest history of the countries of the Middle East, camels served as the ideal means of desert transportation in peaceful times,[51] as well as in times of war.[52] They were sturdy bearers of mighty burdens, able to walk easily on the hot desert sands because of their flat, padded, calloused paws, and, of course, especially adept at traversing long distances without water.[53] Ownership of many camels was an indisputable sign of wealth.[54]

The role played by the horse in ancient Israel was an interesting and somewhat paradoxical one. On the one hand, horses served as practical means of transportation, notably for rulers and men of nobility. Joseph[55] and Absalom[56] ride in horse-drawn chariots, as does Naaman, captain of the hosts of the king of Aram.[57] The dead body of Amaziah, king of Judah, is returned to Jerusalem borne upon horses.[58] Horses would appear to have been common in

Jerusalem. The royal palace boasted a special "horse-gate,"[59] and one of Jerusalem's gates was also known as the "horse-gate."[60] Solomon alone is said to have had forty thousand horse-stalls[61] and apparently trafficked in these animals.[62]

But the horse's most prominent role was that of an animal of war.[63] Virtually all of Israel's powerful enemies are depicted as using steeds in warfare for pulling chariots or as mounts for cavalry units.[64] Isaiah describes the mighty Assyrian army as being composed of infantry, chariots, and cavalry.[65] It is, indeed, curious that scant references exist to the use of war-horses on the part of the Israelites, in spite of Solomon's extensive supply of steeds.[66]

Why? It may be assumed that in the popular mind horses did not rate very favorably. They are conspicuously absent from among the animals owned by the patriarchs, and their debut amidst the Children of Israel came about as war-steeds of the enemy, notably the Egyptian enemy. Indeed, the only direct reference to horses in the entire Pentateuch comes in the form of an exhortation warning the Israelites of the attendant dangers when their kings will seek to acquire multitudes of horses with which to wage war.[67] Later, the prophet Samuel reiterates the same warning.[68] By divine command Joshua hamstrung Canaanite horses,[69] and later David did the same to captured enemy steeds.[70] Perhaps it was this negative association of the horse as an animal of war that inspired the aforementioned messianic vision of Israel's future king mounted upon an ass rather than a royal steed.[71]

Animals as a Source of Food

Scripture repeatedly refers to the promised land as "a land flowing with milk and honey."[72] Milk was a staple food item in the biblical era, with both goat's milk and sheep's milk popularly used.[73] Jael found it a fitting drink with which to drug a weary enemy officer,[74] and Joel's eschatological prophecy envisions an abundance of milk flowing down from the hills.[75] We read of such common milk by-products as butter, cream, and cheese.[76]

Curiously, eggs are rarely referred to in Scripture. Indeed, the prohibition against removing eggs from a nest in the presence of the dam comprises the sole reference to eggs in all the Pentateuch,[77] and it is, in part, the basis upon which the rabbis later declared eggs from a clean bird to be permissible as food. [78]

Hunting was a significant activity in biblical times,[79] and Scripture states specific rules concerning the consumption of food acquired in the hunt. The list of wild animals permissible for food includes the hart, gazelle, roebuck, wild goat, ibex, antelope, and mountain-sheep,[80] but Leviticus[81] explicitly states: "If any Israelite or any stranger who resides among them hunts down an animal or a bird that may be eaten, he shall pour out its blood and cover it [the blood] with earth."[81]

Although hunting was clearly permitted, and enjoyed popularity as the royal sport of the ancient world and the favorite pastime of noblemen and kings, the Bible does not record one single king of Israel indulging in the hunt![82] On the contrary, a derogatory attitude toward hunting is evident in Scripture. Esau, the hunter, is unfavorably contrasted with the more civilized Jacob, the herdsman.[83] The literary image of the hunt is a terrifying one in biblical writings, with powerful metaphors denoting the aggressor's inexorable pursuit of his victim, but almost invariably, sympathies clearly lie with the latter.[84] The respectable and approved manner of dispatching an animal for food was not via the hunt, but rather as part of a sacrificial ceremony.

Furthermore, although Noah is given full permission, after the flood, to consume the meat of fauna,[85] the slaughter of animals for food seems to have been uncommon. On economic grounds alone, practical necessity dictated that an agrarian society preserve as many domestic animals as possible for agricultural labor. For the poor, meat-eating was, no doubt, almost always a rare occasion, indeed a "sacrifice," literally and figuratively. More will be said of this later. The main food items of the biblical era seem to have been vegetarian in nature, the seven species of agriculture,[86] as well as "grain, wine and oil,"[87] and Deuteronomy, while permitting the eating of flesh, speaks of the desire for meat as a luxury, "when the Lord thy God shall enlarge thy borders."[88]

The dietary laws of Israel further limited the consumption of meat. Only quadrupeds which chewed their cud and had parted hoofs, such as the cow, sheep, goat, gazelle, and hart, were fit for food, these being by and large the herbivorous ruminants.[89] Animals possessing only one of the two required characteristics, however, such as the camel, rockbadger, and pig, were forbidden, as, of course, were animals which neither had split hoofs nor chewed their cud. Animals which died of natural causes were prohibited,[90] as were those torn by wild beasts.[91] All blood was to be removed from the flesh of the slaughtered animal, and the fat surrounding the kidneys and abdominal viscera was forbidden.[92] The sciatic nerve, along with the sinews of the hindlegs of an animal, was not to be eaten,[93] and the act of seething a kid in its mother's milk was outlawed.[94] All this will be elaborated upon later.

Only fishes possessing both fins and scales were permitted as food,[95] while the majority of insects were forbidden, with the exception of certain species of locusts.[96] Indeed, all land creatures which crawled on their bellies or moved on many feet were prohibited for food.[97] Numerous birds were outlawed, notably predatory fowl and wild waterfowl.[98]

As we observed earlier, there is no way of ascertaining precisely how often meat was eaten during the biblical era. One would suspect, however, that meat meals were reserved for special occasions or for the tables of the prosperous. Meat was deemed a delicacy. The prophet Amos describes the wealthy as reclining upon beds of ivory and eating of calf and lamb meat,[99] and on several occasions lamb and kid-flesh are singled out as exceedingly desirable portions.[100] Young cattle specially fattened for food were known as "fatted calves"[101] or "calves of the stall."[102]

Meat was clearly a treat reserved for special guests and momentous occasions.[103] Abraham entertains his three mysterious herald-visitors with servings of tender calf meat;[104] Isaac asks his son Esau to prepare venison so that he may bless him before his death;[105] and in describing God's goodness to Israel, Moses depicts the Lord's feeding them the fat of lambs and rams of the breed of Bashan, along with he-goats.[106] Samuel selects a special cut of meat for Saul,[107] and Abigail prepares a feast of meat for David and his men.[108] Adonijah slaughters animals and feasts upon them in honor of his ascension to the throne.[109] Gideon prepares meat before an angel of the Lord,[110] and Isaiah envisions God Himself preparing "a feast of fat things, a feast of wine on the lees, of fat things full of marrow."[111] Elsewhere the prophet describes a scene of feasting and merriment as "slaying oxen and killing sheep, eating flesh and drinking wine, let us eat and drink, for tomorrow we shall die."[112]

The Bible rarely mentions fish as a source of food, and scriptural personalities are never described as partaking of fish meals. Perhaps the Israelites are even fantasizing somewhat when they wistfully look back upon their sumptuous fish meals in Egypt![113] Of course, desert life precludes a frequent fish-menu. Not only is fish rarely obtainable, but it spoils quickly, rendering shipment over long distances impossible. Only coast-dwellers could enjoy fish with regularity. However, reference is made to the "fish-gates" of several cities, particularly in later scriptural books,[114] along with mention of the importation of fish by foreign merchants.[115] In prophetic writings and wisdom literature, allegorical use is frequently made of the art of fishing,[116] and such diverse fishing devices as nets,[117] traps,[118] spears,[119] and rods[120] are alluded to.

Similarly, Scripture rarely refers to the eating of bird meat, but the abundance of terms describing means of apprehending fowl—snares, spring-traps, slings, nets, decoys[121]—testifies to bird-trapping as having been a common pursuit. The Israelites feast upon quail in the wilderness,[122] fatted fowl are a part of King Solomon's menu,[123] and fowl is served at the table of the governor Nehemiah.[124]

However, the eating of meat *in excess* seems to have been frowned upon, and is viewed as gluttony. Scripture is critical of the Israelites for lusting after the "flesh-pots of Egypt,"[125] although it is not the flesh diet per se that is objected to in the context.[126] The aforementioned passage from Amos rebukes the rich, who "eat lambs from the flock and calves from the midst of the stalls,"[127] and Ezekiel's vivid and threatening imagery calls forth: "Set on the pot, set on it, and also pour water into it; gather into it the pieces belonging to it, even every good piece, the thigh and the shoulder; fill it with the choice bones. Take the choice of the flock, and pile also the bones under it; make it boil well, that the bones thereof may also be seethed in the midst of it."[128] Proverbs warns: "Be not among winebibbers; among gluttonous eaters of flesh, for the drunkard and the glutton shall come to poverty,"[129] and Micah condemns the wealthy classes in strong figurative terms for cannibalistically devouring the poor.[130]

Animals as Sacrifices

The sacrificial cult, embracing both public and private rituals in which animals were slaughtered and their meat and viscera consumed or consecrated to God, was a complex institution which has been investigated and reinvestigated by numerous biblical scholars.

Robertson Smith, for example, saw in the sacrifice of animals a drama of the "rite of blood brotherhood." The meat was consumed in an act of communion, a covenant, a "bond of troth and fellowship to all the effects for which kinsmen are permanently bound together,"[131] and he viewed this blood-kinship between the deity and man as the cornerstone of the Israelite sacrificial cult.

However, at the same time, Smith and later scholars recognized that the covenant between Israel and God was not a true expression of blood-kinship. It was, rather, a contractual relationship, a type of contract or bond conceived of in moral and legal terms. Within such a framework there is no need or place for any animistic bond linking the divine powers to the community of humans. There is, rather, a servant-lord relationship underlying the act of sacrifice.[132] The God of Israel is entitled to the sacrifices of His people much as the lord-sovereign receives tribute from his servants and subjects. In return God's beneficence is extended to the faithful.

Similarly, Roland de Vaux rejects some of the popular theories purporting to explain the purpose of sacrifices, e.g., the sacrifice is a gift to a malevolent or selfish deity, a magical means of uniting with the deity, or a meal taken by the deity.[133] He views these theories as unsatisfactory because they neglect the strictly religious significance of Israelite sacrifice and presuppose a far cruder concept of God and man's relationship with God than ever existed in Israel. He proceeds to comment that:

> Sacrifice is the essential act of external worship. It is a prayer which is acted, a symbolic action which expresses both the inferior feelings of the person offering it, and God's response to this prayer. It is rather like the symbolic actions of the prophets. By sacrificial rites, the gift made to God is accepted, union with God is achieved, and the guilt of man is taken away. But these effects are not achieved by magic: it is essential that the external action should express the true inward feelings of man, and that it should be favourably received by God. Failing this, sacrifice is no longer a religious act.[134]

Thus, although a sacrifice is a gift to God, as God is the sovereign to whom the entire earth belongs, and it is only fitting that man should pay tribute to the Lord, there is an act of "desecration" involved in the gift-giving. By giving a portion to God, man "desecrates" the remainder and uses it for his own purposes. Furthermore, there is an ethical dimension to the sacrificial cult, for man deprives himself of his most valued possessions, i.e., domesticated beasts, in seeking God's beneficence.

This idea of "gift" is combined with the dimension of "communion" with God, "which results from sharing the same possessions, from sharing a common life, and from the practice of hospitality."[135] Clearly sacrifices also had expiatory value, notably the sin and expiatory offerings which sought to reestablish man's covenant with God. But whatever the purpose of a given offering, be it propitiatory, tributary, or purely thanksgiving in nature, all offerings consisted of the presentation of some possession as a tribute to God.

Although meal-offerings and wine-libations were also part of the sacrificial scheme, animals, as man's prized possessions, comprised the essence of the sacrificial cult, with both large and small cattle, pigeons and turtledoves being prescribed as offerings. Fatlings (animals especially fattened for meat) were deemed highly desirable offerings, as they represented the choicest gift that could be brought to the Lord.[136] Virtually every type of major offering involved animals; propitiatory offerings, both of the "sin" and "guilt" variety,[137] burnt-offerings,[138] and the continual burnt-offerings for special occasions,[139] peace-offerings,[140] votive offerings,[141] free-will offerings,[142] and installation offerings.[143] The standard procedure for the sacrifice involved placing one's hands upon the animal, slaughtering it, collecting its blood and conveying it to the altar, and finally the aspersion of the blood and the burning of the dedicated portions.

Scripture records the offering of animals by Abel,[144] Noah,[145] Abraham,[146] and other personages from the very first chapters of Genesis until the very end of the Second Commonwealth in 70 C.E.,[147] as the sacrificial cult was a dominant means of religious expression for the Children of Israel. Even when the Roman armies besieged Jerusalem, the daily *tamid* sacrifice was offered until a paucity of lambs forced its cessation.[148]

The question has been raised as to whether certain animals may have had "entertainment" value or "ornamental" value for their masters. But it is doubtful whether people commonly kept certain species of fauna simply as pets. This was a luxury for kings and the immensely wealthy. Mention is made of apes and peacocks which are carried to King Solomon by his fleet of Tarshish ships,[149] and Tiglath-Pileser III receives in tribute birds whose wings were dyed purple and sheep whose wool was dyed blue.[150] It is reasonable to assume that exotic fauna and creatures with singularly striking coloration were desirable as showpiece pets, but how many ordinary people could possibly have afforded to acquire or maintain them?

In all other respects, however, the animal served the average man as a functional commodity, and, as we shall attempt to demonstrate, it was just that—a useful *commodity*. On the biblical stage of life it is man who plays the dominant role. Animals are the supporting players; more often than not, merely man's baggage. They suffer for man's sins and are the innocent victims of his misfortunes. Indeed, in the sacrificial cult they are often made to suffer the punishment rightly deserved by their human masters.[151] As God rewards and punishes men for their acts, animals, more often than not, accompany their masters to their fates, be they the victims of plagues[152] or the spoils of battle.[153] Even the psalmist, imbued as he was with God's providential care for all of His creatures, could proclaim: "O fear the Lord, ye His holy ones, for there is no want to them that fear Him. The young lions do lack and suffer hunger; but they that seek the Lord want not any good thing."[154] God provides for his righteous human subjects, while animals, incapable of appreciating his Word, are forced to suffer deprivation.

2

DEMYTHOLOGIZATION

The Demoted Animal

It is possible to theorize that the relatively minor role delegated to the animal kingdom by Scripture is due, in part, to Scripture's radical demythologization of the animal kingdom, a demythologizing that results in the Bible being virtually bereft of any totemistic elements.

A brief word concerning totemism is in order. In the ancient world totemism was an all-pervasive force. Man felt a deep kinship and mystic bond with fauna, and many clans even traced their physical origins to animals. These ancients who viewed animals as their progenitors often conceived of them as possessing human souls and being endowed with the power to influence human affairs.[1] Indeed, some scholars maintain that totemism was the original religion of the Semitic peoples.[2] In any event, in the ancient Near East "the realm of nature and the realm of man were not distinguished."[3] For the pagan, there simply was no such thing as an inanimate world; life was pulsating within all of nature. The pagan worshipped nature. This meant not only the worship of the *gods* of nature, but also reverence for specific *entities* of nature, including animals, which were deemed to be sacred. As long as a natural landscape was permitted to exist, wild animals constituted a great danger to human populations, and the attendant fear also found expression in animal cults and animal totems. The ancients endowed animals with divine and demonic powers, often choosing to embody their gods within the forms of animals. These animals were either direct objects of worship and devotion or appropriate symbols for the venerated deities. In either case, the multitude of theriomorphic gods in many cultures testify to powerful totemistic elements among the pagan religions of antiquity.

The ancient Egyptians, for example, worshipped Thus, the sacred Apis bull, as their god of fertility. This animal, believed born of a cow which had been fertilized by a ray from heaven, was venerated as a deity, and upon its death was mummified. Egyptians also worshipped the bull Mnevis, the buck of Mendes, and the ram of Khnum, and, looking upon rams as sacred beings, refrained from sacrificing them.[4] Significantly, the paschal animal slaughtered by the Israelites prior to their exodus from Egypt was a ram! Cat images abounded in Egyptian temples, for the cat was an animal sacred to the goddess Baste, and the sun god, Re, was also closely associated with cats. Interestingly, the cat is not mentioned at all in Scripture. Other deified animals were the serpents Apophis, Wazit, and Selket, and the sacred scarab beetle, Ra.

It is noteworthy that even those Egyptian deities normally represented in human form were often endowed with prominent animal traits or an admixture of human and animal features. Thus Horus bore the head of a falcon, Anubis the head of a jackal, and Hathor the horns of a cow. Sebek was a crocodile-headed man, and Sekhmet a lioness-headed woman. Furthermore, these gods were themselves endowed with sacred animals. The lion and the hawk were sacred to Horus, the jackal to Anubis, the dog-headed ape and the ibis to Thoth, the swallow to Isis, the cobra to Ra, the pig and the hunting dog to Set, the ram to both Ra and Osiris, and the sacred scarabaeus (kheper) to the sun god, Ra.[5]

The bull was the popular symbol of fecundity in the ancient world. The Ras Shamra texts refer to El, the chief god of the Ugaritic pantheon, as "the bull" or "father bull El," and Baal bears upon his headgear the horns of a bull.[6] Astarte, the Caananite fertility goddess, was associated with a lion or depicted with a bull's head, and in the Ugaritic myth, Baal, the weather-god of the Semites, has sexual relations with a heifer. The Chaldeans represented the seven evil deities in the form of oxen, and, paradoxically, the ox-form came to also represent divine protection. Not surprisingly, the god of the seafaring Philistines, Dagon, was depicted as a fish with a human head.

Now the recognition of mystic bonds uniting animals and men was a phenomenon not unique to the ancient Near East. It was universal. In his fascinating analysis of the profound effect that the discovery of cooking had upon relations between "sky and earth," Claude Levi-Strauss cites New World Indian myths which also vividly portray the mutual interpermeability of animality and humanity.[7] The deepest mysteries of nature—fertility, sustenance, and death—were all concretized and embodied in the forms of selected beasts. Indeed, ancient zoolatry was the divine manifest within the animal, the deity incarnate within the beast. Not surprisingly, the ancient world would often pay these sacred animals the same homage normally reserved for the gods themselves.

In marked contrast, the religion of Israel conceived of God as being absolutely transcendent—over, above, and beyond nature—while nature and the creatures of nature were relatively devoid of any divinity. In the Bible, even "man remained outside nature, exploiting it for a livelihood, offering its first-fruits as a sacrifice to God, using its imagery for the expression of his moods; but never sharing its mysterious life."[8] The animal, on the other hand, functions in a perfunctory and natural role as an animal, either bearing the burdens of domestication or moving about freely in the wild. But in either capacity it has no intimate or mystical relationship with either man or the cosmos. It is simply an animal.

Scripture seems to be virtually bereft of any real totemistic elements. Although names of plants and animals are abundantly found in the Bible, they comprise less than one percent of all personal names! In all of Scripture only twenty-two Hebrews are found to bear the names of animals. Although a few clans are known by animal names,[9] no practical significance need be attached to the fact. At most they simply recall the nomenclature of vestigial totemism. Significantly, the names of fauna borne by clans and individuals comprise both clean and unclean varieties in almost equal quantities.[10] This is something one would not expect to find if the animals did, indeed, represent special taboos or sacred entities. By the same token, the twenty-three towns within Israel's borders bearing the names of animals include both wild and domestic beasts, clean as well as unclean animals.[11]

One must be cautious in postulating possible totemistic origins on the basis of "animal names" for people and places. Natural poetic usage would dictate that an abundance of flora and fauna names would appear, particularly in the Bible, where animals appear as an integral part of the natural landscape. Jacob and Moses are obviously employing poetic metaphor when they compare several of the tribes of Israel to animals.[12]

To state the obvious, Scripture rigorously outlaws any form of animal worship. Not only the worship, but even the depiction of visual representations of animals as objects of adoration is strictly forbidden.[13] It is only on rare occasions that we encounter cases of animal worship taking place in ancient Israel. Ezekiel's vision of "all kinds of creeping things and loathsome beasts"[14] being displayed upon the Temple walls in the Assyro-Babylonian manner is an extraordinary case,[15] as are such incidents as Hebrews eating swine,[16] or mice and their broth[17] and wringing the necks of dogs.[18] These practices, recorded in disgust by the prophet, most likely reflect the growth of mystery cults in Israel in the period of decline prior to and after the destruction of the First Commonwealth. Similarly, we read of Josiah's removal of "the horses that the kings of Judah had given to the sun" from the entrance to the House of the Lord,[19] and of traces of demon or satyr worship that may have involved animals cults.[20]

The most striking scriptural account describing and vigorously condemning animal images in worship involves, of course, the erection of a golden calf. While Moses is upon Mount Sinai for a forty-day period, some Israelites demand of Aaron: "Make us a god who will go before us."[21] Aaron complies by fashioning a golden calf, a portable image of a calf overlaid with gold, proclaiming: "This is thy god, O Israel, who brought thee up out of the land of Egypt."[22] Jeroboam, the first king of Samaria, constructs two calves of gold in Beth-El and Dan, saying to his subjects: "Behold thy gods, O Israel, which brought thee up out of the land of Egypt."[23] Similar calf-images appear in the temple of Micah and at Gilgal.[24]

As has been noted, many Semitic peoples used the ox or bull as a symbol of worship. These are often referred to as "calves," probably because the representations were, indeed small in size, owing to the scarcity and costliness of gold as a metallic covering. But quite possibly these calves were merely fetishes rather than actual objects of worship, and Jeroboam's calves may not have been true symbols of the deity but rather pedestals for the deity![25] It is conceivable that animal figures were not true objects of idolatry in ancient Israel. They may have been employed as iconolatrous images—as representations of the presence of the deity, rather than the deity itself. Erecting a calf on the vacant throne of God may have provided the popular mind with a necessary visual device for sensing the presence of the deity.[26] The bull represents great power and strength,[27] and its presence in artistic representations, such as Solomon's laver,[28] was probably due to this quality rather than any sacred character. Likewise, the representation of lions upon the steps of Solomon's throne would symbolize the power of the king as a judge.[29]

In summary, the use of animal images in Israel was greatly limited. On the infrequent occasions when they do appear, their function would seem to have been to supply a concrete visual correspondence to biblical anthropomorphism. Rarely if ever do they appear to have been true objects of worship. Animal symbols, disengaged from their original pagan significance, can easily lose any idolatrous associations which they may have once possessed and become purely artistic objects.

The Animal in Magic

The ancient religions were heavily saturated with magic. Ancient man sought to manipulate and influence his environment by means of incantations and "religious" acts, and the animal kingdom figured prominently as the means whereby the desired effects were to be realized. In homeopathic or imitative magic, animals were often employed, or worn as charms, to ward off evil or enhance the powers of the wearer.[30] The consumption of the blood of certain creatures was believed capable of endowing one with supernatural powers. When ancient man dressed as an animal or used the parts of certain animals, he could actually believe that he had achieved a transformation into that particular animal.[31]

Certain species of fauna were deemed to be taboo out of a sense of awe, or "numinosity," while other wild beasts were worshipped and presented with human sacrifices in the hope that disasters could thereby be averted. Another belief of sympathetic magic was that a man's soul could be bound up with that of an animal, and upon the death of that animal the man would also expire. Some animals were believed to possess human souls and were thereby endowed with special powers over other humans.

A variety of fauna were employed in the art of divination and augury. *Menahesh* (Lit. "he who observes the hissing or the movement of the serpent") is a generic term denoting one who specializes in discerning omens. Augury originally referred to the art of foretelling the future by means of observing the flight patterns of birds, for the ancients regarded birds as special harbingers of both good and evil. Thus the crowing of a cock assures Themistocles of victory at Artemisium, and the advent of vultures causes Romulus to proclaim himself king of Rome. Widespread popular belief held the raven to be a bird of omen, and endowed snakes and dogs with prophetic gifts. But the sounds and movements of most any animal could be used in divination.

In marked contrast, biblical magic is unique in that it characteristically lacks any mythological basis. True, from time to time men of God employ certain magical devices, but never does God Himself! Furthermore, whatever the nature of these magical acts, they are not ends in themselves but rather manifestations of God's power, or, at times, means of authenticating God's messengers and prophets before their audiences.[32] Scripture expressly prohibits the practice of all magical arts—divination, soothsaying, augury, sorcery, charming, medium wizardry, and necromancy—considering the practice of any of them to be idolatrous.[33] Magic itself is viewed as an abomination before the Lord.[34]

In view of these prohibitions, it may seem puzzling that certain seemingly magical acts are deemed permissible by the Bible. But what is striking is the total lack of animal participation in biblical magic practices. Significantly, not one auguristic ceremony depicted in Scripture (whether performed by an Israelite or a pagan) involves animals or birds.[35] We do find references to divination by means of arrows,[36] sticks or staves,[37] and hydromancy.[38] Divining by means of the sound of the wind rustling in the trees is mentioned,[39] as is divination by means of the study of certain bodily organs, notably the liver,[40] but fauna are conspicuously absent from the list. Scripture nowhere hints at any bonds of sympathetic magic linking humans to the animal kingdom and making their lives contingent upon the lives of fauna.[41] No biblical animal is endowed with "numinosity," or any power of coercion over a human.

Animal Protagonists of the Deity

Ancient pagan sources describe a dramatic primordial battle transpiring between the deity and some powerful sea-monsters who challenge his authority. In Babylonian mythology the very origin of the universe is traced back to such a colossal encounter between Marduk and the fishlike monster Tiamat. Other ancient traditions, giving different names to the combatants, record similar encounters.[42] Now a few biblical passages, notably in the prophetic and poetic portions of Scripture, also appear to echo some primordial encounter between God and a sea-monster known as Rahab, the lord of the sea,[43] or Leviathan,[44] or Tannin.[45] But these are merely echoes. The Bible has completely demythologized this ancient tale. It contains neither theogony nor primordial encounters between God and any supernatural creature challenging His authority. The surviving echoes are only poetic allusions employed for the greater veneration of the one supreme God.

Furthermore, it is significant that the creation narrative in Genesis, which as a rule only refers to general categories of animals, pointedly refers to God's having created the *taninim* (sea-creatures).[46] They are singled out by name. Why? Perhaps Scripture's purpose here is to emphasize that these enormous creatures of the deep are merely subservient creations of God, rather than rival powers or deities. The psalmist describes mighty Leviathan as God's "plaything"—"there is Leviathan whom Thou has formed to sport therein"[47]—and pictures the sea-monsters as offering homage to God—"Praise the Lord from the earth, you sea-monsters and all deeps."[48] This is a far cry indeed from the original Leviathan, the terrifying hydra-headed monster of the ancient cosmogonies.[49] It is only in post canonical writings that the dragon emerges as the symbol for a powerful adversary,[50] and the *behemoth,* described in Job[51] (and usually rendered as "a giant marsh-dwelling creature" or as "hippopotamus"), emerges in the Apocrypha and the pseudepigraphic writings as the male counterpart of Leviathan.[52]

In a similar manner, the Bible totally demythologizes the serpent. In the ancient Near East, particularly among the Egyptians, the serpent was worshipped as a deity symbolizing fertility. Buzo or Wazit, the serpent goddess of Lower Egypt, symbolized royalty, while Apophis, the chief of the evil gods of Egypt, was also represented by a serpent. Paradoxically, this creature was capable of both destroying and mending, afflicting and curing.[53] Although the serpent in Genesis plays an undeniably powerful role as the tempter of Eve, Scripture is careful to emphasize that he is, nevertheless, merely one among the many in the category of the "the beasts of the field that the Lord God had made,"[54] and later he is cursed "from among all beasts of the field."[55] In other words, for all of his apparent powers, the serpent is still merely one of the many animals God has created, nothing more. He may be shrewd and cunning, but he is in no way demonic, nor is he endowed with any supernatural powers. The serpent of the Bible is a totally demythologized creature, completely helpless before the wrath and power of God.

Even the episode describing the erection of a bronze serpent by Moses, in order to cure those Israelites who had been bitten by fiery serpents, serves more to emphasize faith in God as an efficacious cure than to call attention to any magical powers inherent in a serpent.[56] The eventual destruction of the bronze serpent at the hands of King Hezekiah[57] reflects the ire of the religious authorities when it apparently did become an object of veneration for later generations.[58]

The Animal in Ritual

Now at times a certain aura or mystique does seem to surround certain scriptural animals, notably those involved in several dramatic ritual-purification ceremonies. However, upon closer examination, these animals prove to be not the *source* of cleansing or purification, but rather merely the *vehicle* for the achievement of this desirable state. We shall consider a few examples.

The Scapegoat

Leviticus describes the selection of two he-goats, one designated for God, one for Azazel.[59] The former was sacrificed "to make atonement," while the latter was driven off into the wilderness. It may be tempting to view the scapegoat as a surrogate or substitute for the life of the human being who has transgressed, but more accurately, the animal is merely the vehicle for the removal and disposal of the taint of transgression. The significance of the ceremony is not the goat itself, but rather the transgressions that it bears off into the wilderness. Only after a full public confession on behalf of the entire community[60] was the animal dispatched into a land which is "cut off."[61] Although the scapegoat is dedicated to, or for, Azazel,[62] the goat is dedicated to the Lord alone, who is the all-powerful agency in this drama of atonement.

The Red Heifer

The Book of Numbers describes a means of ritual purification for individuals or utensils rendered impure by contact with, or proximity to, a corpse or a grave.[63] A cow, free from blemish and not yet yoked, was slain outside the camp of the Israelites, and its ashes are described as having the power to effect purification. Paradoxically, the red heifer both purified and defiled, for its ashes, mixed in springwater to produce the purification compound, rendered unclean those coming in contact with it, and at the same time purified the defiled individual. Did the ceremony of the red heifer symbolize the atoning power of blood, or did its red color represent the eradication of sin from the Israelite camp?[64] In either event, the crucial aspect here is Israel's relationship with God and the rectification of her uncleanliness. The red heifer is merely the vehicle for the removal of uncleanliness.

The Eglah Arufah

An even more complex ritual ceremony involved the *eglah arufah*.[65] When an unsolved murder had occurred, the elders of the nearest settlement would proclaim their innocence of any complicity in the crime while participating in a ceremony in which the neck of an unworked heifer was broken. The meaning of this ceremony is possibly related to the notion that "the land shall have no expiation for blood that is shed except by the blood of him who shed it."[66] In other words, the blood of the innocent pollutes and harms the soil upon which it is spilt, possibly resulting in famine.[67] Now in the case of an unknown murderer who can never be brought to justice, the entire earth could conceivably be cursed in this manner! Therefore, the ceremony may have sought to effect a transference of the pollution to a limited and isolated area by transferring the basic impurity from the human remains to the corpse of the animal. In this way expiation takes place with minimal damage to the earth.[68] Of course, it is also possible that the purpose of this ceremony was principally, if not purely, dramatic in nature, to provide the community with a vivid, multidimensional experience emphasizing the preciousness of human life and the enormity of the crime of murder.

Be that as it may, the death of the animal does not, in reality, constitute any magical expiation for the crime. Rabbinic tradition ordains the death of the murderer, should he be subsequently identified.[69] Furthermore, in addition to the powerful ethical implications inherent in this rite (the elders must not only profess their innocence as to both committing and witnessing the crime,[70] but must also proclaim themselves guiltless of any neglect in providing food and sustenance to the unfortunate victim), the culminating declaration of the elders attributes the ultimate power of forgiveness and atonement exclusively to God, not to any ritual ceremony involving an animal. They pray: "Forgive, O Lord, Thy people Israel, whom Thou has redeemed, and suffer not innocent blood to remain in the midst of Thy people Israel."[71]

Granted that animals are prominently featured in these dramatic rituals, they are, however, functionaries rather than mediators, "means to an end" rather than determiners of the end-result.

Animal Representations

Other esoteric animal representations are similarly bereft of any true significance. The cherubim, for example, are mentioned several times in the Bible. They are stationed as guardians at the entrance to the Garden of Eden.[72] Two wooden cherubim, overlaid with gold, rest upon the ark of the Covenant,[73] and God is poetically described as "He who sits upon the cherubim."[74]

The cherubim have been identified with the winged animal creatures appearing frequently in the religious artwork of the ancient Near East, notably the griffin, an animal constituting an amalgamation of the most powerful beasts of earth and air, the lion and the eagle. But neither Genesis nor Exodus supplies a description of the cherubim or relates them in any way to the animal kingdom. Only Ezekiel, in a mystical vision, attributes human and animal features to the cherubim.[75]

Seals were extensively used in antiquity as means of identifying property and ensuring privacy. They were believed to possess magical powers, and many bore representations of mythical figures and deities. The scarab seals of Egypt symbolized the sacred scarabaeus beetle, venerated by the Egyptians. One of these, the dung beetle (*scarabaeus sacer*), was the symbol of resurrection because of its habit of laying eggs within the dead bodies of other beetles! The Israelites, of course, also sealed their documents,[76] and several prophets employ the imagery of the seal as representing the sacred and inviolate.[77] Yet the Bible gives no description at all of any seal, and nowhere associates seals with the forms and figures of animals.[78]

Animals appear in several biblical dream sequences, but they play no magical role. They appear merely as symbols and images within the dream fabric, and it is the quality of presagery or prophecy associated with dreams that renders the symbol worthy of interpretation. In oneiromancy, animals are simply part of the symbolism of the dream-substance, no more.[79]

Scripture deems it a terrible fate for the dead to be denied an honorable burial, and the abandonment of one's body to wild beasts and birds of prey is viewed as a clear indication of divine displeasure and punishment.[80] But Scripture never alludes to any demonic factors at work when a corpse is consumed by beasts. Such lurid descriptions add vivid literal or poetic imagery to the truth that, ideally, one should be buried honorably in the earth,[81] preferably in one's own family tomb.[82] Similarly, exhumation from the grave was viewed as a degradation for the deceased, conceivably an indication of punishment from above.[83]

Nor should the fact that impurity is associated with animals (their corpses are a principal cause of impurity) be viewed as evidence of their embodying demonic powers. The flesh of prohibited animals is never described as being potentially destructive by virtue of magical or demonic taints. Blood and fat are prohibited because they belong to God, and are, in essence, the life of the animal. Certain creatures are forbidden for consumption because they are "abominations" or "loathsome," but Scripture never imputes destructive powers to such animals. This stands in marked contrast to the heathen cults, where "uncleanliness" is deemed a destructive magical power alien to the gods and dangerous to man. In the Bible "impurity is no more than a condition— one might almost say a religious-aesthetic state,"[84] and does not denote the demonic or supernatural.

Although other sacrificial cults of antiquity emphasized the fact that sacrifices are designed to feed the gods and that these deities are in need of the "vitality" of the bodies of animals, Israel's sacrificial system does not countenance such a notion. Such descriptive phrases as "God's food,"[85] "bread of God,"[86] and a "pleasing odor to the Lord,"[87] as well as references to "the Lord's table,"[88] are no more than linguistic fossils. Technical religious terminology is often archaic, and always conservative, retaining terms that no longer signify what they once may have meant.

The God of the Israelite religion is unique in being a nonmythological God, reigning supreme over the world, unencumbered by, or captive to, any preexistent power or being. There is no theogony in the Bible; God maintains no familial relationship with any other being and is neither challenged nor threatened by any creature.

It therefore follows that the animal kingdom in Scripture is devoid of any of the power, mystery, or divinity it enjoyed in pagan literature. The animal has been demythologized. Even those most mysterious and elusive of all creatures, the *shedim* (demons) and the *seirim* (satyrs or goats), are relegated to the habitat of open fields or ruins,[89] where they can work no evil, play no role in human affairs, and surely constitute no threat at all to God. Paradoxically, the *shed* sometimes served as a protector and benefactor in the popular mind.

Even if one grants to the more sophisticated pagan the benefit of the doubt, and assumes that he, too, did not *really* believe animals to be gods or the guardians of gods, but merely used the image or form of the animal in a representational, symbolic function, nevertheless, because the deities were depicted *visually* rather than described *verbally,* the animal came, indeed, to represent the god. It surely came to possess, in the popular mind, the powers of the god.

In contrast, Israel represented God by words, by figures of speech rather than figures of wood, stone, or brass. Consequently the animal became a descriptive entity rather than a visual one, and, needless to say, a powerless entity. The most prominent role played by the world of fauna in Scripture, indeed the *only* prominent role given to the animal, is a descriptive one. The animal is a valuable and vivid figure of speech, employed literally and symbolically by lawgiver, poet, prophet, and visionary in describing God, man, and the world.

POETRY AND PROSE

While it is true that animals play a relatively minor role as *living* characters in the biblical drama, their role is a major one in biblical literary imagery. The Bible is replete with such imagery, for it contains numerous pictorial and graphic representations of reality, almost invariably preferring concrete example to abstract formulation. It is in biblical imagery, notably in poetry and proverb, that animals figure prominently, along with the other common and elemental figures drawn from natural life experiences.

Scripture depicts God with strikingly concrete imagery. He is described in varying contexts as a father,[1] husband,[2] judge,[3] king,[4] warrior,[5] winnower,[6] husbandman,[7] smelter,[8] builder,[9] teacher,[10] healer,[11] harvester,[12] giver of rain,[13] leader of the blind,[14] wayfarer and stranger,[15] as well as the shepherd of a flock.[16] It is therefore not surprising to find God also portrayed with imagery drawn from the world of fauna.

> As an eagle that stirreth up her nest,
> Hovereth over her young,
> Spreadeth abroad her wings, taketh them,
> Beareth them on her pinions.[17]

> I bore you on eagle's wings.[18]

> He will cover thee with His pinions,
> And under His wings shalt thou take refuge.[19]

God is also depicted as a lion,[20] as a leopard,[21] and as a bear lying in wait for its prey;[22] and the wrath of the Lord is compared to that of a she-bear bereaved of her cubs.[23] In Balaam's orations, God is to Israel "like the lofty horns of the wild ox."[24] Now clearly, God is not being compared to the animals themselves. It is rather the *deeds* of God that are described and compared to the deeds of specific animals in particular circumstances.

Similarly, Israel is portrayed as being an unfaithful wife,[25] a wild vine,[26] God's servant,[27] God's beloved,[28] a bride,[29] a vineyard,[30] as well as, from the world of fauna, sheep,[31] a wild ass,[32] well-fed stallions,[33] fatted cows of Bashan,[34] a turtledove,[35] an untrained calf,[36] and a worm.[37] By means of such concrete imagery the concept of God and His covenant with Israel was related to the life experiences of the Israelites, notably those embodied in the world of nature.

It would be a mistake to see in this literary deployment of animals anything more than an effective literary device. There are no mythological overtones here, for the animals are simply animals, used descriptively, and often didactically, notably in folk-proverbs and riddles,[38] or in animal tales. The animal is an appropriate symbol or metaphor because its traits are well-known to man from his practical observations of his natural surroundings.

Thus an attacking army swarming upon its victim is reminiscent of a swarm of bees.[39] Flocks of goats suggest an apt metaphor for the flowing hair of the maiden of the Song of Songs,[40] while the same simile is elsewhere applied to the undermanned army of Israel.[41] The stately march of the he-goat is noted,[42] and this animal, often the leader of the flock, is frequently used as a symbol for men of wealth and leadership.[43] The wild ass is depicted as a shy and cautious animal, endowed with fleetness of foot,[44] while the heifer is a symbol of sexuality,[45] stubbornness,[46] as well as beauty.[47]

A brief excursion into the complexity of animal literary symbolism discloses interesting observations of, and attitudes toward, several species of fauna.

For example, one of the jackal's prominent traits is its habit of prowling and scavenging in desolate ruins. Therefore, when prophets predict the destruction of cities and nations, they refer to these areas as being future haunts for jackals.[48] Conversely, the messianic era is described by Isaiah as one in which the desolate abodes of jackals will suddenly sprout forth vegetation,[49] and the jackals themselves will be the beneficiaries of abundant waters from which they will drink.[50]

Although the ram was only one of the many sacrificial animals in ancient Israel, it is often singled out in prophetic orations to emphasize the religious imperative of adhering to ethical obligations along with ritual sacrificial duties.[51] Perhaps the central role played by the ram in the story of Abraham's binding of his son, Isaac, upon the altar is a factor in the prominence of the ram as a symbol for the sacrificial cult.

Fish rarely appear in biblical literary symbolism. This is possibly due simply to the fact that very little could be discerned about the character and behavior of creatures of the sea that would render them apt subjects for metaphor, except for the obvious fact that they are hunted and captured. Thus Israel's entrapment in captivity is compared to that of a fish in a net,[52] and God's indictment of His people is tantamount to fishermen and huntsmen pursuing their prey with the inevitability of successful capture.[53] Ezekiel's vision of the future fittingly incorporates the image of the waters of the Dead Sea being so sweetened as to permit fish to thrive therein,[54] while the fecundity of fish is implied in Jacob's blessings for his grandchildren. Ephraim and Manasseh.[55]

Poetic allusions often emphasize the close similarities between humans and animals. When Jacob blesses his sons, he compares Judah to a lion's whelp,[56] Issachar to a large-boned ass,[57] Dan to a serpent in the path,[58] Naftali to a hind let loose,[59] and Benjamin to a wolf that raveneth.[60] Balaam's orations compare Israel to a "people that riseth up as a lioness, and as a lion does he raise himself up,"[61] and David, in his moving eulogy, laments Saul and Jonathan as being swifter than eagles and stronger than lions.[62] Shimei son of Gera, who curses David, is deemed a "dead dog,"[63] and Hazael modestly refers to himself as a dog, one clearly unworthy of greatness.[64]

The dog is one of the few animals almost invariably spoken of in negative and derogatory terms. There apparently was little personal relationship between biblical man and the dog. Although a certain degree of domestication of the animal had surely been achieved, and some dogs may have served a useful purpose as sentinels,[65] biblical imagery almost invariably depicts the dog in unflattering terms. Dogs are described as being noisy,[66] greedy,[67] stupid,[68] filthy,[69] and feeding upon carcasses and blood.[70] As has been observed, the term "dog" is applied as an insult to humans.[71] Furthermore, "dog" appears to have been a derogatory designation for male prostitutes.[72]

The worm is the standard symbol of worthlessness and insignificance. God bids a helpless Israel to "fear not, thou worm Jacob,"[73] and the psalmist laments: "But I am a worm and no man; a reproach of men, and despised by the people."[74] Bildad concludes his oration to Job by observing:

"Behold, even the moon hath no brightness,
and the stars are not pure in His sight.
How much less man, that is a worm,
and the son of man, that is a maggot."[75]

The swine is the metaphorical symbol of disgust par excellence. A beautiful woman who is bereft of discretion is aptly compared to a golden ring placed in the snout of a swine.[76] Swine epitomized the food that was forbidden to the Israelites as detestable, and Isaiah describes apostate Jews spitefully participating in heathen rites consisting of the consumption of swine-flesh,[77] while the First Book of the Maccabees depicts attempts to coerce pious Jews to eat pig-meat.[78] Swine were also held in abhorrence by the Phoenicians and shunned by the Egyptians, and later Mohammed also forbade his followers to partake of pig-flesh.[79]

The asp is employed as a frightening and deadly figure of speech. Deuteronomy describes the wine of Israel's foe as the "cruel venom of asps,"[80] and the Book of Job depicts a most agonizing punishment in store for the wicked, namely, that he will be forced to suck the poison of asps and the digested food will then be transformed into the gall of asps.[81] The scorpion was also notorious for its poisonous stings, causing great pain and possible death to both man and beast. Therefore Rehoboam, king of Israel, when asked by a delegation of his subjects to reduce their economic burdens, retorts sarcastically: "My father has chastised you with whips, but I will chastise you with scorpions."[82] We find God Himself encouraging a fearful Ezekiel to take courage even though the people confronting him are as thorns and scorpions.[83]

Among the animals affectionately singled out by Scripture for their positive traits and virtues are the dove, the gazelle, and the hind. The dove was a beloved symbol of beauty and purity. She is the bird who brings to Noah the glad tidings of the cessation of the flood.[84] The maiden of the Song of Songs is praised as "my dove, my dove, my perfect one,"[85] and her eyes, as well as the eyes of her lover, are compared to doves.[86]

The delicacy of form and beauty of movement of the gazelle is also employed in the love imagery of Song of Songs: "My beloved is like a gazelle . . . Thy two breasts are like two fawns that are twins of a gazelle."[87] As these animals were highly prized as prey by their hunters, Isaiah employs the "chased gazelle" as a symbol for an oppressed people,[88] although it is noted that the gazelle's great speed renders it elusive prey for the hunters.[89] The lovely and graceful hind is used metaphorically in describing the wife of one's youth,[90] while in a more practical vein, her attribute of surefootedness[91] and the process of her calving are described.[92]

But as a rule biblical imagery declines to generalize about animal species and refrains from presenting specific fauna in either totally laudatory or totally deprecatory terms. Few creatures are depicted as being totally beneficent or wholly evil, and most species function in a dual capacity for illustrative and poetic purposes.

For example, the *nesher,* or eagle, king of the birds, was the natural counterpart of the lion, king of the beasts.[93] As would be expected, the eagle's regal appearance and superior power are frequently emphasized. The Bible describes the impressive sweep of its wings in flight,[94] its awesome speed,[95] and its characteristic manner of swooping down to attack its victims.[96] Israel's enemies are often compared to the eagle as an attacking bird of prey.[97] Yet

Scripture also dwells upon the eagle in its role as a solicitous parent, for it builds its nest high upon the rocks,[98] and rears its young with great devotion.[99] Therefore God's protective concern for the Children of Israel is expressed in similar terms:

> As an eagle that stirreth up her nest
> Hovereth over her young,
> Spreadeth abroad her wings, taketh them,
> Beareth them on her pinions.[100]

The bull symbolizes the enemies of the psalmist[101] and the rulers of the gentile nations,[102] yet it also appears in a laudatory context in Deuteronomy as the symbol for Joseph.[103]

The locust, a terrifying creature which caused mass destruction in the ancient world by laying waste fields and countryside,[104] is an apt metaphor for swarming armies of human attackers destroying their enemies' land.[105] Their numbers are countless, as the stars in the skies and the sands upon the seashore.[106] They are likened to charging horses of war,[107] and their voracious appetite makes them appropriate symbols for unsatiable greed.[108] They are the harbingers of God's day of retribution upon the earth.[109] However, because of their small size, they are, paradoxically, also symbols of weakness and insignificance,[110] and so the self-deprecating Israelite spies imagine themselves appearing as grasshoppers in the eyes of the giant inhabitants of Canaan.

The swift, agile,[111] cunning,[112] fierce[113] leopard denotes a mighty kingdom,[114] and the powerful enemies of Israel.[115] However, a prophet also muses, in a different vein, on the permanence and immutability of the leopard's spots, paralleling man's own apparently permanent and immutable propensity to do evil.[116]

Along with seven synonyms for the king of the beasts, there are over one hundred and fifty references to lions in the Bible, many of them metaphoric and allegorical in nature. The most powerful and impressive of all carnivores, the lion is the standard symbol, not only of strength and courage, but also of majesty and royalty.[117] Many biblical personalities and several Israelite tribes are compared to the lion as a symbol of kingship,[118] and as the king was also the administrator of justice in ancient times, the lion was a prominent ornamental figure for thrones.[119] As has been noted, God, as the supreme judge, is also depicted as a lion;[120] His roar is like that of a lion,[121] and His people, the Children of Israel, are also likened to a lion.[122] But the foes of Israel are also represented as roaring lions,[123] and the psalmist frequently designates evil oppressors as lions.[124]

The serpent was held in fear and contempt. Scripture refers to its poisonous bite[125] and to the art of serpent-charming,[126] and when Isaiah describes the messianic days as the time when "dust shall be the serpent's food,"[127] he clearly denotes an era when serpents will no longer constitute a threat to humans. As would be expected, the serpent is a frequently used symbol for the wicked, notably Israel's enemies, who are as "serpents and adders which cannot be charmed,"[128] but it is also employed to describe the tribe of Dan in a flattering metaphor,[129] and serpents were the Lord's agency in punishing the Children of Israel.[130] Again, it should be emphasized that while the serpent figured prominently in ancient pagan myths as a deity, in Scripture there is hardly an echo of its possessing any cultic significance.

Complex metaphors accrue around the horse. Animated descriptions depict its attributes of strength,[131] speed,[132] sure-footedness,[133] hardness of hoof,[134] as well as its capacity for leaping[135] and stamping,[136] and its tendency to neigh out of excitement and passion.[137] Metaphorically, its beauty is likened to that of a woman,[138] its need of a bridle is equated to man's need for self-control,[139] and its habit of plunging headlong into battle is an apt simile for the manner in which the wicked impulsively pursue their aims.[140] The neighing of the horse evokes the image of men lusting after their neighbor's wives[141] or the joyful excitement of the victorious soldier plundering the spoils of battle.[142] On the other hand, the crooked and ineffective manner in which a steed attempts to run upon rocks suggests to Amos man's perversion of justice.[143] Horses are featured in such miraculous events as the ascension of the prophet Elijah in a chariot drawn by steeds of fire,[144] Elisha's servant's vision of a fiery horse,[145] and Zechariah's vision of celestial steeds.[146] In the messianic era, horses are to be "consecrated to God,"[147] and the apocryphal literature contains several accounts of supernatural horsemen.[148]

However, the horse also appears as a negative symbol. The Israelites, as a pastoral people, had little need for horses; moreover, the horse came to play a prominent role in idolatrous processions, and symbolized the bellicose nature of the pagan world.[149] Both prophet and psalmist rebuke their people for placing their trust in the might of steeds rather than in the will of the Lord.[150] Zechariah envisions the eradication of all war-horses and chariots in the messianic era,[151] and, as has been noted, depicts the messianic king seated upon an ass, not a horse of war.

In mastering the mystery of flight and soaring in the heavens, the bird has appeared to both ancients and moderns as being closer to God than all of His other creatures,[152] and many a biblical poet was able to closely identify with these winged creatures:

Oh, that I had wings like the dove!
Then would I fly away and be at rest.

O deliver not the soul of Thy turtledove
unto the multitude of the wicked.[153]

In several traditions, the bird is compared to a human soul,[154] and the psalmist, in referring to the soul, sings: "Flee to your mountain, ye birds."[155] Exiles returning to their homeland are like doves returning to their dovecotes,[156] and the wanderer who remains far from home is like a bird far removed from its nest.[157]

The great variety of species among fowl contributed to a great variety of literary images. The owl, because of its habit of frequenting desolate areas and emitting plaintive and mournful sounds, is an apt figure for depicting conditions of desolation and ruin,[158] while the ostrich, also an inhabitant of forlorn areas,[159] is accused of being a stupid creature,[160] lacking in devotion toward its young.[161]

While several books of the Bible have their own "favorite" animal symbols and metaphors, there is, as would be expected, an overall consistency in the use of animals to illustrate concepts and values. One could classify such usage thematically. For example, the "enemies of Israel" are like bulls, dogs, lions, and the horns of a wild ox.[162] They swarm around Israel like bees,[163] their teeth and roar are those of a lion,[164] they snort and neigh like horses,[165] and approach their prey as do the lion and the vulture.[166] When the theme of "desolation" is depicted, characteristic animals making their appearance are the jackal,[167] ostrich,[168] pelican,[169] and bittern,[170] along with wild cats, ferrets, and wild dogs,[171] as well as owls and ravens.[172]

Scripture often focuses on unusual traits of animals to effectively illustrate religious truths. The raven, a scavenger, attacks the young and helpless among other species of animals.[173] However, it has the reputation of being an inadequate provider in meeting the needs of its own offspring. The survival of young ravens is therefore attributed to God's personal providential care, for "who provides for the raven its prey, when its young ones cry to God, and wander about for the lack of food?" asks the Book of Job.[174] The psalmist praises the Lord because "He gives to the beasts their food, and to the young ravens which cry,"[175] an obvious reference to the special care needed by this species of bird.

When the prophet Isaiah depicts the peaceful conditions of the messianic era, he eloquently portrays the unusual state of harmony that will come to exist among all of the members of the animal kingdom:

And the wolf shall dwell with the lamb,
And the leopard shall lie down with the kid;
And the calf and the young lion and the fatling together;
And a little child shall lead them.
And the cow and the bear shall feed;
Their young ones shall lie down together;
And the lion shall eat straw like the ox,
And the suckling child shall play on the hole of the asp,
And the weaned child shall put his hand on the basilisk's
    den.[176]

The great variety and varying characteristics of animals rendered them fitting subjects for moralistic teachings. The First Book of Kings attributes to King Solomon the authorship of three thousand parables and one thousand and five songs employing flora and fauna as the principal characters.[177]

The Book of Proverbs contains striking examples of the use of animals in moral and religious teachings. We are told, for example, that wealth "grows wings, like an eagle it flies away into the sky."[178] The lazy person is advised:

Go to the ant, thou sluggard
Consider her ways and be wise.
Which having no chief, overseer, or ruler,
Provideth her bread in the summer,
And gathereth her food in the harvest.[179]

The fittingness of the industrious ant as a subject is further due to the practical wisdom manifest in her habit of amassing an ample food supply during the summer months in preparation for the severe winter.

The ants are a people not strong,
Yet they provide their food in the summer.
The rock-badger are but a feeble folk,
Yet they make their houses in the crags.
The locusts have no king,
Yet go they forth all of them by bands.
The spider thou canst take with the hands
Yet is she in king's palaces.[180]

A number of the vivid descriptions of animals found in Job are likewise didactic in nature.[181]

However, fables or animal tales with moral implications are rare in the Bible, and the animal's didactic role is a limited one. Plants and animals occasionally appear in parables,[182] but biblical literature does not contain an abundance of this genre of writing. It is more characteristic of rabbinic literature.

Let it be emphasized again that even when extraordinary and unnatural animal imagery appears, as in Ezekiel's visions,[183] the animal is merely being used allegorically. There is no intrinsically supernatural quality to the animal itself. Likewise, the colorful and bizarre beasts of Daniel's apocalyptic visions are merely symbolizing monarchs and their kingdoms.[184] It is, of course, always possible that subtle allusions to popular myths and folklore may be present in some of the poetic deployments of animals as figures of speech,[185] but such allusions are literary rather than literal. The effectiveness of Scripture's use of the animal as a literary device is dependent upon the animal's being recognizable to the audience in all of its natural features and behavioral characteristics as an animal. The demythologized animal was totally recognizable to all.

KINSHIP AND COMPASSION

In spite of the dedeification and demythylogization of the animal kingdom, and the reduction of the animal to a "literary device" and background player in the biblical drama, it could be argued that Scripture not only displays but actually promotes feelings of deep kinship and compassion toward the world of fauna. Perhaps the process of demythologization actually facilitated the expression of these sentiments by highlighting the basic characteristics and similarities that exist between man and beast.

The institution of the sacrificial cult, for example, mirrors an interesting paradox. Man is obviously the master, and the animal the victim-subject. Man's duty and privilege is to live and to sacrifice; the animal's fate and destiny, on the other hand, is to die as the sacrificial victim. Yet, paradoxically, the sacrificial rites and restrictions actually emphasize man's kinship with the animals he sacrifices, and bring to the fore the elements which he shares in common with them.

The prohibition against consuming blood is one such example. Blood is, of course, the basic necessity of life. Indeed, "blood is life,"[1] and God Himself is the direct source of life.[2] Furthermore, blood, because it is life, possesses the power of atonement.[3] Therefore, the blood of animals, possessing the special qualities of life and atonement, rightly belongs to God, and is not to be eaten by man.[4]

Possibly the apotropaic function of blood is also a factor in its prohibition. Not only can blood ward off evil,[5] but it also purges various forms of impurity and expiates sin, though its effectiveness in mediating forgiveness is not due to any innate power, but rather to the will and power of God.

Suet, or fat of the omentum, is also prohibited as food,[6] presumably because, like blood, it was regarded as the "seat of vitality."[7] The reserved portions of a sacrifice normally excluded the omentum, the kidneys with their fat, and the appendages to the liver, along with the fat tail of sheep.[8]

The biblical laws of impurity further emphasized basic similarities between the bodies of humans and animals. One of the principal causes of impurity (along with leprosy and sexual emissions) is contact with the corpses of humans and animals. Granted that the degree of impurity in a human corpse is greater, nevertheless the carcasses of all beasts are also in a state of impurity except for those animals slaughtered for sacrifice or consumption.

Whatever interpretations or explanations one chooses to advance for such prohibitions, the fact remains that animals, like man, possess the divine quality of life, and their blood, like the blood of man, has remarkable powers. Purity and impurity are likewise associated with both man and beast.

The Dietary Laws

Biblical law clearly endorses man's right to consume as food the flesh of animals. Yet here, too, considerable restrictions are imposed upon the consumer. Unquestionably there was a connection between man's sacrifice of animals and his eating of their flesh. Indeed, the very legitimacy of consuming the meat of an animal is, in part, dependent upon its sacrifice on an altar. Thus Leviticus condemns as murder the slaughter of animals outside the precinct of the altar of the sanctuary.[9] Unauthorized slaughter is deemed unlawful bloodshed, and the perpetrator is deserving of divine punishment! It is only when animals fit for sacrifice are slaughtered at the altar, and their blood drained, that their flesh may be legally consumed. Wild animals or birds procured in the hunt must have their blood similarly drained into the earth.[10] As sacrificial animals are to be clean[11] and free from major blemishes,[12] so only clean species of animals are permitted for consumption. The prohibition involving the blood and fat of the sacrificial animal is equally applicable to the animal that is to be eaten, and the blood must be thoroughly drained before the animal's flesh may be consumed.[13] Although the "sons of Noah" are permitted to eat meat once the blood has been removed,[14] the Israelites appear to have been required to have the blood drained at a sacrificial altar,[15] and thus the sacrificial ritual would seem to have been a necessary prelude, as it were, to the eating of meat.

This is not to imply that every act of slaughter had to be a bona fide sacrifice, and that every eating of meat was a cultic occasion. It is rather difficult to envision, for example, the thief who steals an ox or sheep and slaughters it for food as participating in a sacrificial ritual to God in the process![16] But when Saul's troops wish to consume the flesh of animals, he legitimizes the act by requiring that the animals be slaughtered upon a rock altar.[17] Profane slaughtering, as such, would appear to have been forbidden.

Perhaps a distinction should be made between a genuine sacrifice and a quasi-sacrifice performed as a prelude to the slaughtering of an animal for food, but some ceremony of the latter type seems to have accompanied the eating of flesh. The very term *zevah* seems to denote both a family meal of meat as well as a sacrifice,[18] a religious celebration culminating in a meal. Pilgrim feasts featured the consumption of meat as part of the communal meal following the festive sacrifice. Some rabbis insisted that even in the wilderness, the Israelites were only permitted to eat of the flesh of animals which had been sacrificed upon an altar, and their appropriate parts consumed by fire and given to the priests.[19] Peace-offerings often culminated with the offerer enjoying a communal meal[20] held at an especially ordained site.[21]

There is, of course, a prominent communal aspect to a sacrifice. When covenants or alliances were established between men, tradition ordained the breaking of bread together.[22] We find the Israelites commanded by God to bring offerings after the conquest of Canaan and "to eat in the presence of the Lord your God,"[23] the sacrifices constituting, as it were, a prelude to the meal (of the sacrifice).

Sacrifices are clearly required by biblical law. But is the eating of meat similarly required? Clearly it is not. Furthermore, the cultic requirements for slaughter actually serve to severely limit the amount of meat which can be consumed.

Many theories have been proposed to explain the rationale of the dietary laws, ranging in nature from hygienic to moralistic, from totemistic to nationalistic. But Scripture states simply that these laws are to be obeyed in order that Israel should be a "a holy people unto the Lord," and "distinguished from other nations by the avoidance of unclean and abominable things that defile them."[24]

However, one ought not to discount moralistic factors. As has been noted, Scripture does not hold the hunter in high esteem, and although ancient art depicts the rulers of Egypt and Mesopotamia as personally involved in the royal sport of lion-hunting, no king of Israel is ever described participating in this or in any hunt.[25]

Furthermore, when the early pages of Genesis detail the divine plan in which all creatures are to live in harmony, man is told that he may eat from "every plant yielding seed which is upon the face of the earth, and every tree with seed in its fruit."[26] Now meat is obviously excluded from this prescribed diet! It is only after the flood that Noah and his descendants are permitted to partake of the flesh of animals—"Every moving thing that liveth shall be food for you; as the green herb have I given you all"[27]—with the restriction that blood must not be consumed.

Is this accommodation due to the fact that Noah and his sons, by virtue of having saved the animals from certain death in the deluge, are now partners, as it were, with God in the creation of these species?[28] Is meat now permitted to man as a concession to his apparent inability to maintain the spiritual standards (such as vegetarianism) imposed upon him in the Garden of Eden? Or was flesh-eating permitted to the survivors of the flood simply because there was nothing else extant upon the earth that could be eaten? We do not know. But in any event, man is now permitted to eat meat, albeit with certain restrictions.

But *must* he eat meat? On occasion, yes, but only as part of certain specific rituals, such as the partaking of the paschal and *Hagigah* offerings, and priestly sacrificial functions. But in a broader sense, is there a divine decree *demanding* of man that he butcher and consume the flesh of fauna? Should meat be part of his standard, normal diet? Not at all.

Quite the contrary. The crucial passage in Deuteronomy reads: "When the Lord thy God shall enlarge thy border, as He hath promised thee, and thou shalt say: 'I will eat flesh,' because thy soul desireth to eat flesh; thou mayest eat flesh, after all the desire of thy soul."[29] Now rabbinic tradition perceives in this text a clear indication that it is *man's desire* to eat flesh, not God's decree that he is to do so, and attributes an unflattering connotation to this lust for flesh.

Certain aspects of eschatological thought are also significant in this context. Eschatology and cosmogony are obviously interrelated, the former being a futuristic projection of the latter. The eschatological depiction of the messianic era therefore bears a striking similarity to the period when Adam and Eve lived in the Garden of Eden. Again, a futuristic idyllic setting is envisioned where nature will give of her blessings in great abundance, and *all* creatures will live together in harmony, with none feeding upon the flesh of the other.

Both Isaiah and Hosea[30] depict the messianic era in the figurative language of a new Garden of Eden wherein all animals will coexist peacefully: "The wolf and the lamb shall feed together, and the lion shall eat straw like the ox; and dust shall be the serpent's food."[31] No longer will enmity exist between man and the animals, for the Lord proclaims: "I will make a covenant for them with the beasts of the field and with the fowls of heaven and with the creeping things of the ground."[32]

The majority of such prophetic visions seem to depict an exclusively vegetarian diet for man:

And it shall come to pass in that day that
mountains shall drip sweet wine, and the hills
shall flow with milk.[33]

And they shall plant vineyards and drink the
wine thereof, they shall also make gardens
and eat the fruit of them.[34]

And the earth shall respond to the corn,
and the wine and the oil.[35]

Ezekiel's vision of the waters teeming with an abundance of fish is meant to highlight the miraculous transformation of the Dead Sea into a freshwater lake, rather than to encourage fish-dinners![36] Unmistakably, the ideal of the messianic era, like the ideal of the Garden of Eden, envisions a cessation of all enmity between man and the animal kingdom, a state of existence which will find them no longer feeding upon one another's flesh, for all living beings are, after all, the creatures of the Lord.

Kinship

It is only natural that man should feel a certain affinity for the members of the animal kingdom and incorporate them into his own human community. After all, "animals are part of the topocosm . . . that is, of the aggregate of all living beings and inanimate objects which together form the corporate entity and atmosphere of a place. Hence . . . they participate in its fate and future."[37]

The natural tendency among the ancients was to attribute feelings and emotions, not only to animals, but to plants and even to inanimate objects! The pagan religions of antiquity conceived of spirits dwelling in mountains, deserts, and seas, as well as inhabiting the bodies of living beings.

The biblical portrait of the world was quite different. Although its vivid poetic imagery seems, at times, to imbue all entities with life and awareness, clear divisions exist in the Bible between the animate and the inanimate, and striking distinctions are drawn between man and the animal. Still, the biblical topocosm embraces both man and beast, with the former sensing an obvious kinship with the latter. It was only natural for Ezekiel to display this kinship in describing the cataclysmic epoch of Gog, when "the fishes of the sea, and the fowls of heaven, and the beasts of the field, and all creeping things that creep upon the ground, and all the men that are upon the face of the earth, shall shake at My presence."[38]

Such a kinship is based, in part, upon the obvious similarities that exist between humans and animals. Man has always detected, or believed that he detected, emotional reactions in animals not at all unlike his own—elation, disappointment, fear, anxiety, love, hatred, etc. Who could not easily, though uncomfortably, identify with Isaiah's "as a sheep that before its shearers is dumb"?[39] Particularly in a pastoral society, where domesticated animals were in abundance, man spent much time in the company of the lower animals and had ample opportunities to observe and recognize traits held in common.

Some of these were superficial similarities which found expression in poetic imagery. As noted, the beauty of form and delicacy of movement of the gazelle and the hind reminded a lover of his beloved,[40] while the solitary bird flying forlorn far away from her nest symbolized so very well the homeless wanderer among humans.[41] How easy it must have been for the warrior to see a reflection of himself in the power and majesty of the lion.

But there is a deeper dimension to the kinship binding man to beast in Scripture. Both man and animals are doomed to die, for they share in common the fate of mortality, though the former lost an immortality never possessed by the latter.

> For that which befalleth the sons of men befalleth beasts;
> even one thing befalleth them;
> as the one dieth so dieth the other;
> yea, they have all one breath;
> so that man hath no preeminence above a beast;
> for all is vanity.
> All go to one place; all are of
> the dust, and all return to the dust.
> Who knoweth the spirit of man whether it goeth upward,
> and the spirit of the beast whether it goeth downward to the
>   earth?[42]

The frailty and brevity of existence for both humans and animals is an obvious trait held in common. Both man and animal, in contradistinction to plant life, stand in need of God's blessings from the very moment of their creation.[43] Whatever Scripture may choose to compare life to—a mist,[44] a fleeting breath,[45] a cloud,[46] a dream,[47] a shadow,[48] a flower,[49] or grass[50]—both man and beast share this transitory existence, although it is man, of course, who is told he shares the destiny of the beast, and not vice versa.

Biblical terminology reflects this unity of man and beast. *Ruach hayyim* ("spirit of life") can refer to both man and animal,[51] as can *nefesh hayyah* ("living creature").[52] The word *basar* ("flesh") refers literally to the softer parts of the body of an organism, or to the body in general, or to humanity in general.[53] But the phrase *kol basar* ("all flesh") can denote *all* living creatures, animal as well as man.[54] Of course, *basar* refers to food, to the edible flesh of animals,[55] but in a more abstract sense it connotes "frailty," the perishable nature of all living entities.[56]

Scripture extols God's providence as extending over both man and beast and providing sustenance for all:

He giveth to the beast his food, and to the young ravens which cry.[57]

Thou openest Thy hand and satisfieth every living thing with favor.[58]

Man and beast Thou preserveth, O Lord.[59]

Who causest the grass to spring up for the cattle and herb for the service of man.[60]

In whose hand is the soul of every living thing and the breath of all mankind.[61]

The organic unity seen as pervading all of life, and the reality of animals comprising part of the basic topocosm of all life, is beautifully expressed in the Book of Jonah when the king of Nineveh proclaims a public fast, ordering the animals to be clad in mourning sackcloth, just like their human counterparts, and to cry out mightily to God.[62] But, of course, God's covenant with

Noah specifically includes animals along with humans: "Behold, I establish My covenant with you . . . and with every living creature that is with you, the fowl and the cattle and every beast of the earth with you."[63]

Inherent in "covenant" is "responsibility," and Scripture does not spare animals from responsibility for their deeds. The doctrine of reward and punishment is basic to the Bible, functioning on an individual, national, as well as universal level. Retributive justice is extended to beasts as to men, for they, too, are subject to this law, and at times animals would seem to be treated as though they were coequal with men.

Many examples can be cited. When Adam and Eve are punished for their sin of disobedience, the serpent, too, is condemned to crawl on its belly and cursed with remaining in a state of perpetual enmity with man.[64] During the course of God's revelation to the Children of Israel at Mount Sinai, animals, as well as humans, are threatened with punishment should they touch the mountain.[65] The ox that gores and kills a human is stoned to death,[66] reflecting the admonition in Genesis, "And surely your blood, the blood of your lives, will I require; at the hand of every beast will I require it."[67] The inherent assumption here is that an animal, like a human being, bears blood-guilt. In cases of sexual contact between man and beast, both the former and the latter are put to death,[68] with the animal rape victim actually being punished more severely than the human rape victim![69] But it might be advisable to qualify the term "punishment" in this context. After all, the animal has come to symbolize the degradation of a human being, and its death may more accurately be viewed as the eradication of a degrading symbol than as the infliction of a punishment per se.

In any event, it should be noted that punishing animals for their crimes was not an uncommon practice in the ancient world,[70] and Plato even dictates retribution for *in*animate objects, not to mention beasts![71] It is interesting that earlier Mesopotamian legal codes dealing with identical cases of goring oxen do not exact punishment from the animal.[72]

But the fact that animals are subject to rules of responsibility and punishment should not imply that there is always a "reason" for the animal's punishment. In Scripture, beasts often seem to suffer the fate of their masters simply by virtue of the fact that they are the chattels of their masters. What, for example, were the sins of the Egyptian cattle who perished along with their masters?[73] What culpability did the firstborn cattle of Egypt incur to warrant their demise?[74] The animals of the era of the flood are perhaps included in the phrase "*all* flesh had corrupted their way upon the earth,"[75] and therefore they will be blotted out from the face of the earth along with man.[76] But what precisely could have been their offense? Interestingly, rabbinic tradition attributes to them sexual offenses.[77] However, why should Jeremiah condemn beasts to die along with the defenders of Jerusalem?[78] Is it plausible to attribute to them the same transgressions that caused their masters to be expelled from Judea? Hardly. The animal, often, is simply an innocent victim, suffering for man's misdeeds along with man.

On the other hand, animals share with man both the privilege and the responsibility of being God's special messengers. Ravens are bidden to feed the prophet Elijah,[79] lions are sent to kill a rebellious prophet[80] and the new inhabitants of Samaria.[81] In the visions of Ezekiel,[82] the beasts of the field are commanded to consume the remains of tyrants, thereby assisting to remove traces of evil from the earth.[83] She-bears function as God's agents when they kill the children who are guilty of mocking the prophet Elisha.[84]

It is true that many of these "agency" roles played by animals are perfunctory and unthinking roles. But on another level, some scriptural passages seem to exalt the virtues of animals far above those of humans! Isaiah contrasts Israel's failure to acknowledge God with a beast's unerring knowledge and recognition of its master,[85] and Jeremiah sadly muses on the fact that while the bird's homing instincts unerringly lead it to its proper path and destination, Israel lacks such an elemental ability, and is therefore incapable of properly following in the path of the Lord: "Yea, the stork in the heaven knoweth her appointed times; and the turtle [dove] and the swallow and the crane observe the time of their coming; but my people know not the ordinance of the Lord."[86]

Solomon the wise is extolled for his ability to speak of trees, beasts, fowl, creeping things, and fishes.[87] Obviously, a special degree of wisdom and sensitivity is needed in order to fathom the mysteries of God's other creations—creatures whose ways are as inexplicable as some of the mysteries of the human mind and heart.

There are three things which are too wonderful for me,
Yes, four which I know not;
The way of an eagle in the air;
The way of a serpent upon a rock;
The way of a ship in the midst of the sea;
And the way of a man with a young woman.[88]

But ask now the beasts, and they shall teach thee;
And the fowls of the air, and they shall tell thee;
Or speak to the earth, and it shall teach thee;
And the fishes of the sea shall declare unto thee![89]

Scripture admits that fauna can, at times, possess a sensitivity superior to that of their human counterparts. After all, animals can perceive spirits with an ability lacking in humans;[90] witness the case of Balaam's ass detecting the presence of God's angel while his master remains oblivious of the divine visitor.[91]

Compassion

Note was made of God's special act of compassion in providing food for the young ravens. However, Scripture describes all living beings as the direct beneficiaries of divine kindness and wisdom.

The psalmist depicts such diverse creatures as the stork, wild ass, ibex, and even Leviathan living in harmony under God's providential care, and how the Lord "maketh darkness and it is night, wherein all the beasts of the forest do creep forth. The young lions roar after their prey, and seek their food from God."[92]

God's providence is a recurrent theme in Psalms.

All of them wait for Thee,
That Thou mayest give them their food in due season,

Thou givest it to them, they gather it;
Thou openest Thy hand, they are satisfied with good.[93]

The Lord is good to all; and His tender mercies are over all His works.[94]

The eyes of all wait for Thee, and Thou giveth them their food in due season.[95]

Rabbinic tradition elaborates upon this theme, emphasizing God's role as the concerned benefactor of all dimensions of life: "The Holy One, blessed be He, sits and sustains [all life], from the horns of the wild oryx to the eggs of lice."[96]

God is praised for having created a world with varied terrain, suitable for diverse creatures and their specific needs: the lion dwells in the thicket of Jordan,[97] the dens of the lion are the mountains of Lebanon,[98] while the viper and flying serpent dwell in the desert.[99] The psalmist sings: "As for the stork, the fir trees are her house, the high mountains are for the wild goats; the rocks are a refuge for the conies."[100] The wild ass dwells in the wilderness and salt-lands,[101] while nocturnal birds make their abode in desolate areas.[102]

Bearing more directly upon the theme of "compassion for the beast" are articles of legislation promulgated by Scripture which would appear to benefit the animal. To be sure, one must be cautious in seeking to discern rationales for biblical ordinances vis-à-vis the animal, for Scripture often declines to supply any rationale for its legislation. Yet, in contrast to many of the pagan religions of antiquity, which rarely sought correlation between the god and the good,[103] the religion of Israel saw all divine legislation as being, by definition, of benefit for His creatures. A strong case can certainly be made for the animal having been designated by Scripture to be a deserving recipient of divine beneficence.

At times, animals are the beneficiaries of legislation directed to man. For example, the obligation to rest upon the Sabbath is extended to all domestic animals and beasts of burden.[104] They too are to enjoy Sabbath repose. Similarly, when Scripture proclaims

that fields are to lie fallow during the Sabbatical year, it emphasizes that the produce is to be enjoyed by the beasts of the field as
well as the poor.[105] The emasculation of animals as well as men is
forbidden by the Bible.[106]

Other legislation, directed specifically toward fauna, seems to
have been motivated by strong feelings of compassion for the
animal. We shall cite several examples.

Humans are permitted to eat the flesh of animals,[107] but they are
forbidden to eat an animal that is still alive: "But flesh with its life,
its blood, you shall not eat";[108] i.e., while the life and blood are still
in it, an animal must not be consumed. It is forbidden to consume
a portion of a living creature and then proceed upon one's way
while the animal dies a slow, agonizing death.

Deuteronomy forbids the muzzling of an ox while he treads
grain upon the threshing floor,[109] for the animal is entitled to enjoy
food as would any human laborer,[110] and rabbinic tradition interpreted the term "ox" as a generic phrase incorporating *all* animals.[111] Cornhill comments with admiration upon this passage:

> What a truly humanitarian sentiment finds expression in this
> law, *Thou shalt not muzzle the ox when he treadeth out the corn.*
> The brute should not perform hard labor and at the same time
> have food before its eyes without the possibility of eating
> therefrom. I remember some time ago to have read that one of
> the richest Italian real-estate owners, at the grape-harvest, fas-
> tened iron muzzles to his miserable, fever-stricken workmen,
> so that it might not occur to these poor peasants working for
> starvation wages under the glowing sun of Southern Italy, to
> satiate their burning thirst and their gnawing hunger with a few
> of the millions of grapes of the owner.[112]

Man is enjoined against taking both mother and young from a
bird's nest. Only after the mother-bird departs may the young be
taken, for "when the mother is sent away, she does not see the
taking of her young ones, and does not feel any pain."[113] It is
interesting to note that this is the first recorded legislation in
history for the protection of birds![114]

Scripture likewise forbids the slaughtering of mother cattle and their young on the same day,[115] and seething a kid in its mother's milk.[116] The yoking together of an ox and an ass is prohibited by the Bible,[117] presumably because of differences between the species in strength, gait, and endurance that might cause difficulties for the weaker of the pair.

The Israelite is commanded to be vigilant for the well-being of a lost animal: "Thou shalt not see thy brother's ox or his sheep driven away and hide thyself from them; thou shalt surely bring them back unto thy brother."[118] Furthermore, the animal must be cared for indefinitely in the absence of its owner. Similarly, an animal fallen beneath the weight of its burden must be assisted to rise,[119] the Bible emphasizing that these rules are applicable even to the beast of one's enemy![120]

A touching expression of compassion for the feelings of a beast appears in the celebrative narrative of Balaam's ass. The Lord grants the gift of speech to the dumb animal, and the ass plaintively asks her master why he has smitten her three times: "Am I not thine ass upon whom thou hast ridden all thy life long unto this day?"[121] Balaam is condemned by the angel of the Lord for having struck the poor animal.

According to the Book of Proverbs, one of the descriptive traits of a righteous man, along with caring for the poor,[122] pleading their cause,[123] and giving generously to the needy,[124] is his tending to the needs of animals. Thus, "a righteous man regards the *nefesh* ["life"] of his beast, but the tender mercies of the wicked are cruel."[125] *Nefesh* literally means "soul," and on several occasions the term refers specifically to a desire for food.[126]

This quasi-definition of a righteous man as one who is sensitive to the needs of animals finds echo in many writings.

If I know a man is cruel to his beast, I ask no more questions about him. He may be a noble man, or a rich man, or a polite man, or a sensible man, or a learned man, or an orthodox man, or a church man, or anything else, it matters not; this I know, on the sacred word of a wise king, that being cruel to his beast, he is a wicked man.[127]

God Himself proclaims in the closing verse of the Book of Jonah: ". . . and should I not have pity on Nineveh, that great city, wherein are more than sixscore thousand persons that cannot discern between their right hand and their left hand, and also much cattle?"[128]

No animal is more lovingly or compassionately portrayed in Scripture than the sheep and her lambs. The primary occupation of the Israelites during the early biblical period was that of sheepherding, and Scripture emphasizes that many of Israel's heroes and leaders were herdsmen of sheep.[129] In the words of the psalmist, "He chose David also His servant, and took him from the sheepfolds; from following the ewes that give suck He brought him, to be shepherd over Jacob His people, and Israel His inheritance."[130]

The relationship between shepherd and sheep, and the special bond uniting them, is beautifully portrayed in the Bible. The shepherd's responsibility toward his flock is depicted in detail: leading them to water and to pasture,[131] guarding them from predators[132] and robbers,[133] nursing the ill and seeking out the lost from among the flock,[134] and even carrying baby lambs in his bosom, while gently leading the nursing mothers.[135]

When the prophet Nathan rebukes David for his indefensible crime in causing the death of Uriah so that he could take the slain man's wife for himself, he skillfully and movingly portrays for the king, a former shepherd, a story about the love of a poor man for a little ewe-lamb. Nathan describes how the man reared it as he did his own children, for "it did eat of his own morsel and drink of his own cup, and lay in his bosom, and was unto him as a daughter."[136] Such, indeed, was the bond of love that could exist between shepherd and flock, between man and animal in biblical days.

When Esau offers to accompany his brother, Jacob, on his journey, the latter clearly desires to find some pretext to avoid having to travel with him. He declines the offer, commenting, by way of explanation, that his flocks could not possibly keep pace with Esau's fast-moving military entourage. Granted, this may be no more than a pretext; nevertheless Jacob's tender description of his flock is worth noting:

> My lord knoweth that the children are tender, and that the flocks and herds giving suck are a care to me; and if they overdrive them one day, all the flocks will die. Let my lord, I pray thee, pass over before his servant; and I will journey on gently, according to the pace of the cattle that are before me and according to the pace of the children, until I come unto my lord unto Seir.[137]

The weak and defenseless sheep, constantly in need of care and protection,[138] was a fitting symbol for a weak and defenseless human being. Isaiah, in depicting the distress of the persecuted "servant of the Lord," conceives of him "as a lamb that is led to the slaughter, and as a sheep that before its shearers is dumb."[139]

Indeed, the sheep became the ideal symbol for the people of Israel, with the master shepherd being none other than God Himself. Thus the psalmist proclaims:

> The Lord is my shepherd, I shall not want.
> He maketh me to lie down in green pastures;
> He leadeth me beside the still waters.
> He restoreth my soul.
> He guideth me in straight paths for His name's sake.
> Yea, though I walk through the valley of the shadow of death,
> I will fear no evil,
> For Thou art with me;
> Thy rod and Thy staff, they comfort me.[140]

In Isaiah's chapter of consolation, God is described "even as a shepherd that feedeth his flock, that gathereth the lambs in his arm, and carrieth them in his bosom and gently leadeth those that give suck."[141] With similar imagery, Jeremiah prophesies: "And I will gather the remnant of My flock out of all the countries where I have driven them, and I will bring them back to their fold. . . . I will set shepherds over them who will feed them; and they shall fear no more, nor be dismayed, neither shall any be lacking, saith the Lord."[142]

Ezekiel presents a vivid allegory wherein the shepherds of the people of Israel are rebuked for having neglected their human flocks. The prophet announces that God Himself will assume the role of the personal shepherd to His people and will seek them out and rescue them from their dispersal. He will care for the crippled, give sustenance to the weak, and feed all of them upon fat pastures. In matchless prose, the prophet depicts an ideal paradise for the flock under the care of their compassionate divine shepherd.[143]

Such, in prose and poetry, in legal enactment and didactic parable, is the scriptural emphasis upon the need for having compassion for the beast. William E. H. Lecky, in analyzing the prohibitions against plowing with an ox and an ass, and against muzzling an ox as he treads corn, concludes that "tenderness to animals is one of the most beautiful features of the Old Testament."[144]

THE DELICATE TOOL

However persuasively one may attempt to state the case that biblical man sensed a deep kinship with the animal kingdom, and related to it with compassion, the case falls well short of being convincing.

Granted that the destiny of man and animal is the same. Granted that both man and animal are part of God's handiwork. Granted that Scripture can, and does, at times, speak lovingly of certain fauna. We should, nevertheless, recognize certain basic realities in Scripture that render the animal more akin to man's tool than his equal partner in life.

Even if all biblical legislation vis-à-vis the care and treatment of animals were to be interpreted in a purely "ethical" light, as being expressly for the benefit of the animal (and we shall attempt to demonstrate that this is not always the case), it is significant to note that such legislation is strictly limited to domestic animals! In other words, there is a utilitarian factor here that must not be overlooked. Man is nowhere commanded to feed *wild* birds or to supply *wild* animals with their needs. His responsibilities are limited solely to domestic species, e.g., the ox, the ass, the donkey, etc., species with whom he is involved in a practical working relationship, and upon whose well-being he himself is dependent.

As noted earlier, the biblical portrait of the animal kingdom is neither objective nor all-encompassing. Emphasis and prominence are given only to specific species, those species necessary to man for his own survival or comfort. Although there are unmistakable references to God's supplying *all* manner of creatures with their sustenance, such references are more accurately manifestations of God's greatness and power than exhortations to mankind to follow the Lord's example as sustainer of wild beasts and birds. After all, no biblical hero is ever depicted as feeding a baby raven, or any wild animal for that matter! Nowhere does biblical legislation demand such deeds as acts of holiness or piety. The concern of Scripture is primarily limited to the working animal. The animal's master is obligated to treat him kindly and considerately, but obviously, in the long run, this constitutes sound and practical advice which is ultimately for the benefit of the human master and in his own best interests.

Upon closer examination, a *practical* rather than *ethical* purpose may well underlie much of the legislation pertaining to domestic animals. The exhortation to lead a lost ox, sheep, or ass back to its master, even if that master happens to be one's enemy, is surely impressive.[1] But is it for the benefit of the animal? Perhaps the primary purpose of this legislation is the restoration of lost *property* to its rightful owner, even a rightful owner whom one detests! One can similarly interpret the command to assist in the loading and unloading of beasts of burden.[2] Here, too, the preservation of another's property and valuables may well be the dominant factor, not easing the discomfort of the beast per se. Man needed his domestic animals, they were the indispensable commodities of an agrarian and pastoral society. "Where no oxen are, the crib is clean, but much increase is by the strength of the ox."[3]

Even the prohibition against consuming an animal before it is dead,[4] which would seem to have obvious and powerful ethical implications, might also be interpreted more narrowly as ensuring compliance with the restriction against consuming blood.

True, meat consumption was not common in ancient Israel, but this was probably due to *practical* rather than *spiritual* factors. It was clearly impractical to frequently slaughter domestic animals for food when they were of greater value to man in supplying him with the basic necessities of life in the form of dairy-foods, labor, wool for clothing, etc. The correlation between meat-eating, cultic gatherings, and sacrifices is understandable; as meat could not be preserved, it was necessary for the entire animal to be consumed at a single sitting, hence the advisability of inviting guests to help in the consumption of sacrifices.[5]

Although the Bible refers to such ascetic practices as fasting and abstaining from wine, there is no mention of people regularly abstaining from meat. With the aforementioned exception of Daniel's abstention from flesh, wine, and "pleasant bread" during a mourning period,[6] Scripture fails to mention vegetarianism among the practices of pietists.[7]

If there is a single unifying principle underlying many of the biblical injunctions urging abstinence, and limiting man's authority to manipulate or destroy members of the animal kingdom, the principle is not one of ethical consideration for fauna. It is rather to be found in the conviction that the earth and all its inhabitants rightly belong to the Lord.[8] Man must therefore not interfere with the creations of God's world. He must not cause any alteration or confusion in God's natural order; on the contrary, he is bidden to preserve the authenticity and purity of all species of life.

As God is the creator of all, He alone is the rightful owner of all His creatures. As the ultimate source of all life, all life clearly belongs to Him.

For every beast of the forest is Mine,
And the cattle upon a thousand hills.
I know all the fowls of the mountains;
And the wild beasts of the field are Mine.
If I were hungry, I would not tell thee;
For the world is Mine, and the fullness thereof.[9]

Needless to say, the wanton destruction of any of God's creatures is forbidden. Suicide, as well as murder, is outlawed.[10] A besieging army must even refrain from cutting down the fruit trees of the enemy![11] Even legitimate use has its limitations.

For all its variations, the sacrificial system possesses a fundamental, underlying unity—the principle of extending to God a portion of that which He has given to man; of submitting a tribute, as it were, to the divine benefactor. For if all things belong to God, what right does man have to partake of the Lord's possessions at all?

Out of necessity man must, indeed, partake of the bounty of the earth. Food is necessary for survival, and so man is *permitted* to eat of vegetation,[12] and later even of the flesh of animals,[13] with the restriction that the life-blood of any animal belongs to God, and must not be consumed. However, ideally God's world should not be abused at all, and so the idealized portrayal of the messianic era depicts an age in which man and animal are no longer carnivorous. Furthermore, even here and now, while man is permitted to partake of God's bounty, he must, nevertheless, first participate in certain redemptive ceremonies. Hence, the institution of firstlings among animals, firstborn among humans, and first-fruits among the annual crops. A brief digression is warranted.

Firstlings and Firstborns

As God is entitled to the first born males of all living creatures (firstborns were considered the most efficacious of sacrifices),[14] they must be consecrated to Him. However, in the case of a human firstborn or that of an unclean animal, the sacrificial rite is disallowed, and in its stead the tribute is ransomed, usually in monetary form.[15] The redemption of the firstborn among men saw the substitution of the tribe of Levi for the firstborn, who were theoretically obligated to function in some sort of cultic service,[16] for in principle the firstborn belong to the Lord.

First-Fruits

Even man's consumption of herbs and fruits was not without limitation, therefore the first-fruits of the field were also deemed God's possessions,[17] as were prime portions of all grain, oil, and newly shorn wool and coarse material.[18] Since God "quickens" the soil by sending rain, He is entitled to a portion of the produce. Therefore, man is denied the right to eat of fruit trees during the first three years, and the fruit of the fourth year must be presented to God as a praise-offering.[19] Man must also participate in a redemptive ceremony wherein the first-fruits of the field, corn, wine, and oil, were to be offered as a feast-offering to God.[20]

Likewise *hadash* ("new corn") was not to be eaten until the second day of Passover, when the *omer* was offered in the Temple of Jerusalem.[21] Scripture further prescribes that every seven years the land is not to be worked but must lie fallow. The poor and animals were free to eat of the vineyards and groves,[22] but the owners of fields were forbidden to sow their fields, prune their vineyards, or reap any crops at all.

Granted that in such procedures there may be practical benefits accruing in terms of agricultural efficiency and the amelioration of social ills and economic imbalances,[23] but more is involved. The Sabbatical year emphasizes *restitutio in integrum,* permitting the land to revert to a state of undisturbed rest, and the Jubilee legislation underscores the recognition of the fact that the land belongs to God, and no one has the authority to permanently appropriate the land of the Lord,[24] "for the land is Mine; for ye are strangers and settlers with Me."[25]

The weekly Sabbath, as well as the Sabbatical year, undeniably contains aspects that may be beneficial to the beast. However, the welfare of the beast is hardly the primary factor. What is crucial is the recognition that both beasts and fields are part of God's domain. Man may derive benefit and sustenance from them, but he is obligated to cease from any exploitation of them, because rightfully they do not belong to him. Man is a tenant upon earth, not an owner, and the human tenant has limited rights to the Lord's property.

As complex as the institution of tithing may be, the same motif is clearly reflected. The owner (God) exacts payment from the tenant (man). Thus the Bible legislates an obligatory tithe upon the Children of Israel, from the fruits of the trees to the seed of the earth, to the cattle upon the land.[26] The social and institutional benefits accruing from tithing are substantial. Deuteronomy describes the tithing of corn, wine, and olive oil, and its distribution to Levites, strangers, orphans, and widows in the third and sixth years, and its consumption in Jerusalem in the first, second, fourth, and fifth years of the Sabbatical cycle.[27] Tithes are given to the Levites, who in turn tithe to the priests.[28]

In the narrative portions of Scripture, property tithes are donated for sacred purposes and as religious tribute. We find tithing to Melchizedek, the priest-ruler of Shalem, and Jacob vowing to tithe to the Lord at Beth-El.[29] The tithe is occasionally referred to as "holy to the Lord,"[30] and tithes of animals and sheep cannot be redeemed, as they are designated to be sacrificed. It would appear that tithing is related to the tradition of consecrating first-fruits to the Lord. It is a mathematically precise form of the latter, and, indeed, parallel passages in Deuteronomy employ the terms "tithe" and "firstling" interchangeably.[31]

We note, in passing, that the institution of tithing is reflected in paying homage to God not only as the creator of nature but as the active agency in history. Even the spoils of war were deemed rightly the Lord's, as He is the ultimate source of all military victories,[32] and the obligation to dedicate all firstborn to God is explained as a result of God's having spared them when He smote the Egyptian firstborn.[33]

But what is especially pertinent for our purposes is the examination of examples of so-called ethical treatment of animals in the light of another ramification of God's ownership of the world, namely, the prohibition against interfering with the natural pattern and order of life that has been established by the Creator.

Perhaps we could describe this concern for noninterference as an essential aspect of what Scripture means when the word "holiness" is employed. Conformity to the rules of holiness carries with it the reward of prosperity, with both man and animal enjoying the blessings of fertility,[34] while disobedience results in barrenness and confusion.[35]

Now "holiness" obviously embraces many moral and ethical values (chapter 20 of Leviticus, enjoining the Israelites against the practices of deceit, affirms the basic principle of holiness—integrity and discrimination—as opposed to inconsistency, confusion, and the violation of principles), but it also embodies the notion of completeness, wholeness, pattern, and even "cleanliness" in a physical dimension.

For example, "dirt" is disorder. Why? Because it offends against order. Therefore hygiene and ritual purification play such an important role in the religion of Israel. Cleansing actually involves the reestablishment of order in one's environment, while unclean-liness is matter that is out of place. Cleansing imposes order and system, therefore "dirt is the by-product of a systematic ordering and classification of matter, insofar as ordering involves rejecting inappropriate elements."[36] Order implies pattern; it also implies restrictions, for it limits the selection of appropriate entities and responses.

The idea of physical wholeness and perfection is emphasized in the institution of the sacrificial cult. The priest himself must be without bodily imperfections, the animals to be offered must be free of blemishes. Self-mutilation is outlawed in biblical law, and purification ceremonies are mandated for a variety of circum-stances, such as childbirth, and diseases such as leprosy and ailments characterized by bodily discharges. The idea of "holi-ness" was given physical expression in the notion of wholeness of body and limb.

This aspect of the "holiness" concept is extended to apply to categories of living species. When all living organisms, human as well as flora and fauna, are bidden by God to reproduce and propagate, Scripture is careful to emphasize "after its own kind"; let the propagation be strictly "after their own kind." In other words, each species should reproduce its own kind faithfully, restricting itself in sexual selection. Fertility has to be controlled—such is Scripture's message to the Israelite.

For the pagan religions, fertility was a central drama to be reenacted by man with all the creativity imaginable. But for the religion of Israel, fertility rules and regulations were set down by God, the one and only creative power of the world. The pagan was unrestricted in his fertility cults; intermingling of the species was even encouraged. For the Israelite, any deviation from a species reproducing "after its own kind" was abhorrent. Thus Scripture outlaws such human sexual perversions as homosexual-ity and bestiality.[37] Interestingly, in the latter case, the word *tebhel* is used, a term literally connoting "confusion," "mixed-up."

Similar restrictions are placed upon plant and animal propaga-tion. The Bible commands the Israelite: "Ye shall keep My statutes. Thou shalt not let thy cattle gender with a diverse kind;

thou shalt not sow thy field with two kinds of seed; neither shall there come upon thee a garment of two kinds mixed together."[38] It should be noted that the specific prohibition against mixing wool and linen together involves an animal and a vegetable product![39]

It is significant that Deuteronomy, when repeating the prohibition against hybridization and the wearing of clothing of "mingled stuff," juxtaposes between these two prohibitions the exhortation, "Thou shalt not plow with an ox and an ass together."[40] As we have seen, this particular injunction can easily be interpreted as stemming from a sense of solicitude for the smaller and weaker ass, obviously at a disadvantage in pulling the plow alongside an ox, but perhaps the real thrust of this passage is to be seen, rather, within the general context of prohibitions against intermingling different species![41]

Working diverse species of animals together was seen as an unnatural act, one with dangerous potential.[42] Holiness implies conformity to specific classes and genres of being, and the responsibility of maintaining the integrity and purity of these classes. Practically speaking, the offspring of any such union is almost invariably incapable of further procreation. Hybrid plants, similarly, are unable to thrive on their own root system and therefore yield unsatisfactory seed.

"Thou shalt not seethe a kid in its mother's milk," warns Scripture on three separate occasions.[43] Some have proposed "ethical sensitivity" as the factor in this ruling, although the possible pagan roots of this practice seem to indicate that other factors are involved.[44] Maimonides, for example, in interpreting this passage as directed against a prevalent pagan rite, notes how on two of the three occasions it occurs in the context of presenting first-fruits, suggesting to him the possibility that the Israelites are adjured not to prepare their food in such a pagan manner. Can this not also be, however, a prohibition against intermingling such diverse sources of sustenance with fertility overtones?[45] The religion of Israel emphasized a concern for not distorting or adulterating the purity of God's world, while paganism often stressed rites of intermingling, and celebrated the ceremonial joining of diverse species as a "creative" enterprise.

Now what would constitute the ultimate "adulteration" of God's world if not the fusion of the two ultimate opposites, life and death? Milk symbolizes life. How then could it possibly be employed as the medium for the death of the entity it has nourished? The ultimate barbarity would be to cook a kid in its mother's milk. "It is," as Philo wrote, "the height of savagery to slay on the same day the generating cause and the living creature generated."

Closely aligned with the prohibition against creating unnatural combinations of flora and fauna is the obvious interdiction against the destruction of any species of fauna or flora. Planting diverse species together increases the danger of the dominant or hardier breed killing off the weaker growth. Leviticus forbade castration by excluding such animals from being offered as sacrifices,[46] and Judaism was probably unique in prohibiting the emasculation of man or beast. Later, rabbinic law forbade the impairment of the male reproductive system of fauna,[47] and one sage maintained that castration is a violation of one of the seven basic laws of humanity.[48] But it would appear to be the preservation of the species and noninterference with creative processes that are the central factors here, not compassion for the individual creature.

Even the passage enjoining one from snatching baby birds in the presence of the mother-bird, which would decidedly seem to be motivated by sensitivity for the parent-bird's maternal feelings, may have had as its basic goal the avoidance of any possibility, however minute, of causing the extermination of an entire species of bird at one time. If the mother-bird was taken, the eggs would not hatch, or the young would die of hunger. But if the mother is sent away, the eggs or fledglings may safely be taken on the assumption that the mother-bird will most likely lay more eggs. Perhaps this principle lies behind the prohibition against slaughtering a parent animal and its young on the same day.[49] Is it ethical sensitivity to the specter of a parent animal agonizing over the death of its young, or concern that an entire species, or family of species, created by God to endure, might thereby be eradicated from the earth?

Perhaps here too may lie an echo of the interdiction against cooking a kid in its mother's milk. It is morally obscene to commingle life and death in virtually the same space and time frame. Let not the mother-bird and its chick die together. Let not the mother and the young, who have just participated in the drama of life, now share together the slaughterer's knife. Not all would agree, however. One scholar, in analyzing the legislation concerning the mother-bird, concludes that "it rests upon the idea that one may have 'right of user' in the bird to the extent of sharing its produce; but one may not claim entire possession of it."[50]

To return for a moment to the theme of "pattern" as an integral part of "holiness," perhaps some of the dietary restrictions of Israel would fit appropriately into this rationale for holiness legislation. The Israelites are permitted to eat the meat of domestic animals, cloven-hoofed, cud-chewing ungulates. Such livestock were clean and required no purification for the person coming in contact with them. Other creatures, possessing only one of the two required characteristics, do not wholly fit into the approved plan and are therefore forbidden.

Following the threefold classification of fauna in Genesis (those of the earth, the water, and the firmament), Leviticus defines "permissible" fauna as those who fit *wholly* and *properly* into a given classification. Such are the earth creatures of four legs whose manner of locomotion is walking, hopping, or jumping; the fishes of the waters possessing scales who swim with their fins; and, in the firmament, two-legged fowl capable of flying with their wings.

However, any fauna not equipped for appropriate means of movement in its prescribed element is forbidden on the grounds that it is unclean; i.e., its behavior runs contrary to the ideal of holiness.

What constitutes an inappropriate means of locomotion in a prescribed environment? Numerous examples are given in Scripture: water animals without fins or scales,[51] four-footed flying creatures,[52] two-legged, two-handed creatures that go on all fours like quadrupeds,[53] animals whose mode of locomotion is creeping, crawling, or a perverse swimming pattern,[54] animals seeming to possess hands for front feet which are used for walking.[55] Such creatures could be termed "ambiguous" and are, therefore, declared to be unclean.

Now all of these unclean animals must be avoided because they apparently fail to fit into the orderly scheme of the divine pattern. Since all entities must ideally conform to God's plan and pattern, these creatures are ambiguous and anomalous, and their marginal status is incompatible with order and holiness; thus they are undesirable.

As noted, other biblical injunctions vis-à-vis animals also reflect this concept of holiness as integrity and purity. It is perverse to seethe a kid in its mother's milk, it is wrong to plow with an ox and an ass together.

In all of these areas, aesthetics and moral revulsion may also play a role. Not inconceivably, hygiene may also be a factor, or there may be traces of anti-pagan polemic, but many of these injunctions are prefaced by the command "be holy," and their violation is deemed an abomination. It is in the context of "holiness" that they may, perhaps, be best understood.

A minor though interesting problem which remains difficult to understand, however, involves the peculiar status of meat which is deemed fit for consumption. How should such meat be defined? The Bible, on the one hand, clearly forbids the touching or handling of the corpses of animals. These must be avoided. On the other hand, the Bible clearly forbids the eating of a creature that is yet alive! What then is the status of a piece of meat which is eaten, as it is neither "dead" nor "alive" in a technical sense? Is its status akin to that of plant-life? One can only speculate.

But to return to our basic question and rephrase it in negative terms, Does the mistreatment of animals constitute a bona fide *sin* or *transgression* in Scripture?

The Bible employs a vocabulary of some twenty different words to denote "sin," the three most popular terms, *het, pesha,* and *avon,* occurring over eight hundred times in biblical literature. Virtually all aspects of life are encompassed in this vocabulary—juridical, moral, and social transgressions, as well as cultic or ritual infractions. The biblical portrait of man is a realistic one. Perfection of behavior is deemed all but impossible, "there is no man who does not sin."[56] The Pentateuch forbids cursing the deaf or placing a stumbling-block in the path of the blind. Repeatedly, the poor, the widow, the orphan, and the stranger are singled out as the defenseless classes, deserving of special compassion, and those who mistreat them are vigorously condemned. But no similar condemnation is leveled against those who mistreat helpless animals! The word "sin" is virtually nonexistent in this context! Similarly, in the prophetic writings, where people are strongly castigated for their transgressions, we fail to find one instance of a prophetic rebuke for sins committed against animals! The concern of the prophets was exclusively with man's relationship to his fellow-man, not his conduct toward beasts.

The prophetic view of the ideal society, like that of the psalmist,[57] is one of a society based on righteousness,[58] but the animals are just not included among those deserving of righteousness. Amos, who sees national survival as being directly contingent upon the social morality of a nation (and records many a violation of the rules of morality), fails to include any immorality toward animals in his list. Jeremiah, who condemns all levels of society for their crimes against the weak and defenseless, nowhere makes any mention of cruelty to animals.

Is this because the Children of Israel behaved in a consistently compassionate manner toward their beasts? That is hardly likely. It could be argued that man sins against his fellow far more frequently than against his beast. Crimes of passion and cruelty are obviously directed primarily at other humans, for torturing and mistreating a person are often motivated by practical purposes. One tortures an enemy in order to set an example for others, one mistreats a laborer in order to impress other laborers with the importance of performing their tasks properly. In the case of animals, however, such punitive behavior is hardly practical. Nevertheless, it is only logical to assume that some cruelty toward, or at least some neglect of, the beast must have taken place. Yet no mention of this appears in the prophetic writings.

The word "love," employed to denote a full gamut of relationships between human beings, and between humans and God, is never used in describing a man-beast relationship. Nor should this be surprising. Scripture employs such terms, notably the term "righteousness," within a *legal* framework, with the righteous and the wicked pitted against one another as legal adversaries standing before judges.[59] The animal obviously has no place in such a juridical setting, and it would have been ludicrous to use such terminology in describing the "rights of beasts." The prophets of Israel employ the concept of righteousness to denote specific forms of inter*personal* behavior, which, if lacking, could undermine the stability of a society and endanger its survival.[60] It was the person, not the animal, who mattered, by definition.

Needless to say, the prophetic objections to animal sacrifices have nothing at all to do with any feelings of compassion for the sacrificial animal.[61] Nor, indeed, do the prophets object to sacrifice per se, for Isaiah is also critical of prayer that is bereft of the proper ethical commitment.[62] What concerned the prophets was that any rite, minus right, is wrong; that sacrifices unaccompanied by corresponding ethical behavior were empty gestures. They demanded moral obedience along with ritual devotion,[63] but nowhere in Scripture is there the slightest objection to animal sacrifices on ethical grounds.

On a more mundane level, goads were used on animals occasionally, goads tipped with iron,[64] but apparently no objections are raised against this practice. In agrarian and pastoral societies, old and feeble beasts were invariably put to death, for economic realities did not permit keeping such useless animals alive. Nowhere is any opposition to this practice recorded in Scripture.

This is not to say that the ancient Hebrew could not, or did not, feel compassion for his animals. He surely did. But this was not a central or serious concern in his life. Even in the case of Balaam and his long-suffering ass, where compassion for the animal is so beautifully expressed, the main purpose of the narrative is totally unrelated to "kindness for animals." The ass is a side-issue in this particular drama.

Similarly, in Eliezer's test to select a suitable wife for Isaac on the basis of whether she would offer to quench his camel's thirst as well as his own,[65] the point is not kindness to the animal per se. Eliezer merely assumes that a maiden who exhibits compassion toward his beast probably possesses other moral and ethical traits desirous in a wife. Now this insight may well be an accurate one. Both logic and experience seem to indicate that one who habitually practices cruelty to animals is also apt to be insensitive to the feelings of fellow humans. Zulma Steele, the biographer of Henry Bergh, founder of the American Society for the Prevention of Cruelty to Animals, states: "The child that serves its apprenticeship to inhumanity by tearing off the wings of a fly, or robbing a bird of its eggs, when arrived at maturity insults the poor, beats his inferiors and shows the same cruelty intensified by age which characterized his earlier training."[66] William E. H. Lecky comments that "it is a very unquestionable and a very important truth that cruelty to animals naturally indicates and promotes a habit of mind which leads to cruelty to men, and that, on the other hand, an affectionate and merciful disposition to animals commonly implies a gentle and amiable nature."[67]

But this does not imply that animals deserve, *in their own right,* to be treated compassionately. It is surely deemed admirable to do so, but the Bible refrains from imposing legislation for the humane treatment of animals.

The animal was, indeed, a valuable entity, but primarily as property, and the Bible treats the animal as property. When Saul hews a yoke of oxen into pieces, ordering the Israelites into battle with the threat "Whosoever cometh not forth after Saul and after Samuel, so shall be done to his oxen,"[68] both the deed and the threat were highly effective though admittedly cruel. Oxen were valuable animals and were seldom sacrificed.

When one human being kills another, the murderer is subject to death. Even the murder of a slave is to be avenged, because the slave, too, is created in God's image and the murderer is guilty of sacrilege, but one who intentionally kills an animal is liable only to pay for the value of the animal.[69] Clearly, there is an immense difference between the value of a human life and the value of an animal. The animal is essentially a piece of property, little more, akin more to a tool than to a slave.

True, Ecclesiastes seems to repudiate man's claim of superiority over animals by describing both man and animal in purely biological terms.[70] Biological and then chemical dissolution is, indeed, the common fate of both man and beast, but the thrust of the Bible is clearly against this point of view. It is the unique dimension of the human being that elevates him above the animal.

> When I behold Thy heavens, the work of Thy fingers,
> The moon and the stars, which Thou hast established;
> What is man, that Thou art mindful of him?
> And the son of man, that Thou thinkest of him?
> Yet Thou hast made him but little lower than the angels,
> And hast crowned him with glory and honour.
> Thou hast made him to have dominion over the works of Thy hands;
> Thou hast put all things under his feet.[71]

One should also be cautious when interpreting Scripture's beautiful prose and poetic descriptions of animals. What may appear, at times, to be "pure compassion" for the beast is perhaps more accurately a literary device emphasizing God's power and wisdom, or a dramatization of an historical event.

For example, Joel's prayer evoking the sufferings of starving animals is moving in its eloquence.

> How do the beasts groan, the herds of cattle are perplexed,
> Because they have no pasture; yea the flocks of sheep are made desolate.
> Unto Thee, O Lord, do I cry; for the fire hath devoured the pastures of the wilderness,
> And the flame hath set ablaze all the trees of the field.
> Yea, the beasts of the field pant unto Thee;
> For the water brooks are dried up, and the fire hath devoured the pastures of the wilderness.[72]

But the intent of the prophet's message is to describe the totality of destruction on the day of God's wrath, not to single out the animal kingdom for special compassion. Likewise, when the Lord causes vegetation to sprout forth again, Joel bids the beasts to rejoice.[73]

Such powerful literary imagery is indisputably effective in a prophetic exhortation, but it hardly reflects any honest prophetic concern for the welfare of the beast.

Whitehead attributes the reluctance of premodern science to experiment with nature to its Greek-influenced perspective of nature as being imbued with divinity. Nature could be contemplated but not manipulated. Modern science, however, under the influence of the Protestant mind, has absorbed the scriptural view of nature as being a creation of God for the use of man rather than a divine entity. This is our conclusion as well.

The crux of the issue is that the animal should perhaps be viewed more as a tool than as a divine creation. The pagan world, viewing nature as a divinity, endowed animals, as a part of nature, with divinity. The religion of Israel, viewing the world as a product of God's artisanship, saw the animal as an intricately shaped and valuable tool loaned to man for his use. To be sure, man's use of the living tools loaned out to him by the Creator-Craftsman is limited. He must not misuse the tools or disarrange them. Needless to say, he is forbidden to destroy such tools without the craftsman's permission, and he is obligated to care for them.

Wolfson, in contrasting the popular religion of the Greeks with that of the Hebrews, writes that the gods "as producers of things are described after the analogy of animal beings as procreators, begetting by a natural process of natural generation, other gods, the world, and also human beings."[74] To this we may add, "and animals."

The Bible, in contrast, describes God as the master artisan, creating tools for man's use, including animal-tools. This is not to say that the poetic imagery of God, the benevolent shepherd caring for His flock of living beings, is not a valid description. Surely it is, but the biblical process of demythologizing and dedeifying the animal had its effect. The image of God that dominates is that of God the artisan, instructing man how best to use and care for the tools of nature, the animals.

In summary, for most ancients, fauna were objects of worship, endowed with prescience, sanctity, and demonic powers. It was therefore not unusual for these creatures to be venerated and worshipped. But the animal kingdom, as a whole, did not merit attention or concern. In contrast, the religion of Israel dedeified fauna. There was no reverence, and certainly no worship of the beast, but neither was the beast mistreated. As God's most delicate tool, animals were entitled to rights and protection.

It is only proper to conclude on this note, for the obvious question is whether the dedeification of nature by the Israelites had a detrimental effect on their sensitivity toward nature and the degree of compassion with which they held the creatures of nature. In other words, did Scripture's "debasing of nature" lead to a corresponding lack of sensitivity, reverence, or concern for the world of nature among the Children of Israel?

Quite the contrary, we would suggest. In fact, "nowhere in the ancient East do we find such sublime concepts and descriptions of nature as in Israel."[75] Perhaps it was precisely *because* Israel did not worship nature that she was able to appreciate the beauty, symmetry, and variety of nature experiences for what they really were, and treat fairly the world of fauna; neither fearing nor revering, but caring, and with fairness, exerting the right and responsibility of "stewardship."

PART

II

A RABBINIC PORTRAIT

REMYTHOLOGIZATION

If the biblical view of fauna can be described as one of *de*mythologization, the rabbinic attitude can often be characterized as one of limited and cautious *re*mythologization.

As has been noted, in Scripture, the animal plays a minor and unexciting role. It is occasionally depicted in either utilitarian or aesthetic terms, but most often it merely serves as part of the natural background for the biblical drama. Rarely is there any sense of mystery or awe associated with the animal. There is nothing to fear or revere in fauna, for neither the divine nor the demonic is intimately associated with the animal kingdom.

In rabbinic thought, however, notably in Midrash—the specific genre of rabbinical literature abounding in biblical exegeses, sermonica, and aggadic discourses of an ethico-religious nature—the emerging image of the animal is far more colorful and mysterious.

The midrashic literature is immense in size and varied in scope. Its compilation dates span a full millennium, from such early classical amoraic Midrashim as *Genesis* and *Leviticus Rabbah, Lamentations Rabbah,* and *Pesikta de-Rav Kahana,* to such late anthologies as *Yalkut Shimoni* and the *Midrash ha-Gadol.* However, it reflects many ancient oral traditions, and contains early aggadic material originating in the main among Palestinian Jewry from the period of the Second Temple until the time of the redaction of the Talmud.

These varied aggadic traditions, along with certain halakhic (legal) rulings, comprise the essence of the composite picture which we term a "rabbinic portrait of fauna."

83

Bizarre Creatures

The ancient world abounded with fables of mythical creatures embodying fantastic and grotesque qualities, and rabbinic folklore also depicts several curious specimens from the then-current monster menagerie. Indeed, some aggadic passages depict members of the animal kingdom so incredibly striking in their features that they are more easily portrayed graphically than described literally. As a matter of fact, some of them appear to be identical to the primeval monsters which challenged the sovereignty of the creator deity in pagan cosmogonies but were rendered harmless in the Bible. However, now some of their previous powers are returned to them, and they reemerge in midrashic literature in their former glory.

Leviathan

While the biblical Leviathan is a vague, innocuous creature, and while early tannaitic literature contains virtually no mention of him at all,[1] eschatological portrayals in the apocryphal literature[2] and later midrashic utterances depict Leviathan as the most awesome and powerful of all large creatures of the sea. According to legend, there were originally two Leviathans, male and female, which were formed on the fifth day of creation, but God was forced to kill the female beast, lest the reproduction of their species lead to the destruction of the entire earth.[3] Leviathan's size is so immense that the weight of the earth rests easily upon one of his fins,[4] and his thirst so great that only the waters of the Jordan are capable of quenching it.[5] Additional midrashic embellishments provide him with sustenance from a special stream emanating from Paradise,[6] and a sea-goat is reported sighted whose horns bear the inscription, "I am a little sea-animal, yet I traveled three hundred parasangs to offer myself as food to the Leviathan."[7]

The monster's hot breath causes the waters of the sea to seethe and boil as in a cauldron. Its scales are like steel, and its fins cast forth such radiant light as to render the sun all but invisible,[8] while the brightness of its eyes illuminates the dark waters in which it swims.[9] Leviathan's body emits a malodorous stench which could easily have choked to death all living creatures, were it not for the fact that the monster's odor is neutralized by the perfume of paradise.[10]

Rabbi Johanan, the source for many of the legends concerning Leviathan, describes an elaborate banquet at which time the flesh of Leviathan will be served as a feast for the righteous,[11] particularly those pious individuals who refrained from attending or participating in pagan sporting events.[12] One source attributes the monster's death to lethal combat with a second gargantuan beast, Behemoth, while another version traces the animal's demise to the hand of God Himself, in keeping with the scriptural passage, "Thou shalt crush the heads of Leviathan, Thou gavest him to be food to the folk inhabiting the wilderness."[13] In any event, Leviathan's flesh will comprise the menu for a sumptuous messianic feast, with the leftovers amply supplying Jerusalem's marketplaces for many days thereafter. Nor will his hide go to waste. It will be used to manufacture clothing for the righteous and fabric for their tents, which will be spread as a luminous canopy around the walls of Jerusalem.[14]

Behemoth

The history of Behemoth, Leviathan's terrestrial counterpart, bears similarity to that of Leviathan. God also fashions this creature on the fifth day of creation,[15] and ensures that it, too, is incapable of breeding, lest the earth be destroyed by its immense size and powers. It occupies an area of one thousand hills and is in need of immense quantities of food and drink.[16] As the waters of the Jordan are inadequate in quenching its thirst, a special river, Yubal, flows from Paradise to sustain it.[17] The beast's eventual fate is similar to that of Leviathan, for it too will be served as food to the pious in the end of days.[18]

Other Creatures

The size of Ziz or Bar Yokni,[19] the legendary king of the birds, is even more impressive. When standing in the waters, its head extends up to the sky! Moreover, the depth of the waters was such that an axe which had fallen in them seven years earlier had yet to touch bottom![20] One of Ziz's eggs once fell to the earth and shattered, resulting in the instantaneous flooding of sixty cities and the destruction of three hundred cedar trees. The immense wingspan of this fowl was capable of eclipsing the light of the sun.[21] Ziz performs several valuable services in that it provides a buffer between the earth and the powerful southern storm winds, while its deafening cry causes birds of prey to cower in terror and therefore desist from preying upon weaker species of fowl.

But Ziz's eventual fate, like that of Leviathan and Behemoth, is a culinary one. Its flesh, too, will be consumed at the future repast of the righteous as a reward for those who abstained from the eating of unclean species of fowl. Indeed, Ziz will constitute the ultimate table delicacy of all, as its flesh comprises all known tastes. The very name, Ziz, stems from the fact that it possesses the taste of this *(zeh)* and that *(zeh)*.[22]

Rabbah bar bar Hana, who testifies to having seen this great bird, also relates having encountered a day-old gazelle as large as Mount Tabor, whose excrement obstructed the Jordan River, an enormous fish which was mistaken for an island because of the sand and meadows which covered its back, and another fish whose bulk was so immense that when washed ashore upon its death, it demolished sixty coastal towns and inadvertently supplied an additional sixty communities with food. One of its eyeballs alone purportedly filled three hundred kegs with oil. Finally, Rabbah bar bar Hana describes a frog the size of sixty houses, which is consumed by a snake, which is, in turn, swallowed by a raven![23]

Elsewhere, we encounter the Phoenix (possibly the *hul* or *malhan),* a bird which enjoys the gift of immortality as a reward for its having refused to eat of the forbidden fruit in the Garden of Eden. Every thousand years, it reverts to the size and appearance of an egg, and again commences its growth to maturity.[24] This creature's immense wingspan helps to filter and diffuse the heat of the sun's rays, thus making life possible upon the earth.

The *reem,* a beast too gigantic to fit within the confines of Noah's ark, was permitted to mate but once in seventy years so that it could reproduce itself before dying. David, once mistaking the *reem* for a mountain, climbed upon it, and while helplessly suspended high upon its horns, fervently prayed to God for deliverence, vowing, in return, to erect a Temple to the Lord which would tower as high as the horn of the *reem*.[25]

In addition to the aforementioned creatures, rabbinic legend also endows several scriptural fauna with impressive origins and characteristics.

For example, the serpent in the Garden of Eden is clearly a demythologized creature in the Bible, simply "one of the animals." Midrashic lore, however, glorifies his status and endows him with humanlike traits, i.e., the possession of a keen intellect, the ability to stand erect as a human, and status as king over all the animals.[26]

The ram sacrificed by Abraham in the stead of his son, Isaac, is also depicted as an extraordinary creature, created on the twilight of the Sabbath eve, and destined to play a significant role in Israel's future history. Its ashes comprised the foundation of the future altar upon which the Yom Kippur expiatory sacrifice was performed, its sinews served as the strings for David's harp, its skin became the girdle of the prophet Elijah, while its horn was destined to herald the culmination of the revelation at Mount Sinai, as well as proclaim the ingathering of Israel's exiled to their homeland.[27]

The deeds of other biblical creatures are similarly elaborated upon. For example, Balaam's ass, gifted with the power of speech, was especially created for its role on the sixth day of creation. Noah's dove is depicted as actually being able to converse with the Lord, and she eloquently declares: "May my food be as bitter as the olive but entrusted to Your hand rather than be sweet as honey and dependent on a mortal."[28] The fish that swallowed Jonah was no mere large fish. It, too, was especially created by God in order to perform its mission, for its immense size spaciously housed the prophet, while its eyes served him as windows during his tour of the undersea world.[29] A unique one-horned creature known as the *tahash* was also brought into existence for a singular purpose, so that its skin could be used as the material for the tabernacle erected by Moses in the wilderness.[30] The golden calf which was worshipped by the Israelites at the foot of Mount Sinai was also endowed with special properties. It was not merely an inanimate object but possessed the gift of life and could actually skip and move about at will![31] The snakes of the desert of Shur possessed such great lethal power that a bird flying overhead could be destroyed should its shadow pass over one of them.[32] Finally, we read how King Solomon was capably served by a remarkable entourage of fauna, notably a giant eagle which transported him to obscure and distant lands and a large sea-turtle upon which he rode at his coronation.[33] Other mystery creatures, such as *ha-shesuah*, the cloven, with double spinal columns and backs, have unclear functions to perform.[34]

But perhaps the most bizarre of all the creatures was the *shamir*. Although neither talmudic nor midrashic sources clearly describe it as a living creature, medieval Jewish scholars identified it with a species of insect, most likely a worm.[35] It too was created upon the sixth day of creation during the twilight hours and was the size of a barley-corn.[36] However, it possesssed the remarkable ability to cut into the hardest of substances, even diamonds. Moses first employed it in the engraving of the names of the twelve tribes upon the high priest's breast plate; however, its main mission was to be the hewer of giant stones for the building of Solomon's Temple. Without the *shamir*, the Temple could not have been built, for the Israelites were forbidden by God from using any implements of iron in its construction.[37] As the *shamir*'s sharp edges could easily cut through any receptacle, it was wrapped in wool and safely stored in a lead basket containing barley bran.[38]

The "mystique" of the animal kingdom was further enhanced by the folk belief in "spontaneous generation" as a means of propagation; i.e., the conviction that living beings can emerge from putrified animal or vegetable matter. This led to the interesting observation that certain species of mice,[39] vermin,[40] and salamanders[41] do not breed! How then do they originate? Their origins are attributed to the soil itself, to perspiration, or to food matter, or, in the case of the salamander, to a continuously burning fire!

It is stated in the Talmud that "the male hyena after seven years turns into a bat, the bat after seven years turns into an *arpad* [possibly a variant species of bat], the *arpad* after seven years turns into *kimmosh* [a species of thorn], the *kimmosh* after seven years turns into a thorn, the thorn after seven years turns into a demon. The spine of man after seven years turns into a snake."[42]

The Talmud refers to the "Book of Creation," probably a collection of esoteric mystical teachings, which enabled Rabbah to actually create a man! And in this context we are informed of the fact that Rabbi Hanina and Rabbi Oshaya would sit every Sabbath eve and occupy themselves with the "Book of Creation" by means of which they created a three-year-old calf which they then ate!

Joshua b. Hananiah purports to have been able to create a deer and a gazelle out of gourds and watermelon, and claims to have once witnessed the transformation of a stone into a live calf! However, this latter occurrence is explained away on the basis of "sleight of hand," and the rabbis dogmatically state that "if all the human beings were to join together, they would be unable to create one gnat and imbue it with a soul."[43]

Certain creatures, such as the hare, were believed to be capable of undergoing sexual metamorphoses in the course of a lifetime. Possibly this explains the recorded custom of advising sterile women to consume the stomach of a hare as a cure-treatment for their sterility,[44] a practice against which the mother of Samson is warned.

Some legends effectively blurred distinctions between plants, animals, and human life by describing creatures endowed with bizarre combinations of morphological characteristics from all the diverse spectra of life-forms. Perhaps the most fascinating of such creatures was the *adne hasadeh,* a plant-man or mandragon root. It is described as species of ape-man with leaves sprouting forth from its head.[45] Its navel was attached to the ground by means of an elongated umbilical cord from which it drew its sustenance as would a plant or a tree. Severing the cord would be tantamount to cutting off a plant from the earth; it would cause instantaneous death.[46]

There is reference to the existence of dolphins, which are described as being half-human and half-fish[47] and mention is made of the existence of mermaids.[48] The barnacle goose was believed to have metamorphosed[48] from barnacles, and is depicted as attaching itself to trees by means of its bill.[49] Other birds were conceived of as actually growing on trees and bearing the appearance of fruit. Rabbenu Tam, a twelfth-century legal authority, replied in the affirmative when asked if such fowl required ritual slaughter in order to be eaten.[50]

Rabbinic legend endows early man with certain animallike traits and characteristics. Adam is purported to have sported the tail of an animal,[51] and from the generation of Enosh, all men are reputed to have had apelike faces,[52] with their fingers remaining unseparated until the era of Noah.[53] Some sources depict the countenances of Adam, Seth, and Enosh as having been initially God-like in appearance, but as a result of idolatrous practices, ensuing generations came to bear some of the characteristics of apes.[54] Others claim that half-man, half-animal mutations, along with apelike creatures, were among the offspring of Adam and the decadent generations of Enosh.[55]

God punishes some of the builders of the tower of Babel by transforming them into apes,[56] and a singular legend, appearing only once in rabbinic literature,[57] and possibly based upon an apocryphal version of the Book of Daniel, has God punishing King Nebuchadnezzar for his arrogance in deeming himself a deity, by transforming the king into a beast, the upper part of his body an ox, the lower, a lion.

On a more mundane and natural level, certain remarkable similarities are noted between man and the animal kingdom. We are told, for example, that human flesh has the same specific gravity as the flesh of an ass.[58] The intestine of swine is deemed similar to the human intestine, and therefore prayer and fasting are decreed in communities in which an epidemic has broken out among swine.[59] It is also noted that he-goat blood is more akin to human blood than to the blood of any other animal.[60]

Magical Creatures

A word of introduction is in order at this point. The use of animals in effecting magic and magical cures was not always viewed as an illegal activity. True, the Bible is vigorously opposed to sorcery, deeming magic to be an abomination or, at least, a manifestation of sheer vanity.[61] Yet, while denying any independent power or efficacy to sorcery, the Bible does, under appropriate conditions, approve of modified sorcery and those divinations which are in keeping with God's authority. Similarly, the Talmud, although equating magic with "idolatry,"[62] and denouncing magical cures as "the customs of the Amorites,"[63] records the practice of various forms of magic, some critically, some approvingly.[64] It would appear that when the rabbis felt that certain magical practices were actually effective and had a natural basis in fact, they did pemit them on the pragmatic grounds that "whatever does, indeed, cure effectively is not to be prohibited as a custom of the Amorites."[65]

This ambivalence is understandable. Magic is a complex phenomenon and need not always constitute a challenge to God's power and authority. On the contrary, the efficacy of magic could conceivably be viewed as either a manifestation of the greatness of a wonder-working God or merely as a harmless series of acts which may foretell events but in no way cause or alter their occurrence. An individual's employment of magic may signify nothing more than his desire to simply seek out signs and omens to safely lead him through a hostile and perilous world.

In the area of divination, we encounter attempts on the part of some rabbis to differentiate between permissible forms of divination (*simanim*) and forbidden forms (*nahash*); not surprisingly, animals play an important role in both categories.[66]

We read of divination by means of the flight and cries of birds, the shrieks of weasels, the croaking of ravens, and the movement of snakes, foxes, and deer across one's path.[67] Divination is selective, however. Rabbi Ilish refuses to take heed when a raven warns, "Ilish, run away, Ilish, run away," but he does take seriously a similar message from a dove.[68] Animal manifestations in dreams or waking hours were believed to herald future events. Dreaming of a white horse or a snake was deemed to be a beneficial omen,[69] while a hart crossing one's path or a fox passing on one's left side was a portent of evil for the wayfarer.[70] To the popular mind, a howling dog signified the advent of the angel of death.[71] As Longfellow phrased it:

In the Rabbinical book it saith'
the dogs howl with icy breath,
Great Sammael, the Angel of Death,
Takes through the town his flight.[72]

On a more practical level, certain animals, or the parts of certain
animal bodies, were used as antidotes for a variety of illnesses and
dangers. Thus applications made from the bodies of snails were
used to treat scabs, flies to treat hornet-stings, mosquitoes for
serpent bites, serpents for headsores, and spiders for treating
scorpion stings.[73] Others attempted to cure scorpion stings by
treating the patient with stork-gall,[74] and a more elaborate treatment for snakebite consisted of the application of snake-flesh, the
embryo from a white she-ass, and crushed gnats.[75] The blood of a
foal was recommended as a cure for jaundice,[76] and salamander
blood spread upon one's body was believed to be an effective
protective agency against fire. The efficacy of this latter procedure
was, no doubt, based on the aforementioned assumption that
salamanders originate in fire, and the Talmud records that Hezekiah's mother saved him from the flames of Moloch by smearing
salamander blood over his body.[77] Cataracts were treated with a
solution made from seven-colored striped scorpions mixed with
stibium.[78] The egg of an edible locust, the *chargol,* was placed in
the ear to protect one from earaches,[79] while the physician Min-
yomi recommended the juice of goat kidney in treating an ear-
ache.[80] Goat's milk was highly recommended for treating many
illnesses.[81]

Animal parts were also believed to be effective in warding off
evil spirits. Some recommended hanging a fox's tail upon a
horse's forehead as protection against the "evil eye," while "if one
wishes to see the evil spirits, he must take the afterbirth of a
firstborn black cat, which is the daughter of a firstborn black cat,
burn it, and grind it into a powder, and put the ash in his eye."[82]

Folk-medicine antidotes to combat the "demons of blindness"
employ animals in a number of dramatic ceremonies. For example, the powers of the day-demon, *shabriri,* may be counteracted
by consuming seven pieces of red meat from the insides of animals

which have been placed on the shards of blood-letters, provided that one subsequently breaks the shards.[83] A far more elaborate ceremony, apparently involving sympathetic medicine, is designed to thwart the night-demon, *shabriri*. The foot of the blind person is tied to the leg of a dog with cord made from hair, while chidren rattling potsherds chant "old dog, stupid cock." The dog is then fed seven pieces of raw meat from seven houses upon a dung pile. The person then unties the cord from his foot and proclaims: "*Shabriri* of so-and-so . . . leave so-and-so," while blowing into the dog's eye.[84] This cure for *nyctalopia* (night-blindness) is possibly an example of curing by transference, acting on the assumption that as one can be infected by others, so can one similarly transfer his ailments to others—in this case, to an animal.

The supposedly efficacious treatment for *celichetha* (possibly a migraine headache)[85] is to slaughter a wild cock over the side of the patient's head that ails him and to hang the bird's body upon the doorpost. The patient then rubs his head against the bird when entering and leaving the house.[86] The bird's blood is also recommended for treating the eye-ailment *barkith*.[87]

A recommended cure for insomnia is the wearing of the tooth of a dead fox; conversely, one who sleeps too much should wear the tooth of a living fox.[88] For *pika* (a disease of the anus) the prescription is to melt the fat of a goat which has not borne any young and to apply the substance to the diseased area.[89]

In fairness, it should be pointed out that the use of animals and animal-matter in the treatment of illness was not unique to Israel. It merely reflects the pharmacology of all peoples of antiquity. Not merely antiquity. Even into the sixteenth century, an apothecary was legally required to maintain in stock such items as "woodlice, rain worms, ants, vipers, scorpions, frogs and crabs; also the skull of a dead person who was not buried, the bone from the heart of a hart, sparrow-brains and hare brains, teeth of wild pigs and elephant skin, frog hearts, fox lungs, wolf-intestines, etc."[90]

Also, in fairness, it must be said that some animal cures may actually have been effective. The Midrash[91] refers to a man who suffered from foot diseases and was advised to plaster his feet with the excrement of cattle.[92] According to a modern physician, this may well have proven to be an effective treatment for the ailment.[93] But effective or not, most of the cures we have thus far discussed reflect the "folk" medicine, as opposed to the "legal" medicine, of the people, although the two categories are not always clearly differentiated. In any event, the folk mind permitted and even encouraged the animal to play a prominent role in this area.

Animals as Demons

Although there is only one reference to harmful spirits (*mazzikim*) in the entire Mishna,[94] and demonology is discussed only rarely in the Palestinian Talmud, the Babylonian Talmud contains extensive references to demons and other assorted malevolent spirits which inhabit man's universe with him. According to one source, it is fortunate that these entities are invisible, for "if the eye could see them no one could endure them. They surround one on all sides. They are more numerous than humans, each person has a thousand on his left and ten thousand on his right."[95]

Among the descriptions of demons which appear are several which bear distinctive, though often composite, animal characteristics. The *ketev yashud tzohorayim* is a winged demon with the horns of a goat,[96] while the bizarre *ketev meriri* possesses the head of a calf with a single revolving horn and an eye in its heart. It is covered with scales and hair, and it rolls about like a ball.[97] The *sheiyyah* resembles an ox,[98] while other demons are black goatlike creatures,[99] and still others are seven-headed dragons.[100] Interestingly, the footprints of *mazzikim* are reported to be similar to those made by cocks.[101] King Solomon is the subject of numerous legends involving demons and vampires, some of whom assume animal forms while interacting with humans. Satan himself is depicted as dancing between the horns of an ox,[102] and was believed capable of assuming the guise of an animal in order to entice men into danger or wrongdoing.

For example, How was David enticed to sin with Bathsheba? Satan disguised himself as a bird hovering over the king. When David cast a dart at it, he inadvertently shattered a nearby wicker screen, thus exposing the beauty of the bathing Bathsheba to his view.[103] On another occasion, Satan assumes the guise of a deer, thereby leading the pursuing David on a hunt deep into Philistine territory, where he is attacked by Ishbi, Goliath's vengeful brother.[104]

Animal Worship

The rabbis were well aware of the widespread veneration for certain species of animals and the use of their representations as objects of reverence and worship. They inform us that "if the names of all the idols were to be enumerated, all the donkeys in the world would not suffice to carry them."[105] Indeed, rabbinic sources record the pagan worship of eggs,[106] roosters and doves,[107] small worms,[108] and other species of animals.[109] The term *neevad* (a deified animal) occurs frequently in rabbinic literature.[110]

The Talmud relates how, after the fall of Samaria, the new inhabitants of the area persisted in animal-worship rites. The Babylonians served a hen, the people of Cuth and Hamath a cock and ram respectively, while the Avvites worshipped a dog and an ass, and the Sepharvites a mule and a horse.[111] The Talmud classifies the following bizarre ceremonies as Amorite practices: saying to a raven, "scream,"and to a she-raven, "screech and return me thy tuft for my good"; saying, "kill this cock because it crowed in the evening" or "kill this fowl because it crowed like a cock"; breaking eggs against a wall in front of dancing fledglings; stirring eggs before fledglings; dancing and counting seventy-one fledglings in order that they should not die.[112]

The sages were keenly aware of the powerful "attractiveness" and "allure" of animal worship, whether in the literal sense of actually paying devotion to a creature or in the broader sense of seeing supernatural powers vested within it, and many a *midrash* inveighs against inadvertently succumbing to such temptations.

The rabbis taught, for example, that "as soon as she [Balaam's talking ass] finished speaking, she died, so that people should not say, 'This is the animal that spoke,' and so make of her an object of reverence."[113] The rabbis further emphasize that in the episode of the bronze serpent in the wilderness, the power to cure or kill was, in reality, not vested in the animal itself. Only God responded to those who prayerfully gazed up at the animal configuration.[114] Later, the sages approved of Hezekiah's destruction of the bronze serpent, presumably precisely because it had the potential of becoming a tempting object for veneration.[115]

Such examples notwithstanding, the rabbinic period did witness the remythologization of the animal kingdom. It may have been a limited remythologization during the mishnaic era, but in subsequent centuries, midrashic literature reflected an apparently growing aura of magic and mystery surrounding the animal.

AN INITIAL RATIONAL AND EMPIRICAL OVERVIEW

A legitimate question seems to have arisen at this point. On the basis of the preceding data, is one justified in theorizing that the animal now plays a new role of far greater importance in human life, a role of mystery, if not reverence? In other words, did remythologizing the world of fauna elevate the animal's status far above what it had been in the biblical era?

Apparently not. The materials cited in no way attempt to deify, glorify, or magnify the role of the animal kingdom, nor do they even represent a distinctively "Jewish" perspective. Quite the contrary. Such teachings represent essentially an amalgamation of many elements common to the ancient world. For rabbinic observations concerning the animal kingdom fall into the general category of "natural science," and much of rabbinic natural science was a *popular* knowledge shared in common with the other peoples of the ancient Mediterranean world, notably Greco-Roman society.

Far more significant is another body of information concerning fauna which can be culled from rabbinic sources. Much of this information was acquired as a result of careful observation of, and experimentation upon, fauna. Such observation and experimentation was motivated by the practical needs of an agrarian society, as well as the religious needs involved in determining the ritual fitness of animals vis-à-vis the dietary laws of Israel. A number of such observations appear perceptive even by contemporary standards, and all of then presuppose treating the animal simply like an animal, without awe or reverence—simply like an animal.

It may be of interest to cite several of the practical observations of the animal kingdom that appear at random in rabbinic literature.

All fishes which have scales have fins.[1]

All mammals which have horns have cloven hoofs.[2]

All mammals which have no upper teeth chew the cud and have a cloven hoof, with the exception of the young camel.[3]

The only mammal which has a cloven hoof but does not chew its cud is the swine.[4]

Male partridges sit upon the eggs laid by the female.[5]

A lion will attack a human being only when extremely hungry.[6]

Parasitic worms inhabit the bodies of certain fish.[7]

The lifetime of a fly is less than a year.[8]

A locust becomes blind when its proboscis is broken.[9]

Scorpions breed sixty young at one time.[10]

Serpents shed their skin periodically, and their venom loses its potency as they age.[11]

Rancid oil applied to a plant acts as a repellent against worms.[12]

Roosters are able to shatter glass by crowing into it.[13]

The human body is infected with hosts of worms which inhabit different organs.[14]

Fish reproduce by means of external insemination,[15] with permitted species laying eggs, while prohibited ones breed alive.[16]

Those species with external testicles bear live young, while those with internal testicles lay eggs. Similarly, among birds, when the male possesses external genitalia the female gives birth, when the male's genitalia are internal, the female lays eggs.

The recognition that flies may be carriers of disease is reflected in Rabbi Johanan's admonition to "beware of the flies of a man afflicted with *ra'athan*" (a severe skin disease, possibly a form of leprosy). Similarly, we are informed that Rabbi Zera refused to sit in the same draft with one suffering from this affliction, while Rabbi Eliezer never entered his tent, and Rabbi Ammi and Rabbi Assi never partook of eggs coming from the alley in which he lived. Interestingly, Rabbi Joshua ben Levi attached himself to these sufferers and studied Torah with them, confident that no illness would befall him. He cites the passage "A lovely hind and a graceful doe,"[17] proclaiming: "If [the Torah] bestows grace upon those who study it, would it not also protect them?"[18]

Fear of snake-poison led to a rabbinic prohibition against drinking water that had been left uncovered overnight,[19] and some recommended the boiling of such water.[20] Jews were advised against eating of the flesh of animals bitten by snakes, even if the flesh was cooked.[21] Moreover, one is cautioned against eating figs, grapes, cucumbers, or gourds that have holes in them, lest the holes were made by snakes.[22] Finally, one is cautioned not to walk barefoot in a house where cats dwell. Why? Perhaps the cat ate a snake and spat out the bones, and by stepping on the bones one might become infected with the snake's poison![23]

Another practical fear concerned rabid animals. The rabbis described the symptomology of a rabid dog as follows: an open mouth dripping saliva, ears hanging down, tail curled between legs, slinking along the side of the road, and having a hoarse, barely audible bark. One is cautioned to discard any garments against which the rabid animal may have rubbed itself.[24]

It is of interest to note Rabbi Matia ben Heresh's leniency in permitting one who has been bitten by a rabid dog to eat the lobe of its liver, obviously a nonkosher item,[25] a procedure apparently akin to contemporary antitoxin therapy. Some heathen physicians in the ancient world, notably Dioscorides and Galen, also believed in such curative procedures.[26]

A fascinating observation is made by Samuel of Cappadocia to the effect that birds have scales on their legs similar to the scales of fish, a fact that led Bar Kappara to conclude that birds were created out of the alluvian mud![27]

Rabbinic observations of the natural world at times appear to be even more sophisticated than those of their "enlightened" Greco-Roman contemporaries. For example, non-Jewish scholars of antiquity, including even the great Plato,[28] taught that women were capable of giving birth to animals, a notion which remained popular well into the Middle Ages! This phenomenon was explained as being due either to direct impregnation of the woman by the beast or to her having been frightened by an animal while in her pregnant state, so that the fetus emerged in the form of an animal. The Talmud, on the other hand, proclaims that sodomy with an animal is completely *un*fruitful, declaring that "no animal can become pregnant from a human being, and no human being can become pregnant from an animal."[29] Therefore there is no mention in rabbinic literature of a human being giving birth to an animal, or vice versa, although the rabbis do discuss cases of women aborting fetuses *resembling* birds or beasts.[30]

Another fascinating rabbinic observation concerns *dolphanim*, presumably dolphins. The sages recognized that dolphins possess many mammalian characteristics, notably that they "are fruitful and multiply like human beings" or that they reproduce and grow up like human beings.[31] This has been interpreted to mean that they have sexual intercourse in the manner of humans, give birth alive, and nurse their young.[32]

Granting the existence of a "practical" approach to the animal kingdom on the part of the rabbis, granting further a rational manner of observing fauna on their part, what then do we make of some of the previously cited incredible-sounding selections from animal folklore?

As noted earlier, some rabbinic animal folklore, bordering upon the incredible, reflects ideas common to other ancient cultures. Thus the aforementioned mice comprised in part of flesh and in part of earth[33] are also described by Ovid and Pliny,[34] and an Egyptian fable depicts voles as originating out of the mud of the flooded Nile.[35] Aristotle believed that bedbugs generate from body humidity, lice generate from meat, and fleas emerge out of dry decay.[36] Pliny also endows salamanders with the ability to extinguish fires, attributing this to their being ice-cold![37]

Descriptions of ape-men and centaurs, along with elaborate accounts of man-animal affinities, were part of the common culture of the times, and their appearance in Jewish folklore should be neither surprising nor significant. The belief that the raven impregnates its female by spitting semen into her mouth[38] was also held by Aristotle,[39] and both Pliny[40] and the Talmud[41] describe the existence of a remarkable little lizard capable of terrorizing the mighty scorpion. The same account depicts the elephant in fear of the mosquito, the lion frightened by the gnat, the eagle intimidated by the swallow, and no less a figure than mighty Leviathan himself in terror of the tiny stickleback! The Alexandrians believed a small animal, the leontophonus, capable of killing lions simply by urinating upon them.[42] The notion of the weak triumphing over the mighty among the animal kingdom was a motif common to many civilizations in the ancient world.

What is significant, however, is the fact that although most of the thinkers of the ancient world believed in metempsychosis (the transmigration of the soul), and envisioned human souls transmigrating into the bodies of birds and beasts, the sages of the Talmud nowhere refer to the notion that man and animal can share a soul.

As for the practice of "magic" among the Jews of the rabbinic period, it must again be emphasized that there was probably no "distinctive Jewish form of magic" in the talmudic age,[43] but, rather, an eclectic collection of ideas and practices common to the Mediterranean world, and influenced by Egyptian, Babylonian, and Persian folklore. These ideas and practices reflected belief in an "intertwined" universe, a close-meshed state of unity of life in which all living creatures exist in a condition of mutual interdependence. In such a "unity" it is only natural to expect that careful observation and proper manipulation of the animal kingdom can provide valuable insight into, and exert powerful influence upon, the state of human affairs. Portents of future events were eagerly read into or out of daily happenings in the animal world.[44]

Eagles were deemed to be divinatory birds, and Cicero regarded ravens flying to one's right and crows flying to one's left as beneficent omens.[45] Artemidorus of Daldos compiled detailed lists of oneirocritica (dream interpretations) dealing with the appearance of insects in one's dreams.[46]

But the fact that Jews viewed a given animal as an omen or a means of divination in no way implies the existence of either the "divine" or the "demonic" within that animal. Divination also involved the study of the placement of the stars, planetary configurations, the movement of ferryboats, and, more understandably, the recitation of scriptural passages by young schoolchildren,[47] the latter testifying, perhaps, to the latent power of prophecy that may exist in children.[48]

Some rabbis denied altogether the efficacy of divination by means of the cries of birds,[49] and the Third Sibylline Book flatly declares that "the Jews do not consider the omens of flight as observed by the augers."[50] Compared to their contemporaries, there is evidence that the Jews made limited use of quasi-magical devices.

It should be reemphasized that the entire civilized world of the time fully believed in the efficacy of charms and magic, and even the rabbis, who as a rule forbade such Amorite practices, occasionally permitted them when convinced that a given magical procedure was actually effective. But, of course, at this point "magic" was no longer "magic" any more; it was, rather, a legitimate part of the natural science of God's world, involving at times the plant or animal kingdom. When it came to talmudic medicine, embodying as it did both folklore and scientific observation, both Raba and Abayye were in full agreement that "nothing done for the purposes of healing is to be forbidden as superstitious."[51]

But this in no way imputes mystique or magical power to the animals or animal parts used in medicine. It is simply that "animals and beasts, reptiles and insects, were created for human therapy."[52] These are merely the "materials" of healing legitimately available to man.

It is significant, however, that Jewish tradition introduced limitations in these areas. "There is not a single instance in all of Jewish literature of the prescription of blood for internal medicine,"[53] and the internal consumption of animal parts was a rarity among Jews. Non-Jewish medicine, on the other hand, was frequently characterized by the use of such "cures." Similarly, in spite of the widespread belief that certain repugnant foods, notably animal excrement, had curative powers, the rabbis severely limited the use of such obnoxious compounds,[54] and discouraged *dreckapotheke*, or "filth pharmacy."

Indeed, in rabbinic literature animal folklore frequently seems to be consciously directed against the folklore of other nations and seeks to emphasize moral and ethical values instead of reaffirming popular superstitions. For example, the ancient world saw in the advent of a weasel an evil omen and a frightening symbol of impending disaster. A man would deem his journey doomed should he encounter a weasel on his travels. But the rabbis ridiculed this belief,[55] and chose to emphasize instead (on the basis of a play on words between *haled* and *hulda*[56]) that the human inhabitants of the world are similar to weasels. Why? "Because just as the weasel drags and stores up and does not know for whom he stores, so the dwellers of the world drag and store, drag and store, not knowing for whom they store up, as it is written: 'He reapeth up riches and knoweth not who shall gather them.' "[57]

Perhaps it is in contradistinction to the Persian belief that certain animals created by the deity Ahiran are totally noxious and useless, if not dangerous,[58] that the rabbis emphasize that even those creatures which would appear to be totally repugnant possess beneficial qualities, and therefore the snail is a cure for scabs, a crushed housefly is an antidote for hornet-stings, a mosquito neutralizes viper poison, vipers cure headsores, and spiders can neutralize the stings of scorpions.[59]

Other, nominally insignificant creatures are described as having been brought into being by their Creator to fulfill historic missions. So the gnat, which lives for only one day, was destined to cause the death of the tyrant Titus, by crawling into his brain via his nostrils.[60]

It is true that rabbinic tradition attaches importance to certain animals appearing in dreams, but no more significance than would attend any other dream subject. Some of the standard rabbinic interpretations for animal manifestations are the bird as a symbol of peace, the ass as a symbol of salvation, a white horse as the harbinger of good fortune, and an elephant as an omen for wondrous future events. These are often related to scriptural allusions as well as the natural traits of some of the creatures.[61]

A further point should be raised vis-à-vis some of the striking aggadic utterances concerning beasts of incredible size and strength. Did the rabbis truly intend *all* of their statements of this genre to be taken literally? Is it fair to treat these descriptions as sober and serious depictions of fauna? Or, in so doing, are we not really rendering a disservice to rabbinic poetic imagery and aesthetic-symbolic teachings? Not only is it true that "the danger of confounding popular belief with the belief of the people is great," but popular beliefs in the form of folk motifs are often employed allegorically by scholars in order to transmit social, ethical, or political truths.[62]

> In the world to come there is neither eating, drinking, nor procreation, neither barter nor envy, neither hatred nor strife; but the righteous sit with crowns on their heads and enjoy the splendor of the *Shekhina,* for it is said: "And they saw God and did eat and drink"; that is, their seeing God was meat and drink to them.[63]

This utterance, attributed to Rab, would hardly seem to anticipate a gargantuan feast where the righteous will be served the flesh of Leviathan and Behemoth.

Should we take literally the statement that when the lion of the forest of Ilai roared, the tower of Rome, four hundred parasangs away, shook, women in Rome miscarried, and at a distance of three hundred parasangs, Caesar toppled and fell from his throne?[64] Was there, indeed, such a vocally endowed lion in Judea? Perhaps. However, a more plausible interpretation of the passage might seek political or military rather than zoological implications. Indeed, later rabbinic interpreters understood such accounts as dreams or allegories, or cryptic allusions to political or military events.[65]

Rabbah bar bar Hana's wondrous tales of fantastic beasts are impressive, but some of his own contemporaries were singularly *un*impressed with him, as is evident in their response: "Every Abba is an ass, and every bar Hana is a fool."[66] Scholars of ensuing generations saw cryptic messages and allegorical teachings in bar bar Hana's fantastic adventures and miraculous encounters.[67] Are there implications of a demonic nature in the talmudic admonition to beware of an ox emerging from the meadow "because Satan is dancing between his horns"? Not at all, according to one expositor; this is a mere figure of speech denoting a mad ox![68]

Aggadic materials were not always taken literally or seriously, and what appears to be a *re*mythologizing of the biblical *de*mythologization of the animal kingdom is perhaps more accurately a mere *poetic* or *symbolic* remythologization. If there is any real doubt as to the matter, one has only to consider the conspicuous lack of any real dimension of terror or fear in the narratives depicting the gigantic land, sea, and air monsters. After all, God Himself sits and sports with Leviathan,[69] and, in the final analysis, mighty Leviathan is made to endure the indignity of being the subject of a discussion vis-à-vis *kashrut,* of its fitness to be included as part of the cuisine for the messianic banquet.[70]

Some of the same factors possibly apply to the apparent identification of certain members of the animal kingdom with demons. Although most rabbis did not question the reality of demons and took their existence for granted, many statements pertaining to demonology might well be taken symbolically or metaphorically. Moreover, even those who took demons seriously did not always view them as malignant creatures. They were deemed more mischievous than diabolical. Such beliefs were, as we have noted, a part of the natural science of the ancient world. Even Aristotle believed in demons! The sages of Israel simply incorporated such current "scientific" data into their own thought system.

The fact that some demons are depicted as having animal traits (in Arabic literature the *jinn* invariably possessed animal characteristics) seems to have had no practical significance. True, fanciful descriptions exist of goatlike spirits. But do we find any corresponding practical consequences manifesting themselves in terms of special reverence and awe for the common goat? Not at all; the goat remained a goat.

The relationship of the sages to the animal world was respectful, but not reverential. It was a relationship predicated upon practical need, and the rabbis were dispassionate and rational observers of fauna, with an eye to utility, not awe. Numerous illustrations can be cited.

Some sages, notably Simeon b. Halafta, performed interesting scientific experiments upon animals. He succeeded, for example, in treating dislocated hips in fowls, investigating the nesting habits of hoopoes,[71] and determining the effect of high temperatures upon the feathers of birds. When his hen lost its down, he was able to stimulate the growth of feathers once again by wrapping it in a leather apron and placing it in an oven where it was safely exposed to heat.[72]

In another interesting experiment, Rabbi Simeon spread his coat over an anthill, and when an ant emerged, had it marked for identification. The ant reentered the anthill, presumably to inform its fellow ants that it was safe to emerge as there was now shade protecting the anthill from the rays of the sun. But in the interim Rabbi Simeon had removed his coat, and the ants, upon being exposed to the sun's fierce rays, turned in rage upon the unfortunate messenger ant and killed it. Rabbi Simeon drew the conclusion that the ant community lacks a king or central authority figure,[73] and comments elsewhere on the highly developed olfactory sense possessed by ants.[74]

An interesting example of ecological control appears in connection with a colony of ants which were causing damage to a field. Other ants were procured from a distance of several miles away and placed upon the local nest of harm-causing ants. The ant colonies then proceeded to destroy one another in the fight that ensued.[75] In a rather imaginative development, we read in the Talmud of the use of large ants as surgical clamps![76] The ants would be permitted to bite into the margins of a wound and then their bodies would be severed so that only the mandibles remained, holding firmly to the margins of the wound.

No less a personage than the scholar Rab spent eighteen months with a shepherd in order to gain first-hand experience in understanding the eye diseases of animals (in order to better understand which blemishes would render firstborn animals unclean)[77] and the skilled physician Samuel comments on the poisonous venom of serpents and discusses with meticulous detail the organic diseases which would render animals unfit for consumption.[78]

As has been noted, the complex and intricate halakhic requirements pertaining to the ritual fitness of animals to be slaughtered for food necessitated a thorough knowledge of zoology, particularly as regards organic diseases and injuries to birds and beasts. A *mishna* in the tractate *Hullin* enumerates no less than eighteen defects which render cattle unfit for human consumption. The rabbis were able to discern malformations in the lungs of such animals by inserting a tube into the animal's trachea, thereby inflating the lungs. The sages were skilled in the postmortem examination of such animals and well-versed in the sphere of comparative pathological anatomy, notably the morbid anatomy of the lungs and pleura, and the effects of lesions and perforations.

The Talmud contains an interesting account of one such postmortem examination in veterinary medicine. A sheep belonging to Rabbi Habiba was observed dragging her hindlegs as she walked. Some thought this was due simply to rheumatism, but Rabbi Habiba disagreed, attributing the condition to neurological causes, namely, a divided spinal cord. A postmortem examination by the rabbis verified Rabbi Habiba's diagnosis of paraplegia.[79]

According to a distinguished medical authority and student of talmudic medicine, the rabbis made significant contributions in the field of medical pathology, a branch of knowledge in which even the ancient Greeks were deficient.[80]

We read for example: "Samuel said in the name of Rabbi Hiyya, If a man breaks the neck bone of an animal [after it had been slaughtered but before the life departed from it], he thereby makes the meat heavy, robs mankind, and causes the blood to remain in the limbs."[81] This is precisely the case when vasoconstriction, which is controlled by the medulla oblongata, is abolished, thereby causing the blood vessels to dilate and the blood to remain within the small and medium-sized vessels. The purchaser is thus defrauded when he pays for meat that is heavy with blood.[82]

As far as is known, the earliest record of a tracheotomy in Semitic sources is found in Rabbi Jose b. Nehorai's account of a lamb whose windpipe had been cut. A tube made of reed was inserted into the animal to close the hole, and the lamb recovered.[83]

The rabbis accurately concluded that injuries to the gastrointestinal tract as a result of which food or fecal matter can extravasate into the abdominal cavity are a threat to the creature's life.[84] The sages recognized what even Aristotle failed to note, that in animals the upper anatomical knee joint has its curvature posteriorly, while the ankle joint has its curvature anteriorly,[85] and Rabbi Hiyya correctly observes that an animal may have one or even three kidneys on a congenital basis.[86] Surely these random observations and "discoveries" more accurately reflect a detached clinical attitude than one of reverential awe for the animal subject.

What hardly merits any discussion is the bizarre accusation leveled by certain Greek and Latin writers to the effect that Jews (and early Christians) worshipped the ass! Whether this calumny was purely malicious in intent or merely ignorant and misguided has long been a matter of interesting scholarly debate,[87] but in either event, it is totally without foundation. No evidence at all exists to support the accusation.

However, what is accurate is that although the Talmud and the tannaitic Midrashim condemned image-making, some animal representations appear in the Greco-Roman period. Among the more popular representations are scenes of birds eating grapes (a symbol of immortality), lions guarding the scrolls of the Torah or facing wine cups, fish, dolphins ox-heads, and peacocks gathered around wine goblets, but no one seriously views these as having been objects of worship! These forms, along with the Helios head at Bet Shearim and the zodiac figures at Hammath-Tiberias, whether conventional symbols of immortality or borrowed symbols from current religious mystery cults, seem to have been highly popular, if controversial, art themes. It is even possible that not all rabbis were opposed to them. Rabbi Johanan and Rabbi Abun did permit frescoes and mosaics in synagogues,[88] and the Palestinian Talmud records the fact that prior to the destruction of the Temple of Jerusalem in 70 C.E., all manner of likenesses were found in Jerusalem, except, of course, for human images.[89]

We referred earlier to the postbiblical era as one characterized by a cautious and limited remythologization of the animal kingdom; more accurately, perhaps, a *poetic* remythologization. This may have been facilitated in part by the fact that the Jewish people in the first centuries of the common era were far removed from idolatrous practices, and there was therefore no need for vigorous polemics. It is significant that the rabbis devote little time or attention to assailing heathen mystery rites. Presumably, they felt little need to do so.[90]

Only in specific areas, notably procedures relating to the sacrifice of animals, do the sages impose special restrictions as to the locale and manner of slaughtering, so that their procedures should clearly differ from the gentile procedures and bear no similarity to the sacrificial ceremonies for the pagan deities.[91]

Overall, a poetic remythologization of bird and beast could be safely tolerated. It consitituted no real threat to the supremacy of man, and carried within itself no practical implications vis-à-vis the powers of the beast. To the popular mind the animal was neither divine nor demonic, it was merely subordinate to man, created by God to serve him.

FOLKLORE

Proverbs and Narrative Fables

Coextensive with rabbinic legend and lore describing the "super-normal" beast was a far more extensive literature depicting the "normal" beast, mostly in the form of proverbs and narrative fables.

We use the phrase "normal" in describing such fauna because, for the most part, they retain their essential natural characteristics. Indeed, they are easily recognizable precisely because they conform in feature and in personality to the accepted stereotypes of their respective species. Of course, in animal fables the animals usually possess the power of speech and are able to communicate with the wisdom (or stupidity) of humans, but this is merely an effective literary device in this genre of literature. The fabulist seeks to convey certain truths about human affairs and relationships, and endowing animals with the gift of speech is merely an effective means to this end.

Proverbs

Some proverbs serve to illustrate simple animal traits.

Hang the heart of a palm tree on a pig and it will do the usual thing with it[1] [i.e., take it to a dung heap].

It can be in Babylonia and see a corpse in Palestine[2] [such is the keen eyesight of the vulture].

110

[Even] when the ox's head is in the feeding-bag, climb up on the roof and throw away the ladder from under you[3] [One should never trust oxen].

A weight of sixty minas of iron is suspended upon the proboscis of a gnat[4] [such is the virulence of its sting].

The intent of most descriptive proverbs is obvious.

Gabble like geese . . . cry like a crane.[5]

A dog when hungry is ready to swallow even his own excrement.[6]

When one dog barks he will find other dogs to bark with him.[7]

Though a duck keeps its head down while walking, its eyes look afar.[8]

A lion does not roar over a basket of straw but over a basket of flesh.[9]

Other proverbs illustrate human traits by way of analogy to the animal kingdom.

He never controlled two fleas[10] [a weak person].

A mouse lying on coins[11] [a miser].

One who cannot hit the donkey hits the saddle[12] [a coward].

He placed his money upon the horns of a stag[13] [the stag sheds its horns often, therefore the man made a foolish investment].

There are many old camels laden with the hides of young camels[14] [the old often manage to outlive the young].

Unflattering, but obvious is the advice that "If someone tells you that you have donkey-ears pay no attention; but if two people say so, order a halter."[15]

Man-wife relationships are succinctly and cynically stated.

No man can live in the same basket with a snake.[16]

If the dog barks, enter. If a bitch, leave.[17]

Many aspects of human nature are seen reflected in the nature of animals.

Every bird dwelleth according to its own kind, and so does man according to his like.[18]

The cat and the weasel prepare a feast with the fat of the unfortunate one[19] [even the worst enemies are capable of uniting in common cause against a mutual foe].

More than the calf wishes to suckle, does the cow wish to give milk[20] [the teacher wishes to teach even more than the student wishes to learn].

The evil inclination resembles a fly[21] [as unwanted flies persist in returning even after being driven away countless times, so does man's evil inclination persist in repeatedly haunting him].

Which farmer could not easily identify with the observation that "when the ox is plowing, on his forward journey he weeps, but on his return journey he eats the young green from the furrows."[22]
The inherent similarity between man and beast is employed by Rabbi Samuel b. Isaac in the name of Rabbi Eliezer in relating the seven "vanities" of Ecclesiastes to the seven stages in human life:

At a year old he is like a king seated in a canopied litter, fondled and kissed by all. At two and three he is like a pig sticking his hands in the gutters. At ten he skips like a kid. At twenty he is like a neighing horse, adorning his person and longing for a wife. Having married, he is like an ass. When he has begotten children, he grows brazen like a dog to supply their food and wants. When he has become old, he is [bent] like an ape.[23]

The utilitarian value of animals is expressed in obvious terms, "Dwell not in a town where no horses neigh and no barking of dogs is heard,"[24] and with subtlety, "the ram alive produces only one sound; dead, seven sounds"[25] (wind instruments were made from the ram's horns, flutes from its thigh bones, lute and harp strings from its intestines, while its wool was used in making the pomegranates in the high priest's vestments against which golden bells were struck to make a tinkling sound).

Certain species of fauna were especially appropriate subjects for proverbs. The fox, for example, is often contrasted with the lion. Although he lacks the inherent grandeur and power of the king of the beasts, he is sly and cunning, and skilled in the art of self-preservation. But the lion is the legitimate heir to the mantle of greatness. Therefore,

Be rather the tail among lions than the head of foxes[26] [better to play a role of lesser magnitude among the great than to be a leader among the mediocre].

The lion has become a fox[27] [a man has declined in greatness and his lofty reputation is no longer deserved].

Lions are before you, and you inquire of foxes[28] [you ask questions of mediocre people instead of inquiring of the great scholars].

A fox in its hour . . . bow down to it[29] [pay honor even to a lesser personage in his hour of glory].

The proverbial stupidity of the ass renders him a particularly apt subject for ridicule.

If the earlier [scholars] were sons of angels, we are sons of men; and if the earlier [scholars] were sons of men, we are like asses.[30]

An ass feels cold even in the summer solstice.[31]

If thy neighbor calls thee an ass, put a saddle on thy back.[32]

Guilt by association also rendered the ass-driver well worthy of ridicule. Therefore "an ass-driver's question" was a figure of speech denoting a foolish question.[33]

The Narrative Fable

Animals are excellent subjects for fables, for they offer distinct advantages to the fabulist who employs them. To begin with, animal fables are usually vivid and striking narratives which can be easily comprehended and appreciated even by an uneducated audience, and are easily recalled and transmitted to others. One need not be a sophisticate or a bookish scholar to appreciate a fable; quite the contrary.

Furthermore, the animal fable is an effective vehicle for the propagation of ideas that might otherwise be too difficult or too dangerous to advance. There is a "safety" factor inherent in such a fable because animal subjects can be made to mouth rebellious or treasonous doctrines without arousing the ire of the ruling powers. Therefore the animal tale proves to be an effective means of protesting against the injustices of society while yet granting to the narrator relative immunity from censorship and safety from reprisal. The disarming charm of many an animal fable, along with its subtle ambiguities, renders even the harshest of messages somehow less objectionable to its target.

This may explain, in part, the infrequency with which the fable appears in Scripture, notably in the prophetic writings. The prophets preferred direct exhortation to subtlety, and perhaps the seriousness of their message would have been inappropriately clothed in the charm and playfulness characteristic of most animal fables. More in keeping with our analysis, however, is another factor. The animal was intimately associated with the heathen religious rites of the ancient world. It would have been incongruous to expect the prophets of Israel to deliver their powerful anti-pagan exhortations while at the same time utilizing humanlike animals to illustrate their prophecies. The biblical mood of demythologizing hardly permits this luxury.

The rabbinic period, however, in permitting the emergence of a cautious remythologization, was far more hospitable to the animal fable. Indeed, it could well afford to be. For although the fable's *thematic factor* may have involved animals, the all-important *functional factor* of most fables involved teachings and morals pertaining to purely human endeavors. The animal's role was didactic, not magical; it was merely the vehicle for the communication of truths, not their source.

Rabbinic literature contains thirty-six animal tales known as "fox tales," although the fox is featured in less than a third of them. Mention is made, however, of numerous other animal stories. Hillel[34] and Johanan ben Zakkai[35] were acknowledged masters of the animal tale, and Rabbi Meir was reputed to have had a repertoire of three hundred fox fables,[36] as was Bar Kappara.[37] The latter's collection of parables was so spellbinding that on one occasion a crowd of enchanted listeners forgot to partake of their sumptuous dinner, so engrossed were they in his recitations.

Aesopian and Indian fables were also well-known in the ancient Mediterranean world,[38] and many an ancient fable underwent interesting adaptations and metamorphoses, as timely morals were prefixed or appended to such older narratives to make them relevant to the current audience. The popularity of certain fables was so great that fable-tellers sometimes take for granted that their audience knows the content of a given fable and therefore feel no need to recount it! For example, "Said Rabbi Ammi: 'Come and see how great are the men of faith. From what is this derived? From the incident of the weasel and the well. If it is so with the one who trusts a weasel and a well, how much more so with one who trusts in God.' "[39] Now the listeners obviously comprehended the fabulist's point because the episode of the weasel and the well was common knowledge. Fortunately for us, most fables and animal narratives are recounted in full, and spiced with elaborate detail.

Ancillary Animals Highlighting the Greatness of Biblical Heroes

Among the extensive cycle of legends surrounding King Solomon, and dramatizing his superior wisdom and cunning, are a series of dramatic stories featuring animals. Solomon's dominion over the animal kingdom was a common theme,[40] with the monarch reputed to have spoken the language of all creatures,[41] although early midrashic literature prefers to interpret this gift rationalistically.[42]

One legend concerns a man who gives milk to a thirsty serpent on the promise that he would be rewarded for his kindness with a handsome treasure. Instead, the ungrateful serpent coils itself around its benefactor's neck and threatens to kill him for allegedly stealing the treasure. When the two appear before Solomon for adjudication, the king cleverly orders the snake to uncoil itself from its victim. The Scripture-quoting serpent declares: "I will kill him, for the Holy One, blessed be He, commanded me: 'And thou shalt bruise their heel.' "[43] But Solomon inquires of the man: "Did not the Holy One, blessed be He, command that 'they shall bruise thy head'?" Whereupon the man crushes the serpent's head. The narrative concludes with the proverb, "Even with the best of snakes, crush its head."[44]

A later variation of the tale has an old man taking a half-frozen snake to his bosom in order to warm and revive it. The ungrateful serpent wishes to kill its benefactor, and an ox and an ass concur with its evil intent on the grounds that humans are unfair to their working-beasts. Again, Solomon saves the man from certain death by persuading the serpent to descend, whereupon it is killed.[45]

The building of the Temple in Jerusalem entailed Solomon's acquiring the *shamir*. However, the Lord of the Sea had entrusted it to the care of the *dukhiphath* (hoopoe bird), which had safely concealed it. But Solomon's messengers tricked the bird by placing glass over the nest containing its chicks, thereby forcing the bird to fetch the *shamir* from its hiding place in order to cut the glass.[46]

In contrast to these tributes to the wisdom of Solomon, another fable takes him to task for his lack of humility. Solomon overhears the queen of the ants warning her subjects against his troops. When asked why she fears them, she replies that her ants are distracted by them and therefore are unable to fulfill their obligation to offer praise to the Lord. The queen ant then reproves Solomon for remaining seated upon his throne while she stands on the earth. Holding her in his hand, the boastful king then inquires of the ant whether in all of creation there is anyone comparable in greatness to himself. The ant calmly replies that she is superior to Solomon, for God has obviously sent him to hold her in his hand! The enraged king flings her to the earth, proclaiming: "Dost thou know whom I am? I am Solomon, the son of David." Replies the ant: "I know that thou hast been formed from a corrupted drop, therefore be not proud." Whereupon King Solomon bows low in shame.[47]

Another story has Solomon apprehending a bird which has been overheard chirping boastfully to its companion-bird that it is capable of destroying Solomon's tower of Zion. The monarch castigates the bird: "You miserable, broken-winged gnat that you are, how could you set out to destroy this strong tower where my seat is?" But the bird wisely replies: "Solomon, where is that intellect of yours? Where is your understanding? Do you not know, and has nobody told you, that it is the habit of those who love, to say all kinds of great and wonderful imaginings to the beloved one, just in order so that she should love him in return. Why, all I was doing was telling tall tales to my love in order to find favor in her eyes."[48]

Origins of Traits and Relationships among Animals

A number of fables, in seeking to explain animal behavior, present moralistic teachings with obvious implications for the human audience.

The enmity between the cat and the mouse is attributed to the mouse's evil intention to devour the cat. God therefore punishes the mouse by ordaining that it be food for the cat, but pledges to protect its species from extermination.[49]

Another fable describes the dog and the cat as having originally been good friends. However, they decide to go their separate ways when their food supply becomes depleted, pledging never to share the same master. But the dog later violates his end of the bargain by accepting the invitation of the cat's master, Adam, to dwell with him and the cat. The enraged cat refuses to live together with the dog even though the latter assures her that he will not interfere with her privileges in any way. The result has been constant warfare between the cat and the dog unto this day.[50]

Why are there apparent seams alongside the mouth of the mouse? This is a result of the cat's having pursued the mouse while they were on Noah's ark. The terrified mouse found refuge in a hollow too small to permit the cat entrance. However, the latter was able to reach in with its paw and rip flesh from the mouth of the mouse. Noah then sewed up the mouth of the mouse with a hair from the swine's tail.[51]

Why is the steer's nose free of hair? Because Joshua kissed him upon that spot in gratitude for his having borne Joshua's heavy frame throughout the long siege of Jericho.[52]

Why is the raven's gait so awkward? It stems from his envy of the dove for her graceful walk. In trying to imitate her, the raven broke the bones of his feet and became incapable of resuming his normal manner of locomotion. The result—an awkward, hopping gait. The obvious moral of this story—he who is unhappy with his own lot often loses even that in his desire to attain more.[53] The camel's lack of prominent ears is similarly attributed to his insatiable desire to possess horns.[54]

Why does the eagle soar high in the air, closer to the heavens than any other species of fowl? The answer is an involved one. When the eagle attempted to eat another bird after departing from Noah's ark following the flood, it was sentenced to death by the rest of the fauna, clipped of its wings and feathers, and cast into the lion's den. But God protected the eagle from harm, and in order to protect it from the vengeful creatures, enabled its wings to grow again and carry it higher in the sky than any other species of fowl.[55]

Other legends describe how potentially dangerous creatures are rendered harmless to man, as when the serpent loses its physical as well as mental powers, the mole is made blind, and the frog toothless.[56]

The Nature of Animals

A number of rabbinic fables highlight the psychological and "spiritual" nature of certain species of animals.

For example, numerous tales extol the crafty wisdom of the fox. One such account depicts how the angel of death is ordered to cast one pair of each species of fauna into the waters. But the fox fools the angel of death by pointing to his reflection in the waters and pretending to be in mourning for his comrade fox which has already been drowned. The ruse effectively convinces the angel of death that a representative fox has already been cast into the waters, and he releases the captive fox. Later Leviathan discovers the deceit that has been perpetrated and sends a delegation of fish to fetch the fox. The fish swim homeward carrying the fox on their backs, having employed the ruse that he is to be their new ruler. But the suspicious fox prods the truth from the fish and then informs them that regrettably he cannot be killed, because "foxes do not carry their hearts around with them," and he persuades them to return him safely to the shore so that he may procure his heart. Once safe on dry land, the fox tauntingly declares: "Oh, ye fools, if I could play a trick on the angel of death, how much easier was it to make game of you!" Even Leviathan is forced to concur that "in truth, the fox is very wise, and ye are fools."[57]

Rashi attributes to Rabbi Meir the story of a shrewd Scripture-quoting fox who persuades a wolf to join the Jews in their Sabbath festivities. The unwanted Sabbath guest, the wolf, is attacked and severely beaten by the menfolk of the community. When it seeks to avenge itself by killing the fox, the latter explains most convincingly: "It is no fault of mine that you were beaten, for they have a grudge against your father, who once helped them in preparing their banquet and then consumed all the choice bits."

"And I was beaten for the wrong done by my father?" cried the indignant wolf. "Yes," replied the fox, " 'The fathers have eaten sour grapes and the children's teeth are set on edge.' However," he continued, "come with me and I will supply you with abundant food." He led the wolf to a well which had a beam suspended across it, from either end of which hung a bucket attached by means of a rope. The fox climbed in the upper bucket and descended into the well while the lower bucket was drawn up. "Where are you going?" asked the wolf. The fox, pointing to the cheeselike reflection of the moon, replied: "Here is plenty of meat and cheese, get into the other bucket and come down at once." The wolf did so, and as he descended, the fox was drawn up. "And how am I to get out?" demanded the wolf. "Ah," said the fox, " 'The righteous is delivered out of trouble and the wicked cometh in his stead.' Is it not written, 'Just balances, just weights'?"[58]

The dog is the subject of many negative observations in rabbinic literature. Jews contemptuously nicknamed their idols "dogs"[59] and were warned that "no man should breed a dog unless it is kept on a chain." One may, however, breed a dog in a town adjoining the frontier if he keeps it chained during the day and permits it to roam free only at night.[60] Rabbi Eliezer the Great declared that he who breeds dogs is like he who breeds swine.[61] We read of a woman who miscarried due to a barking dog,[62] and of the far more common fear of rabies.[63]

But dogs are given their due for possessing rudimentary intelligence and, on occasion, like the fox, real craftiness. For example,

Rabbi Tanhum b. Marion said: "There are dogs in Rome that know how to deceive men. A dog goes and sits down before a baker's shop and pretends to be asleep. When the shopkeeper dozes off, he dislodges a loaf near the ground [thus scattering the pile of loaves], and, while the onlookers are collecting the scattered loaves, he snatches a loaf and makes off."[64]

However, the loyalty and devotion of dogs toward their masters is also noted. We are informed that dogs differ from cats in that they recognize their masters, while cats do not.[65] According to Rab, the sign of protection which God gave to Cain was a dog![66]

The Jerusalem Talmud cites as one of Rabbi Meir's fables the story of a dog who observed a serpent poisoning the curdled milk of its master. The dog barked frantically, but to no avail, as its master failed to heed its warnings and set out to partake of the milk. The desperate dog hastened to consume the food itself, thereby dying an agonizing death while saving the lives of its master and his fellow shepherds. The grateful shepherds buried the faithful dog with funerary honors and erected a monument to its memory.[67] Interestingly, a similar tale is told of a pet snake which tries to warn its master against eating garlic powder which has been contaminated by another snake. The loyal snake eats the contaminated food and dies, so that the master's life is saved.[68]

Didactic Creatures

In commenting upon Rabbi Johanan's claim that Rabbi Meir knew three hundred fox-fables, Hai Gaon wrote:

Know that these fables contain moral lessons which are presented as if they emanated from the mouths of the beasts of the field, like the writings of the Hindus which are called *Kitab Kalila wa-Dimna,* and which contain moral lessons, wise sayings, and metaphors in the form of animal fables. As for these fables of Rabbi Meir, each was attached to a biblical verse which expressed a similar idea.[69]

Indeed, animal fables and parables are, for the most part, didactic; they seek to instruct, to exhort, and to inspire the human listeners.

Joshua b. Hananiah dramatically employs an animal tale to calm a throng of Jews who are protesting the sudden reversal of Hadrian's earlier decision to rebuild the Temple in Jerusalem. He successfully dissuades them from rebelling against the emperor by telling them the tale of a crane who removed a thorn from the tongue of a lion. When the bird asked the king of the beasts for a reward, it was informed that its having emerged alive from out of the lion's mouth constituted a sufficient reward in and of itself.[70]

Rabbi Joshua's moral was not lost upon the crowd: be thankful for Hadrian's benevolent policies, and do not be so foolhardy as to press him for further benefits.

A pagan philosopher asked Rabbi Gamliel why God is so angry at idolaters and yet refuses to take out His wrath upon the objects of idolatry. Rabbi Gamliel replied with a parable. A prince named his pet dog after his father, the king, and would swear "by the life of the dog, my father." When the king heard of this behavior he was aghast. But against whom did his anger turn, against the dog or against his son? Surely only against his son, for the dog, after all, was blameless![71]

When the Roman authorities issued a decree forbidding Jews from studying and practicing the Torah, Rabbi Akiba assembled his students and publicly taught them Torah. Pappas b. Judah said to him: "Akiba, are you not afraid of the government?" Akiba replied with a parable.

A fox was once walking alongside of a river, and he saw swarms of fishes going from one place to another. Said he to them: "From what are you fleeing?" They replied: "From the nets cast for us by men." He said to them: "Would you like to come up unto the dry land so that you and I can live together in the way that my ancestors lived with your ancestors?" They replied: "Art thou the one that they call the cleverest of animals? Thou art not clever but foolish. If we are afraid in the element in which we live, how much more in the element in which we would die!" So it is with us. If such is our predicament when we sit and study the Torah, of which it is written, "For that is thy life and the length of thy days," if we go and neglect it, how much worse off we shall be.[72]

For those who fear the insecurity of freedom, Rabbi Levi relates the story of a free bird who envies a caged bird because the latter is provided with all the food it needs, while the free bird must scrounge about, often unsuccessfully, for its sustenance. But the caged bird hastens to point out that it is at the mercy of its keepers and may well be killed on the morrow.[73]

For those who are despondent and despair of divine liberation from their oppressors, the fable is told of a lion who invites his friends to join him in a banquet hall, above which is stretched out a canopy made from the skins of numerous evil beasts which he has killed. When asked to sing a song, the fox proclaims: "What he showed us with respect to those above, he will show us with respect to those below" (i.e., the lion, who has destroyed the evil beasts above us, will also successfully destroy the evil beasts all around us) and proceeds to affirm that as Bigthan and Teresh were destroyed by God, so will the wicked Haman meet his end at the hand of God.[74]

Mordecai's challenge as how to deal with the wicked Haman is the perennial challenge faced by Israel in a heathen world.

The nations of the world demand that Israel worship their gods or else face annihilation, but God will surely punish her severely for the sin of idolatry; what then is Israel to do? Israel's dilemma is likened to that of a thirsty wolf who knows that a net is spread out for it at a well. If he drinks of the water he will be ensnared, but if he abstains from drinking he will die of thirst! What then is he to do?[75] One can almost sense here an appeal on Israel's part to God for compassion and understanding when Israel, at times, appears to be guilty of idolatrous practices. She does not transgress willfully, she simply has no other choice if she is to survive!

The sobering and saddening truth that life must inevitably end in death, and that "As he came forth of his mother's womb, naked shall he go back as he came," is given a vivid interpretation by Genibah.

It is like the fox who found a vineyard which was fenced in on all sides. There was one hole through which he wanted to enter, but he was unable to do so. What did he do? He fasted for three days until he became lean and frail, and so got through the hole. Then he ate [of the grapes] and became fat again, so that when he wished to go out he could not pass through at all. He again fasted another three days until he became lean and frail, returning to his former condition, and went out. When he was outside he turned his face and gazing at the vineyard, said, "O vineyard, how good are you and the fruits inside! All that is inside is beautiful and commendable, but what enjoyment has one from you? As one enters you, so he comes out." Such is this world.[76]

Haman's rise to power and subsequent downfall were connected by the rabbis to the passage "For the wicked shall perish and the enemies of the Lord shall be as the fat of lambs,"[77] because lambs are not fattened for their own benefit, but for slaughter.

So the wicked Haman was raised to greatness only to make his fall greater. It was like the case of a man who had a sow, a she-ass, and a filly, and he let the sow eat as much as it wanted, but strictly rationed the ass and the filly. Said the filly to the ass: "What is this lunatic doing? To us who do the work of the master, he gives food by the measure, but to the sow who does nothing he gives as much as she wants." The ass answered: "The hour will come when you will see her downfall, for they are feeding her up not out of respect for her but to her own hurt." When the Calends [the first day of the Roman month, usually observed as a feast-day] came around, they took the sow and stuck it. When afterwards they set barley before the filly, it began sniffing at it instead of eating. The mother then said to it: "My daughter, it is not the eating which leads to slaughter but the idleness."[78]

Haman's stupidity in seeking to destroy the Jewish people is illustrated by the story of the

bird which made its nest on the edge of the sea, and the sea swept away its nest, whereupon it said: "I will not move from here until I turn the dry land into sea and the sea into dry land." What did it then do? It took water from the sea in its mouth and poured it on the dry land, and it took dust from the dry land and cast it into the sea. Its companion came and stood by it and said: "Luckless unfortunate, with all your labor what will you effect?" So God said to the wicked Haman: "Stupid fool, I said that I would destroy them, and even I, in a way, was not able, and you want to try!"[79]

Animal characters give to a fable a built-in sense of ambiguity which permits varying interpretations to exist for any given fable and enables a single fable to be applicable to differing political climes, crises, and personalities. For example, the *Sifre* describes two sheep dogs who are enemies under normal circumstances but unite in fighting a common enemy, the wolf, who attempts to sieze their lambs.[80] At first glance this could be interpreted as part of a sermon urging the diverse feuding factions in Judea to unite in fighting the common enemy, most likely Rome. But in its context in the *Sifre,* the message would seem to be that the common enemies, Midian and Moab (the fighting dogs), pool their efforts against Israel (the wolf). Yet another version of the same fable is associated with the proverb, "The weasel and the cat prepare a feast with the fat of the unfortunate one."[81] In other words, oppressors are always ready and able to overlook prior enmities in order to join forces in destroying a defenseless victim, presumably the mouse.[82]

Rabbi Simlai, in the midst of a discussion dealing with messianic expectations, comments on the passage in Amos, "Woe unto you who desire the day of the Lord, to what end is it for you? It is darkness and not light,"[83] by relating the story of the cock and the bat who sat through the night awaiting dawn. The cock remarks that it is sensible for himself to look forward to the break of day, but what possible benefit could the blind bat derive from daylight?[84] Not suprisingly, Rabbi Simlai's dictum has been interpreted by some as a subtle anti-Christian or anti-pagan polemic.[85]

To return for a moment to the didactic role of the animal. This didactic capacity is at times a direct one, for the biblical passage "Who teaches us more than the beasts of the earth, and makes us wiser than the fowls of the heaven" was also interpreted to mean "who teaches us *by* the beasts of the earth and makes us wise *by* the fowls of the heaven."[86]

Therefore Rabbi Johanan could state that had God not given the

Torah to Israel, many necessary moral qualities could have been learned simply by observing the behavior of animals. To be specific, modesty could have been learned from the cat (presumably from her cleanliness habit of covering her excrement with dust), honesty from the ant (who never encroaches upon the storage areas of other ants), chastity from the dove (who practices monogamy), and good manners from the cock, who first coaxes and then mates. (When the cock desires to have sexual relations with its mate, he promises her a beautiful cloak reaching all the way to the ground. Later, when she reminds him of his promise, he dramatically shakes his comb and proclaims: "May I be deprived of my comb should I not purchase it when I have the means.")[87]

Even the locust has a valuable lesson to teach man, the lesson of unity and discipline in the manner in which it divides up into bands. Furthermore, the grasshopper teaches man a powerful spiritual lesson in that it sings steadily throughout the summer months until it is claimed by death and its belly bursts. Though this creature is surely well aware of its imminent fate, it nevertheless sings on. Man, likewise, should fulfill, in love and joy, all of his duties toward the Creator, even while being mindful of his own mortality.

The stork, too, has lessons to teach, for he is a model of family purity, as well as a merciful and compassionate bird. Even the lowly frog serves as an inspiring example of self-sacrifice in that he is willing to offer himself up as food to famished creatures who are dependent upon a diet of aquatic animals, fulfilling thereby the injunction: "If thine enemy be hungry, give him bread to eat; and if he be thirsty, give him water to drink."[88]

Solomon's admiration for the ant and his admonition to humans to "consider her ways and be wise"[89] was interpreted by Rabbi Tanhuma as referring to the ant's habit of storing away food in far greater abundance than her immediate needs would warrant. Why does she do so? Because she says: "Perhaps God will grant me [more] life, and I will have food in readiness."[90] Rabbi Simeon b. Halafta recounts how when one ant dropped a grain of wheat, no other ant would pick it up. The moral drawn was that if the ant, who has no judges or police officers, nevertheless refrains from taking another's property, how much more so should man refrain from robbery, seeing that human society does establish judiciary personnel.[91]

Animals were also believed by some to be endowed with such acute sensitivity that humans could learn of future events by observing their behavior. For example,

It happened that a man was plowing when one of his oxen lowed. An Arab passed by and asked: "What are you?" He answered: "I am a Jew." He said to him: "Unharness your ox and untie your plow" [as a mark of mourning]. "Why?" he asked. "Because the Temple of the Jews is destroyed." He inquired; "From where do you know this?" He answered: "I know it from the lowing of your ox." While he was conversing with him, the ox lowed again. The Arab said to him: "Harness your ox and tie up your plow, because the deliverer of the Jews is born." "What is his name?" he asked; and he answered: "His name is 'Comforter.' " "What is his father's name?" He answered: "Hezekiah." "Where do they live?" He answered: "In Birath 'Arba in Bethlehem of Judah."[92]

According to the Midrash, Balaam's speaking ass died shortly after her conversation with her master.[93] Why? As noted earlier, one interpretation deemed this to be necessary so that people should not transform her into an object of reverence. But another explanation justifies the animal's demise on the grounds that otherwise people would have exclaimed: "This was the animal that degraded Balaam." The Midrash continues:

This serves to inform you that the Holy One, blessed be He, has consideration for the dignity of mankind, and, knowing their needs, He shut the mouths of the beasts [i.e., created them dumb]. For had they been able to speak, it would have been impossible to put them to the service of man or to stand one's ground against them. For here was the ass, the most stupid of all beasts, and there was the wisest of all wise men, yet as soon as she opened her mouth he could not stand his ground against her!

To conclude our discussion of the didactic role played by animals in rabbinic literature, we turn to the dove. In a far more symbolic vein, the dove continued to be the symbol par excellence for Israel,[94] and based on the passage "Thou hast dove's eyes,"[95] the rabbis extolled its virtues in obviously didactic terms.

As the dove is chaste, so the Israelites are chaste.

As the dove stretches out her neck to the slaughter, so do the Israelites.

As the dove atones for sins, so do the Israelites atone for the nations.

As the dove is faithful to her mate for a lifetime, so the Israelites are faithful to God.

Just as the dove is saved only by her wings, so are Israel saved only by the precepts.

Just as the dove never abandons its cote, even upon the loss of its young, so Israel continues to observe the festivals even though its Temple is lost.

Just as the dove produces a fresh brood every month, so does Israel produce fresh learning and good deeds monthly.

Just as the dove goes far afield and yet returns to its cote, so the Children of Israel return to their land.[96]

In perhaps the highest possible tribute of all, the rabbis sometimes endowed the human soul with the form and movement of a dovelike bird.[97]

Religious Creatures

In suggesting that humans would do well to learn certain vital moral lessons and basic religious truths by observing the behavior of animals, the rabbis occasionally went so far as to endow animals with "religious" sentiments and a fervent desire to serve their Creator. It is therefore not unusual to find animals playing a pivotal role in the unfolding of divinely ordained events, and God will frequently call upon fauna to function as His emissaries in dispensing divine justice upon mankind.

Sometimes the animal seems to function consciously and discerningly as God's messenger, but often its role is a perfunctory and unthinking one.

For example, God brings about Zedekiah's capture at the hands of the Babylonians by causing a deer to lead the pursuing troops on a chase to the precise locale of the king's hiding-place, and at the exact time that Zedekiah emerges from hiding.[98] We read of a serpent which is sent to kill a deceitful priest who hides beneath the altar of Baal.[99] Swarms of worms (or possibly ants) emerge from *manna* (the heavenly food) and crawl about conspicuously, thereby testifying to the guilt of those Israelites who transgressed God's command by storing away quantities of the *manna*.[100] The Philistines who captured the holy ark are punished by the Lord by means of swarms of mice which tear apart their sexual orifices and entrails, spread plagues, and destroy the crops of the land.[101] When Og, king of Bashan, lifts a mountain over his head with which to crush the Israelites, God summons an army of ants to rescue them. The ants promptly bore a hole in the mountain so that it slips around the giant's neck.[102] The Israelites are able to vanquish the Amorite army with the assistance of hornets which afflict the enemy troops.[103] Not infrequently, attacks of wild animals were interpreted as divinely ordained events,[104] although it is surely questionable whether the beasts involved had a true awareness of their mission.

Occasionally, however, animals manifest great discernment and discrimination in fulfilling their tasks. Thus snakes and scorpions refrain from attacking the Israelites during their desert journeys,[105] while discerning lions refuse to harm Daniel but do kill his enemies.[106] In an interesting vignette, the Talmud credits a venomous serpent with preventing a potential thief from absconding with the linen cloak belonging to Rabbi Eliezer b. Pedath while the rabbi was engrossed in the study of Torah in the lower market of Sepphoris.[107]

David and Solomon are the beneficiaries of several acts of kindness performed by discerning animals at God's bidding. A dove wails and plucks out her plumes in order to warn Abishai that his brother, David, is in danger of losing his life,[108] while a lion and a deer team up to rescue young David and help him to escape from the monstrous *reem*.[109] Solomon's intimate ties with the animal kingdom are, predictably, beneficial to him. He enlists the aid of birds to shade his troops from the hot sun,[110] and is served by a giant eagle which transports him upon her back and faithfully fulfills numerous perilous errands for the monarch.[111]

Animals are portrayed as ministering to the dead by protecting corpses and helping to provide honorable burial for them. Thus Abel's dog faithfully stands guard over his master's body so that no beast may disturb it, and flocks of birds and clean animals perform the burial rites.[112] Since a corpse cannot be moved on the Sabbath, Solomon commands eagles to stand guard over the dead body of his father, David,[113] while another tradition records that a flock of birds provided shade for the multitudes gathered to pay their final respects at David's funeral.[114]

The prophet Hosea, who dearly longed to die and be buried in Israel, was forced to spend his last days in Babylonia. As his deathbed wish, he asked that his bier be placed upon the back of a camel which would then be permitted to roam freely, and that his burial-site be wherever the camel chose to stop. Upon Hosea's death his instructions were followed; the camel bearing his body proceeded directly to the Jewish cemetery at Safed, and there the prophet was buried.[115]

Because of their conscious desire to do the Lord's bidding, we are told that Noah had no need to expend any energy in gathering the animals into his ark. All thirty-two species of fowl and three hundred and sixty-five reptilian varieties entered immediately upon God's bidding.[116] Later, when God commands the birds and beasts to feast upon the flesh of tyrants and thereby eradicate evil from the world, the Midrash observes that these creatures, which had so eagerly entered the confinement of the ark, would surely be willing to obey all of God's commandments.[117]

Sometimes a sense of ironic poetic justice characterizes the choice of specific animals to do the Lord's bidding. Since the serpent was the first creature to speak slander, God decreed that slanderers who failed to learn their lesson from his punishment should themselves be punished by serpents.[118] The Midrash adds that "although the serpent eats dainty delicacies, all his food changes into dust. The Israelites, on the other hand, eat only *manna*, but it is transformed into many delicacies. Therefore, let the serpent, who eats many types of food which have but one taste, come and punish those who eat one type of food which has many tastes."[119]

It would be appropriate at this juncture to state a point of perspective, which, though obvious, nevertheless merits assertion. However impressive some of the preceding excerpts appear to be, their principal intent is not to extol the virtues of the animal kingdom per se. The animal is merely a useful and efficient instrument in the unfolding of providential destiny, but it is God, with His extraordinary wisdom, who is the master in bringing together diverse creatures to help achieve His will with delicate harmony. "Samuel saw a scorpion borne by a frog cross a river and then sting a man, so that he died. Thereupon Samuel quoted, 'They stand forth this day to receive Thy judgments' " (i.e., the scorpion is unable to swim, the frog cannot sting, but God's will is achieved through their cooperative effort).[120] A more elaborate version also appears:

It once happened that a man was standing at the riverside and saw a frog carrying a scorpion and transporting it across the river. Said he: "This creature is designated for the performance of a mission!" She carried it across the river, and after it had gone and performed its mission, she brought it back to its place.

The sound of wailing was heard in the city: "so-and-so was bitten by a scorpion and died."[121]

Even when we encounter remarkably discerning and sensitive beasts, the kudos rightly belong to the Creator, whose superior wisdom endows even such limited creatures with extraordinary powers.

It is in this connection that another lesson, perhaps more subtle, is developed in rabbinic thought; to wit,

even those things which one may regard as completely superfluous in the creation of the world, such as fleas, gnats, and flies, even they are included among the creations of the world. The Holy One, blessed be He, carries out His purpose through everything, even through a snake, a scorpion, a gnat, or a frog.[122]

It is possible to cite striking examples of this theme.

Rabbi Jannai was sitting and lecturing at the gate of his town, when he saw a snake coming on in great haste, slithering to and fro, from side to side. "This [snake] is going to carry out a mission," observed he. Immediately a report spread in the town, "So-and-so has been bitten by a snake and died."

Rabbi Eliezer was sitting to ease himself in a privy, when a Roman came and drove him away and sat down. "This has a purpose," remarked he. Immediately a snake emerged and struck and killed him [the Roman].[123]

A later version records Rabbi Eliezer rebuking a serpent with the words, "Serpent, serpent, turn back, for the man whom you are going to slay has already repented and regrets the evil he has done," and explaining to his colleagues that the serpent had been instructed from heaven to kill a sinner, but now that the sinner had repented, no punishment was to be administered.[124]

Perhaps the most dramatic of such episodes is recounted by Rabbi Aha:

The Holy One, blessed be He, carries out His errands with the help of all, even through the instrumentality of a serpent, even through that of a frog, and even through that of a scorpion, aye, even through that of a mosquito. The wicked Titus entered the interior of the Holy of Holies, his sword drawn in his hand, slashed the curtain, brought two harlots, and, spreading out a scroll of the law beneath them, cohabited with them on top of the altar. . . . He began to utter revilings and blasphemies against heaven, and said: "The case of one who makes war with a king in the desert and vanquished him cannot be compared with that of one who makes war against a king in his own palace and vanquishes him." . . . The Holy One, blessed be He, said to him: "Villain! By thy life I shall inflict punishment upon thee by means of a trifling creature which I created during the first six days of creation." Thereupon the Holy One, blessed be He, beckoned to the sea, and it ceased from its fury. When he reached Rome, all the citizens of Rome came out and lauded him with the words: "O conqueror of the barbarians!" Immediately afterwards a hot bath was prepared for him, and he entered and bathed. When he came out they mixed him a cup of wine. The Holy One, blessed be He, brought in his way a mosquito, which entered into his nose and gnawed its way up until it reached his brain. It began to bore in his brain, so he ordered: "Call the doctors and let them split open the brain of that man and ascertain what it is whereby the God of this nation inflicts punishment upon that man." Forthwith the doctors were summoned. They split open his brain and found in it something resembling a young pigeon which possessed a weight of two pounds![125]

David is described as having once questioned the Lord's wisdom in creating such "useless" creatures as spiders and wasps. Of what possible benefit or service can these loathsome insects be? By way of reply, God causes David's life to become endangered when he flees from Saul, and in desperation he hides himself in a cave. As Saul's troops draw near, a spider obligingly spins its web across the cave's mouth. The soldiers notice it and therefore desist from searching the cave's interior, reasoning that if anyone was hiding therein, he would surely have broken the web in order to enter. On another occasion, a wasp-sting causes the sleeping giant, Abner, to stir in his sleep, moving his heavy legs and thereby freeing a trapped David. David now realizes that he owes his life to these "useless" creatures, and he praises the Lord for having created them, admitting that each and every creature serves an indispensable purpose in the divine schema.[126]

Religious Devotion among Animals

When David completes the composition of the Psalter, he boastfully exclaims: "O Lord of the world, is there another creature in the universe who like me proclaims Thy praise?" A frog promptly approaches the king and declares: "David, do not be so pleased with yourself, for I say more songs and praises than you do, and furthermore, every song I sing can have three thousand parables told about it."[127]

The notion that members of the animal kingdom, like humankind, utter paeans of glory to God is, of course, a biblical one, but its development in midrashic literature is extensive and striking. In many respects, however, this is a perfectly natural development. After all, animals once possessed the power of speech, and their silent thoughts are still discernible to wise and sensitive humans. Furthermore, if even trees, plants, and inanimate objects are endowed with the capacity to praise the Lord, it is only natural for animals to be able to do so as well.

Birds, notably the cock, are given the honor of singing the principal songs of praise to God, but animals also join in the chanting of scriptural passages in homage to their Creator. Even dumb fishes and frogs and mice chant appropriate verses as their praise to the Lord.[128]

This portrait of the animal world united in lifting up their voices in prayer to their Creator is a genuinely Jewish concept[129] which finds its ultimate expression in the *Perek Shira*, an ancient *braita* which apparently underwent modifications through the years.[130] *Perek Shira* depicts numerous species participating in the chanting of scriptural passages, exhorting one another to greater piety and religious devotion.[131]

Many of these prayers are beautifully appropriate to the nature and disposition of the respective species, and represent the sort of utterances that the "dumb" creatures would emote in their hearts. For example, the sea-monsters appropriately intone, "Praise the Lord from the earth, ye sea-monsters and all deeps,"[132] while the fish declare that "the voice of the Lord is upon the waters, the God of glory thundereth, even the Lord upon many waters."[133] The early-rising cock proclaims, "How long wilt thou sleep, O sluggard? When wilt thou arise out of thy sleep?"[134] while apt passages for the dove and other birds are "O my dove, that are in the clefts of the rock, in the covert of the cliff, let me see thy countenance, let me hear thy voice; for sweet is thy voice, and thy countenance is comely,"[135] and "Yea, the sparrow hath found a house and the swallow a nest for herself, where she may lay her young; Thine altars, O Lord of Hosts, My king and my God."[136] The persecuted and defenseless hare sings a prayer of thanksgiving, "But as for me, I will sing of Thy strength; yea, I will sing aloud of Thy mercy in the morning; for Thou hast been my high tower, and a refuge in the day of my distress,"[137] while the crafty and dishonest fox is presented with the passage "Woe unto him who buildeth his house by unrighteousness, and his chambers by injustice; that useth his neighbor's service without wages, and giveth him not his hire."[138]

At times these prayers represent more than poetic exercises, for we also encounter testimony to the *efficacy* of the prayers of animals, and one rabbi attributes the defeat of the army of Sennacherib and the deliverance of Jerusalem to the fact that the prayers uttered by the beasts of the field caused the attacking army to flee.[139]

Religious Observance among Animals

Along with their devotion to God in the form of prayer, animals are also depicted as serving their Master by seeking to fulfill precisely the same ritual and ethical obligations incumbent upon humans.

Thus the ass of Pinhas b. Yair starves itself for three days because it refuses to eat barley until it can ascertain that tithing has taken place,[140] while Hanina b. Dosa's donkey refuses to eat or drink from items which have been stolen.[141] Rabbi Yose's ass, when hired out for a day's labor, refused to return home unless it had the precise amount of hire placed upon its back. Once it stubbornly refused to enter its stall until a pair of shoes placed upon it were removed for the shoes were not the rightful property of its master.[142]

Most impressive is the story of the plowing heifer sold by its impecunious owner to a pagan. When the new master attempted to plow with it on the Sabbath day, the animal lay down beneath the yoke and refused to budge, notwithstanding the beating it received from its incensed master. The pagan assumed that the animal's peculiar behavior was due to its being emotionally upset in grieving for its previous owner, but the Israelite perceived that the true cause for the animal's refusal to work was its desire to observe the Sabbath. He therefore said to the pagan:

"I will come and raise her." When he came, he whispered into her ear, "Heifer, heifer, you know well that when you were mine, you plowed all the week and you rested on the Sabbath, but now, through my sins, you have passed to a pagan master. I beseech you, rise and plow." The heifer did so at once. The pagan then said to him: "I beg you take your cow away, because I cannot always come to fetch you to raise her. But now I will not leave you until you tell me what you said to her, in her ear. I wearied myself with her and beat her, but she would not get up." The Israelite then began to appease him and said: "It was neither witchcraft nor magic that I did, but thus and thus did I whisper in her ear, so that she rose and plowed." At once the pagan was struck by fear, and said: "If a heifer, which has no speech and no sense, could recognize her Maker, shall not I, whom my Creator formed in His own image and to whom He gave understanding, acknowledge Him?" Straightway he went and became a proselyte. He studied and acquired the merit of Torah, and they used to call him, "John, son of the heifer," and to this day our rabbis pronounce rulings which he gave. Now if you are astonished that a heifer should bring a man under the wings of the *Shechina*, reflect that it is through a heifer that Israel can be purified.[143]

Numerous other "inspirational" stories of devotion to God also feature animals in the central role.

In the classic confrontation-competition between the prophet Elijah and the prophets of Baal, a pair of twin bullocks were selected, one designated to be offered to God, the other to Baal. While Elijah's bullock went willingly to the altar of the Lord, the animal designated for Baal refused to budge from its place in spite of the strenuous efforts of no less than eight hundred and fifty priests of Baal to dislodge it. When Elijah attempted to persuade the reluctant animal to follow the priests, it said to him: "We two, yonder bullock and myself, came forth from the same womb, and we took our food from the same manger. But now he has been destined for God as an instrument for the glorification of the divine name, while I am to be used for Baal, as an instrument to enrage my Creator." Elijah replied: "Bullock, bullock, fear not! Do thou but follow the priest of Baal that they may have no excuse for their failure, and then thou wilt have a share in that glorification of God for which my bullock will be used." The bullock was persuaded by this argument, but insisted that it at least be led to the heathen altar by the prophet Elijah himself.[144]

Animals are credited with playing an interesting role in the drama wherein God inflicts physical ailments upon the Philistines for having taken the holy ark from the Israelites. The Philistines harnessed the ark to nursing kine, and although the kine yearned deeply for their young, they nevertheless proceeded to march directly on the road to Judea, thereby proving to the Philistines that their afflictions were the direct result of their having confiscated the ark from the Hebrews.[145] Furthermore, the kine proceeded to sing a song of praise to God as they went on their way with their precious cargo.[146]

Rabbinic legend elaborates upon the role played by animals when God visited the plagues upon the Egyptians. The frogs, in particular, distinguished themselves in performing the Lord's will. Not only did they excel in tormenting the Egyptians, but they even cast themselves into the fiery ovens! Their behavior later served as an inspiration to Hananiah, Mishael, and Azariah, who, when threatened by Nebuchadnezzar with being thrown into a burning furnace unless they worshipped his idols, proclaimed:

If the frogs, which were under no obligation to glorify the name of God, nevertheless threw themselves into the fire in order to execute the divine will concerning the punishment of the Egyptians, how much more should we be ready to expose our own lives to the fire for the greater glory of His name.[147]

At the very dawn of history, fauna stand aghast at the enormity of Cain's crime of fratricide. Cattle, beasts, and birds alike recognize the terrible wrong that was perpetrated in destroying life and demand that Abel's murder be avenged. It became necessary for God Himself to defend Cain before the animals and explain that "Cain's judgment shall not be as the judgment of other murderers. Though Cain did, indeed, slay, he had no way of knowing the enormity of his crime. Henceforth, however, all who slay will be slain."[148]

Responsible Creatures

Any depiction of the animal as occupying a religious universe as well as a physical universe in common with man must inevitably carry with it certain implications vis-à-vis the law of retribution. Irrespective of the obvious differences between the two, just as man is subject to the basic religious law of reward and punishment, so must be the animal.

The rewards and punishments for animals differ greatly in magnitude. For example, we are informed that because the dogs obeyed the divine command, "But against any of the Israelites shall not a dog whet his tongue, against man or beast,"[149] the Lord rewarded them by giving them meat which is unfit for human consumption. A midrash concluding Perek Shira explains that the reason why greedy dogs are granted the privilege of uttering shira is because this is their reward for not whetting their tongues against the Israelites. The dogs are further merited in that the holy parchments for the Torah scrolls, *mezuzot,* and phylacteries are all tanned with their excrement![150]

Because the asses willingly carried upon their backs the raiment and jewelry of the Israelites during the exodus from Egypt, God declares as their reward that "the firstling of an ass thou shalt redeem with a lamb,"[151] while the clean birds, as well as the animals that participated in the burial of Abel, merited that two blessings would be recited over them at the time of their slaughter and when their blood was to be covered.[152]

On other occasions, the reward bestowed upon an animal is the supreme gift of life itself. After Cain kills his brother, Abel, a unique dilemma presents itself: what to do with Abel's dead body? After all, this is man's first encounter with death! A raven supplies the answer by way of example as it buries the dead body of another bird. In gratitude to the birds, God personally undertakes the task of feeding baby ravens. Why should these birds be in need of divine solicitude? A fascinating answer is given. We are told that parent ravens often neglect their brood because the fledglings are born with white feathers and the parent birds are, therefore, incapable of recognizing them as their own offspring. God Himself, therefore, assumes the responsibility of caring for the young ravens until such time as their plumage darkens and the parent birds are capable of recognizing them as their own, and caring for them.[153]

The aforementioned frogs who willingly entered the hot ovens of Egypt were rewarded by God in that they were able to survive their ordeal and live to return to the river, whereas the other frogs perished.[154] The *milhan* (phoenix), a fowl, is granted the gift of eternal life because it alone refused to join the other creatures of the Garden of Eden in partaking of the forbidden fruit.[155] It is interesting to note that the *milhan* birds were given a special sanctuary-city in which to live, at the suggestion of the angel of death. They would thereby remain pure and not be persuaded to sin by their decadent contemporaries.

Chastity is a significant virtue meriting reward among members of the animal kingdom. The epoch of the flood was characterized by a universal state of corruption upon the earth, pervading animal as well as humankind. In the same way that Noah and his family were spared the ravages of the deluge by virtue of their piety, so those animals who survived did so by virtue of their own high moral standards. They are depicted as refraining from copulating with diverse species and consciously restricting themselves so that they would mate exclusively with their own kind.[156] Such chastity is well worthy of divine recompense, for "God, praised be His name, does not deprive any creature of its reward. Even the mouse which guarded its family and did not intermingle with other species received a reward."[157]

But relatively minor virtues are also handsomely rewarded by the Almighty. The Talmud suggests another reason for the fact that the *urshana* (phoenix) is blessed with immortality—its considerateness toward Noah. Whereas other animals were exceedingly demanding and insistent upon enjoying their full comforts, and continually besieged Noah with their complaints, the *urshana* declined even to ask him for food, so concerned was it not to disturb Noah.[158]

But as animals share God's rewards with humans, it is only proper that they also be subject to His punishments. Mention was made of a dog which persisted in chewing upon the shoes of the rabbis. The sages, unaware of the culprit's identity, pronounced a ban of excommunication upon the guilty party, whereupon the dog's tail promptly caught fire and was burnt.[159] On a broader level, midrashic teachings emphasize that the curse of mortality was visited upon the animal kingdom for their having joined Adam and Eve in partaking of the forbidden fruit, that the horses of the Egyptians perished along with their riders for having pursued the Israelites,[160] and that the birds of the generation of the deluge were destroyed because they permitted themselves to be fattened up as cuisine for the wicked.[161]

Significantly, retribution for animals is not only a theoretical or aggadic issue. After all, biblical law ordained the killing of any animal that took a human life,[162] and the rabbis required a court of twenty-three judges to administer the sentence.[163] However, such an execution took place only if the animal killed "intentionally," but should it be guilty of accidental homicide, its life was to be spared. Furthermore, if the beast had intended to kill one individual and instead caused the death of another, some argued that it should not be liable to any punishment at all. Such, indeed, were precisely the distinctions introduced in cases involving homicides committed by human beings![164]

Not only were domestic animals destroyed for killing humans, this was also the penalty for wild beasts, such as wolves, lions, bears, leopards, panthers, and serpents.[165] We read of a cock that was stoned to death for killing a newborn infant. It apparently picked out the child's brains, possibly mistaking the pulsating fontanel for a moving insect.[166]

A similar penalty was carried out against animals involved in sexual relations with humans. On three occasions Scripture invoked a stern prohibition against bestiality,[167] decreeing death for *all* the participants, while the Levites on Mount Ebal pronounce a solemn curse upon "he that lieth with any manner of beast."[168] Legend describes how the extensive corruption of the generation of the flood resulted in people actually writing out marriage contracts between themselves and animals,[169] how Balaam committed sodomy with his ass,[170] and how Artaxerxes shared his throne with a bitch.[171]

Such fears were taken seriously, as were the attendant precautions. We read of Rabbi Judah's opposition to the hiring of bachelor shepherds to tend small livestock,[172] and how widows are advised not to rear dogs in their homes, lest they be suspected of immoral practices.[173] Heathen shepherds in particular were prime candidates for suspicion, and Jews are cautioned not to have them tend their cattle, lest the shepherds engage in carnal relations with the animals.[174] Some bizarre incidents are, indeed, documented. Rabbi Hanina records how a heathen sodomizes a goose and then proceeds to eat it,[175] and references are made to a case of sodomy with a bitch,[176] and a sexual assault upon a young girl by a hunting dog (or possibly an ape).[177]

There is no reason to doubt that animal offenders were, indeed, punished for their "crimes." It was appropriate, considering the fact that they shared the religious and physical universe of man with him. It should be noted, however, that this was common practice among the peoples of antiquity, when even inanimate objects were occasionally sentenced to punishment in courts of law![178]

Of more lurid interest, but of interest nevertheless, is the fact that the practice of trying animals was carried to extremes in medieval Europe. Among the more interesting facets of the medieval legal process were the frequent criminal prosecutions of animals. The courts had biblical authority for these remarkable trials. In 1456, a pig was sentenced to be burned in the Rhineland for having killed and eaten a small child. Another pig died for the same offense in Amsens in 1643, also at the stake. Sometimes the animals were first put to torture: according to one theory, so that their grunts and squeals could be interpreted as confessions, but according to another, only because torture had become an integral part of any legal proceeding. The *lex talionis* was usually observed: if a dog bit a man, the dog was held down and the man allowed to bite him back, and so on.

Animals, even insects, were allowed to have lawyers. The insects (usually fleas, lice, or locusts) had to be given three days' notice before trial and some representatives would be brought into court, duly notified, and then freed to effect service upon others. The main issue during the trial was whether the creatures were simply obeying the will of God ("I will send wild beasts among you which shall destroy you and your cattle and make you few in number"), or whether they had criminal intent. This was always a difficult matter to prove and was a source of much judicial consternation.

To emphasize the anthropomorphic nature of the offense, the animal was sometimes dressed in clothes and tied in a sitting position during the trial. In 1386, a pig in Falaise, Normandy, that had torn the face and arm of a small child was dressed in clothes and sentenced to be maimed in the same manner as the child. In 1685, a wolf in Austria that had killed several people was dressed in clothes, wig, and beard. His snout was cut off and a human mask tied over it during the trial. He was sentenced to be hanged.

If a man committed bestiality, true to biblical precedent, both he and the creature were killed. Cotton Mather describes the death of a Mr. Potter in New Salem, Connecticut, who, in 1662, kept a harem of a cow, two heifers, three sheep, and two sows. His harem was first hanged before his eyes, a sight that reduced Potter to tears, and then Potter suffered the same fate.

The courts, as time passed, gradually grew more reasonable in their treatment of accused animals. An Austrian dog that bit a man was sentenced to only a year in jail in 1712. In 1750, Jacques Ferron of Vanves, France, and his she-donkey were arrested for bestiality. The court reluctantly agreed to hear the testimony of character witnesses, and the she-donkey was lucky enough to have a good one. The prior of a convent pointed out that the donkey "has always been virtuous and well-behaved and never given occasion for scandal. This is clearly a case of rape." The court agreed, and only the unfortunate Ferron was hanged.[179]

Although such colorful detail is lacking in the area of rabbinic animal-trials, there is no record that any of the blatant anthropomorphisms and torture techniques of medieval Europe were a part of rabbinic court procedures.

To summarize this unit, it is apparent that the "religious" nature imputed to the animal bears a striking similarity to that of the human. Both man and animal possess religious sensitivities and are subject to religious responsibilities. The animal is undeniably "humanized" in folklore and is featured by the fabulist in human-like roles. Yet both its prominence and its similarity to humans should be suspect. For in the main, it is not the animal per se that really matters, but what the animal represents to man. Thus if animals manifest authentic religious sensitivity toward their Creator, surely man should! If God rewards and punishes a beast, how much more so will man be requited for his deeds! There is, undeniably, much that man can learn from the animal kingdom in the pages of rabbinic folklore, but on most occasions the animal is merely an object lesson used to make a point.

9

COMPASSION FOR THE CREATURE

Notwithstanding the fact that rabbinic folklore usually employs the animal as a pedagogic device designed to teach man lessons about himself, this folkloristic portrait of the "normal" animal as a "humanized" animal, possessing religious sensitivities, sentiments, and responsibilities akin to those of humans, is often accompanied by admonitions to humans to treat animals with a compassion normally reserved for fellow-humans.

These admonitions take many forms. They are manifest indirectly in the form of expositions on biblical texts which emphasize the concern of God, as well as scriptural and rabbinic heroes, for the well-being of the animal. They also appear directly in the form of halakhic rulings which specifically enjoin compassionate treatment for the fauna.

God's Concern for the Animal

Psalm 145, which features the passage "and His tender mercies are over *all* His works" (emphasis added), was recited by the Jew three times daily.[1] God was viewed not only as the creator of all life but as the constant provider for all living entities, as He who "sustains all creatures, from the horned buffalo to the eggs of vermin."[2] Moreover, this task is personally administered to by the Creator, for "the Holy One, blessed be He, sits in the heights of the universe and distributes food to all creatures."[3]

God's extraordinary solicitousness is necessary owing to the peculiar characteristics of certain species of fauna. For example, the verse "He giveth to the beast his food and to the young ravens

144

which cry"[4] is the subject of a most interesting interpretation. Why, indeed, are the young ravens singled out for special mention by the psalmist? As we noted earlier, the parent raven is negligent in caring for her young, presumably because she fails to recognize them as her own, owing to the fact that the young birds are born with white feathers. God therefore personally provides food for the fledglings by causing maggots to spring forth from their excrement. The baby birds are sustained for several days until such time as their feathers turn black and they become recognizable to their parents, who then proceed to care for their needs.[5]

The list of other creatures in need of special assistance is a long and fascinating one, and God faithfully assists them all. As she-bears lack breasts with which to nurse their young, the cubs are miraculously enabled to derive nourishment by sucking upon their paws! As baby jackals are in danger of being devoured by their own parents, God equips them with veils upon their faces so that their nursing mothers fail to recognize them.[6] As most dogs can barely scrounge up enough food for their sustenance, God endows them with stomachs capable of retaining food for three whole days.[7] As wild goats hesitate to pause to drink from waterholes lest their enemies, lying in wait, attack and kill them, God causes frightening sounds to emanate from their horns and terrorize their adversaries. The goats may thus safely stop for nourishment.[8]

Even legendary beasts are the beneficiaries of divine solicitude. The monstrous reem, for example, has a twelve-year pregnancy period. During the twelfth year she is no longer capable of standing and collapses on her side. But God, in His mercy, sustains her by causing dribble to pour forth like a fountain from her mouth, irrigating the land upon which she lies so that it sprouts grass. She is thus able to graze upon it until giving birth.[9]

Why has the camel a short tail? Because it feeds upon thorns, and a long tail would easily become ensnared. Why has the ox a long tail? Because it feeds on the plains and must protect itself against gnats. Why are the feelers of locusts flexible? Otherwise they would be blinded should their feelers break against trees. Why do the lower eyelids of chickens close upwards? Because the birds perch on elevated roosts at night, and were their eyelids to close downward, they would be blinded by smoke rising from below.[10]

God is merciful to animals as He is to man, and knowing that animals cannot depend upon the assistance of man when giving birth, He has therefore endowed them with the capacity to give birth on their own, without need of human assistance.[11]

In the course of emphasizing that both prayer and honest labor help provide for one's sustenance, an interesting comment is voiced, one not without a trace of envy for animals.

> Rabbi Simeon b. Eliezer said, "In my whole lifetime I have not seen a deer engaged in gathering fruits, a lion carrying burdens, or a fox as a shopkeeper, yet they are sustained without trouble, though they were created only to serve me, whereas I was created to serve my Maker. Now, if these, who were created only to serve me, are sustained without trouble, how much more so should I be sustained without trouble, I who was created to serve my Maker."[12]

Rabbi Simeon sadly attributes his own difficulties in procuring a livelihood to the fact that he had sinned before God.

In an interesting homiletical exposition, "rain" is held to be of even greater importance than God's revelation to Israel at Mount Sinai! Why?

> A philosopher asked Rabbi Joshua b. Hananiah: "At what time are all men equal and do the nations worship God!" He replied: "On the day when all rejoice." "When is that?" asked the other. "When the heavens have been shut up, and all are in distress, and the rain comes down, and all rejoice and praise God." Rabbi Tanhum b. Hiyya said: "The falling of rain is greater than the giving of the Law, for the giving of the Law was a joy only to Israel, while the falling of rain is a rejoicing for all the world, including the cattle and the wild beasts and the birds."[13]

God, the champion of animals, espouses their cause, and cares for their welfare with the same solicitude manifested toward humans. For example, the angel of the Lord who blocked Balaam's path and rebuked him for having struck his ass is referred to as "the angel of mercy."[14] A *midrash* describes a group of men taking their cattle aboard a ship. They will surely jettison their animals in the event of stormy weather, in order to save their own lives. Not so would be the behavior of God, emphasizes the *midrash,* for just as the Lord is merciful to man, so is He merciful to the beast. God pities man and beast alike, as it is written: "God remembered Noah and the animals that were with him in the ark."[15]

Rabbinic literature contains a fascinating collection of stories featuring Alexander of Macedonia. In one of these episodes the African king, Kazia, is appalled at the cruel and unjust manner with which Alexander adjudicates disputes. The king inquires of Alexander,

> "Does the sun shine in your country?" "Yes," he said. "And does rain fall in your country?" "Yes," he replied. "Perhaps, " said the other, "there are small cattle in your country?" ["Yes," he answered.] He exclaimed: "Oh, woe to that man! It is because of the merit of the small cattle that the sun shines upon you and the rain falls upon you. For the sake of the small cattle you are saved!" Hence it is written, "Man and beast Thou preservest, O Lord," as much as to say, "Thou preservest man, O Lord, because of the merit of the beast."[16]

One *midrash* attributes the saving of the city of Nineveh to the fact that its wicked inhabitants separated parent animals from their young and then threatened God: "If You will have no pity upon us, we will show no compassion toward the animals." The Lord's compassion for the animals was so great that He was forced to succumb to this form of blackmail and relented on His threat to destroy Nineveh.[17]

A bizarre legend with somewhat apologetic overtones concerns King Saul's refusal to obey the divine command to destroy the animals of the Amalekites. Granted, Saul erred in disobeying God's orders, but why would the Lord make such a demand in the first place? What possible crimes could the innocent beasts have been guilty of? We are told, by way of reply, that the animals were, in reality, not animals, but Amalekite warriors who by means of sorcery transformed themselves into the forms of animals. Therefore, God could order their destruction. Otherwise, one would presume, God would never have demanded the death of innocent fauna.[18]

Biblical Man's Concern for the Animal

God's solicitousness for the beast is reflected in the behavior of the many biblical heroes who seek to emulate His ways.

For example, the rabbis describe Noah, the custodian of the ark and its animal menagerie, as not being content with a perfunctory and indiscriminate feeding of the animals. The Scriptural passage "He that is wise wins souls"[19] is applied to Noah in praise for his extraordinary care of all the fauna. Noah was careful to feed each species its appropriate food at the proper time interval. Therefore he chopped straw for the camel, barley for the ass, vine tendrils for the elephant, and prepared grass for the ostrich and cistus for the gazelles. He is pictured as being unable to sleep, neither by day nor night, owing to his perpetual preoccupation with the proper care of his "passengers."[20]

A similar emphasis is reflected in the following dialogue between Abraham and Melchizedek.[21] Abraham inquires: "How is it that you emerged safely from the ark? Only Noah and his sons were present there, so to whom could you have been charitable?" Melchizedek replies: "To the animals, birds, and beasts. We did not sleep but provided each with its proper food throughout the night."[22]

The appellation *zadik,* "one who practices charity," is bestowed upon only two biblical figures, Noah and Joseph. Why should they alone merit this distinction? Because they provided food for both humans *and animals* in times of famine and emergency.[23]

The mark of a righteous man is his concern for the well-being of his beast, and so the rabbis emphasize the fact that Joseph was instructed by his father, Jacob, to determine "whether it is well with thy brethren and well with the flock,"[24] and the Israelites in the wilderness were similarly concerned over the well-being of their flocks as well as themselves.[25] Conversely, mistreatment of animals is condemned in the strongest terms. Adam is rebuked for having failed to communicate to the fauna the prohibition against eating from the Tree of Knowledge, and is therefore held responsible, at least in part, for their sin.[26] The wicked inhabitants of Sodom are described as having practiced cruelty toward birds as well as humans, and the heinous behavior of the sons of Eli the priest included their violation of the injunction concerning the "bird's nest."[27]

The sequence of the passage in Deuteronomy, "And I will give grass in thy fields for thy cattle, and thou shalt eat and be satisfied,"[28] is revealing as to priorities. Rashi interprets it to mean that "you shall trim your wheat (corn) all the rainy season, and cast it before your cattle, and if you will withhold your hand from it thirty days before the harvest, it will not give you any the less of its corn" (than had you kept it all and not fed your cattle with it).

An exceedingly touching legend describes the distraught father Jacob demanding of his sons that they apprehend the ferocious animal allegedly responsible for having devoured his son Joseph, so that he may personally avenge Joseph's death. The sons apprehend a wolf and bring it before their father for punishment. Jacob castigates the beast and is about to destroy it when God miraculously grants to the animal the power of speech. The wolf proceeds to eloquently defend itself against the charge, insisting on its complete innocence. Significantly, the wolf points out that it, too, has a missing child, a cub, which it fears has been killed. Convinced of the wolf's innocence, and feeling a deep sense of kinship with a fellow bereaved parent, Jacob promptly frees the animal.[29]

A quaint rabbinic comment points out that great as was the happiness of the Israelites at the time of their exodus from Egypt, the exultation of the Egyptians was even greater, for now they would be spared the pain of future plagues. The situation is compared to that of a corpulent man riding upon an ass. The portly rider surely rejoices in being able to dismount and rest upon journey's end, but his joy does not begin to approximate that of the weary ass, finally freed from its heavy burden.[30]

A *midrash* records with sympathy the plight of a donkey whose master has purchased a neck of beef. All the way home, the hungry donkey longingly eyes the beef, anxious to be fed. Once home, however, the master ties up the donkey and suspends the beef at an elevation where the animal cannot reach it. The rabbis comment that such a master is to be rebuked with the words, "You wicked man, all the way home he runs after it, and now you withhold it from him!"[31]

Of particular interest is the rabbinic observation that God tests a man's leadership potential in the crucible of solicitousness for animals, and those desirous of becoming shepherds of men must first prove their worth by being compassionate shepherds of sheep. It is significant that Moses and David, Israel's greatest leaders, both were tenders of sheep in their youth.

Moses is depicted as enabling young and weak animals to feed first so that they could consume the tender and juicy grass so vital to their health and growth. Only after they were provided for would Moses lead the stronger animals of the flock to graze in terrain suitable for them. What signal moment in the life of Moses convinced God that he would make a worthy leader for the Children of Israel? It occurred while Moses was tending the sheep of his father-in-law, Jethro. A young kid suddenly broke away from the rest of the flock and ran off. Moses pursued it furiously for a great distance and finally discovered it thirstily drinking water from a distant well. Moses muses to the little animal, "I did not know that you ran away because you were thirsty, now you must be weary," and he gently lifts the animal upon his shoulders and carries it back to the flock. It was this episode that caused God to proclaim: "Thou hast compassion for a flock belonging to a man of flesh and blood. As thou livest, thou shalt pasture Israel, my flock."

In a similar vein, God declares: "David knows how to tend sheep, therefore he shall be the shepherd of my flock, Israel." The Lord was impressed with David's gentleness in caring for his flocks, for he, too, would lead the young lambs to pasture on tender grass and provide the older sheep with less juicy herbs, while the rams adequately subsisted upon tough weeds.[32]

Tzaar Baalei Hayyim

Underlying these varied legends, homilies, and scriptural interpretations concerning animals is a central principle in rabbinic
literature, the principle of *tzaar baalei hayyim,* lit. "pain of living
beings." This concept, although nowhere enunciated in Scripture,
was accepted as a biblical ordinance, derived, in part, from the
passages enjoining one to assist in unloading burdens from beasts
and returning lost animals to their masters,[33] and applied to a
variety of circumstances in which men and animals come in
contact. Israel's observance of biblical legislation vis-à-vis the
animal was seen as a hallowing and distinctive mark, for Israel was
unique in her sensitivity to *tzaar baalei hayyim.* Thus Rabbi Levi
proudly cites the scriptural prohibitions regarding plowing with
diverse creatures,[34] muzzling,[35] and the bird's nest[36] as evidence of
the fact that "all Israel's actions are distinct from the corresponding actions of the nations of the world."[37]

Many other biblical ordinances pertaining to animals were
interpreted by the rabbis as being within the spirit and purport of
tzaar baalei hayyim. Indeed, some rabbis imputed the motive of
"kindness to animals" to a number of scriptural injunctions where
Scripture itself is silent as to the reason for the injunction.

For example, "And whether it be cow or ewe, ye shall not kill it
and its young both in one day"[38] is interpreted by *Targum Pseudo-
Jonathan* (the Palestinian *Targum*) as an act of mercy: "Sons of
Israel, O my people, just as I in heaven am merciful, so shall you
be merciful on earth; neither cow nor ewe shall you sacrifice along
with her young on the same day."[39] *Leviticus Rabbah* similarly
interprets this as an act of righteousness, and evidence that God
has compassion upon animals just as upon humans: "It is written,
'a righteous man regardeth the ways of his beast.'[40] 'A righteous
man' applies to the Holy One, blessed be He, in whose Torah it is
written, 'Whether it be cow or ewe, ye shall not kill it and its
young both in one day.' "[41] This prohibition was extended to
apply to the slaughter of a father and calf as well,[42] and the edict
against sacrificing an animal less than eight days old[43] was interpreted in the light of permitting mother and child to stay together
for at least this minimal period of time.[44]

Philo Judaeus (20 B.C.E.–40 C.E.), the renowned philosopher of Alexandria, and author of numerous allegorical interpretations of Scripture, expounds eloquently upon these passages:

And he [Moses] extends his principles of humanity and compassion even to the race of irrational animals, allowing them always to share of those benefits as of a pleasing fountain; for in the case of domestic animals, with reference to flocks of sheep and of goats and herds of oxen, he commands the people to abstain from using those animals which are just born, or from taking them either for food or under pretense of sacrificing them. For he looked upon it as a proof of a cruel disposition to plot against such creatures the moment they are born, so as to cause an immediate separation between the offspring and the mother, for the sake of the pleasures of the belly, or on account of some absurd and preposterous unpleasantness which the soul fancies. Therefore, he says to the man who is about to live in accordance with his most sacred constitution. "My good man, there is a great abundance of things of which you are permitted the enjoyment, to which there is no blame attached; for, perhaps, it would have been pardonable if it were not so, since want and scarcity compel men to do many things which otherwise they would not intend. But you ought to be pre-eminent in temperance and the practice of all virtues . . . by all which considerations you ought to be rendered humane, avoiding receiving in your mind anything which is wrong. And why in addition to the pains which the animal bears in parturition, should you inflict other pains from external causes by the immediate separation of the mother from her offspring? For it is inevitable that she will resist and be indignant when they are thus parted, by reason of the affection implanted by nature in every mother toward her offspring, and especially at the time of their birth; since at this time the breasts are full of milk-like springs, and then if through want of the child which is to suck them the flow of milk receives a check, they become hardened by being distended by the weight of the milk, and the mothers themselves are overwhelmed with pain. Therefore, says the law, give her offspring to the mother, if not for the whole time, still at all events for the first seven days, to rear on her milk, and render not unprofitable those fountains of milk which nature has bestowed upon her breasts . . . the most tender and reasonable food for a tender creature, which, though it is only one thing, is at the same time both meat and drink. For inasmuch as part of the milk is of a watery nature, it is drink; and inasmuch as part of it is of a somewhat solid nature, it is meat; and it is endowed with these characteristics from a prudent foresight to prevent the lately born offspring from suffering disaster, through want, lying in wait for it at different times, taking care thus that by the one and same application of each kind of food, it may escape those cruel mistresses, hunger and thirst.[45]

On the basis of the passage "Thou shalt not take the dam with the young,"[46] Rabbi Berekiah taught in the name of Rabbi Isaac that "just as the Holy One, blessed be He, bestowed His compassion upon beasts, so also has He compassion upon fowl."[47] Clearly he sees the purpose of this commandment to be compassion for fauna. In a similar vein, Philo attributes the purpose of the ordinance "Thou shalt not plow with an ox and an ass together" to the fact that "they are unequal in point of strength. He takes care of that which is weaker in order that it may not be oppressed and worn out by the greater power of the other."[48] It is therefore not surprising to find the sages expanding the ordinance by declaring "an ox and an ass" to be generic terms including *all* species of beast.[49]

Likewise the ruling requiring one to assist in removing the burden from an animal crushed beneath its weight was interpreted broadly to apply to the beast of a non-Jew as well.[50] Why? Because the rabbis viewed the injunction to relieve the suffering of an animal as being biblical in origin, and therefore also applicable to animals outside of the Jewish community.[51] The sages further emphasize that "if one is bound to load, though no suffering of dumb animals or financial loss is involved, how much more so as regards unloading, seeing that both suffering of dumb animals and financial loss are involved."[52]

Rabbinic tradition reaffirms and indeed emphasizes that a laboring beast is entitled to its hire much as is a human laborer. Therefore, as workers are permitted to eat of the produce of the field, so should be animals,[53] and muzzling a beast clearly violates this right and inflicts suffering upon the animal. "In the same day shalt thou give him his hire"[54] was homiletically interpreted to apply to a laboring beast as well as a laboring man.

Halakhic problems arising from the prohibition against muzzling[55] were dealt with in a manner most sensitive to the feelings and needs of the beast.

For example, an unmuzzled animal laboring amidst *terumah* (heave-offering portions of the harvest given to the priests by Israelites and Levites)[56] would surely be tempted to eat of the forbidden consecrated food. However, it would be unthinkably cruel to muzzle the animal! What then could be done? The problem was solved by authorizing the placement of a feeding bag upon the beast, which would contain a type of food similar to that which the animal was harvesting. In this manner the unmuzzled beast could happily satisfy its hunger and yet not disturb the sanctity of the *terumah* trodden out at its feet.[57]

The sages were well aware that an insensitive or unscrupulous master could easily find ways of fulfilling the letter of the law while violating its spirit, by imposing a nonphysical or indirect form of muzzling upon the beast in order to deprive it of its rightful hire. Moses Maimonides paraphrases the stern talmudic prohibition against such practices, and the sages' extension of the term "muzzling" to protect the rights of the beast:

If a man said to a heathen: "Muzzle my cow and thresh with it"; or if a thorn happened to be stuck in the animal's mouth and he threshed with it while it was unable to eat, or if he caused a lion to lie down nearby [thus frightening the animal so that it could not eat], or if he caused the animal's offspring to lie down nearby [so that the animal would not eat], or if the animal was thirsty and he failed to give it drink, or if he spread leather over the threshing floor so that the animal was prevented from eating, all this is forbidden.[58]

Rabbinic regulations concerning the feeding of fauna and the castration of animals further reflect the sages' sensitivity. Thus the scriptural passage "And I will give grass in thy fields for thy cattle, and thou shalt eat and be satisfied"[59] was interpreted to imply that it is forbidden for a human being to eat and drink until he has first provided food for his animals.[60] The inference was drawn that even one who is a guest in another's home must not partake of any nourishment if he has not yet fed his own animals at home.[61] In the course of their analysis of the scriptural narrative, the rabbis explain that the reason why Levi was the brother who discovered Benjamin's money in his sack is that the pious Levi insisted on feeding his donkey prior to partaking of his own meal.[62] Eliezer ha-Kapar forbids the purchasing of either a domestic animal or a wild beast unless the purchaser is certain that he can provide it with proper sustenance.[63]

As far as castration is concerned, although it was commonplace in the ancient world for men to castrate animals in order to enhance their appearance and improve their working habits, the Israelites were unique among the nations of antiquity in banning this practice. Any deliberate impairment of the reproductive organs of fauna was forbidden,[64] and according to one source, the prohibition against emasculation is one of the basic Noahide laws, thus possessing universal validity.[65] "Anyone who castrates a human being, or a domesticated or wild animal, or a bird, whether large or small, male or female, is punishable."[66] Even unclean animals were not to be maimed in this manner,[67] and the very act of inflicting a blemish upon an animal was forbidden.[68]

The Jewish farmer undoubtedly suffered great economic hardship because of the prohibition against castration, and we read of rabbinic disapproval of the crafty practice of some Jewish farmers in having kindly gentiles "steal" their calves, castrate them, and then return them![69]

The Sabbath and the Animal

Although the Sabbath rules governing man and animal are few in number in the Mosaic code, numerous rabbinic regulations came into being to fortify and augment the institution of the Sabbath, with the rabbis themselves admitting that such "laws concerning the Sabbath are as mountains hanging by a hair, for they have scant scriptural basis but many laws."[70] Such multitudinous restrictions clearly served to curtail and limit the Jew's activities upon the Sabbath, so that it became a unique day of rest.

However, Jewish law clearly and firmly dictated the principle *pikuah nefesh doheh et ha-Shabbat*—"danger to life casts aside the Sabbath"—and ordained that the Sabbath may be, and indeed *must* be, desecrated whenever one's life is threatened.[71] It is important for our purposes to note that this principle was often extended to apply to the life of the animal as well. Furthermore, as the rabbis attributed a biblical origin to *tzaar baalei hayyim,* an animal's discomfort and suffering were also deemed sufficient cause for superseding Sabbath legislation.

To illustrate, if an animal falls into a dike on the Sabbath, not only must provisions be made for its sustenance, but one is permitted to place pillows and bedding in the dike so that the animal may ascend. Now technically speaking, the latter activity may constitute a clear violation of rabbinic law, but the law is here superseded by the biblical principle enjoining that the animal be spared pain.[72]

Not only is one permitted to assist an animal in the process of giving birth on the Sabbath, but in order to ensure that the animal's maternal instincts will operate effectively, "a lump of salt was brought and placed in its womb so that it might remember its travails and have mercy upon it; and we sprinkle the water of the afterbirth upon the newly born animal so that its mother might smell it and have pity upon it."[73]

Even those items designated as *muktseh* (lit. "set aside") and normally prohibited for Sabbath handling were permitted to be served as food for animals on the Sabbath.

> Our rabbis taught: We may handle *hazab,* because it is food for gazelles, and mustard, because it is food for doves. Rabbi Simeon b. Gamliel said: "We may also handle fragments of glass, because it is food for ostriches. . . . bundles of straw, bundles of branches, and bundles of young shoots, if one

prepared them as animal fodder, may be handled; if not, they may not be handled. . . . Bones may be handled because they are food for dogs; putrid meat, because it is food for beasts; uncovered water, because it is food for a cat."[74]

Although tying and untying knots is an inappropriate Sabbath activity, one may untie bundles of sheaves if they are to be used as animal fodder.[75] Similarly the law permits one to salvage from a fire on the Sabbath a given quantity of foodstuffs for animals as well as for oneself,[76] even though theoretically one should not save even those items which it is permissible to handle. Blankets and saddles could be placed upon a beast in order to protect it from the elements and stinging insects,[77] and the animal could be exercised on the Sabbath in order to alleviate its pain.[78]

In the same manner that *tzaar baalei hayyim* supersedes the prohibition of *muktseh,* so it supersedes the prohibition against *nolad* (the handling of newly created objects first appearing on the Sabbath), and therefore a gentile can be instructed to milk cows on the Sabbath.[79]

Such leniencies ought not to be taken lightly. The fourth commandment clearly requires that one's cattle observe the Sabbath rest, and a master was fully accountable for the Sabbath observance of his beast. A *mishnah* describes the dilemma of a traveling Jew when Friday evening nightfall descends upon him:[80] "He must give his purse to a gentile, and if there was no gentile with him, he must put it on the ass. Later, in the courtyard, however, he must remove the burden [from his animal so that it may rest]."[81] Clearly the animal, like the master, is obligated to rest upon the Sabbath.

The Killing of Animals for Food and Sport

Is it proper for man to kill animals in order to consume their flesh? Is it necessary?

As we have noted, the idyllic state of man as portrayed both in the prehistorical setting of the Garden of Eden and in the milieu of the "end of days" is that of a vegetarian being. Man partakes of vegetation, not flesh.

Genesis Rabbah contains an interesting legend which explains that the destruction of the animals in the flood took place as retribution for their having enticed man to eat of their flesh, thereby causing him to sin![82]

Is meat deemed essential for man's survival? Apparently not, according to a legend depicting the Israelites, dissatisfied with their diet of *manna,* demanding of Moses and Aaron that they be given meat to eat. God angrily rebukes them: "You have demanded two things. You desired bread and I gave it to you because man cannot live without it. But now, filled to your satiety, you demand flesh!"[83]

The word "desire" clearly has a negative connotation for the rabbis when it appears in the crucial passage in Deuteronomy permitting the eating of flesh: "When the Lord your God shall enlarge your border, and you shall say, 'I will eat flesh,' because your soul *desires* [emphasis added] to eat flesh."[84] "Lust" would probably be a more appropriate translation of the Hebrew than "desire." And although the sages nowhere prohibit the eating of flesh, rabbinic legislation does propose and reinforce certain crucial limitations and procedural requirements pertaining to the killing of animals.

Ever Min haHai

The injunction forbidding one from severing a limb from a living animal, presumably for food purposes, was derived from several scriptural passages,[85] and was included among the seven Noahide commandments meriting universal adherence.[86] In other words, the rabbis conceived of this act as being so barbarous and incredibly cruel that all humanity, Jew and non-Jew alike, are obligated to abhor its practice.

Hunting for Sport

Rabbinic texts contain several references to hunting, but significantly, they never describe hunting for pure sport. There is always a utilitarian purpose underlying the hunt. Animals are hunted for food,[87] for economic profit,[88] for domestication purposes,[89] or they are destroyed as menaces or pests.[90] But the rabbis disapproved of the wanton destruction of fauna as a sporting exercise. Nimrod and Esau, the two biblical hunters, were cast into the mold of villains, and Josephus records rabbinic opposition to Herod's hunting exploits with horses.[91]

Hunting was an activity associated with the pagan world; it was a sport for gentile rulers, not Jewish leaders, and the rabbis could not even conceive of the possibility of Moses ever having been a hunter![92] The passage "Happy is the man that has not walked in the counsel of the wicked"[93] was applied to the Jews who refused to attend circus spectacles in which animals were forced to fight one another to the death.[94]

Secular Slaughtering Must Be Modeled after Sacred Slaughtering

The relationship between secular slaughtering and sacred slaughtering was an intimate one. Indeed, it would appear that at certain times in Israel's history (notably when the Israelites were wandering in the wilderness), meat consumption was permissible only in the context of sacred sacrificial slaughtering, and it was not until their entry into the promised land that the Israelites were permitted to slaughter animals purely for consumption. "Owing to the fact that in the wilderness Israel was forbidden from eating the 'flesh of desire,' Scripture comes and permits it to them, stipulating only that it be ritually slaughtered."[95]

As noted earlier, King Saul is pictured as rebuking his troops for having eaten meat prior to the blood having been sprinkled upon the altar,[96] possibly reflecting the view that it was only in times of war that meat from a sacrifice was permissible as food.[97]

Although, generally speaking, meat can be eaten without the bringing of a formal sacrifice to the altar, the sacrificial requirement forbidding fat and blood was to be observed upon one's table as well. *Targum Yerushalmi* emphasizes that "in all your dwellings you shall eat neither fat nor blood; for that should be sacrificed upon the altar of the Lord."[98] Similarly, the verse "then thou shalt kill of thy herd and thy flock which the Lord has given you, as I have commanded thee"[99] is interpreted by *Torat Kohanim* to refer to the fact that profane slaughtering must follow the previously commanded rules and regulations prescribed for sacred slaughtering.

What did the rules and regulations prescribed for sacred slaughtering entail for the rabbis? Obviously that only certain species of animal, fowl, and fish were permissible as food, and that any permitted beast or fowl must only be slaughtered in a rigorously prescribed manner.

The scriptural list of permissible and forbidden classes of fauna is clarified and further augmented by the rabbis with meticulous detail. For example, attention is paid to the status of animals which fail to exhibit the clean or unclean characteristics of their parents,[100] the status of certain species of worms or grasshoppers,[101] as well as means of identifying and distinguishing cattle from beasts on the basis of their horn formation.[102]

Rules are established concerning the by-products of animals. For example, eggs of clean fowl are considered permissible, while eggs of unclean fowl are forbidden. Similarly, the milk of unclean animals is prohibited, although honey is permitted, even though the bee itself obviously is not.[103] The rabbis apparently approved of bee honey because they viewed it as a secretion of pure plant nectar ingested by the bee, while they forbade wasp and hornet honey on the grounds that these insects secrete their own saliva into the honey.

Rabbinic tradition distinguishes between two types of blood, the *dam hanefesh,* or life-blood, which is found in the heart and which flows from the animal during the process of slaughtering, and the languidly flowing blood which is located in various tissues and organs. Although both types were forbidden, the penalty for consuming the latter is less severe.[104]

The rabbis interpreted the injunction not to seethe a kid in its mother's milk as implying that it is forbidden to boil *any* manner of meat with milk, and explained the threefold repetition as stressing a threefold prohibition: not to cook the two together, not to eat them after the cooking, and not to derive any profit from the mixture.[105]

Philo writes movingly that the Torah

looked upon it as a very terrible thing for the nourishment of the living to be the seasoning and sauce of the dead animal, and when provident nature has showered forth milk to support the living creature which it had ordained to be conveyed through the breasts of the mother, that the unbridled licentiousness of man should go to such a height that they should slay both the author of the existence of the other and make use of it in order to consume the body of the other. The man who seethes the flesh of any one of them in the milk of its own mother, is exhibiting a terrible perversity of disposition and exhibits himself as wholly destitute of that feeling, which, of all others, is most indispensable to, and most nearly akin to, a rational soul, namely compassion.[106]

Shehitah

The only approved manner of slaughtering an animal for food was by means of shehitah, cutting the animal at the throat. Shehitah was based on a passage in Deuteronomy, "thou shalt kill of thy herd and of thy flock . . . as I have commanded thee,"[107] and by speculating on the etymology of shahat and zavah, the rabbis concluded that one could slaughter an animal only by cutting it at the throat.[108] What is significant is the fact that this means of slaughter was evidently considered to be the most painless manner of causing death to an animal.[109]

In the course of a discussion concerning capital punishment, the question is raised, "Whence is it deduced that execution by the sword must be at the neck?" Rabbi Nahman, answering in the name of Rabbah b. Abbuha, cites the scriptural verse "but thou shalt love thy neighbor as thyself" as meaning: "choose for him an easy death."[110] Presumably, this "easy death," which was held to be the least painful way of executing a human being, was also deemed the most "humane" way of dispatching an animal.

Indeed, this manner of slaughtering would appear to cause a swift and relatively painless death, by severing the trachea, esophagus, jugular vein, and carotid artery. Presumably the sharp incision of the knife would lessen the animal's agony, while the instant and profuse loss of blood would render the beast unconscious.

The rabbis further specified that the sharp slaughtering knife be completely smooth, without any nicks or dents, and the *shohet* (ritual slaughterer) was obligated to carefully inspect it prior to the slaughtering by rubbing his finger and fingernail over its edges and sides.[111] It was ordained that the movement of the knife during slaughter should betray no hesitation or interruption (*shehiyyah*), no undue pressure (*derasah*), no digging or burrowing (*haladah*), no slipping or cutting outside of the specified area (*hagramah*), and no tearing or laceration of the tissues (*ikkur*). For Moses Maimonides this was ample evidence that "the law enjoins that the death of the animal be as easy and painless as possible."[112]

Later generations demanded that the *shohet* himself be not only skilled and knowledgeable in his craft but also an individual of exemplary character and piety. He came to be viewed as a religious functionary in the full sense of the word, possessing religious obligations toward both his human clientele and his animal subjects. The following vignette is illustrative:

> Several *Hasidim* of Kolomeyer complained to the Sadagurer that the *shohet* was a miserly and inhospitable man. The rabbi exclaimed: "And do you eat the meat from his *shehita?*" This question was equivalent to a prohibition and henceforth no one purchased meat. The *shohet* came to the rabbi and said: "Where do you find that a *shohet* must be hospitable?" The rabbi replied: "We find in the Talmud that some persons are born with a passion for shedding blood. One becomes a murderer, a second, a soldier, a third, a *shohet*. The question arises: Why do we make use of meat from an animal killed by a man who is like a murderer? The whole *shehita* legislation has been formulated in order to prevent brutal treatment of the animal, and what is more brutal than to let it perish at the hands of a near-murderer? The answer is that a *shohet* should have a good heart, notwithstanding his love for shedding animal's blood; he thus may be trusted to avoid brutality in shedding this blood. Thus if a *shohet* is kind to his fellow-man, he may be trusted to slaughter animals in a mild manner. But if he is unkind, he is in truth a

near-murderer who cannot be trusted to observe the kind methods of slaying animals prescribed in the law."[113]

It is not difficult to discern an ethical dimension within the dietary laws of Israel. It would appear to reflect the conviction that the life of an animal also contains a measure of inviolability. Fauna are not there simply "for the taking"—man must not indiscriminately and indifferently butcher the animal kingdom in order to satisfy his own lusts. The concession permitting him to eat flesh is therefore a limited one. Only certain species of fauna, slaughtered under certain prescribed conditions, may be legitimately consumed at one's table. Otherwise, the animal kingdom is inviolate, and their abuse forbidden.

In the preceding pages we have tried to emphasize the sense of concern and compassion for animals that emanates from rabbinic sources. No discussion of this theme, however, would be complete without reference to two rather remarkable citations, quite dissimilar to one another, yet emphasizing the common kinship of man and beast.

The first citation appears in the form of an exegesis upon the scriptural passages describing how Adam, while bestowing names upon all the fauna, is unable to find a helpmeet for himself among them, and then, upon the creation of Eve, exclaims: "This is now bone of my bone and flesh of my flesh."[114]

A striking interpretation is given to these verses: namely, that Adam initially approached the members of the animal kingdom in his search for a mate but found them all to be inadequate![115] The fact that an animal is not suited to be man's sexual partner and life-companion is not surprising and is hardly the point. What is remarkable is the intimation, however lacking in seriousness, that God could possibly have intended for animals to share such an intimate relationship with human beings!

Can such a notion possibly strike a responsive chord in the listener? Presumably it can, and did. The Judean farmer and animal-tender surely spent many pleasant hours with his cattle. Animals are patient and sympathetic listeners. They do not interrupt. Neither do they nag, argue, or contradict. Their demands are simple and predictable, their devotion total, and often selfless. In short, they possess many virtues often lacking in human spouses! Both scientific observation and casual everyday vignettes abound with examples of humans who develop deep and intensive feelings of affection for their pets and working animals. Some individuals actually prefer the companionship of animals to that of humans. Surely all men have felt, at some time, an unspoken but deep sense of kinship with members of the animal kingdom. Preposterous as may be the notion of an animal as a mate for a human, it is an idea not always unaccompanied by a slight wistfulness.

The second citation consists of a dramatic episode in the life of Rabbi Judah haNasi. The Talmud records how this sage was forced to endure excruciating pain for a long period of time. When the question was raised as to why such a pious soul should be afflicted with such intense sufferings, the following answer was given:

> A calf was being taken to the slaughter, when it broke away, hid its head under Rabbi's skirt and lowed. "Go," said he, "for this wast thou created." Thereupon they said [in heaven], "Since he has no pity, let us bring suffering upon him."

Rabbi Judah's pains did not depart until one day his maid-servant attempted to sweep away some weasels she had discovered while housecleaning. (Another version speaks of his daughter attempting to kill some creeping animals which had crossed her path.) Rabbi Judah rose to the animals' defense. "Let them be," he said to her, "for it is written: 'and His tender mercies are over all His works.' " Said they (in heaven), "Since he is compassionate, let us be compassionate to him."[116]

Years later, Rabbi Judah's grandson, Gamliel, proclaimed: "Whosoever has compassion upon his fellow-creatures, upon him will God have compassion."[117]

This is a powerful narrative. The personage involved is no less a scholar than the eminent Rabbi Judah the Prince, redactor of the

Mishnah. Punishment and absolution are clearly contingent upon compassion toward animals. Moreover, some of the animals are creatures of no utilitarian value at all to the rabbi, yet their treatment is of overwhelming importance!

But the narrative is also a troubling one. Is there justification in concluding from it that one has a moral obligation to rescue *any* animal designated for slaughter? After all, is it not permissible to eat the meat of kosher animals which are properly slaughtered? Or is it, ideally? Why then should Rabbi Judah be condemned from heaven for not interfering in what is a legitimate undertaking. Yet he *is* condemned. He is clearly judged guilty of having shown no pity toward the frightened calf, and is severely punished for failing to emulate Him whose "tender mercies are over all His works."

10

A FURTHER RATIONAL AND EMPIRICAL OVERVIEW

The story of Rabbi Judah the Prince and the unfortunate calf is poignant and touching, but it appears to have had no practical implications at all for the practice of slaughtering animals for food. In all of classical rabbinic literature there is no record of this episode ever having been raised as an argument against the killing of animals for food. It was not until centuries later, in the geonic era, that such implications were discussed.

Sherira Gaon receives the following inquiry:

If Rabbi Judah was punished because he handed a calf over to the slaughterer, and was again rewarded because he protected a dumb creature from death, should we not learn from this not to slaughter any animal and not to kill harmful animals?

Sherira replies:

Animals that are harmful as snakes, lions, wolves, must always be killed; on the other hand, animals that do us no harm, and are not needed for food or medicine should not be killed. The dumb animal (the weasel) does not belong to the harmful animals and such animals are defended and protected from death. To save a calf that we need for nourishment is not required of us. Rabbi Judah was not punished for a crime, but was punished because, had he shown mercy and pity to the animal, many persons would have learned a good lesson thereby. It would have been merciful on the part of Rabbi Judah to at least delay the

166

slaughtering for a few days, and those who might have seen Rabbi so conduct himself, would have learned therefrom to be merciful. Those, however, who saw Rabbi surrender the animal and take no pity on it, despite its seeking protection, those would become hard-hearted in their relations to both man and beast.[1]

Sherira's reply is clear. Slaughtering animals for food is perfectly permissible. Rabbi Judah was, therefore, not guilty of any crime. He did err, however, insofar as he had an opportunity to teach others the value of compassion and declined to do so. He failed to respond to a dramatic moment which he could have used to vividly illustrate to others the duty of man to be merciful to beasts.

One wonders whether this dramatic moment should be regarded as akin to the situation of a human prisoner who escapes his fate on the execution day. Presumably, some ancients would have attributed the escape to divine benevolence, and Roman jurists might even have spared him from death on these grounds. Perhaps Rabbi Judah should have done the same for the condemned animal victim!

In any event, the issue of vegetarianism as an ideal is not a factor here. In all of rabbinic literature there is scarcely a trace of vegetarianism. Quite the contrary. Some rabbis doubted that meat-consumption had *ever* been forbidden to mankind, and maintained that even Adam was permitted to eat flesh, although, according to one interpretation, he was served roasted meat that had been prepared by angels, for he himself was forbidden to slaughter animals.[2]

Others took Adam's "vegetarianism" for granted but declined to attribute it to any ethical factor. Why, then, was Adam limited to a diet of fruits and vegetables? Because originally animals, like humans, were destined to live forever. But when the decree of death was visited upon all flesh, including animals, it was now permissible to eat animals. Why not? They will die anyway![3]

It should also be noted that vegetarianism was not viewed by all authorities as being the state of affairs in the hereafter. Aside from the many legends concerning a sumptuous messianic banquet featuring exotic cuisine, we find the interesting observation that God Himself will, in the hereafter, declare all unclean animals to be clean![4]

To whatever extent asceticism may have existed in the rabbinic period (and it was decidedly not a common practice among the rabbis),[5] it was not characterized by a specific abstention from meat per se. Rabbis such as Zeira and Simeon bar Yohai, who were renowned for the frequency with which they fasted, did so for reasons totally unrelated to vegetarianism.

Far more typical and representative of rabbinic Judaism than asceticism was Rab's observation that "man will have to give account in the future for every permissible enjoyment offered to him which he has ungratefully refused."[6] The eating of meat was clearly a permissible form of pleasure, for "there is no joy without meat and wine,"[7] and it was deemed meritorious for one to enhance the joy of the Sabbath and festivals by partaking of meat and fish.[8]

Such was the extolled practice of many leaders of Israel. Rabbi Hiyya, for example, describes the immense wealth of a certain individual. When asked how he came to merit such affluence, the man replies: "I was a butcher, and whenever I saw a choice animal, I would always say: This is for the Sabbath meal."[9] Rabbi Abba would spend thirteen silver coins every Friday at thirteen different butchershops in order to acquire the finest meats in honor of the Sabbath, and Shammai the Elder would set aside choice animals for Sabbath consumption.[10] Fish, too, was a popular Sabbath repast, and workers would be sent home well before nightfall in order to fill a cask of water and complete the broiling and frying of their fish prior to the kindling of the Sabbath lights.[11]

A dramatic story is told concerning a man named Joseph, popularly known as "Joseph who honors the Sabbath." It was foretold that Joseph would someday inherit all the property of a wealthy gentile neighbor. The apprehensive neighbor proceeded to sell off his properties and purchased a precious stone which he fastened securely in his turban. However, as he was crossing a bridge one day, a powerful gust of wind blew off his turban and carried it into the river, whereupon it was promptly swallowed by a fish. The fish in turn was caught by a fisherman, who was then advised to take it to "Joseph who honors the Sabbath," as the latter customarily purchased the most expensive fish for his Sabbath table. Joseph indeed bought the fish and was amazed to find inside it the precious stone, which he subsequently sold for a substantial amount of gold denarii. Not so amazed was a certain old man who proclaimed: "He who lends to the Sabbath, the Sabbath repays him."[12]

Genesis Rabbah records the tale of a poor Jewish tailor who paid the exorbitant sum of twelve denarii for a single fish on the eve of the Day of Atonement, thereby outbidding the governor's servant.[13] The astonished governor summoned the Jew to his chambers and incredulously inquired: "A Jewish tailor can eat a fish at twelve denarii?" Replied the poor Jew: "Sir, we have one day when all our sins of the year are forgiven, and we honor it greatly."

We read of a teacher of young children who is praised for his having taught the children of the poor as well as those of the wealthy, without ever having exacted tuition payment from the former. He is also lauded for his practice of bribing reluctant students to better their dismal academic achievements by promising them fish from his own fish pond![14]

On a more professional level, the fishing industry, centered in Lake Tiberias, though flourishing in the Jordan and the Mediterranean as well, was an extensive one during the mishnaic and talmudic periods. Acco apparently served as the commercial center for fish-trading, with "bringing fish to Acco" serving as the equivalent of "carrying coals to Newcastle." However, the fish connoisseur Rabbi Yose b. Halafta concluded that the taste of Acco fish was inferior to that of fish caught at Sidon, which in turn could not compare with the delicious fish caught at Aspamia.[15] Dried and salted fish was transported long distances, and Tarichaea, the "town of salted fish," is known in Hebrew as *Migdal Nunaiia* ("the fish tower").

Meat and fish, symbols of honor and joy, obviously constituted an integral part of the Sabbath and festival delight, and of any festive meal honoring guests. The only cause for hesitation about eating meat was economic rather than ethical in nature. Meat was expensive! We find the wealthy Eleazar b. Azariah cautioning individuals of moderate means to restrict their meat-eating to the Sabbath unless they were certain they had the means to afford it as part of their daily diet.[16] He taught that one who possesses one *maneh* should buy a pound of vegetables for his stew, if he has ten *maneh*, he may buy a pound of fish for his stew, with fifty *maneh* he may purchase a pound of meat, while only the man with one hundred *maneh* may have a pot set upon his hearth on a daily basis. Rabbi Nahman's impecunious response to this advice was: "As for us, we must even borrow to eat."[17]

The Midrash comments with irony that on the first day one feeds his guests geese and chickens, on the second day, fish, on the third day, meat, and on the fourth day—legumes.[18] Rabbi Judah b. Ilai's ironic advice to gourmands was to "sit in the shade [*batzel*] and eat onions [*batzal*], but don't eat geese and chickens though thy heart may crave them."[19] In a similar vein, a folk proverb cautioned that "he who eats fat tails [*allitha*] will be compelled to hide from creditors in the attic [*alitha*], but he who eats cress [*kekule*] is able to quietly relax in the town's assembly place [*kikle*]."[20]

Perhaps this partially explains Mar Zutra's caution to parents that they not accustom their sons to partake of meat and wine,[21] and the advice that "a person should not eat meat except after such preparation as this."[22]

Interestingly, the "rebellious son" who was a *zolel* and *sobeh* (usually translated as a "glutton and drunkard")[23] is defined as one who consumes an *excess* of meat.[24] Strong scriptural support for this could be adduced: "Be not among winebibbers; among gluttonous eaters of flesh. For the drunkard and the glutton shall come to poverty."[25]

But meat was also regarded as a highly nutritious "health food," so much so that people were advised to purchase it even on credit.[26] It was inconceivable to envision life without this nutrient. Rabbi Simeon b. Gamliel taught that since meat and wine were only reserved for festive occasions, then we ought not to partake of them since the Holy Temple has been destroyed. However, the authorities do not impose a law by which most people could not survive.[27]

The "health" benefits of a flesh diet are detailed and numerous in rabbinic literature. *Bassar shumen* ("fat meat") was said to straighten the stature and give light to the eyes,[28] and came highly recommended as an aphrodisiac,[29] though convalescents are cautioned to avoid it, lest it cause relapses to occur.[30] Spleen was considered an important food for the development of strong teeth, though one is warned to merely chew but not swallow it, as it is not easily digested.[31]

Rab recommends the consumption of meat after venesection (bloodletting), because meat from a "strong animal" adds to one's own strength,[32] and Rabbi Zeira promptly proceeds to purchase meat for himself following his bloodletting.[33] On the other hand, Samuel the physician advises against eating fowl meat after phlebotomy,[34] and fish and pickled meat are similarly discouraged by the rabbis.

Meat was deemed particularly beneficial for pregnant women and their unborn children,[35] and we are informed that "one who eats meat and drinks wine will have children of a robust complexion."[36] Red meat broiled on coals, along with undiluted wine, was prescribed for sunstroke, and fat meat broiled on coals, with undiluted wine, was recommended for treating chills.[37]

On the other hand, fowl meat was considered an ideal food for the aged and feeble,[38] and those recuperating from illness or injury were advised to eat chicken, as it is easily digested: "When I was healthy I ate lentils and green vegetables; now, however, I can only tolerate eggs and chicken."[39] The following advice is given to parents: "He who desires his daughter to have a bright complexion, let him, on the approach of her maturity, feed her young fowl and give her milk to drink."[40]

The lung of a goose was said to "brighten the eyes"[41] (the rabbis noting the similarity between *reah* ["lung"] and *meirah* ["to brighten"]). Not surprisingly, goose-lung became a highly desirable food item, bringing a price of four zuzim in the market place, whereas the rest of the goose could be purchased for a mere zuz!

A fish diet was highly recommended for nursing mothers, as well as for those suffering from eye ailments,[42] and it was prescribed as a health food for the ailing.[43] Fried fish was recommended for spleen ailments,[44] and small fish were deemed beneficial for the bowels, for the general strengthening of the body, and as a stimulant for propagation.[45]

An interesting dispute between Rab and Samuel concerns a poor man who has let blood and is in need of food. Samuel urges him to purchase red wine, as this will aid to replenish the lost blood. Rab, however, advises the purchase of meat, for meat will provide all needed nourishment.[46]

Mental acumen was held by Rabbi Nahman to be a function, at least in part, of nutrition. He informs us that he was once incapable of rendering a correct legal decision until the following morning. Why? Because he had neglected to eat ox-meat the previous evening![47]

Suffice to say, a fish and flesh diet comes highly recommended by the sages for the good health of all.

In fairness, one can also cite several rabbinic comments which would appear, upon first glance, to discourage a regular diet of flesh. One reads, for example: "At first the Israelites were like hens picking in a dung-hill until Moses came and designated for them an appropriate time for feasting [i.e., morning and evening, a diet of quail]. Here the Torah intimates a matter of good form, that one should only eat meat at night."[48]

Now is this teaching meant to seriously limit meat-eating to the nighttime? The context of the discussion concerns the exegesis of the biblical passage "And Moses said: 'This shall be when the Lord shall give you in the evening flesh to eat, and in the morning bread to the full.' "[49] Perhaps the intimation here is that one ought not to be guilty of gluttony and therefore should refrain from making each and every meal a meat meal.

More revealing, perhaps, is Rabbi Judah the Prince's prohibition against an ignoramus eating meat. Rabbi Judah cites the passage "this is the law of the beasts . . . that may be eaten,"[50] and concludes that one who is a student of the Law may eat meat, while an ignoramus may not.[51] Now it would be tempting to see in this comment a reflection of Rabbi Judah's poignant personal experience with the runaway calf. Could he be seeking to restrict meat consumption to sensitive, intelligent human beings *only?* Or is Samuel Edels (MaHaRShA) correct in interpreting this to be merely an expression of concern that ignoramuses may not be aware of the intricate rules of *kashrut* pertaining to the slaughtering, soaking, and salting of meat. We shall see how later scholars, more sympathetic to vegetarianism, interpret Rabbi Judah's statement as severely limiting the eating of flesh on "moralistic" grounds, but it is difficult to discern any real evidence for this conclusion.

It is undoubtedly true that the rules of *kashrut* limit the species of animals which are permissible for food. But is it the real intent of the law to benefit the animal kingdom by limiting meat consumption? No rabbinic source put forth such a claim.

Admittedly, some Jewish thinkers perceived ethical intent in the dietary laws. Aristeas eloquently extolled them for helping to tame man's instinct for violence, and explained the prohibition against eating birds of prey as symbolizing the prohibition against one human being "preying" upon his neighbor.[52] In a similar vein Philo wrote that "the ossifrage is a cruel bird, dropping its young from a great height to dash them upon the stones below; the pelican preys upon its own flesh; hence they are forbidden."[53] But Aristeas and Philo are not really concerned with the welfare of the birds themselves. Their concern is that men might conceivably develop evil qualities by consuming the flesh of such "evil" creatures! It is man's behavior toward his fellowman that is of importance here, not man's conduct toward animals.

A *midrash* explains God's restriction of the Israelites in their choice of meats (while permitting the Sons of Noah a full dietary range) as being of ultimate benefit to the Israelites insofar as they would be richly rewarded in the future for their abstinence.[54] But no mention is made of any benefits accruing to the animals.

It is noteworthy that the rabbis are even silent as to the reason for their insistence on the use of a sharp, nick-free slaughtering knife and a specific locale for the incision and a prescribed manner of cutting. It is surmisable that this parallels the "easy death" of the executed prisoner—surmisable perhaps, as we have noted, but still nowhere clearly stated as such!

It is true that the comment "the commandments were given only to refine humanity" appears in connection with the dietary laws, as if to emphasize an inherently ethical dimension, but it is questionable whether the "animal" is the intended beneficiary of the "ethics."

The implications of the following quotations are obvious.

> For what does the Holy One, blessed be He, care whether a man kills an animal by the throat or by the nape of the neck? Hence its purpose is to refine man.[55]

> What does God care whether a man kills an animal in the proper way and eats it, or whether he strangles the animal and eats it?[56]

Let us turn, for a moment, to the basic purpose of *shehitah* itself. Is it to minimize the pain of the beast? Perhaps, in part. But in view of the fact that the prohibition against eating blood is one of the essentials of proper slaughtering, notably secular slaughtering, could one not argue plausibly that it is the instantaneous and thorough draining of blood that is the primary purpose behind slaughtering an animal at the neck?[57] Never do we find any discussion as to how extensive are the sufferings of the animals being slaughtered and how their pain can be minimized.

Furthermore, the laws of *shehitah* are limited. They are applicable to mammals and birds, but do not apply to fish or to edible locusts.[58] The Talmud refers to numerous fishing implements, but does not seem to concern itself with the question of how to provide the fish with a relatively painless death![59] An unborn fetus found inside its slaughtered mother may be eaten without any need for *shehitah* if it is immediately used for food.[60] (Of course, it could be argued that the fetus was not a living being, by the rabbis' definition of life.)

Even the prohibition against eating from the flesh of a living animal (which is enjoined upon all humanity, not merely the community of Israel) has its limitations. The rabbis apply it only to those animals whose flesh is distinct from the blood, but not to reptiles![61] Is it possible that reptiles were believed to suffer no pain under these circumstances? Apparently some even permitted a quasi *ever min hahai* by allowing for the cutting of a small piece of flesh from the throat of a dying animal so long as it was properly salted and rinsed, and not eaten until after the creature actually expired.[62] This was prescribed as beneficial for one's health, but hardly seems a "humane" way of treating a dying animal.

Several other examples can be cited of procedures involving animals which would seem to fall short of being "compassionate." For example, we read of Rabbi Johanan's abolition of the practice of the "knockers," i.e., those who would stun an ox before slaughtering it. This practice was criticized on the grounds that it was commonly employed by pagans. Apparently the ancients regarded it as a bad omen, and unacceptable to the gods, for a beast to struggle while being slaughtered. It was viewed as unseemly for the animal to appear reluctant to meet its fate. The pagan would therefore render the animal fairly senseless by stunning it. It would appear that some Jews also followed this practice, thereby drawing the ire of Rabbi Johanan, who objected on the grounds that a stunned animal might become blemished and hence unfit for a sacrifice. He advocated, instead, that metal bands be used to hold the animal in place.[63] Now it would seem that stunning a beast would be an effective means of minimizing its pain during slaughtering. But the alleviation of the animal's pain might not have been the primary purpose of the *shehitah* procedures. It may have been quite incidental to the all-important principle of maintaining distinctively Jewish sacrificial procedures.

Heathens would tightly bind their sacrificial animals, presumably for a similar reason. They felt it to be inappropriate for the beasts to manifest any indication of unwillingness to be sacrificed, much less a desire to escape. Such resistance on the part of an animal could lead to the divinities declining to accept the offering. Perhaps it is out of concern that the animal should appear to be a "willing" offering that we read of a man offering a bundle of endives to a reluctant bull in order to make it more willing to draw near to the altar,[64] and we encounter the pathetic episode of a cow being led to the abattoir by means of having her calf walk before her.[65]

The Palestinian Talmud refers to the practice of whipping cattle in order to enhance their skin color and give them the appearance of being fatter than they actually are.[66] A rabbinic source opposes this practice, but not out of any feeling of compassion for the animal. The objection is raised on the grounds that this is an attempt to defraud and deceive potential purchasers.[67]

It is reasonable to surmise that *tzaar baalei hayyim,* the prohibition against causing animals pain, is clearly limited in its scope. True, one must not cause animals pain for no good reason, but at times "good reasons" legitimately exist.

For example, the Talmud teaches that "if one buys aught in a market of idolators, if it is cattle, it should be disabled, i.e., it should have the tendons of the hoofs beneath the ankles cut." The question is promptly raised: "Is there not the prohibition against causing suffering to a living being?" Replies Abayye: "The Divine Law says, 'Their horses shalt thou hough.' "[68] Obviously the Divine Law overrules any thought of *tzaar baalei hayyim.* Similar reasoning justifies the severing of the sinews of horses belonging to a dead king at the royal funeral on the grounds that none should benefit from his steeds.[69]

A subtle distinction is made in the case of Pinhas b. Yair's visit to the home of Rabbi Judah the Prince. Rabbi Pinhas fears to enter the gate because of several white mules standing nearby, and he exclaims: "The angel of death is in this house! Shall I then dine here?" When Rabbi hears of his apprehensions, he goes out to greet his guest and assures him: "I shall sell the mules." But Pinhas objects on the grounds that this would constitute placing a stumbling-block before the blind. Rabbi Judah replies: "I shall hamstring them," but Pinhas protests: "You would be causing suffering to the animals." Finally Rabbi Judah declares: "I will kill them," but again Pinhas objects, this time on the grounds that "there is a prohibition against wanton destruction."[70]

This dialogue is revealing. Pinhas b. Yair sees hamstringing an animal as a clear violation of *tzaar baalei hayyim* if no compelling reason exists for it to be done, and dining at Rabbi Judah's abode does not constitute a compelling reason. Therefore it is wrong to hamstring the mules. But killing the animals does not constitute causing them undue suffering. It merely violates the rule enjoining one against the wanton destruction of items of value.

Viewed from a more balanced perspective, one can call into question the true purpose behind many of the biblical laws pertaining to the animal kingdom. Are they essentially manifestations of God's concern and compassion for His animal creations,[71] or are they, rather, manifestations of a concern for animals only insofar as they constitute the property of man? Is it the animal per se that matters, or the animal as a symbol of man's property, sustenance, and interpersonal relations that is of pivotal importance?

Consider the injunction to return a lost ox or sheep to its owner. This clearly falls under the category of returning lost property, and the rabbis introduce limitations and exemptions into the situation. They inform us that a priest need not assist such an animal if it is within cemetery grounds, nor need an elderly man bother with performing such an undignified task,[72] nor need anyone bother with a lost animal if his time is simply too valuable.[73]

"If thou meet thy enemy's ox or his ass going astray, thou shalt surely bring it back to him again."[74] The ox and the ass are undoubtedly the immediate beneficiaries of such kindness, but the central concern here is the relationship of two human enemies, the finder and the owner. It is in this light that Philo analyzes the consequences of this law being carried out.

> The man who has received a benefit is willingly induced to make peace for the future as being enslaved by the kindness shown to him; and he who has conferred the benefit having his own action for a counsellor, is already most prepared in his mind for a complete reconciliation.[75]

It is with a similar emphasis that *Targum Onkelos* renders the following passage: "If you see your enemy's ass prostrate under his burden, you must not forsake him, you shall surely abandon that which is in your heart against him and shall release it to him."[76]

The rabbis devote considerable attention to a classic dilemma.

One is confronted with two concurrent emergencies: the ass of one's friend is lying down weighted beneath its burden, and the ass of an enemy is standing by in need of being laden with a burden. Which emergency should take precedence?

From the point of view of discomfort to the beast, one's first obligation should clearly be the unloading of the ass of one's friend. The Talmud, however, rules otherwise and ordains that the loading of the enemy's animal should take precedence. Why? In order to crush the evil *yetzer*, i.e., to subdue the evil inclination that would surely make one tend to ignore (if not rejoice in) his neighbor's misfortune.[77] Therefore one must first assist his enemy, and only afterwards his friend, notwithstanding the fact that the latter's animal is suffering, while the former's beast is in no pain at all. The *Tosefta* emphasizes the fact that such behavior may hopefully bring about a change of heart on the part of the enemy and cause the enmity to dissipate.[78] Interestingly, the *Tosefta* adds that one must assist the ass of a non-Jew no less than the ass of a Jew, unless it is laden with "wine of libation," in which event the Israelite would be facilitating the practice of idolatry.

The laws of the Sabbath, as we have noted, do permit a certain flexibility when the animal's welfare is concerned, but it is, in reality, a limited flexibility. One may, for example, *assist* an animal in giving birth on the Sabbath, but one ought not to perform the actual delivery![79] Rabbi Judah permits serving an animal fodder on the Sabbath but rules that one should not put forth the effort to spread the fodder around,[80] and Simeon b. Gamliel forbids serving water that has been left uncovered to animals on the Sabbath because of the possible danger to humans.[81]

Although God is poetically extolled as the One who "sits in the heights of the universe and distributes food to all creatures,"[82] mankind is nowhere instructed to emulate the Creator by doing the same. Only the domestic animal, the beast who is of utilitarian value to man, is entitled to be fed, and the Sabbath laws clearly permit the feeding *only* of these. Thus one is permitted, on the Sabbath, to place food before domesticated geese, fowls, and Herodian doves, but not before bees and doves in dovecotes, for these can presumably fend for themselves.[83]

Furthermore, no domestic beast is entitled to any food so long as humans are in need of sustenance. That is a reasonable enough statement of priorities. But it is carried further in a discussion dealing with the virtues of Rabbi Huna. Mention is made of the fact that on the eve of every Sabbath, he would send a messenger to the marketplace with instructions to purchase all the leftover vegetables and throw them into the river. The question is promptly raised: "Should he not, rather, have had these distributed to the poor?" The reply is that the poor would thereby be led to rely exclusively upon him and therefore would not purchase any provisions for themselves. Then the Talmud asks: "Why did he not give the vegetables to the domestic animals?" The reply: "He was of the opinion that food fit for human consumption may not be given to animals."[84]

It is significant that even the ruling requiring a master to feed his animals before partaking of his own meal was not applicable in the case of *all* animals. We find that dogs were to be excluded on the grounds that they were reckoned as wild animals and therefore undeserving of such privileges.[85]

The Bird's Nest

The precept of the "bird's nest," concluding, as it does, with the promise "that it may be well with thee and that thou mayest prolong thy days,"[86] merits closer inspection. Now this precept carries with it essentially the same reward that is ordained for those who fulfill the commandment of honoring their parents,[87] deemed by the rabbis to be the most important *mitzvah* of all,[88] the gift of longevity. Why? Is it because compassion for a parent bird is equivalent in importance to showing consideration toward human parents? Some would agree, but others have thought otherwise.

So God did not reveal the reward of the precepts, except for two, the weightiest and the least weighty. The honoring of parents is the very weightiest, and its reward is long life, as it is said: "Honor thy father and thy mother that thy days may be long." Sending away the mother bird is the least weighty, and what is its reward? Length of days, as it is said: "that thou mayest prolong thy days."[89]

Some rabbis apparently viewed the selection of the "bird's nest" for meritorious reward as being due precisely to the fact that it is so *un*important! By juxtaposing it to the fifth commandment, they found a vivid illustration of the principle "Be heedful of a light precept as of a weighty one, for thou knowest not the recompense or reward for each precept,"[90] and they could happily muse on how abundantly God would reward those who fulfilled weighty commandments, seeing that even the observance of so minor an ordinance as that of the "bird's nest" merits longevity.[91]

Why is the commandment of the "bird's nest" deemed to be such a minor one? We are not told. But it should be noted that not all scholars are in agreement that the ordinance is motivated by a sense of compassion for the feelings of the mother bird. Rabbi Eleazar declares that it is proper for the mother bird to be preserved, as she is busy with the maintenance and beautification of the world. His comment may display a fine aesthetic sensitivity, but it appears to be somewhat lacking in ethical sensitivity.[92]

It is interesting to note that rabbinic literature records several striking examples of "nonreward" in connection with the fulfillment of this *mitzvah*. Elisha b. Abuya's eventual apostasy is traced to an incident in the plain of Gennesaret when he beheld a man ascend a tree, remove both dam and young in clear violation of the law, and then descend safely and proceed upon his way. Later, Elisha saw another individual follow the scriptural command by taking a young bird only after dismissing the dam, and this person was killed by a snake as he descended from the tree. Elisha was unable to reconcile this injustice with the promise of reward for compliance with the biblical text, and he lost his faith in God. A concluding rabbinic comment explains that the promise of "length of days" will, indeed, be fulfilled, not in this world perhaps, but in the world to come.[93]

We shall detour a bit at this point to consider in greater detail another talmudic discussion regarding the "bird's nest." It reflects not only the complexity and difficulty involved in analyzing rabbinic discussions, but also how frequently the subject under discussion (in this case the "bird's nest") can become quite tangential and secondary to other issues. It well illustrates how cautious one should be in attempting to draw conclusions about rabbinic attitudes toward fauna from isolated rabbinic comments concerning fauna, for the animal itself may be incidental to the real issues under discussion.

Briefly summarized, the discussion is as follows: A *mishnah* contains the cryptic comment, "If one says. . . 'To a bird's nest do Thy mercies extend,' they silence him."[94] The comment is preceded by the statement, "If one says, 'May the good [plural] bless thee,' this is a heretical practice," and it is followed by the observation, "If one says, 'May thy name be remembered for favors' or 'We give thanks, we give thanks,' they silence him."

Another *mishnah* commences: "If one says, 'To a bird's nest do thy mercies extend,' they silence him." This is followed by "[If one says] 'Let thy name be remembered for favor,' or 'We give thanks, we give thanks,' they silence him," and in some versions the phrase "If one says, 'May the good [plural] bless thee,' this is an error."[95]

It would appear that these discussions deal with phraseology of a possibly heretical nature that was employed by sectarians in their prayer formulae.[96] "May Thy name be remembered for favors" might imply that one ought *not* to praise God for evil as for good, in contradistinction to the teaching of a *mishnah*,[97] while the use of the plural *tovim* for "good" and the repetition of the phrase "we give thanks" may hint at the existence of two divinities!

But what heresies can there possibly be in the words "to a bird's nest do Thy mercies extend"? They apparently refer to the biblical injunction requiring one to spare the life of the mother bird and send her away prior to taking her nest of fledglings. What conceivable heresy can there be in referring to this scriptural injunction?

Apparently a difference of opinion exists, because the Palestinian Talmud puts forth two views on the subject. One view, advanced by Rabbi Pinhas in the name of Rabbi Simon, is that the phrase would seem to limit God's kindness to birds while excluding it from humans![98] Some versions apparently used the phrase "*ad* [up to] a bird's nest do Thy mercies extend," and this was understandably objected to by Rabbi Jose in the name of Rabbi Simeon, as limiting God's providence to birds!

Another objection to this phrase is that it seems to attribute motives of compassion to God's decrees. Rabbi Josa b. Bun, the expounder of this view, criticizes those who would interpret "My people, the children of Israel" to mean: "Just as I am merciful in heaven, so should you be merciful upon earth; whether it be a cow or an ewe, you shall not slaughter it with its young in one day."[99]

In a somewhat different manner the Babylonian Talmud also presents these two grounds for objecting to the aforementioned prayer.[100] Rabbi Jose b. Abin claims that it creates jealousy among the works of creation, i.e., God seems to care only for birds, and not for any other creatures.[101] Rabbi Jose b. Zebida contends that it is erroneous to attribute motives of compassion to divine decrees, because all of the commandments are to be implicitly obeyed, whether or not they are perceived to contain any ethical components. This is followed by a cryptic account of one who offered the following prayer in Rabbah's presence: "Thou hast shown pity to the bird's nest, do Thou have pity and mercy upon /us; Thou hast shown pity to the animal and its young, do Thou have pity and mercy upon us." Rabbah observed, "How well this rabbi knows how to placate his master," while Abayye raised the question, "But we have learned that he is to be silenced!" No direct reply is given to Abayye's challenge. The Talmud explains the situation as one in which "Rabbah only tried to sharpen Abayye's wits."[102]

Now what is one to make of these differences of opinion? Do they actually reflect specific attitudes toward birds and animals per se? Probably not.

Rabbi Josa b. Bun may be reacting to the tendency to see specific purposes in all of God's commandments and to justify their observance on the grounds that "just as He is compassionate and gracious, so you be compassionate and gracious." He, like other *amoraim*, may have opposed the trend to propose reasons for scriptural observances on the grounds that this might conceivably have the opposite effect and actually undermine their observance.[103] Thus Rabbi Josa objects to the attribution of motives of compassion to the injunction against the slaughtering of "it and its young on one day," while other sages take to task one who similarly interprets the injunction "unto a bird's nest does Thy compassion extend."[104]

But other explanations for these passages have also been advanced. Some scholars detect here echoes of anti-Christian polemics vis-à-vis the Pauline teachings of law and grace.[105] One view has been proposed that the *mishnah* is in reality discussing a prayer in which Israel is metaphorically compared to a bird which has flown its nest[106] and has nothing at all to do with live birds and their fledglings. Finally, it is not inconceivable that we are dealing here with certain technical aspects of prayer formulae in the *tefillah* and the propriety or impropriety of adding certain formulae of prayer. Possibly the entire discussion stems from Rabbi Josa b. Bun's merely voicing his objection to a rabbinic interpretation.[107]

Whatever the case, it would be presumptuous to attempt to draw any definitive conclusions concerning attitudes toward animals from these sources.

It would be similarly unfair to take at face value some of the aggadic utterances which glowingly extol the wisdom and sensitivity of the animal. The true intent and purpose of these texts may be far removed from any attempt to glorify the role of fauna.

For example, Rabbi Johanan comments that even had the Torah not been given to mankind, one could have learned certain moral values from the animal kingdom; decency from the cat, refraining from theft from the ant, chastity from the dove, and appropriate sexual manners from the rooster.[108] But is it Rabbi Johanan's intent here to extol the ethical sensitivity of these animals? Or is it rather to advocate that man improve his moral conduct by learning even from the lowly creatures of the animal kingdom? Perhaps these observations point to the existence of a form of "natural law," to a genre of ante-halakhic values and modes of behavior which are self-evident and universal, inherent in nature, and therefore capable of being derived by reason or from the observation of natural phenomena. How extensively developed this notion of "natural law" is in rabbinic literature remains an elusive point,[109] but it possibly implies social utility as a rationale for ethical behavior.

Finally, it should be noted that Rabbi Johanan's dictum follows directly upon Rabbi Hiyya's teaching that God endowed various creatures with wisdom so that man might learn from them. (The animals themselves, interestingly, are deemed to be totally oblivious to their own good qualities.)[110] Perhaps Rabbi Johanan is limiting this teaching somewhat, for his statement "Had the Torah not been given, we could have learned, etc.," may actually imply as its corollary, "but since it was given to us, there is clearly no need for man to have to learn anything of value from an animal!"[111] Whatever the case may be, one doubts that the primary purpose of this teaching is to emphasize that man and the animals have similar ethical sensitivities.

Let us consider another example, that of the cow sold by a Jew to a non-Jew, which refused to do any labor on the Sabbath until the Jew whispered in her ear that it was perfectly permissible for her to work on the Sabbath now that she was the property of a gentile.[112] Impressive as the cow's religious sensitivity may be, it is the conversion to Judaism of her new master that supplies the triumphant climax to this tale, not praise for the animal. Perhaps the extraordinary behavior of the asses of Pinhas b. Yair and Rabbi Yose serves merely to illustrate the adage that "even the beasts of the righteous are not allowed by the Holy One, blessed be He, to offend."[113]

Midrashic literature undeniably contains many striking examples of God's concern for the well-being of the animal kingdom, and how this concern manifests itself in the intricate structure of many a creature, and the delicate timing of events which makes possible its survival. However, upon closer examination, the emphasis in a preponderance of these passages appears to be not so much upon God's *compassion* for fauna as upon His *wisdom* and *greatness* in fashioning a world that is such a marvel of perfection.

Such comments are perhaps similar to contemporary scientific observations to the effect that if the earth were but a fraction closer to or further removed from the sun, all life upon earth would surely perish either from heat or from cold. Or, if the chemical composition of the atmosphere were ever so slightly changed, if the chromosome formations were only marginally altered, and so on, then human reproduction and survival would surely be impossible. Is it not reasonable to assume that, in a similar vein, the rabbis were also paying tribute to God for His marvels of nature and existence, and for having created precisely the conditions that were perfectly suited for the survival of human and animal life.

The *Sifre* states:

His work is perfect in regard to all the inhabitants of the world, and there is not the slightest reason for questioning His works. There is not one of them who would speculate and say: "If I had three eyes, or three heads, or three legs, or if I walked on my head, or if my face were turned backwards, how it would benefit me."[114]

The Talmud eloquently elaborates upon God's reply to Job when the latter, convinced that his sufferings were unwarranted, accuses God of having perhaps mistakenly inflicted upon him the punishments intended for another. God retorts to the accusation by describing the exactness and precision of all His wondrous deeds—how each hair has its own sac, each drop of rain proceeds from its own mold in the heavens, and each thunderbolt has its own path. It is in this context that the rabbis inform us that because gazelles normally give birth high upon the pinnacles of rocks, God sends an eagle to rescue their offspring from falling to a certain death in the gorge below. Needless to say, were the eagle a fraction of a second too early or too tardy, the baby gazelle would surely die. Similarly, because hinds possess extremely narrow wombs, God causes a serpent to emerge at the precise moment in order to soften the womb of the hind so that she will be able to give birth.[115]

Rabbi Akiba similarly comments upon the verses in Chapter 11 of Leviticus in which many names of birds, beasts, and crawling creatures are mentioned:

"How manifold are Thy works, O Lord, etc." Thou hast creatures that live in the sea and that live on land. If those that live in the sea go on to the land, they die; and if those that live on the dry land go into the sea, they die. There are creatures that live in fire and creatures that live in the air. If those that live in fire go into the air, they die; if those that live in the air go into the fire, they die. The place of life of the former spells death for the latter; and the place where the latter live spells death for the former. Thus Scripture declares: "How manifold are Thy works, O Lord! etc."[116]

It is first and foremost in tribute to God's greatness that Rab taught: "Of all that the Holy One, blessed be He, created in His world, He created nothing without a purpose. He created the snail [as a remedy] for the scab; He created the fly for the hornet's [sting]; the mosquito for the serpent's [bite]."[117]

Now the rabbis may have been confronted with some of the same quasi-philosophic challenges that confronted the ancient Stoics.[118] One of these was the apparent superfluousness of certain creatures. What possible purpose could God have had in creating seemingly useless and obnoxious insects and reptiles? Did these not constitute an imperfection in His otherwise perfect world? And so Rab emphasizes that *every* creature serves *some* purpose, no creation of the Lord is totally bereft of value, and other sages proclaim that "even things that appear to you wholly superfluous in the creation of the world . . . like fleas, gnats, and flies . . . also form an integral part of the world-creation, and the Holy One, blessed be He, uses them all in His service."[119]

Man-Animal Contrasts

True, the animal is extolled. All living creatures are declared to possess value and purpose, and their existence is due to divine genius and compassion. But it is not really the greatness of the animal which is highlighted in many of the preceding excerpts. The animal is merely one example of the greatness of God, the indirect beneficiary of praise which is rightly His.

Not so man. Man stands far above the animal. He is God's

unique creation, formed directly by the divine hand, in contradistinction to the animals, which sprung from the word of God,[120] and man alone, of all creations, is a microcosm of the entire world.[121] Indeed, it was for man's sake that the world was brought into being.[122]

Hardly any attention is paid to the soul of the animal because "an animal is not mindful of what it does . . . an animal is ignorant of what leads to death . . . an animal is only destined for slaughter and has no portion in the world to come."[123] But rabbinic teachings call special attention to the soul of man, created on the first day of creation[124] after enjoying a complex prehistory in which it was instructed in the ways of the Lord and charged with its earthly responsibilities.[125]

Whereas animals are formed solely from the substance of the earth, God employs the contributions of both heaven and earth in the creation of man, forming his soul from heavenly substance and his body from an earthly composition.[126] Therefore, like the animal kingdom, man must take nourishment, secrete his wastes, propagate his species, and finally die. But he is angellike in that he possesses the gift of speech, intellect, an upright walk, and the glance of his eye.[127] Indeed, man is portrayed as a delicate combination of the celestial and the bestial, and God is depicted as proclaiming: "The celestials are not propagated, but they are immortal. The beings on earth are propagated, but they die. I will create man to be the union of the two."[128]

Obviously, the central point here is not so much man's similarity to, and partial kinship with, the animal kingdom as much as it is an affirmation that man is able to elevate himself about a bestial existence to celestial heights by virtue of his devotion to Torah. As Rabbi Simlai phrases it: "If he observed the Torah and did the will of his Father in heaven, he is like the beings of heaven above. But if he did not observe the Torah or do the will of his Father in heaven, he is like the creatures of below."[129]

This contrast between man and beast is further developed.

Neither the angels nor the animals satisfied God; the former have no evil inclination, the latter have no good inclination.[130]

The good of the one and the evil of the other, therefore, are not the result of their free will. God, therefore, created man, who possesses both the good and the evil inclinations. If he follows evil, he is likened to an animal; if he follows good, he is higher than an angel.[131]

Clearly, man's superiority over the beast is deemed to be the quality of free will with which he is vested, a quality shared neither by animals nor by angels.[132]

Furthermore, the obvious intellectual gap between man and the animals is a formidable chasm with deep religious implications. The activity of supreme importance in rabbinic Judaism was *Talmud Torah,* the study of Torah, an activity obviously limited to the human species alone. Only man can study Torah as a means for the apprehension of God and the attainment of sanctity, as a means of bringing order into a chaotic world and cultivating lives of rational decision-making, as opposed to capriciousness and drift. "For the Talmud the alternatives are . . . reflection or dumb reflex, consciousness or animal instinct. Man, in God's image, has the capacity to reflect and to criticize. All an animal can do is act and respond."[133]

Therefore the lowliest of humans stands far above the greatest of the animals: "The king of the wild animals is the lion; the king of the cattle is the ox; the king of the birds is the eagle; and man is exalted over them."[134] "The Holy One, blessed be He, says to man: 'I have endowed you with *madda* [intellect] above cattle, birds, and beasts.' "[135]

Punishment of Animals

Rabbinic literature puts forth some interesting questions, or, more accurately, challenges, in connection with the issue of punishment of animals. In commenting upon the biblical injunction condemning bestiality,[136] the *mishnah* succinctly raises the obvious question: "If the man has sinned, wherein has the animal sinned?"[137]

Several passages in apocryphal literature appear to challenge the notion that animals can be subject to the laws of judgment as are men,[138] and an aggadic teaching informs us that "when an animal dies, its spirit has rest, but when a human being dies, its spirit has no rest, because he is brought to judgment, and there are enumerated in his presence all his deeds, both good and bad."[139]

Why, indeed, *should* an animal be brought to judgment? Does it possess a humanlike intellect or understanding to be deemed culpable? Is there a divine soul in the animal to begin with that has become corrupted?

The *mishnah's* reply is of quite a different order. "Because the human being was enticed to sin through it [the animal], it should be stoned. Another explanation: So that the animal should not pass through the streets while people say, 'This is the animal on account of which so-and-so was stoned.' "[140]

If the question raises an ethical dimension vis-à-vis the culpability of a dumb, passive beast, the answer concerns itself solely with a practical dimension, that of the virtue of the human community. Clearly it is more important for the human community to rid itself of a disgusting and shameful reminder than to consider ethical questions involving the punishment of animals.

Another example. The Pentateuch records how "the Lord smote all the firstborn in the land of Egypt, from the firstborn of Pharaoh who sat on his throne unto the firstborn of the captive that was in the dungeon; and all the firstborn of cattle."[141] The latter part of the passage posed an ethical dilemma which some rabbis articulated: the human beings had obviously sinned, but what crimes could the cattle possibly be guilty of?

The ethical question is met with a theological response. The reason why the cattle die, we are told, is because they were objects of worship in the eyes of the Egyptians. Had the cattle survived, the Egyptians might have assumed that their gods (i.e., the cattle) were the ones who inflicted punishment upon their firstborn, or that the cattle were mighty deities easily capable of withstanding the same plagues which so ravaged their human counterparts. Therefore it was necessary for the innocent beasts to die. A second response consists of the succinct observation: "Woe to the wicked, and woe to their care-taking [cattle]."[142]

Even if one assumes that the enumeration of the "sins" of the animals in the era of Noah's flood is a response to a similar ethical challenge—i.e., "why should innocent animals suffer because of the corruption of man?"—Philo sees no need for any justification for the death of the fauna in the deluge. He merely points out that all entities were created for the sake of human beings, and exist merely for the service of human beings, and thus, since human beings were being destroyed, animals might just as well be destroyed too! There simply was no longer any need for an abundance of fauna to serve mankind.[143]

The rabbis reinforce this notion by proposing an analogy to the case of a man who arranges a wedding for his son, only to have the unfortunate boy die. The grieving father disposes of all the elaborate wedding preparations, saying: "I have prepared all this for my son. Now that he is dead, what need have I for the banquet? Thus the Holy One, blessed be He, said also: 'Did I create the animals and beasts for aught but man? Now that man has sinned, what need have I of the animals and the beasts?' "[144]

Indeed, it would seem that the entire purpose for the existence of animals, their sole raison d'etre, is the service of mankind. When the angels object to God's plan for creating man, the Lord replies with a question of His own: "Sheep and oxen, all of them, why were they created? The fowl of the earth and the fish of the sea, / what were they created for? Of what avail is a larder full of appetizing dainties, and no guest to enjoy them?"[145]

The very question "why raise such creatures as monkeys, sea-dogs, and porcupines?"[146] contains the intimation that such creatures are clearly of no utilitarian value to man. Hence, why bother with them?

Finally, it was unthinkable for the rabbis that both man and beast should share the same fate. They interpreted Ecclesiastes' sad musing—"For that which befalleth the sons of men befalleth beasts; even one thing befalleth them; as the one dieth so dieth the other; yea, they have all one breath; so that man has no preeminence above a beast, for all is vanity"—to mean precisely the opposite, namely, that man *does* have preeminence over the beast, for God Himself ordains proper and befitting burial for human beings.[147]

Little wonder that moralists should feel compelled to remind man, the apex of creation, not to become saturated in arrogance, for, after all, even the lowly gnat preceded him in the order of creation.[148]

Conclusion

The complexity of the rabbinic portrait of fauna is due, in part, to the fact that such a portrait mirrors an interesting paradox that is inherent in traditional Jewish ethical thought, a paradox rooted in the gap between the ideal and reality.

On the one hand, Jewish ethics emphasized the necessity of one's extending oneself *lifnim mishurat hadin*—beyond the minimal standards of moral behavior—and seeking a higher ethic by which to guide one's life and bring it into harmony with the divine will. Such an ethic may have been more theoretical than practical in nature, but from its vantage point, all of God's creations, humankind as well as animalkind, stand related and interrelated. Aggadic literature emphasizes this Hellenistic notion that God is reflected in the world of nature, in the myriads of His creations. Thus divine obligations are omnipresent, compassion to all living creatures is mandated, and the way of the *hasid* ("pious one") is to expand one's ethical obligations to be all-embracing. The *hasid* strives for the unattainable.

On the other hand, Jewish ethical thought also extols moderation. It is suspicious of, and opposed to, extremism in virtue, as in vice. It suspects superpiety, and is uncomfortable with hyperreligiosity.

This distrust is dramatically mirrored in the rabbinic exposition of a dialogue between the prophet Samuel and King Saul. Samuel rebukes the king for not having killed all of the Amalekites, along with their cattle. Saul responds: "If the Torah enjoined that a heifer should be brought [in atonement] for the death of one soul, how great must be the atonement required for the slaughter of so many? Granted, man sinned. But what sin have the cattle committed? Granted, adults have sinned, but what sin have the minors committed?" A heavenly voice proclaimed: "Be not overly righteous!" Later, when Saul commissions Doeg to slay the priests at Nob, the heavenly voice declares: "Be not overly wicked."[149]

For Rabbi Simeon b. Lakish the moral was obvious: "Whoever is merciful when he should be ruthless, in the end is ruthless when he should be merciful."

A similar lesson in moderation and graduated priorities was preached by Moses to the Children of Israel. The two and a half tribes that were desirous of settling on the eastern side of the Jordan River presented their petition to Moses with the words: "We will build sheepfolds here for our cattle and cities for our little ones." Moses objected to the fact that they referred to the well-being of their cattle before that of their own children.[150]

The thrust of *halakhah* would seem to be the application of moderation to the *aggadic* extolment of the animal kingdom. True, all creatures are entitled to their place in God's great world, and man is obligated to refrain from the wanton destruction of fauna. But while *halakhah* is *fair* to animals, it is decidedly *partial* to humans.

To moderns, *tzaar baalei hayyim* denotes compassion for animals out of a sense of empathy and humane sentiments for the animal's *tzaar*, or "pain." But one wonders whether the rabbis did not interpret *tzaar* in the broader sense of man's responsibilities or obligations vis-à-vis the animal, rather than the animal's pain per se. These responsibilities and obligations were real enough but limited, for man is clearly higher than the animal, his priorities are far above theirs, and therefore his concerns must *always* take precedence over theirs.

Let man, therefore, center all of his efforts and energies in the arena of intrapersonal relations. This is the essential will of God. Let man dream of the ideal, but let him strive for the attainable and attain it.

PART

A MEDIEVAL AND MODERN PORTRAIT

MAN'S SUPERIORITY OVER BEAST

Jewish literature in the Jewish Middle Ages (500–1750) consists primarily of explications upon biblical and rabbinic teachings. These explications take many forms—exegesis, commentary, legal responsa, philosophic treatises, mystical speculation, as well as religious poetry and ethical exhortations. It is understandably difficult to draw a composite portrait of the animal kingdom from such diverse sources and disciplines. We shall, therefore, consider individual portraits painted in different epochs by representatives of the diverse schools of thought. Although they may vary considerably, their composite contribution reflects the traditional portrait of the animal, one of a creature entitled to compassion and concern, but undeserving of excessive compassion or undue concern. The animal is to be treated fairly but not favorably.

Moses Maimonides: A Philosophic and Halakhic Overview

The writings of Moses Maimonides (1135–1214) mirror well the complexity and tension inherent in the traditional portrait of the animal. This may be due in part to Maimonides' formidable literary productivity as both philosopher and legal codifier. His works, therefore, reflect the irreducible tension that exists between philosophy and law, and the obvious fact that the structure of law discourages the emergence of concepts suitable for philosophy.[1] This may also, in part, be a function of the variations in style, mode, subtlety, and sophistication that differentiate Maimonides' code of law, the *Mishneh Torah,* from his philosophic guide, the *Moreh Nebukhim*,[2] as well as of Maimonides' own philosophic bent. However, Maimonides' composite portrait of fauna accurately reflects some of the intrinsic variations within, as well as the dominant thrust of, the traditional rabbinic portrait of the animal.

We shall consider in detail two legal summaries in the *Mishneh Torah*, one pertaining to the loading and unloading of animals, the other concerning itself with prayer formulae related to compassion for fauna.

Maimonides summarizes the talmudic legislation concerning the loading and unloading of the burden upon an animal in need of assistance in both his *Sefer haMitzvot* and the *Mishneh Torah*.

The *Sefer haMitzvot* derives from this legislation two positive commandments and one negative commandment.

Commandment 202 is that wherein He has commanded us that we are to [render assistance in] unloading the burden from a beast which has become fatigued while on the road. This [injunction] finds expression in His words, praised be He. "[If thou see the ass of him that hateth thee lying under its burden, and wouldest forbear to help him], thou shalt surely help with him." In the words of the *Mekhilta*: " 'Thou shalt surely help with him.' . . . this portion of the verse refers to unloading." There it has [also] been said, " '[If thou see the ass of him that hateth thee lying under its burden], and wouldest forbear to help him, thou shalt surely help [with him]' ": We thus infer that in [failing to render assistance] one violates [both] a positive commandment and a negative commandment." That is to say, we are commanded to unload the burden from the beast, and we are [also] admonished not to leave it prostate under its burden . . . so that in failing to render such assistance one violates [both] a positive commandment and a negative commandment. Thus it has been explained that [His words], "Thou shalt surely help [with him]," [establish] a positive commandment.

Commandment 203 is that wherein He has commanded us that in the case of a man who is alone we are to [assist him] in lifting up [his burden] upon his beast or upon himself [even] though it has been unloaded without our assistance; for just as we have been commanded to render assistance in unloading, even so we are commanded to [assist one] in loading. This [injunction] finds expression in His words, praised be He, "Thou shalt surely help him to lift up again." In the words of the *Mekhilta:* " 'Thou shalt surely help him to lift them up again.' [This portion of the verse] refers to loading."

[Commandment 270, negative] We are commanded against leaving a beast lying under its burden, as it is said, "Thou shalt not see thy brother's ass or his ox fallen down by the way, and hide thyself from them."

It is significant that although Maimonides does not propose any rationale for this legislation, the general context and juxaposition of paragraphs places it within the legal context of loss of property and restoration of lost property.

The *Mishneh Torah's* discussion commences with the reaffirmation that one is biblically mandated to unload a burden from a helpless animal.[3] Maimonides then enumerates those classes of individuals who are exempt from this responsibility, but emphasizes that this is a worthy and fitting obligation for men of piety to fulfill. He stresses that although there is no remuneration forthcoming for unloading a beast of burden (one may, however, claim wages for assisting in loading), there is no limit to the number of times one is obligated to assist in the task. Furthermore, in the event that the animal's owner is incapacitated due to old age or infirmity, one must bear the *total* obligation of loading or unloading the beast.

Now up to this point, Maimonides does not suggest any reason for this *mitzvah,* nor does he employ the phrase *tzaar baalei hayyim.* He does use the word *tzaar* (lit. "pain") in paragraph no. 9, but there it appears in a context which is clearly nonapplicable to the beast.

As to the case involving an animal belonging to a non-Jew, while the burden belongs to an Israelite, if the non-Jew was trailing after his beast, one is not obligated to concern oneself. However, if he was not trailing the beast, one is obligated both to unload and to load because of the *tzaar* of the Israelite. Similarly, in the case of an animal belonging to an Israelite and a burden belonging to a non-Jew, one is obligated both to unload and to load because of the *tzaar* of the Israelite. However, if both the animal and the burden are the property of the non-Jew, one theoretically need not concern oneself with the matter were it not for the factor of "enmity" [the non-Jew would resent the lack of assistance from Israelites and hate them].

Now what is one to make of this paragraph?

Several commentators are quick to point out that *tzaar baalei hayyim* is, indeed, the crucial principle here. Joseph Karo[4] (1488–1575) and Joshua Falk Cohen[5] (16th–17th cent.) interpret the passage to imply that one is exempt only from loading the non-Jew's animal in his presence, but, they stress, one *is* obligated to assist in unloading the beast in all of the cases cited precisely because *tzaar baalei hayyim* is of biblical origin.

However, Elijah, the *Gaon* of Vilna (1720–1798), disagrees. He views these interpretations as forced, and claims that a dispassionate, objective reading of the text will disclose that Maimonides clearly does *not* require one to assist in either loading or *unloading* an animal's burden under certain circumstances. On the basis of this ruling, the *Gaon* questions whether Maimonides himself truly believes *tzaar baalei hayyim* to be biblically mandated![6]

The position of Maimonides is somewhat clarified in paragraph 13 of the same chapter, where he writes:

If one encounters two animals, one crouching under its load, and the other's master in need of assistance in reloading it, he should first help in the unloading, because of *tzaar baalei hayyim,* and then load the other. When does this rule apply? Only when the owners are both enemies or both friends of the person in question. But if one is an enemy and one is a friend, he is required to load for the enemy first so that his evil impulse may be subdued [i.e., so that his negative inclinations toward the enemy may be overcome].

The phrase *tzaar baalei hayyim* appears here in the accepted and normal context. The animal crouched beneath its burden is clearly in greater pain than the unladen beast; hence, all other factors being equal, one should first assist it by freeing it of its burden. But Maimonides proceeds to explain that there is a more important principle at stake here than the animal's pain, namely *lakof et yitzro harah*, i.e., to condition one to be able to overcome his negative inclinations. In other words, it is more important to assist one's enemy in loading than to assist one's friend in unloading! Granted, it is the friend's beast which is in pain and merits immediate assistance, but interpersonal relations are more important than the discomfort of beasts. And if, as a result of going to the aid of an enemy in need, enmity will now cease to exist, this is clearly a more compelling state of virtue than that of an animal alleviated of its pain. So rules Maimonides in accordance with talmudic precedent.[7]

In his discussion of laws relating to prayer, Maimonides writes:

Whoever says in his supplications, "He that dealt mercifully with a nest of birds, forbidding the taking of the mother-bird together with the nestlings and the slaughter of a beast and its young in one day . . . may He have mercy upon us," or offers petitions of a similar character, is silenced; for these precepts are divine decrees set forth in Scripture and have not been ordained in a spirit of compassion. Were this the motive, the slaughtering of all animals would have been prohibited.[8]

In his Commentary to the Mishnah Maimonides similarly dismisses as absurd the notion that the purpose of this *mitzvah* is God's compassion for birds, and he cites it as representative of an entire genre of commandments for which there simply is no apparent reason.[9]

Some scholars have commented upon the apparent contradiction between Maimonides' insistence in the *Mishneh Torah* that no motive of compassion lies behind these commandments and his eloquent statements to the contrary in the *Moreh Nebukhim*. For in the latter work, after affirming the necessity of slaughtering animals for food (Maimonides believed that animal-flesh, along with herbs, comprises man's natural food), he emphasizes that the Torah's concern was "to kill them in the easiest manner, and it was forbidden to torment them through killing them in a reprehensible manner by piercing the lower part of their throat or by cutting off one of their members."

Maimonides continues:

It is likewise forbidden to slaughter "it and its young on the same day," this being a precautionary measure in order to avoid slaughtering the young animal in front of its mother. For in these cases animals feel very great pain, there being no difference regarding this pain between man and the other animals. For the love and tenderness of a mother for her child is not consequent upon reason, but upon the activity of the imaginative faculty, which is found in most animals just as it is found in man. This law applies in particular to *ox* and *lamb*, because these are the domestic animals that we are allowed to eat and that in most cases it is usual to eat; in their case the mother can be differentiated from her young.

This is also the reason for the commandment "to let [the mother] go from the nest." For in general the eggs over which the bird has sat and the young that need their mother are not fit to be eaten. If then the mother bird is let go and escapes of her own accord, she will not be pained by seeing that the young are taken away. In most cases this will lead to people leaving everything alone, for what may be taken is in most cases not fit to be eaten. If the Law takes into consideration these pains of the soul in the case of beast and birds, what will be the case with regard to the individuals of the human species as a whole? You must not allege as an objection against me the dictum of [the sages], may their memory be blessed: "He who says, 'Thy mercy extends to young birds, etc.' " For this is one of the two opinions mentioned by us—I mean the opinion of those who think that there is no reason for the Law except only the will [of God], but as for us, we follow only the second opinion.[10]

Such apparent inconsistencies in Maimonides' writings supply scholars with stimulating hours of analysis and speculation. But it should be emphasized that the subject matter of Maimonides the codifier is, by definition, given quite a different emphasis than that of Maimonides the biblical commentator and philosopher, and most likely the *Mishneh Torah* and the *Moreh Nebukhim* are intended for different reading audiences and therefore address themselves to dissimilar challenges.

Actually, Maimonides' attitude toward animals is a consistent one. In the *Mishneh Torah* he is bound by rabbinic legal precedents which he records faithfully and dispassionately. It would be futile and fruitless to attempt to infer any personal sentiments on his part vis-à-vis animals from his code. In the *Moreh Nebukhim,* Maimonides is likewise bound—only this time by powerful philosophic convictions concerning the nature of fauna and their place in the divine scheme of things.

A. The *Mishneh Torah* reflects accurately the halakhic portrait of the animal kingdom. Therefore, on the one hand, we find the "rights" of animals clearly enumerated.

For example, one is forbidden to castrate neither man nor beast,[11] and one is permitted to attend to the needs of animals on the Sabbath and festivals, even when certain religious restrictions would seem to be compromised. Thus one may break off straw and grass to feed one's cattle,[12] and may move animal fodder about.[13] One is permitted to dismount from an animal on the Sabbath even if one mounted her deliberately, and to unload an animal's pack because of *tzaar baalei hayyim*.[14] If an animal falls into a cistern or an irrigation canal on the Sabbath and it is impossible to provide her with nourishment, one is permitted to place blankets and pillows beneath her so that she may ascend.[15]

The sages' ruling permitting the lifting out of both a mother animal and her young on a festival, even though there obviously is no intent to slaughter them both, is explained by Maimonides as being an example of subtlety for the sake of *tzaar baalei hayyim*.[16] On a festival one is permitted to pull off flies adhering to an animal and to assist in the delivery of a calf, or to place the calf's afterbirth over it in order to stimulate maternal love for the calf.[17]

Maimonides records the rights of the animal, clean or unclean, to eat while it is working:

> If a man said to a heathen, "Muzzle my cow and thresh with it," or if a thorn happened to be stuck in the animal's mouth, and he threshed with it while it was unable to eat, or if he caused a lion to lie down nearby, or if he caused the animal's offspring to lie down nearby, or if the animal was thirsty and he failed to give it to drink, or if he spread a skin over the threshing-floor in order to prevent the animal from eating . . . all this is forbidden.[18]

At times Maimonides' language displays sentiments of genuine warmth and compassion for the animal. He summarizes the rules requiring one to feed his servants and animals before sitting down at the table for his own meal,[19] and emphasizes that such behavior causes one to emulate God Himself, whose compassion extends to all creation, "for His tender mercies are over all His works." Maimonides concludes by observing that "he who shows mercy to animals will in turn be shown mercy by God." This reference, apparently to the episode of Rabbi Judah the Prince and the unfortunate calf, caused Rabbi David Ibn Abi Zimra (1479–1589) to comment that Maimonides' piety prompted him to interject his own personal emphasis within this legal section.[20]

But on the other hand, Maimonides' code also clearly reflects the legal disadvantages of the animal kingdom, and the severe limitations placed in the way of total compassion for the beast.

For example, on a festival it is forbidden to drip the afterbirth over a calf of an unclean animal in order to stimulate maternal feelings. Why? We are informed simply that "there is no need for it!"[21] The injunction not to take the dam with its young is applicable only to clean, nondomesticated birds; other fowl, however, are not entitled to have the dam released.[22] Finally, we are taught that on the Sabbath one is permitted to feed only those animals one is duty-bound to feed, such as domesticated animals, or nondomestic fowl, such as doves, which are reared indoors. But one may not put food or water in front of creatures which one has no obligation to feed, such as swine, or doves reared in a dovecote, or bees.[23]

Significantly, Maimonides rules with those sages who limit the prohibition against *ever min hahai* as being applicable only to "clean" animals![24] He also comments that one who removes only flesh from the limb of an animal is not guilty of violating the prohibition against eating the *limb,* but is liable only on account of consuming *terefah,*[25] and that eating less than an olive's bulk of flesh renders one exempt from any penalty.[26] It is even ruled permissible to cut a portion from an animal after *shehitah* has been performed but before life is extinct, provided that one salts the meat thoroughly, rinses it well, and waits until the animal expires.[27]

Now, clearly, all of these rulings are based on talmudic precedent. They splendidly illustrate the careful application of halakhic categories of thought to the details and variations of circumstances. But somehow a sense of real compassion for the animal seems lost in many of these discussions. After all, nonkosher animals also suffer pain, and are not minute mutilations also painful?

Jewish tradition is undeniably quite specific in setting down provisions as well as restrictions for "animal rights." Maimonides is faithful to the letter of these laws but hardly seems very concerned about furthering the spirit of mercy and compassion for dumb beasts.

With all his genius for organization, Maimonides obviously did not deem it necessary to create a special category or subdivision within the *Mishneh Torah* to be entitled *Hilkhot Tzaar Baalei Hayyim.* Instead he is content to scatter the specific bits of legislation beneficial to beasts under whatever legal categories they best fit without choosing to highlight them in a special section. However, in fairness to Maimonides, neither does the halakhic tradition to which he is bound. Furthermore, Midrash obviously plays virtually no role at all in the *Mishneh Torah*, and it is primarily in the midrashic literature that the animal is "humanized."

B. Maimonides' own philosophic convictions, as expressed in the *Moreh Nebukhim*, also structure and limit any feelings he may have had vis-à-vis the sufferings of animals. For there is a philosophic principle of great importance in Maimonidean thought, one also espoused by most medieval Jewish philosophers, which determines to a great degree his attitude toward animals. Stated simply it is this: God is concerned for the well-being of the individual human being as well as that of the human species, but God is not concerned over the fate of the individual animal. His providential care is limited to the survival of animal *species* only, not individual animals. This principle merits examination in greater detail.

Maimonides enumerates four prevalent theories concerning divine providence, each of which he refutes and rejects: (1) the theory of Epicurus, attributing all events to mere chance; (2) that of Aristotle, insisting that divine providence exists only on a general level toward the species as a whole, but not on an individual level to a single member of the species—in other words, the circumstances befalling individual humans and individual animals are attributable to mere chance; (3) the theory of the Islamic Asherites, believing that divine providence extends to all beings, animate as well as inanimate, individuals as well as entire species; and (4) that of the Mutazilites, affirming divine providence for all individual living beings, animals as well as men, but not for inanimate objects.

Maimonides then puts forth his own position: that individual providence *does* exist, but is limited to human beings only! For providence is a function of the degree of divine overflow present in an individual, i.e., the degree of development of the intellect, clearly a human enterprise. Maimonides explains:

For I for one believe that in this lowly world—I mean that which is beneath the sphere of the moon—divine providence watches only over the individuals belonging to the human species, and that in this species alone all the circumstances of the individuals and the good and evil that befall them are consequent upon the deserts, just as it says: "For all His ways are judgment." But regarding all the other animals and, all the more, the plants and other things, my opinion is that of Aristotle. For I do not by any means believe that this particular leaf has fallen because of a providence watching over it; nor that this spider has devoured this fly because God has now decreed and willed something concerning individuals; nor that the spittle spat by Zayd has moved till it came down in one particular place upon a gnat and killed it by a divine decree and judgment; nor that when this fish snatched this worm from the face of the water, this happened in virtue of a divine volition concerning individuals. For all this is in my opinion due to pure chance, just as Aristotle holds.

Maimonides proceeds to elucidate this in his reading of Scripture.

I have never found . . . a text mentioning that God has a providence watching over one of the animal individuals, but only over a human individual. . . . For this reason, killing them [animals] and employing them usefully, as we wish, has been permitted and even enjoined.[28]

Now Maimonides' position in denying divine providence to the individual animal is not to be construed as an "anti-animal" position! It is a philosophical perspective, not one of personal prejudice. Animals do not, after all, possess a rational soul as do men. Moreover, Maimonides comes close at times to denying even to certain human beings the gift of divine providence, for he maintains that the degree of divine providence is a function of the degree of "divine overflow" present in an individual. This "divine overflow" from God to man accounts for intellectual cognition and the differences in intellectual rank between individuals. Ideally, both the rational and the imaginative faculties of man are reached by the "overflow," but often this is not the case.

Maimonides clearly spells out the consequences.

Now if this is so, it follows necessarily . . . that when any human individual has obtained, because of the disposition of his matter and his training, a greater portion of this overflow than others, providence will of necessity watch more carefully over him than over others. If, that is to say, providence is, as I have mentioned, consequent upon the intellect. Accordingly, divine providence does not watch in an equal manner over all the individuals of the human species, but providence is graded as the human perfection is graded. . . . As for the ignorant and the disobedient, their state is despicable proportionately to their lack of this overflow, and they have been relegated to the rank of the individuals of all the other species of animals.[29]

Now this is not to imply that Maimonides denies that animals can experience pain. As we have seen, he did not feel that limitation of intellect renders a mother animal incapable of suffering agony upon beholding the slaughter of her young. Quite the contrary. He states that often there is no difference between the pain experienced by humans and that felt by animals. He comments, for example, upon the regulations concerning *shehitah*:

As necessity occasions the eating of animals, the commandment was intended to bring about the easiest death in an easy manner. For beheading would only be possible with the help of a sword or something similar, whereas a throat can be cut with anything. In order that death should come about more easily, the condition was imposed that the knife should be sharp.[30]

The commandment concerning the slaughtering of animals is necessary. For the natural food of man consists only of the plants deriving from the seeds growing in the earth and of the flesh of animals, the most excellent kinds of meat being those that are permitted to us. No physician is ignorant of this. Now since the necessity to have good food requires that animals be killed, the aim was to kill them in the easiest manner, and it was forbidden to torment them through killing them in a reprehensible manner by piercing the lower part of their throat or by cutting off one of their members, just as we have explained.[31]

But a reservation should be introduced at this point. It is not kindness to the animal per se that is of supreme importance to Maimonides in such cases. His emphasis is rather upon the acquisition of habits of kindness that will enhance relations between human beings, and the avoidance of the cultivation of noxious habits that will vex and pain other humans. Thus Maimonides concludes his discussion of the commandment of the "bird's nest" with the observation that "if the law takes into consideration these pains of the soul in the case of beast and birds, what will be the case with regard to the individuals of the human species as a whole?"[32]

He addresses himself to an interesting philosophical dilemma: If God's providence does not extend to the individual fauna, why then is man bidden by the Torah to manifest kindness toward individual members of the animal kingdom? Maimonides replies:

In order to perfect us so that we should not acquire moral habits of cruelty and should not inflict pain gratuitously without any utility, but that we should intend to be kind and merciful even with a chance animal individual, except in case of need "because thy soul desireth to eat flesh," for we must not kill out of cruelty or for sport.[33]

Even the prohibition against the reprehensible practice of eating a limb cut off from a living animal is justified by Maimonides on the grounds that such an act "would make one acquire the habit of cruelty."[34]

In summary, Maimonides' concern is clearly not the animal per se. Kindness toward animals is not an end in itself, but rather a training ground for the perfection of interpersonal relationships. It is therefore perfectly understandable why one should sooner assist in the loading of an enemy's ass than in the unloading of a friend's burdened animal. Similarly, it would be misleading to attribute a motive of compassion to the rule forbidding the taking of a mother-bird together with her nestlings, for the ultimate benefactors of such training in compassion would be other human beings. Furthermore, Maimonides viewed "intellect" as the supreme value to be cultivated, with ethical practice as a means to an end, but not ultimately as significant as man's intellectual development—though he surely viewed insensitivity and cruelty as interfering with one's attainment of intellectual perfection.

There may also be a trace of a polemical aspect to Maimonides' position vis-à-vis animals, particularly as pertains to his disagreement with the Mutazilites. The Mutazilites dealt with the philosophical question of how a just and beneficent deity could possibly permit injustice to take place in His world by causing innocent creatures to suffer pain. They attempted to solve the dilemma by postulating that God's rewards and compensation extend to animals for whatever pain they may have endured upon earth. Both Saadiah Gaon[35] (892–942) and Samuel ben Hofni[36] (d. 1034) concurred with this position, as did Sherira (ca. 900–1000) and Hai Gaon (939–1038), but Maimonides disagreed. He argued that although some *Geonim* believed that animals will be compensated for their sufferings in the hereafter, the notion is erroneous, and, claims Maimonides, is nowhere to be found in all of rabbinic literature![37] Is one justified on this account in attributing antianimal sentiments or an indifference to their lot to Maimonides? Hardly. The issue was purely philosophical. The Mutazilites were making a theological statement, not proposing a new policy of "kindness toward animals." Maimonides, in turn, is merely responding to their views on a philosophic level.

Limitations in Divine Providence

In their discussions dealing with divine providence, medieval Jewish philosophers spoke of both *hanhagah*, the universal providence which determines the natural order of the world as a whole, and *hashgahah*, the individual providence bestowed by God upon his specific creations.[38] As regards this latter category, there was virtually universal agreement among them, for a span of several centuries preceding and following Maimonides, that whereas divine providence extends over individual humans, it is limited to the classes of species among animals. This position, clearly articulated by Maimonides, appears to have been a basic principle in the writings of virtually all, both rationalists and mystics, philosophers and legal commentators.

For Moses Hayyim Luzzatto (1707–1747) this was easily understandable, for it was a matter of simple logic.

> Since man is unique in that he is rewarded for his deeds . . . the providence that applies to him must be different from that over all other species. The providence over any other species exists only to maintain that particular species within the bounds and limitations that God desires. He thus oversees each individual creature of that species only with respect to its effect on the species as a whole, but not as an individual. The individual merely fulfills the purpose of maintaining the species as a whole.
>
> This is not the case, however, with regard to man. Besides what each individual experiences as part of the human race as a whole, providence is also extended to him individually, for his own sake. He is thus judged individually for his deeds, and decrees are issued regarding him as an individual, according to all the details of his situation.[39]

This position stems essentially from the conviction that man stands superior to the animal, and that superiority is reflected in man's unique soul.

Aristotle's tripartite division of souls into vegetable, animal, and human (with the first two limited to powers common to both man and beast, such as growth, nutrition, perception, and movement, while the human soul is uniquely gifted with the power of intellect) was accepted by a number of Jewish philosophers and theologians, including Isaac Israeli (855–955), Saadiah Gaon, and Yehuda Halevi (1086–1141). Solomon Ibn Gabirol (1021–1069) phrases it poetically: "Thou hast formed man from a pinch of clay and breathed into him a soul, and didst impart to him the spirit of wisdom whereby man is distinguished from the beast."[40]

Man's uniqueness and superiority over the beast were seen as both evidence and rationale for the fact that God's providence, on an individual level, extends only to human beings. These philosophers may have differed as to the underlying reasons for this phenomenon. Is "intellect" the crucial factor here, with providential concern being a function of, and perhaps directly proportional to, the development of one's active intellect and one's striving to attain a "knowledge of God"? So thought Abraham Ibn Daud (ca. 1110–1180) and Gersonides (1288–1344), and, of course, Maimonides. Gersonides carefully summarizes the prevalent views concerning divine providence and rejects the commonly held notion that God's providence extends to each and every human being, advocating instead that it is bestowed only upon certain individuals and in proportion to their attainment of the active intellect,[41] essentially the position of Moses Maimonides. However, according to Hasdai Crescas (1340–1410) the degree of divine providence is dependent upon the degree of one's ethical perfection,[42] while Abarbanel (1437–1509) viewed divine providence as a simple act of grace, bestowed by God, irrespective of one's intellectual achievements or moral character. In any event, the animal is clearly a nonrecipient of such divine benefits.

The commonly held portrait of the animal was hardly a flattering one. Isaac Israeli described the animal's soul as bereft of any true intelligence. How, he muses, can one otherwise explain why an ass coming to quench its thirst at a river will flee from its own shadow, while at other times it will willingly invite certain death by approaching a lion? Since animals lack the rudiments of a basic intelligence, God neither rewards nor punishes them for their behavior, concludes Israeli.

Abraham bar Hiyya (1065–1136) taught that man alone possesses an immortal soul. Whereas the Bible describes all other forms of life as being created by means of various substances, man alone is created directly by the Lord and empowered to exercise dominion over all others. He concurs that man alone is subject to the laws of retribution, for animals, with their limited intellect, possess neither merit nor guilt.[43]

It is interesting to read Saadiah Gaon's rationale for the permissibility of butchering animals for food—one that has a polemical "anti-pagan" ring to it.

> Among the advantages, again, that result from the prohibition against the eating of [only] certain animals is the prevention of any comparison between them and the Creator. For it is inconceivable that God would permit anything resembling Him to be eaten or, on the other hand, that [the eating of such a being] could cause defilement to man. This precept also serves to keep man from worshipping any of these animals, since it is not seemly for him to worship what has been given to him for food, nor what has been declared unclean for him.[44]

For Nachmanides (1194–1270) and Recanati (late 1400's–1500's), man's right to slay individual animals for food is justified simply on the grounds that man's superior intellect grants him preeminence over the animal, which merely functions intuitively. Joseph Ibn Zaddik (d. 1149) describes man as combining all the attributes and skills of the entire animal kingdom, and additionally being endowed with a unique immortal soul and the capacity to reason. Since animals are not rational beings, they are not required to obey any laws and can be neither rewarded nor punished for their actions. Ibn Zaddik observes that man is clearly permitted by God to kill lowly creatures such as animals.

The *Sefer haYashar* (1200's) phrases man's superiority over the beast poetically:

> We see animals with their bodies bent and man with an erect posture. From this we derive that the animal's soul is from the dust and is thus drawn toward its element, therefore is the animal's body bent earthward. But the soul [of man] is drawn upwards, striving to ascend to its source.[45]

The nineteenth-century exegete Samson Raphael Hirsch described the nature of animal as though he were summarizing the dominant medieval philosophical position.

They have innate instinct, and this instinct is the voice of God, the will of God for them. Accordingly what they do in accordance with this Divine Providence which rules within them . . . and they do nothing else, can do nothing else . . . is good, and everything which this instinct keeps them back from doing, is bad. Animals do no wrong, for they have only their one nature that they are to follow. Not so man.[46]

Man alone is created "in the image of God," and although the precise meaning of the phrase has always proven to be elusive,[47] it symbolizes man's superiority over the beast.

Many attribute the uniqueness of man in having been created in God's image to his capacity for speech. Onkelos renders "and man became a living animal" as "it [the breath] became a speaking spirit in man."[48] Likewise Rashi (1040–1105) and Nachmanides seem to identify man's uniqueness with his faculty for speech, and the classic differentiation between man and animal in medieval Jewish philosophy is man's designation as the creature capable of speech. Indeed Saadiah Gaon describes the animal world as the "nonspeakers,"[49] while Halevi designates man as the *medabber*, i.e., "he who speaks," in contradistinction to other forms of life, which are merely *tzomeah* ("animate") or *hai* ("living").[50]

Therefore it is not surprising to find scholars uncomfortable when affinities are noted between man and animal in postrabbinic literature, particularly such an affinity as the animal's alleged capacity for speech.

For example, Maimonides describes the *adne hasadeh* (mountain-men or *bar-nash detur*)[51] as animals purportedly possessing the capacity to speak in a manner similar to humans.[52] Interestingly, the Arabic phrase employed by Maimonides, *al-nanas*, is the Egyptian Arabic term for *kof*, or "ape." Menahem Hameiri (1249–1316) comments that "one can teach an ape seventy languages"![53] Maimonides believed that animals possess an imaginative faculty similar to that of man, and a soul capable of reflection and feeling pain,[54] although he emphasizes that only humans possess the capacity for *hasagah sikhlit*, i.e., intellectual apprehension.[55]

On the other hand, Saadiah Gaon denies that any animal is able to speak, claiming that even such miraculous creatures as the serpent of the Garden of Eden and the ass of Balaam did not actually utter words on their own power. He attributes their apparent communications to an angel and to Satan, respectively, who were functioning on their behalf.[56] Abraham Ibn Ezra (1092–1167) and Nachmanides do accept the fact of the speaking ass, but claim this to have been a singularly miraculous event, while the nineteenth-century scholar Samuel David Luzzatto (1800–1865) emphasizes that the biblical text does not explicitly state that the ass actually spoke words![57] Most likely, he concludes, Balaam was able to perceive verbal content in its natural braying. Suffice to say, man and man alone is gifted with the power of speech, and it is inconceivable, not to mention uncomfortable, to endow animals with similar powers.

Scattered through the writings of Joseph Albo (d. 1444) are several theories purporting to explain the nature of man's superiority over the beast.

Man, who is the end of all the lower creatures, is nobler and more perfect than all, since in him are combined all the earlier forms.[58]

In the lower animals the only perfection that is expected of them is the perfection of existence; as soon as they come into existence, the good of which they are capable is attained and completed, and no other good is expected of them.[59]

As for irrational animals, they are devoid of reason.[60]

Because of these factors, declares Albo, "reward and punishment for lower animals concerns itself merely with the preservation of the species."[61]

What then of the vivid biblical and rabbinic passages which would appear to emphasize precisely the opposite: namely, that God does manifest concern and compassion for all fauna, and that He "nourishes both the horns of the wild ox and the ova of the lice"?[62]

These passages are, for the most part, interpreted to apply to the *species* of animals, not to *individuals*. The author of the *Sefer haHinnukh* (late 13th cent.) declares:

> The providence of God, blessed be He, over all His creatures extends in the case of the human species to the individual, as it is written, "For His eyes are upon the ways of man, and all his steps does He see" [Job 34:21]. In the case of all other living creatures it extends to the species in general; that is, God's desire that the species be perpetuated. [63]

In discussing the law prohibiting the slaughter of an animal and its offspring on the same day, the *Sefer haHinnukh* comments:

> The purpose of this commandment is that a man should take to heart the fact that God's providence extends generally to all species of living creatures, and that by His providence over them will they continue to exist forever; for divine providence in relation to things constitutes their very existence. Hence none of the species will ever become totally extinct. And though divine providence in the case of the human species extends to the individual, it is not so in regard to other living creatures. [64]

Similarly, David Kimhi (1160–1235?) justifies God's decision to eradicate all living beings from the face of the earth because of man's wickedness on the grounds that animals were created for man, and, furthermore, God's providence extends only to the general species, not individual animals. Since the general species of all animals were to be preserved, [65] it was clearly proper to destroy a great many individual creatures.

It is noteworthy that even kabbalistic literature, which emphasizes the unity of *all* being, and the reality of God's breath permeating *all* of life, admits to gradations of divinity. The further one is from the *En Sof,* "the source," the less pure and more material one becomes. Thus, while the kingdom of fauna stands on a higher rung than the flora kingdom, it is clearly beneath the level occupied by humans. For man alone is the ultimate purpose of all creation, and a microcosm representing in his physical structure the structure of the universe, and one may even foretell future events by means of his physiognomy![66]

Divine providence plays an exceedingly important role in kabbalistic thinking, underlying the hidden order of all planes of creation and determining the minutest detail of every event. Yet here, too, a clear distinction is drawn between man and animal, and the author of the *Zohar* also points out that whereas God's providence extends to individual human beings, it is vouchsafed only to the generic essences of animals, but not to individual beasts.

It is true that Moses b. Joseph Cordovero's (1522–1570) detailed analysis of the question of divine providence raises the possibility that God may, at times, act on behalf of individual members of the animal kingdom, but he emphasizes that "this is not for the sake of the animals themselvs, but for the sake of man . . . for individual providence does not apply to any ox or lamb, but to the entire species together . . . but if divine providence applies to a man, it will encompass even his pitcher, should it break, and his dish, should it crack, and all his possessions . . . if he should be chastised or not."[67]

Only among the Karaites do we find sustained voices being raised in defense of divine providence for the individual beast. Joseph b. Abraham al-Basir (early 11th cent.), the Karaite philosopher, holds forth the promise of rich rewards and compensations in eternity for all animals who have endured pain on earth;[68] and Aaron b. Elijah of Nicomedia (1300–1369) taught that God's providence extends to individual beasts as well as to men. But even these utterances were apparently not motivated by any great sense of compassion or fairness toward the animal. It is, rather, a matter of philosophical consistency. Aaron b. Elijah emphasizes that the true purpose of the biblical legislation enjoining compassion for the beast is to train us to develop qualities of compassion vis-à-vis humans, and he wholly approves of butchering animals for food.[69]

New Rationales for Kindness to Animals

The principle articulated by so many, that providential concern is limited to the general species rather than to the individual animal, finds its logical extension in the interpretations given for the scriptural commandments advocating kindness toward animals.

For why, indeed, should a human being behave kindly toward a single animal when God Himself limits His concern to the general species? Precisely because an entire species might conceivably be obliterated with the death of a single animal!

For example, Nachmanides does not deny that the commandments prohibiting the slaughter of an animal together with its young and enjoining one to spare the mother bird when taking the young reflect an abhorrence of cruelty toward animals. Yet he emphasizes that their central purpose is to ensure the preservation of the species![70] Bahya b. Asher (d. 1340),[71] the *Sefer haHinnukh*,[72] and the *Kol Bo* (late 13th cent.)[73] all concur that such legislation is designed to prevent the possible disappearance, however unlikely that may be, of any form of fauna species.

Related to this is a similar concern that the "purity" of all species be kept intact. This is both Maimonides' and Nachmanides' rationale for the prohibition against plowing a field with a team consisting of an ox and a donkey. Conceivably, these animals will be placed in one stable and may eventually mate together! Such cross-breeding clearly violates the integrity of the Lord's creations.

"Respect the Divine order in God's creations. . . . You should not interfere with the natural order which you find fixed by God in His world for its ultimate good."[74] In such a way, centuries later, S. R. Hirsch summarized the essential purport and underlying unity of the legislation prohibiting the mating of diverse species of animals, the grafting of diverse trees and herbs, the wearing of wool and linen, boiling milk and meat together, and working in the fields with two different species of animals.

Recanati develops the interesting theory that wild animals merit greater respect than domesticated beasts precisely because they exist in a mode and manner more authentically faithful to the laws designed for them by their Creator. Domesticated species, on the other hand, as a result of their subservience to man, are no longer in such close harmony with the laws of nature. This is Recanati's explanation for the ruling limiting the covering of the blood of a dead animal to birds and wild beasts alone.[75] It is noteworthy that Jacob Emden (1697–1776) later advocates precisely the opposite, maintaining that the prohibition against causing suffering to a living being is applicable only in the case of domestic beasts which serve man. Insects, however, which are clearly of no utilitarian value, may be destroyed without mercy.[76]

Another popular rationale for the laws enjoining kindness toward animals was strictly utilitarian: Be nice to an animal, because you will thereby condition yourself to be nice to your fellow humans. For Abraham Ibn Ezra, Abarbanel, Luzzatto, etc., seething a kid in its mother's milk is a barbaric practice that will tend to harden a man's heart and make him cruel. For the *Sefer haHinnukh,* muzzling an ox treading corn is forbidden because of its negative ramifications vis-à-vis the treatment of human laborers.

When a man becomes accustomed to have pity even upon animals who were created only to serve us, and he gives them a portion of their labors, his soul will likewise grow accustomed to be kind to human beings and he will refrain from depriving them of anything that is due them. He will pay them their rightful wages, and he will satisfy them from the fruit of their labors. This is the proper way for a holy and chosen people to follow.[77]

Nachmanides, in analyzing the passage dealing with the "bird's nest," cites Maimonides' observation that as there is no difference between the distress of humans and the distress of animals for their young, we are therefore exhorted to spare the mother bird such agony. But Nachmanides proceeds to develop his own thesis— that all such commandments have as their central purpose the development of sensitivity among human beings for one another.

It was not a matter of God's mercy extending to the bird's nest or the dam and its young, since His mercies did not extend so far into animal life as to prevent us from accomplishing our needs with them, for, if so, He would have forbidden slaughter altogether. But the reason for the prohibition [against taking the dam with its nest, or against killing the dam with its young in one day] is to teach us the trait of compassion and that we should not be cruel, for cruelty proliferates in man's soul, and it is known that butchers, those who slaughter large oxen and asses, are "men of blood"; "they that slaughter men" are extremely cruel. It is on account of this [cruelty] that the rabbis have said; "the most seemly among butchers is a partner of Amalek." Thus these commandments with respect to cattle and fowl are not [a result of] compassion upon them, but they are decrees upon us to guide us and to teach us traits of good character.[78]

Indeed, this is Maimonides' central point as well. "If the Law provides that such grief should not be caused to cattle or birds, how much more careful must we be that we should not cause grief to our fellowmen."[79]

In a similar vein, Solomon Efraim Lunchitz (author of *Keli Yakar*) observes that the injunction regarding the "bird's nest" and the obligation to honor one's parents hold forth the identical promise of reward, "that it may be well with you and enable you to prolong your days." Why? One of the explanations he advances is that when children see their parents behaving compassionately toward a mother bird, they will surely conclude that they are obligated to be kind to their own parents.

In an interesting variation upon the theme, Recanati sees in the "bird's nest" a gentle reminder to God Himself to reconsider His own acts of "cruelty" toward the Children of Israel! This commentator interprets the act of sending off the mother bird to be a cruel one. God should similarly regret His having forcibly removed His divine presence from His children, Israel!

Many a biblical injunction which would appear to be motivated out of a sense of compassion for an animal is given a variety of interpretations, many of which are totally unrelated to compassion. For example, what is the purpose of the laws regulating *shehitah?* True, they cause the animal a minimal amount of pain, but, according to the *Sefer haHinnukh,* they also ensure a quick and thorough drainage of all blood![80] Why must one delay offering a sacrificial animal until it is at least eight days old? So as not to force a painful separation of mother and child? Hardly. According to Maimonides, the reason stems from the fact that such a young animal has no appreciable value, for "it is deficient among those of its kind and is considered disgusting, for it resembles an abortion,"[81] while the *Sefer haHinnukh* also deems such a creature to be unacceptable as an offering because it is not yet totally formed.[82] On the other hand, Jacob ben Asher, author of the *Arba'ah Turim* (d. 1340), cites the talmudic teaching that the symbolic representations of the first seven days would render the animal unacceptable, while the author of *Keli Yakar* extols the virtues of the number eight. Clearly, many rationales have been adduced for this commandment that seem to have nothing at all to do with compassion for the beast.

Even the biblically derived concept of *tzaar baalei hayyim* failed to have much impact in certain areas of "animal rights." For example, Joseph Ibn Habibah's *Nimukei Yosef* (1300's) seems to differentiate between the degrees of pain suffered by animals, claiming that while it is true that extremely excruciating pain constitutes a violation of *tzaar baalei hayyim,* lesser degrees of pain are merely violations of rabbinic injunctions alone. Significantly, Jacob Joshua of Frankfort's *Pnei Yehoshua,* Mordecai ben Hillel (13th cent.),[83] and, as previously noted, the Gaon of Vilna seem to suggest that there is no clear biblical prohibiton against causing an animal pain!

Whatever the case, *Nimukei Yosef* overrules the principle of *tzaar baalei hayyim* whenever it comes into conflict with the honor and dignity of human beings. He raises the question as to why an elderly man is exempted from the obligation of assisting in the unloading of an animal's burden. Obviously, he concludes, it is because such activities are beneath his dignity, and the honor of the elderly takes precedence over the pain of an animal.[84]

There is ample precedent for this notion. The fact that animals may be hamstrung or even mutilated in order to pay homage to a ruler or prince is clear evidence that *tzaar baalei hayyim* may indeed be superseded.[85]

Halakhic authorities were in general agreement that it is perfectly permissible to employ animals as subjects for medical experimentation even though they may be caused great discomfort or even death in the course of the experiment. This is because human welfare clearly overrules the "rights of animals."[86] Some, however, such as Jacob ben Joseph Reischer (ca. 1670–1733), limit such experimentation upon animals to the oral administration of drugs and potions, while forbidding more painful surgical procedures.[87]

Ezekiel Landau's (1720–1793) celebrated responsum on the subject of hunting,[88] while criticizing the activity as "un-Jewish," nevertheless points out that it is theoretically permissible for man to hunt and to kill animals, or to do almost anything to them, so long as he derives some utilitarian value from them. Furthermore, writes Landau, *tzaar baalei hayyim* does not apply to the *killing* of animals. Killing an animal is not forbidden by Jewish law; it is the mistreatment of living creatures that is forbidden. Landau cites as a proof-text the episode of Pinhas b. Yair's visit to the home of Rabbi Judah. Rabbi Pinhas feared to enter the premises because of the latter's white mules. It was deemed cruel to hamstring the animals, but perfectly acceptable to have them killed.[89]

But even obvious mistreatment of animals is justified on the grounds that there is utilitarian value, i.e., religious or economic benefit, for humans. It is therefore theoretically permissible, for example, to use an animal as a wall for a *succah* (a booth constructed for the feast of Tabernacles) and force it to stand in a stationary position! And Rabbi David Halevi *(TaZ)* (1586–1667) permits one to kill an animal in a painful manner by stabbing it through the throat because its uncut skin can be sold in the marketplace for a higher price.[90]

Nonthreatening Symbolism

Thus far the portrait of the animal in postrabbinical literature has not been a particularly colorful one. It would appear to be essentially the demythologized "biblical" animal that has been described, a limited creature of secondary importance in the scheme of things in the eyes of both God and man, a living "tool" brought into existence by God to serve man.

But what of the cautiously remythologized "rabbinic" animal? What of the midrashic passages in rabbinic literature extolling the supernatural qualities and curative powers of certain fauna? What of the deployment of the animal in magical ceremonies, and its association with demonology?

At first glance, all the above would seem to be commonly characteristic of the folk myth, folk medicine, and folk magic pervading Jewish life in the Middle Ages.

Folk myths undoubtedly endowed fauna with extraordinary traits. For example, the bizarre creature of rabbinic legend known as the "plant-man" sprouts forth with elaborate detail. Meir of Kalonymos's vivid description is cited in a commentary upon the Mishnah.[91]

A sort of long string grows out of a root in the ground, and to this string the animal called *yadua* is attached at its navel like a gourd or melon, but the *yadua* has the shape of a man in every particular, face, body, hands and feet. No one can approach closer than the radius of the string, for it uproots and destroys everything within its reach. One may capture it only by shooting at the string until it breaks, whereupon the animal dies.[92]

The mysteries of spontaneous generation were further elaborated upon in the Middle Ages, with the "barnacle goose" playing a significant role. Much speculation centered around its mysterious origins, possibly from shellfish in shallow waters, possibly from the branches of trees. Such speculation found logical extension in halakhic queries: Should this entity be treated as a fowl vis-à-vis ritual slaughter? Or is it, in reality, a fish or a fruit, depending upon which theory of origin one espouses? As noted earlier, Rabbenu Tam insisted on ritual slaughter.[93]

Jewish demonology of the Middle Ages often elaborated upon motifs already present in rabbinic literature, but, notably in the thirteenth century, German, French, and Latin names of demons make their appearance in Jewish lore, testifying to the assimilation of non-Jewish elements into the folk magic of the Jews.[94] Thus we encounter the *estrie*, a black sucking vampire which could assume animal forms, and the *werewolf*, which often took the shape of a wolf in attacking its victims.

The folk belief in magic and sorcery led to the blurring of the demarcations between man and animal, with the former assuming the shapes of the latter, and the latter exerting powerful influences upon the behavior of the former. This was a common motif in non-Jewish circles and is also reflected in Jewish medieval legends.

We encounter in Jewish sources, and in Christian sources, the episode of a man fighting off a cat which attacks him, only to later encounter a severely wounded woman, whom he recognizes as being the human transformation of that same cat,[95] and the terrifying metamorphosis of a human being into a werewolf.[96] The demoness Lilith was also believed to be capable of assuming the guise of wild animals and birds in spreading her terror.[97]

And as for skeptics, Moses of Tachau records how the doubter Abraham Ibn Ezra, who denied the existence of demons, came upon demonic powers in the form of black dogs, an encounter which eventually caused him to take seriously ill and die.[98]

Animals and animal parts are occasionally employed in magical ceremonies in a manner reminiscent of some of the talmudic procedures. For example, we are told that a lock may be opened by striking it with the right foot of a male raven which has been smeared with the fat of a snake.[99] A more elaborate ceremony, involving the casting of a love spell, recommends that one

secure an egg laid on a Thursday by a jet-black hen which had never laid an egg before, and on the same day, after sunset, bury it at a crossroads. Leave it there three days; then dig it up after sunset, sell it, and purchase with the proceeds a mirror, which you must bury in the same spot in the evening "in Frau Venus namen," and say "allhie begrab ich diesen spiegel in der Libe, die Frau Venus zu dem Dannhäuser hat." Sleep on that site three nights, then remove the mirror, and whoever looks into it will love you![100]

The popularity of fauna in dream omina is evident in Solomon b. Jacob Almoli's (Turkey, 16th cent.) *Pitron Halomot,* a volume which underwent several publications and was popular among Ashkenazi Jewry as well, through its 1694 Yiddish translation. It contains a comprehensive glossary of dream symbolism, listing fauna, flora, as well as inanimate objects with their corresponding significance within the dream fabric.

Fauna also played their role as "living" omina. Many animals, dogs in particular, were believed to possess an acute sensitivity, unshared by humans, to the presence of demons. Thus the mundane occurrence of a horse or ass snorting and neighing and refusing to proceed upon its journey would be attributed to the beast's sensing the presence of a demon, or even the angel of death, in its path.[101] The story is told of a saintly man who was never barked at by dogs. When, for the first time, a dog barked at him, he took this to be an omen of his impending death and bade his wife prepare the shrouds for his burial.[102]

The Animal as a Scapegoat

The ancient belief that a human life could be spared via the sacrificial substitution of the life of an animal also found interesting elaboration in the medieval world.

For example, people are cautioned concerning the inherent danger in building a home of stone, or in constructing a domicile upon a parcel of land never before inhabited. A precaution consisted in having a rooster and a hen placed within the house for an interval of time and then slaughtered. In this way, it was believed, the human inhabitants would be spared.[103] The rabbinic observation that dogs are sensitive to the presence of the angel of death found its extension in the notion that should the animal's master push it toward the angel of death, the dog would die, for "the dog then serves as a substitute for the man whom the angel of death has been sent to kill."[104]

The most noteworthy of scapegoat rituals was the rite of *kapparah*. On the eve of Yom Kippur a fowl (usually a cock for males and a hen for females) was raised and thrice circled around one's head while the individual would intone: "This fowl is my substitute, this is my substitute, my vicarious atonement . . . this cock [or hen] will be designated for death, but I shall have life." Although this rite met with disapproval on the part of some of the leading rabbinic authorities—Solomon b. Abraham Adret condemned the ritual as a heathen superstition,[105] Nachmanides also opposed it, as did Joseph Karo, who designated it as a "silly custom"[106]—*kapparot* had the support of many mystics, and it became popular among the masses. Indeed, the choice of a cock had already been advocated during the geonic period on the persuasive grounds that the word *gever* meant both "cock" and "man," and therefore the fowl was the most appropriate substitute for the intended human victim.

There is no need to belabor the point. The folk beliefs and folk practices of medieval Jewry surely incorporated fauna. But two qualifications merit consideration. First, the animal's role was a comparatively limited one in the fabric of magic. Secondly, a distinction should be drawn between a *belief* in magic and the *practice* of magic.

The first qualification is best illustrated by the fact that "the use of parts of the human body and animals in sympathetic magic was very common in medieval Europe, but exceedingly rare in Jewish practice."[107] Needless to say, this was due to a substantial degree to halakhic prohibitions on the use of blood, animal corpses, and the flesh of nonkosher species of animals. It is only rarely that one encounters among Jews love charms prescribing the use of such "sexually active" creatures as the guinea pig, mole, or hen. It is significant that amulets were the most popular magical devices among Jews of the Middle Ages, and the overwhelming majority of Jewish amulets consisted of writings, rather than such popular animal parts as foxtails.

Of even greater significance is the fact that folk superstitions were not practiced by *all* folk. Many such customs were condemned as "idolatrous" by rabbinic authorities, many more as "foolish." Moreover, even among the practitioners of superstition, there were those who clearly did not "believe" in the superstition. *Sefer Hasidim* expresses the thought pithily: "One should not believe in superstitions, but it is still best to be heedful of them."[108] Or, "Superstitions harm only those who heed them."[109]

To return to our earlier question, what impact did the remythologized fauna of rabbinic literature have upon subsequent generations? Undoubtedly there were many who took literally *all* of the rabbinic observations concerning the natural world. Others, however, declined to do so when such observations ran counter to experience and acceptable evidence.

Thus Leviathan and his cohorts, along with the impressive animal menagerie of Rabbah bar bar Hana, were either viewed as singular creatures totally unrelated to the "normal" members of the animal kingdom or allegorized out of any real existence by such diverse commentators as Yom Tov Ishbili, Samuel Edels, and Meir Lebush (*Malbim*). For example, the dramatic story of Titus' painful death through the agency of a gnat which entered his brain[110] is analyzed by Azariah ben Moses dei Rossi (ca. 1511–ca. 1578) as a moral poem illustrating the truth that God can destroy even the mightiest despots with one of His most insignificant creatures.[111]

As for talmudic medical prescriptions involving animals, Sherira Gaon writes:

We must tell you that our sages were no physicians; they only recommended that which experience had proved helpful. Their counsels in this field are by no means laws. You must not, therefore, rely on medicines mentioned in the Talmud. Only he may use them who had been examined and confirmed by experienced physicians, and who has the assurance that at least they can do no harm. Thus our forefathers also teach us that one may employ only those remedies of which it is certain they produce no injurious effects.[112]

Similarly, rabbinic insights into the world of natural science and zoology were not always accepted as factual. Abraham Maimuni (1186–1237), the son of Maimonides, writes in the introduction to his *Haggadah:*

> It does not at all follow that because we bow to the authority of the sages of the Talmud in all that appertains to the interpretation of the Torah in its principles and details, we must accept unquestionably all their dicta on scientific matters such as medicine, physics, and astronomy. We ought to be quite prepared to find that some of their statements coming within the purview of science are not borne out by the science of our times.

Jacob b. Moses Halevi Mollin (1356–1457) discouraged the use of rabbinically prescribed remedies on the general grounds that "we may not employ any of the cures and charms given in the Talmud, for we no longer know how to apply them correctly," and states that the rabbis occasionally erred in their medical observations,[113] a comment with which Akiva b. Moses Eger (1761–1837) concurs.[114] The Tosafists at times ignored talmudic medical prescriptions, not only on the grounds that it is impossible to accurately identify certain herbs, but because "human nature has changed,"[115] and Moses Sofer (*Hatam Sofer*) (1762–1839) explains that the reason why Maimonides' *Mishneh Torah* fails to cite the talmudic prohibition against the roasting of meat and fish together is because "Maimonides tested the matter by investigation and found that conditions had changed."[116]

Suffice to say that for philosophers and legal authorities alike, spanning the centuries, rabbinic observations reflecting a sense of "awe" for the common animal were often not taken literally, and some of the alleged curative powers of animals were also a matter of doubt.

It is legitimate, however, to inquire as to the effect that postrabbinical folk literature had upon the image of the animal. Among the more popular volumes of this type was *Kalila wa-Dimna,* a twelfth-century translation of centuries-old Hindu fables, the *Sefer Sha'ashuim* ("Book of Delight") by Joseph b. Meir Zabara (early 13th cent.), *the Ben ha-Melek ve-ha-Nazir* of Abraham Ibn Hasdai (early 13th cent.), and especially the collection of *Mishlei Shualim* ("Fox-Fables") of Berakiah ben Natronai Krespia Ha-Nakdan (12th-13th cent.), a noted fabulist who authored over one hundred fables.

One may ask whether such animal tales and animal fables did not serve to "humanize" the animal in the minds of listeners and readers. Possibly they did, but this is doubtful, for this genre of literature dealt primarily with the same basic standard themes that were already popular in rabbinic times, drawing upon many *midrashim* as well as the fables of other cultures to illustrate the drama of the human condition by means of animal bit-players. The animal actors in these vignettes are generally made to play their "normal" roles. The fox remains a sly, crafty manipulator, surviving in a hostile world by means of his wits, and often at the expense of his less-cerebrally endowed animal companions, such as the wolf and the bear. Occasionally there are moralistic overtones to the fox-stories, other times craftiness and deceit are highlighted for their own sake, but as a general rule these dramas bear witness to the triumph of brain over brawn which alone enables the weak to survive in a world of giants.

We cite, by way of example, the following selections from the one-hundred-and-seven-fable collection of *Mishlei Shualim*.

An ox once met a lion on his way and fled from him. In deathly terror he heard the lion's angry roars behind him. Crawling barely alive into a cave, he sought safety there. Suddenly in a corner he saw a he-goat. The ox trembled mightily and could not stand on his feet. Astonished the he-goat asks, "Why do you tremble so? We are, after all, like brothers, raised from childhood on the same flock." "Ah," answers the other, "all animals now appear to me like wild leopards and lions. Yesterday, I would not have been afraid of, or hidden from, anyone. Today the lion attacked me, and I tremble before every shadow."

The moral:
He who is persecuted and cast down
Trembles constantly before afflictions and plagues.
In every corner, in every nook,
He senses only danger and terror,
For in everyone he sees deathly hostility.
He always thinks he will be discovered by his enemy;
Before every rustling leaf he runs away in fright.

Near a pond in an open field two deer stand. One tells the other a quiet secret. A stranger would not have understood a word. A man passes by and, in surprise, asks the deer, "Why such stillness? You both stand quite alone and may express your thoughts aloud; no one will overhear your secret." "No," they reply, "we are not telling any secrets. We simply have no strength. Our minds are weakened, and we are glad to do nothing."

The moral:
When fools are silent and do not raise their voices,
They are considered wise, all praise and laud them.
If the fool reveals what he thinks and believes,
He is mocked and laughed at by all.[117]

The *Kalila wa-Dimna* collection occasionally extols the virtues of the animal kingdom above those of its human counterpart. We read, for example, an elaborate tale of how a hermit rescues an ape, a serpent, and a viper from a pit which had been dug by hunters. The animals warn the hermit not to save a goldsmith also trapped in the pit, because "there is none so ungrateful on earth as man," but the hermit takes pity on the helpless goldsmith and rescues him. As the story unfolds, the animals treat the hermit kindly and reward him for having saved them, while the goldsmith jeopardizes the hermit's life by implicating him in the murder of a king's daughter. Fortunately, he is saved from death by the cleverness of the serpent.[118]

Not infrequently animal dramas assume a distinctively "Jewish" coloration. Talmudic and midrashic stories are interwoven with the Indian-Arabic text of *Ben ha-Melek ve-ha-Nazir,* and Ibn Hasdai is an eloquent preacher of prophetic ideals.

Three things grieve me greatly, and the fourth tears my heart to pieces: When the mighty wings of the eagle are cut down and flies spread their wings over his head; when the horns of the ox are broken and timorous little lambs push him about; and when the sick lion must be humbly silent before the little foxes which only yesterday trembled before his shadow. But more terrible than all these is when the man of righteousness and justice is trodden underfoot by vile clods and arrogant barbarians.

The fable poet Isaac b. Solomon Ibn Sahulah (b. 1244) provides the rationale behind the Judaization process that took place.

I saw that many of our people ran after foreign models. They were dazzled by Greek philosophy and are charmed by Arabic fables and various foreign tales. What is strange pleases them most. So I said to them bitterly, "You children of the holy stock, you who stem from the source of eternal light! You have become like Gypsies. Your own treasures you cast into the dust, and chase after foreign playthings and worthless trifles. . . . Behold, I will now create something new. I will take these fables, parables and tales for which you are so eager, stories about beasts of the field and birds of the deserts, and will wrap them not in foreign garments, and weave them together, not with sayings and maxims of foreign sages . . . Ishmaelites, Edomites, Moabites and Arabs—but with the words of our Torah, with the divine parables of our prophets, and with the wise riddles and allusions of our Talmudic sages." . . . And in order that my *Meshal haKadmoni* should please the children also and be loved by them, and that they should eagerly read my stories. I have adorned them with beautiful pictures and illustrations.[119]

Not surprisingly, the animal characters appearing in Ibn Sahu-lah's *Meshal haKadmoni* manifest an impressive degree of expertise in their knowledge of biblical texts and aggadic lore. A deer is expert in talmudic studies, a rabbit proficient in rabbinic codes, and even the hawk discusses the laws of damages in the manner of a student in a talmudical academy.[120]

Some three centuries later, the popular *Ku-Bukh* ("Cow-Book") presented Jewish readers with a similar menagerie of scholarly fauna. A dog courting a cow is rebuked by the latter. The dog indignantly replies:

> But I am pious and honest,
> And do nothing other than the right.
> For I am of good stock,
> My native piety guards me
> For many long years.
> I am descended from the pious and quiet canines
> Who refused to bark in Egypt
> On the night Israel left the land.
> And therefore they received a good reward from God;
> He bade that they be given all the ritually
>   forbidden food
> That they, too, might live in luxury,
> As is proper according to the law.
> Of canine stock, I claim my pedigree
> From all the best and pious;
> From these have I come here.
> The dog named Schlager was my cousin
> And the dog Muftil belongs to my family.[121]

Many fables recount interactions between humans and beasts, with the former often depicted as aiding animals in distress, but, significantly, such acts of kindness are often unappreciated, and a good portion of the time humans suffer at the hands of their ungrateful animal clientele.

As would be expected, the same themes often appear in differ-ent collections of stories with variations in detail. Both *Kalila* wa-Dimna[122] and *Mishlei Shualim*[123] contain accounts of a mouse seeking out a mate for itself. The *Kalila wa-Dimna* version describes a female mouse which has been transformed into a beautiful maiden. The maiden declares: "I desire a very brave and valiant husband with whom none can compare for strength or power." A Nazarite approaches the sun in prayer, beseeching it to marry off the maiden to its master, but the sun refers him to the more powerful ruler of the clouds, who in turn sends him off to the lord of the winds, who refers him to the all-powerful mountain. But the mountain confesses that there exists a power stronger than it, capable of digging into it and penetrating it—namely, the mouse. The Nazarite calls upon divine assistance and the maiden is transformed back into a she-mouse so that she can become the wife of the mountain-boring mouse.

In *Mishlei Shualim,* it is the he-mouse that seeks out a mate for himself. He approaches the sun and courts her with the words: "I love you with an everlasting love, therefore I beg you to come down from above and I shall pay your bridal price and wed you." But the sun declines, explaining: "I am but a servant to the cloud, for whenever it desires, I am clad in darkness." The mouse then proclaims to the cloud: "Indeed, I have toiled and found, O cloud most fair and fine, and by counsel of the sun I wish to make you mine, and I shall never forsake you." But the cloud replies: "He who is high above the high has placed me in the hands of the wind, which bears me wherever it finds to be best, whether north or south or east or west. With might and main it carries me away. Now if a wife like me you desire, you will be wandering to and fro on earth until you tire. Forsake the maid and the lady take, for the wind can make me or it can break. Go to the wind and dwell with her, entice her if you can."

So the mouse approaches the wind and declares: "Have no fear. But haste away to the hills with me, for of all the females I did see in these times and our present age, you are the best and most fit for me, so you be mine and I shall be yours." But the wind answers: "Why do you come to take me? You do not know how abject I be, for I have no strength or power to blow down a wall at any hour, whether of stone or earth it be. I am not strong at all, you see, when a wall is stronger than me. So if it should seem fit to you and you can persuade her to be faithful and true, let her be our citadel and stay."

The mouse then addresses the wall: "Listen to me, for I would have you know the counsel of the sun and the cloud and the wind, and they advise that I should ask you to be sweet and kind to me, so that we may wed, you see." But the wall answered in rage: "They sent you to me to display my shame and reproach. You have come to remind me that they are all of them free to rise up and go down while my stone and wall cannot move at all, and I have neither strength nor power, and any mouse or worm can make me bare and dig into my base and make themselves a ladder and a stair. Though I may be an upthrust wall, they injure me with their mouths and feet as though I had no strength at all, and the mice come here with all their kin and dwell in me, the mothers and their litters. And they have many a hundred nests, and I cannot stand against them at the best. And do you desire a wife like me?" Seeing that his hopes were in vain, the mouse took another mouse for his wife.

Another story making its appearance in several collections concerns a huntsman who captures a bird and prepares to kill and eat it. *Ben ha-Melekh ve-ha-Nazir*[124] describes the bird pleading for its life and promising in return to reveal to its captor the words of wisdom engraved upon a tablet belonging to the prophet Shem: "Do not sorrow for what you have lost, do not seek what you cannot obtain, do not believe what cannot be." Impressed with these enigmatic words of wisdom, the huntsman frees the bird. But the latter mocks him for his foolishness; "How silly you are! If only you knew what you have lost you would weep and sorrow till your very last day . . . if you had slain me as you had in mind, you would have found a pearl in me of the very best kind, as large as an ostrich egg and all your life you would not need to beg but would be richer than all who were before you." When the huntsman hears these words, he beseeches the bird to return, promising that he will guard it from all harm. "O foolish one," replies the bird. "You do not keep the counsel I gave, nor are the words I taught you of any aid. I said you should not seek what you cannot obtain, and not bemoan what is lost and gone, and not believe what cannot be true. You seek for me and cannot come near, you sorrow and moan for what is lost and gone, and you believe what is not worthy of belief. For you believe a stone as large as an ostrich egg can be hidden within me, when an ostrich egg is far bigger than the whole of my body."

A parallel version describes how a certain huntsman once caught a bird that knew seventy languages.[125] The bird said to him: "If you set me free, I shall teach you three wise sayings." "Teach them to me," said the huntsman, "and I shall let you go." "Swear to me," answered the bird, "that you will let me go after I have taught them to you." The huntsman took an oath and the bird said to him: "The first wise saying is: 'After a thing has been done, do not regret it.' The second is: 'If a man tells you something that cannot be done, do not believe him.' And the third is: 'If you cannot climb up, do not weary yourself trying to climb up.'" Then it said to the huntsman: "Let me go," and the huntsman set him free.

The bird flew off, perched on a tree that was loftier than all the other trees, and laughed at the huntsman, saying: "You set me free and you did not know that in my crop I have a pearl that is worth more than a thousand dinars, and it is the only thing that makes me wise." At this, the huntsman regretted what he had done and ran to the foot of the tree and started to climb it. But when he had climbed halfway, he fell and broke his legs and twisted all his joints.

Then the bird mocked him indeed and said: "Fool of the world, you did not act according to the wise sayings I taught you even for a few moments. I told you that once a thing is done you should not regret it, yet you regretted having let me go! And I told you that if anybody tells you something impossible, do not believe him, yet you believed that I have a pearl in my crop! Yet I am only a bird that flies and seeks food all day long. I told you that where you cannot climb you should not tire yourself out trying, and yet you had to run after me till you fell and broke your legs and twisted your limbs! It was said about you in the Book of Proverbs, 'A rebuke enters deeper into a man of understanding than a hundred stripes into a fool.' Many men are wiseacres like you."

Occasionally bizarre and grotesque creatures make their literary appearances, as is the case in Gerson b. Eliezer of Prague's seventeenth-century adventure-travel-novel, *Gelilot Eretz Yisrael*. But no one seems to suggest that these beasts are to be taken seriously, or that they actually possess divine or demonic powers.

Animals do appear more frequently in art-forms, but almost invariably they are confined within the context of religious symbolism. Thus the *parohet* (ark-covering) and Torah covers often bore the forms of such fauna as lions, leopards, gazelles, and eagles, symbolizing Judah b. Tema's dictum: "Be bold as a leopard and light as an eagle and swift as a gazelle and strong as a lion to do the will of the Father which is in heaven."[126] *Hallot* (bread) for Rosh Hashanah were baked in the shape of birds to symbolize Isaiah's promise that "as birds hovering, so will the Lord of hosts defend Jerusalem."[127]

Published books often bore pictures of animals and birds on their title pages, and prayerbooks occasionally depicted the standard zodiac symbols alongside the prayers for rain and dew. But such animal illustrations were symbolic, not real. Furthermore, the majority of these fauna were exotic species, not at all a common part of the urban European landscape. Surely no one expected (or hoped) to encounter lions, leopards, or eagles in the course of a Sabbath afternoon stroll.

12

JEWISH MYSTICISM

The Remythologization

As noted, the man-animal dichotomy articulated by the foremost Jewish philosophers of the Middle Ages emphasized the existence of a formidable chasm separating man from beast. Man's superiority stemmed from his rational and spiritual distinctiveness. He was fashioned by his Creator as a unique creature, endowed with the spark of divinity. No animal could make a comparable claim.

But this was not the total picture. The Jewish mystic chose to emphasize a different dimension of life by stressing the underlying kinship of all living creatures, man as well as beast. A thorough remythologization of the animal transpired in mystical thought, for in the eyes of many mystics, divinity is manifest in *all* of creation, with divine life pulsating as surely in any animal as it does in man. This quasi-pantheistic view of the world served to bridge the chasm, or at least narrow the gap, separating man from beast.

Rabbi Judah heHasid (ca. 1150–1217), elaborating upon selected rabbinic passages, bears testimony to God's providential hand pervading all the world of nature. He observes how diverse species of fowl and beast are equipped, from the moment of birth, with the capacity to thrive in hostile environments. The varying sizes of horns, tails, and hooves among the different species are clearly designed to ensure their optimal chance for survival. Clearly, *the well-being of animals is as precious to God as the well-being of man,* for God has seen fit to endow *all* of His creations with the necessary qualities for their survival.

If variations in physical traits are nothing more than survival mechanisms, God's carefully thought out gifts to His creations to enable them to survive, then what essential difference is there between human life and fauna life? Intelligence? Man's intellectual endowments are clearly superior to the rudiments of intelligence characteristic of even the most "gifted" animals. But why cannot intelligence also be defined merely as a survival mechanism?

To the question "What is the essential difference between man and beast?" most medieval theologians would have replied, "the soul." Man has a soul, beasts do not have souls. Or the response might be that the soul of man is qualitatively unique in its essence, and therefore distinct from the soul of any animal. But at this point the fascinating doctrine of *gilgul neshamot* metempsychosis, or transmigration of souls introduced a new dimension that cast doubt upon any such facile distinction between the souls of man and beast.

Metempsychosis

The belief in metempsychosis was prevalent in the ancient world. Herodotus claims that the ancient Egyptians were the first people to propose the notion of the immortality of the soul and depict human souls as transmigrating into the bodies of animals and birds.[1] Indeed, several chapters in the Egyptian *Book of the Dead* describe human souls entering into the bodies of hawks, swallows, serpents, crocodiles, etc.

Several Greek sects and the Manicheans also subscribed to this belief, and it formed an integral part of Indian philosophy. The Pythagoreans theorized that the souls of human beings occasionally transmigrated into the bodies of animals. This belief was occasionally justified on the simple grounds that many a human being possesses animallike traits, hence, an animallike soul. Although the Talmud contains no clear references to this doctrine, some Jews in the geonic period, notably Anan ben David, the founder of Karaism, also believed in the transmigration of souls.[2]

However, most medieval Jewish philosophers rejected the doctrine, among them Saadiah Gaon,[3] Abraham Ibn Daud,[4] Don Hasdai Crescas,[5] and Joseph Albo,[6] while Halevi and Maimonides fail to discuss it in any of their works. For the Jewish philosopher it was a nonissue, one that hardly merited discussion, but post-rabbinic Jewish thought embraces many currents of thought, and philosophy is only one of them. So, "although the doctrine of transmigration was not accepted by any of the great Jewish writers of the Middle Ages, the mystics employed the belief as the cornerstone of their religious structure."[7]

In Kabbalistic literature, the doctrine found its share of adherents, although the *Sefer haBahir,* perhaps the earliest of Kabbalistic works to refer to it, limits the soul's passage into human bodies alone.[8] Indeed, most of the early Kabbalists denied the universality of transmigration even among humans. They limited the phenomenon to exceptional situations in which the souls of sinners were punished for their transgressions by being forced to inhabit other bodies and thereby endure additional pain until purification would be achieved.

It was not until the late fourteenth century that the notion of *gilgul* was expanded from a limited and specific punishment to become a general principle of existence, with animals, plants, and even inanimate objects designated as possible receptacles for human souls. Therefore, although the *Zohar* itself nowhere refers to a person's soul finding lodging in the body of an animal, later works such as the *Sefer haTerumah* and the *Taamei haMitzvot,* record many such occurrences. The Kabbalists of Safed viewed transmigration as a process necessarily encompassing *all* forms of nature in order to facilitate the processes of "elevation" and "descension" to be undergone by souls.

The idea of transmigration of souls was a valuable and necessary one for the Kabbalists. Proceeding from the premise that all souls have a common divine root, they conceived of the soul as returning to its divine source upon its achieving perfection, but what of the soul which fails to attain such perfection in the course of a lifetime? What of the soul which was unable to achieve its earthly destiny? What of the soul of one who met an untimely death? What of the soul of a dead infant? Such souls are clearly in need of a second or third chance in order to purify themselves for the ascent. Metempsychosis provided them with this opportunity. In addition it offered a dramatic solution to another vexing problem, the problem of how God permits a wicked person to lead an apparently happy and prosperous existence, while his pious counterparts seem to be afflicted with great personal tragedy. This was but a temporary state of affairs, the believer in metempsychosis would maintain, because divine justice would yet be meted out via the transmigration of souls. In such a manner the soul of the wicked is surely destined to suffer, while the soul of the righteous will be elevated to its deserving blissful state.

Lurianic Kabbalah clearly spells out the extent of the involvement of animals in metempsychosis. We are told that not all human souls transmigrate into the bodies of animals. It is only the souls of the wicked who are doomed to inherit animal-forms. These souls are forced to undergo a series of transmigrations in order to cleanse themselves of their iniquities. They are lowered to the level of beasts, plants, and even inanimate objects until such time as they become purified of their sins and then begin their ascent to a human level.[9]

Hayyim Vital (1542–1620), the renowned Kabbalist, records several instances when he witnessed his master, Isaac b. Solomon Luria Ashkenazi (ARI) (1534–1570), pointing to certain objects, plants, and animals, and explaining that they housed a human soul which was being punished for its iniquities. The ARI did not consider this to be a rare or unusual phenomenon either, for as Vital explains:

> Virtually all humans cannot escape from these transmigrations . . . for it is only through transmigration that one suffers to the extent that his sins are atoned for. The extent and nature of the transmigration is directly proportional to the severity of the transgressions . . . therefore even pious and learned people undergo this process.[10]

Detailed expositions on the subject are cited by Luria's disciples. We are informed, for example, that the souls of unrepentant sinners guilty of sexual offenses are assigned to specific animals. The soul of an adulterer is forced to enter the body of a donkey, while the soul of one guilty of commiting incest with his mother cohabits the body of an ass. A homosexual's soul enters a rabbit, one guilty of bestiality, a bat. Luria recounts the episode of a Jew in the tannaitic era whose soul was forced to abide in a female goat as a punishment for having had sexual relations by candlelight.[11]

As for miscellaneous transgressions and their corresponding metempsychotic punishments, those guilty of cruelty to the poor enter the bodies of crows, and Moses Galante of Safed recalls Luria's designating a particular crow as possessing the soul of a cruel tax-collector, and identifying ravens as possessing the souls of Balak and Balaam.[12] Forgers of amulets, along with those who use the name of the Lord in vain, are forced to inhabit the bodies of cats.[13] Hayyim Vital recounts the episode of a soul which mocked the efficacy of repentance and was punished by being consigned to the body of a fish,[14] and Luria recounts the tradition that whoever cuts off his earlocks is transformed into an ox.[15]

Often the punishment aptly fits the crime, literally if not metaphorically. For example, the souls of community leaders guilty of arrogance enter the bodies of bees, notorious for their buzzing about proudly.[16] Those guilty of gazing lustfully at women transmigrate into small birds who must satisfy their passions by gazing from afar at the objects of their desire, while the slanderer, who loudly denounces others, is appropriately forced to inhabit the body of a barking dog.

The motif of the "black dog" appears frequently in the transmigration lore of Kabbalistic literature. Rabbi Luria declares that the punishment meted out to Joseph Della Reina for his having made "practical use" of Kabbalistic secrets was that he was transformed into a black dog,[17] and both the demon Samael and his mate Lilith appear in the Della Reina sagas in the form of black dogs.[18] A similar fate is said to have befallen the soul of Joseph Delpino. ARI interprets the episode of a large black dog severely biting a sleeping Safed housewife as being due to the fact that the dog was, in reality, a vengeance-seeking *gilgul* of a man whom the woman had previously seduced.[19]

Birds are also popular creatures in transmigration lore. Hayyim Vital records a dream in which he observed the pious of the ages dwelling in the form of birds in a beautiful garden. He relates this to the notion that certain animals, particularly birds, possess the power of speech, and sensitive humans who understand their utterances are thereby capable of discerning divine truths in their chirpings. Such birds may well contain the transmigrated souls of humans and are thus able to foretell future events and disclose divine secrets to those perceptive enough to understand.

But, as a general rule, the punishment of those souls forced to transmigrate into the bodies of animals is an exceedingly great one, because the soul is fully aware of its own degradation. However, this mortification process is essential for the subsequent elevation of the soul to its divine source.

At this point in our discussion, a superficial observation might lead one to conclude that Lurianic Kabbalah would probably encourage vegetarianism precisely because many animals are, in reality, not animals at all, but rather creatures in which human souls reside.

Indeed, the Cathari, or Albigenses, a heretical Christian sect, were vegetarians apparently because of their belief that the souls of the wicked transmigrated into the bodies of animals. Isaac Luria himself allegedly prohibited the killing even of noxious insects, and the Kabbalists of sixteenth-century Safed opposed the mistreatment of living creatures presumably because of the belief that they might contain the transmigrated souls of errant humans.[20] Does it not seem logical that vegetarianism would be a natural outgrowth of such convictions? After all, two pseudepigraphic works from fourteenth-century Spain, *Sefer haKaneh* and *Sefer haPeliah,* oppose the slaughtering of animals for food!

However logical, such was not the case. The doctrine of metempsychosis may have encouraged greater kindness toward animals, but it in no way encouraged vegetarianism. It had quite the opposite effect.

Moses b. Joseph Cordovero, one of Luria's mentors, discusses the episode of the calf seeking safety under the cloak of Rabbi Judah the Prince. He observes that it is forbidden to mistreat or abuse any living creature, nor should one kill an animal or even pluck out plant-life unless this be for a specific purpose. The rule of conduct for man is to manifest compassion toward all living creatures; however, and this is the important point, he should be compassionate to animals "unless he is elevating them from one level to the next . . . from the plant level to animal level, from the level of animal to the level of man. Then it is permissible for him to uproot plants and to slaughter animals . . . for he thereby causes them ultimate benefit."[21]

Cordovero relates this process to the psalmist's chant that the whole universe is like a Temple where all sing the glory of God.[22] He explains:

At every rung of the ladder extending from the depths of life on earth to the sublimest regions of the spirit, all the elements reach upwards and strive to come ever closer to the holy, divine source of life and blessing. Indeed, in nature there exists a hierarchical order which extends right down to inorganic elements, differentiated by the measure of the vitality which they receive from the supreme source of the divine light. This sequential connection of the spheres of creation encompasses the mineral, vegetable, animal, and human realms. The continual rise of each constituent occurs step by step. Thus, rain falls on the earth, it waters the earth, it helps the seed to germinate. The seed assimilates and transforms elements in the earth to grow into a plant. The plant is eaten by animals, and the vegetable element, thanks to this transmigration, reaches a level of existence where the soul begins to shine forth on the purely physical world. Ultimately, man consumes the flesh of the animal, which becomes part of man himself. The animal comes ever closer to the source of light contained in the spiritual soul. In this way, the different elements of nature ascend to the threshold of the metaphysical world, where the unfettered human soul will rejoin the heavenly sphere of absolute holiness.[23]

Luria elucidates how this process of elevation through metempsychosis can be facilitated. Souls that have been lowered to the level of plants and animals can be elevated when the plants and animals are eaten by human beings! For they thereby rise to become a part of the human level of existence. This ascent from the inanimate to the plant to the animal, and finally to the human level, is normally a gradual ascent, although at times it can be accelerated, as when a human eats the flesh of an animal which has itself recently consumed vegetation or dust containing a transmigrated soul![24]

In any event, it is clearly "desirable" for man to eat the flesh of animals, for he thereby "frees" their entrapped human souls and helps to restore them to their prior human level of existence. In such cases, vegetarianism is no virtue; indeed it is a disservice to any transmigrated souls residing in animals.

But even independently of the notion of metempsychosis, the eating of meat was deemed a meritorious act, for by eating an animal, one facilitates an alignment of qualities between the consumer and the consumed. Therefore, when the consumer performs righteous deeds, the consumed also shares in the merit. This is in keeping with the concept of ascension and return to the divine source, whereby lower elements strive to achieve less coarseness and greater purity. This elevation is obviously facilitated by the process of eating, whereby they are ingested into the bodies of higher organisms.

Vital recounts a bizarre episode in which a dead man appears to him in a dream and beseeches the rabbi to have mercy upon him and "improve" his sinful soul. Not long thereafter,

> Some farmers brought a calf into the city to be slaughtered. When the wagon came into the city, the calf broke away from the farmers and ran to the house of study where I sat with my colleagues over open books. The calf leaned with its hindfeet against the bench on which we were sitting and with its forefeet on the table upon which the books were lying. It looked straight at me, and tears flowed from its eyes. All around the table were astonished, but I explained to them, "Here is my dream fulfilled."

Vital, realizing that this calf is the transmigration of the dead man whose sinful soul is in need of "improvement," purchases it from its owners and prepares it for slaughter. The calf willingly stretches out its neck beneath the slaughterer's knife, and Vital and his colleagues taste of its meat "for the sake of the commandment," i.e., in order to "improve" its soul. "The following night," relates Vital, "the dead man came to me again in a dream and gratefully said, 'Blessed are you for having given peace to my soul.' "[25]

Centuries later, Hasidic literature describes how animals and birds gather of their own accord around a certain ritual slaughterer. Why? Because they realize that their human souls will be liberated when he slaughters them.[26] A disciple of Nahman of Bratslav (1772–1811) extols the eating of flesh even though he admits that consuming meat strengthens the evil inclination and endangers one's state of spirituality. Why then consume flesh? Because the process of *shehitah* is a meritorious act, freeing transmigrated human souls lodged in animal bodies so that they may become part of the human consumer.[27]

It is in this spirit that M. L. Malbim (1809-1879), in an exegesis of a passage in Genesis,[28] comments:

In the same manner that there is nothing wrong in an animal eating plant life, for the latter benefits thereby in being transformed into the body of the animal, so there is nothing wrong if man consumes the flesh of an animal, for it is thereby elevated to become part of the body of man.

True, there were times when Jews abstained from eating flesh, but for different reasons. The custom restricting the eating of meat and the drinking of wine during the three-week period preceding the fast-day of Tisha beAv is clearly unrelated to vegetarianism. Some connect it with Daniel's similar abstention while mourning over the destruction of the Temple.[29] Others reason that the seventeenth day of the month Tammuz, the first day of this three-week period, marked the breaching of the walls of Jerusalem, initiating the final phase of her destruction; therefore it is appropriate to abstain from symbols of joy, such as meat and wine. Furthermore the daily Temple sacrifices, along with the accompanying wine libations, ceased on the seventeenth of Tammuz.[30] The Kabbalistic custom to refrain from eating meat during the month containing the first four Torah readings of the Book of Exodus should likewise be viewed within the general context of abstaining from food as a mark of personal piety.[31] Similarly, the law requiring an *onen* (a mourner who has not yet buried the deceased) to abstain from meat and wine meals underscores the inappropriateness of such joyful pursuits at such a time.[32]

But clearly, vegetarian practices were not motivated by concern for the animal or dictated by any sense of compassion. The doctrine of metempsychosis, if anything, militated in favor of the consumption of flesh, for one thereby did the animal a favor!

It is not surprising to find that this philosophic outlook, when carried to its logical conclusion, has similar implications vis-à-vis the death of human beings. The phenomenon of death can be viewed as an ultimate blessing for man as well as for beast, because

it is impossible for man . . . to ascend to the higher elevations other than by means of death . . . for death sheds him of his earthly garb of clay and enables him to embrace spirituality and the higher dimension of sanctity that will enable him "to behold the graciousness of the Lord and to visit early in His temple."[33]

13

KINDNESS TO ANIMALS

Mysticism

Mystical literature may not have encouraged vegetarianism, but in emphasizing the common bond linking man and beast and viewing divinity as inhererent in all life, it did help create an intellectual and emotional atmosphere conducive to greater consideration and compassion for animals.

Rabbi Judah heHasid, the principal author of the *Sefer Hasidim*, reflects in his writings the deep piety of the mystics of Franco-German Jewry toward beast as well as man.

The cruel person is he who gives his animal a great amount of straw to eat and on the morrow requires that it climb up high mountains. Should the animal, however, be unable to climb quickly enough in accordance with its master's desires, it is mercilessly beaten. Mercy and kindness, in this instance, have evolved into cruelty.[1]

Man is worthy of divine punishment for causing needless pain to his cattle, as when he places too heavy a burden upon them and strikes them when they are unable to move.[2]

For any suffering he may have caused his fellows, man will be punished, yea, even for needless suffering toward animals. For the man who places a burden upon a beast too heavy for it to bear, or goads it with a whip when it cannot move, will surely be punished, for cruelty to animals is prohibited by Scripture.

And in the world to come God will punish those rulers who wound their horses with spurs . . .[3]

Similarly those who pull the ears of cats in order to cause them to cry are committing a sin.[4]

Several narratives in *Sefer Hasidim* concern insensitive masters who abuse their beasts of burden and are subsequently rebuked by men of piety for their cruelty. Kindness to animals, on the other hand, is invariably rewarded. We read the episode of a snake about to swallow a frog. A man assists the frog to escape by striking the snake over its head with his staff. Later, while he is leaning upon his staff, his thigh becomes infected from the snake venom adhering to the staff. But the grateful frog proceeds to sacrifice its own life in order to save its benefactor's life by sucking up the poison from the infected thigh.

Although much evidence exists that it was the common practice, from times of antiquity, to tie the tails of valuable animals,[5] the *Sefer Hasidim* condemns such acts, not to mention the cutting off of their tails, because animals are thereby rendered incapable of warding off flies.[6]

The dog is singled out for special praise by the author of *Sefer Hasidim*. One is cautioned against mistreating dogs, for they stand in a special relationship to man as benefactors.[7] Therefore, "The Torah ordains that man not consume flesh torn by wild beasts, but rather that he give dogs of such flesh (Exodus 22:30) in gratitude for their defense of his herds and flocks against the wolf."[8]

Sefer Hasidim records the episode of a dog fleeing its cruel master and seeking refuge under the cloak of a sage. The sage refuses to surrender the animal to its master, declaring: "Since this dog sought my protection, you shall not touch it!"—an interesting variation upon, and moral improvement over, the episode of the less-protective Rabbi Judah the Prince and the unfortunate calf.[9]

The *Little Sefer Hasidim* contains the admonition to "refrain thy kindness and thy mercy from nothing which the Holy One Blessed Be He, created in this world. Never beat nor inflict pain upon any creature, beast, bird, or insect; nor throw stones at a dog or cat; nor kill flies or wasps."[10]

Moses Cordovero taught that

> One's compassion should extend to all creation. One should
> neither destroy nor abuse any creature, for all of them were
> created with God's wisdom. One should not consciously up-
> root any plant or take the life of any animal unless it be for a
> purpose—and then one should see to it that their death be an
> easy [painless] one.[11]

Several centuries later, Jacob Emden dealt with the question of
whether the biblical prohibition against cruelty to animals includes such lower forms of life as insects and worms. Emden
concludes with the observation that although killing such noxious
creatures may be technically permissible, it nevertheless should
not be done, and he cites Isaac Luria's teaching that even irritating
insects ought not to be destroyed.[12]

A touching tale is related concerning Isaac Luria. The ARI had
enjoyed the hospitality of an exceedingly gracious host, and upon
departing inquired as to how he could repay such warm hospitality. The host sadly replied that although he and his wife dearly
yearned to have children, his wife had remained barren, and he
beseeched the ARI to cure her of her barrenness. Luria explained
to the man that his wife's inability to conceive was, in reality, a
divine punishment visited upon her. "For what offense?" inquired
the host. Luria then reminded the man how in the past little chicks
would drink from a water cistern in his garden by climbing upon a
little ladder adjoining the cistern. However, the man's wife had
ordered the removal of the ladder, leaving the birds unable to
reach the water, and their plaintive cries of thirst had reached to
the heavens. God therefore had punished the woman for her
cruelty to the young fledglings. The host immediately replaces the
ladder for the baby chicks, and shortly thereafter his wife becomes
pregnant.[13]

Hasidism

In the Hasidic centers of Poland and the Ukraine, Jews had far
greater contact with animals than did their coreligionists of Lithu-

ania or the northern urban German communities. Therefore Hasidic lore frequently centers on fauna.

The "type" of fauna featured in Hasidic lore is also significant. In the agrarian society of ancient Palestine, as well as in the Jewish communities of medieval Europe, the dominant animals with which Jews came in contact were not the sort of species with which one can develop an intimate relationship (cows, chickens, etc.). In other words, Jews were limited for the most part to those animals which were themselves "limited," and the development of any meaningful man-beast relationship was thus precluded. In contrast, the non-Jews in medieval society frequently encountered dogs and horses, creatures with whom humans can more readily relate. In Hasidic tales, it is precisely the horse and the dog which now form part of the common landscape for the Jew.

Furthermore, Hasidic literature, possessing deep kabbalistic roots and pietistic ethical emphases, champions the rights of fauna, for the animal is not only a divine creation but also a manifestation of divine imminence in the world.

Israel b. Eliezer, the Baal Shem Tov (ca. 1700–1760), the founder of Hasidism, taught in pantheistic language that "the *Shekhinah* permeates all four orders in the world: the inanimate objects, the plants, the living beings and man. It is inherent in all creatures in the universe whether they are good or bad."[14]

His disciple, Shneur Zalman of Liadi (1747–1812), expressed the same thought in more poetic terms: "All that man sees—the heaven, the earth, and all that fills it—all these things are the external garments of God."[15] Once, it is related, Shneur Zalman paused to listen attentively to the chirping of birds. His grandson asked him why he would bother to pay attention to such meaningless sounds. The rabbi replied that he heard the very voice of God Himself reverberating in the chirping of the birds.[16]

The Baal Shem Tov explained:

In the upper chariot there is the face of an ox, the face of a man, the face of an eagle and the face of a lion. . . . From the face of the upper ox through the chain of phases, through risings and fallings and many contractions, the life power descends to all the lower animals. From the face of the lion the life power extends down to the lower beasts, and from the face of the eagle it goes to all the lower birds. This is the secret of *Perek Shira*. Similarly, the language of each animal in the upper chariot descends to the lower animals, beasts, and birds. The wise man who can understand and examine everything in its upper source in the upper chariot will be able to comprehend the origin of all and the details and the means of the speech of the animals, beasts, and birds. This is the picture in general.[17]

The mundane scene of an animal grazing in a pasture was a spectacle of cosmic beauty and mystery for the Hasidic masters. Nahman of Bratslav records how every shepherd has a special *niggun* (melody) related to the grass upon which his sheep feed, for each individual animal subsists upon its own special grass and has its own unique melody.

While on a summer's-day stroll through a grassy meadow, Rabbi Nahman turns to a disciple and explains:

O that you might have the privilege of hearing the singing of the paeans and praises of the grasses and plants! Every little blade of grass sings a paean to God without any extraneous motives, without any strange thoughts, without any consideration of recompense. Ah, Ah, how good, how lovely it is when one hears this song of the grasses; it is good to be pious among them.[18]

Elsewhere, Rabbi Nahman says:

How precious and lovely it is to go out at the beginning of spring in the fields when nature awakens from its sleep and to pour out a prayer there. Every fresh blade of grass that grows, every little flower—all merge themselves with the prayer, for they also yearn and long for God.[19]

The legal codification of Shneur Zalman contains examples of pro-animal legislation not to be found in previous codes of law. For example,

If horses are pulling a wagon and they come to a bad spot or to a high mountain and they cannot go on without help, one is bound to help even an alien in order to avoid pain to living things: lest the alien driver beat them excessively in order to make them pull beyond the limits of their strength.[20]

Significantly, Shneur Zalman's *Shulhan Arukh* contains a special section bearing, in part, the designation *tzaar baalei hayyim*, a feature lacking in all previous codes.

The Hasidic masters are featured in an impressive number of tales exemplifying the virture of showing kindness to animals.

We read, for example, how the Baal Shem Tov, during his youthful days of extreme poverty, owned a scrawny, undernourished horse which had barely the strength to pull a laden wagon. As Rabbi Israel was unable to afford the purchase of another animal, he would frequently descend from the wagon and personally assist his horse by pushing the wagon from behind.[21]

A poignant tale describes Zussya of Anapole setting off on a mission to collect funds for the redemption of captives. While stopping at an inn, he happened to notice some caged birds beating their wings against the bars of their cage in a vain attempt to escape. Much to the chagrin of the innkeeper, Zussya opened the cage-latch and freed the "captive" birds, explaining that they, too, were unfortunate captives entitled to their freedom.[22]

Velvel of Zabrig demanded that his wagon-driver desist from striking the horses with his whip. The wagon-driver replied that he meant the animals no harm; quite the contrary, he explained, "I am merely driving away flies with my whip." "If that was your intention," replied Velvel, "then take my handkerchief and use it for that purpose."[23]

When David Lelov (the "Lelever") visited the Lublin Rebbe for Rosh HaShanah, he was mysteriously missing from the local synagogue during the time for the sounding of the *shofar*. An intensive search finally located him in a nearby stable, feeding a horse. Explained the Lelever: "Its owner had departed early for the synagogue and therefore neglected to feed the beast."[24] A similar tale describes Moshe Leib of Sassov observing cattle at a fair which had been neglected by their masters. He proceeded to fetch a pail of water in order to give them to drink. When one of the merchants observed Rabbi Moshe attending to the cattle, he ordered him to feed some of his own calves standing nearby. The rabbi gladly complied with the request.[25]

The motif of the compassionate shepherd as the worthy leader of human flocks is beautifully illustrated in the case of Yaakov Yitzhak of Pshiskha, who loved to spend his hours tending to the needs of sheep and speaking lovingly to them. His uncle, the *Zadik haNistar*, proclaimed: "This lad is destined to be a worthy leader of his people."

Transmigration of Souls in Hasidic Literature

The kabbalistic theme of metempsychosis is a recurrent one in Hasidic literature. Not only are human souls housed in the bodies of animals, even Satan appears before the Baal Shem Tov in the form of a huge black dog![26]

The Rabbi of Belz cautions a *shohet* to be meticulous in his craft, and, by way of warning, points to several dogs, remarking: "You see these dogs, they used to be *shohtim* who abused their privileges and declared unfit meat to be *kosher*."[27] In a twentieth-century manifestation of metempsychosis, the Rabbi of Karlin explains the incessant barking of a dog as being due to the fact that it houses the soul of a soldier who was killed during World War I.[28]

Like their kabbalistic forebears, the Hasidic masters emphasized that the transmigration of the souls of humans into the bodies of animals was neither a capricious nor an accidental phenomenon. Such journeys were always purposeful, and frequently beneficial to the soul. For example, the Baal Shem Tov, in the course of his wanderings, comes upon a giant frog. The frog explains that it houses the transmigrated soul of a renowned scholar which has been forced to spend over five hundred years of suffering in the desert, even though Rabbi Isaac Luria had been successful in mending all other souls of their imperfections and elevating them to their source. When the Baal Shem Tov inquired as to the enormity of the sin that would merit such punishment, the frog explained that the scholar had transgressed by failing to perform the ritual washing of hands with proper concentration, and had since added other sins to the roster. The heavenly court decreed that he repent of his sins, but Satan induced the scholar to become inebriated and therefore incapable of repentance. Eventually his soul was forced to transmigrate into the body of a frog (as the original transgression involved water, the scholar was transformed into a creature which dwells in the water), and it was banished to a forlorn spot where presumably no Jew would be found to aid it in its ascension. The Baal Shem Tov promptly intervened and miraculously enabled the unfortunate soul to depart the body of the frog and ascend to its salvation, where upon the giant frog dies.[29]

Another, even more elaborate tale concerns Rabbi Yudel of Chudnow, son of Rabbi Joseph the preacher, who on the eve of the Sabbath stood on the verge of crossing a body of water, which, unbeknownst to him, was exceedingly deep. A dog rushed quickly into the pond, howling pitifully as it drowned. Rabbi Yudel, moved to tears at the sight of the unfortunate creature, realized that it was impossible to cross the water and therefore decided to spend the Sabbath at a nearby inn. He instructed the landlord to purchase fish for the Sabbath meal, and the landlord procured an extraordinarily large pike. Later that evening Rabbi Yudel fell asleep at the dinner table, whereupon his father appeared to him in a dream and told him:

> Know that I was reincarnated as that fish. An informer whom I always condemned during my life was reincarnated as the dog that drowned. His redemption was that he drowned in order to save you. I was reincarnated as this fish because I persecuted him. The tears which you shed when the dog drowned redeemed me. Be careful, my son, how you eat this fish.[30]

A similar theme, involving the Baal Shem Tov, concerns an informer who is destined to enter the body of a dog upon his death. This calamity is averted, however, when a preacher's eulogy disgraces him, and his humiliation is deemed sufficient punishment in itself.[31]

Another mysterious tale concerns a little horse which amazingly manages to outperform all other beasts in strenuous labors for its master. One day, Reb Motel of Tchernobl inquires of its master as to the nature of a certain debt owed to him, and is informed that the debtor had died penniless. Reb Motel asks that the horse's master transfer the debt to him as a donation, and when the latter agrees, the rabbi declares that the dead debtor no longer has any financial obligations. The horse promptly dies! The bewildered master inquires as to the significance of the annulled debt and the animal's sudden death. Reb Motel explains:

> The man doesn't owe you anymore . . . you see, this man owed you three hundred dollars. He ascended to the other world without having paid you. He failed to complete what he was obligated to do. Therefore God decreed that he should work for you. His soul was born in a horse and he worked for you. You forgave him what he owed you, and so the horse died.[32]

Metempsychosis plays far less of a role among the scholars of Lithuanian Jewry, and their lore is virtually bereft of any references to the transmigration of souls into the bodies of animals. However, an extensive literature exists lauding rabbinic pietists for their great compassion toward fauna. Not surprisingly, many of the vignettes are similar to those found in Hasidic literature.

For example, Rabbi Israel Lipkin (Salanter) (d. 1883) was tardy arriving at the synagogue on the night of Yom Kippur. His delay was caused by the fact that he had come upon a lost, frightened calf while on his way to the synagogue. He had led the animal to its stall in a gentile's barn, where he proceeded to calm its fears and minister to its needs. Only then did Rabbi Israel continue on his way to religious services.[33]

A similar account has Naftali Zevi Yehudah Berlin, (1817–1893) the head of the academy at Volozhin, delaying the recitation of the *kaddish* prayer on Rosh HaShanah until after all his fowl had been fed. Once, when the key was misplaced, this necessitated his waiting until the lock on the chicken coop could be broken. Only after all the birds were fed did the rabbi commence with his own meal.[34] Finally, one comes across the interesting account of how Rabbi Isaac Elhanan Spektor (1817–1896), rabbi of Kovno, gathered scraps of food with which to feed a dog and carried a cat upon his shoulders as he made his rabbinic rounds.[35]

Secular Literature

Works of fiction can be revealing as to the value-system of both author and reader, and the animal's portrayal in secular literature is often a sympathetic one.

It is instructive to focus upon one of the favorite books of medieval Jewry, Kalonymos ben Kalonymos' translation, the *Iggeret Baalei Hayyim* ("The Book of Animals and Men"), a work first appearing in Hebrew in 1316.

In reality, this book was volume twenty-five of a fifty-one-volume encyclopedia composed by an Islamic association known as the Society of Pure Brethren or the Brothers of Purity, whose membership apparently consisted of Jews and Christians as well as Mohammedans.[36]

This association, dedicated to the pursuit of knowledge and the development of the human soul, eclectically embraced the insights of many philosophic systems and religious orders. Its encyclopedia sought to present the sum total of human knowledge in such disciplines as logic, physics, philosophy, mathematics, religion, natural science, etc. The volume translated by Kalonymos ben Kalonymos contains interesting insights vis-à-vis man-animal relationships, presented in the context of an elaborate narrative which we shall briefly summarize.

A ship containing men of differing nationalities and creeds is forced by high winds to land on a mysterious island ruled over by a demon king named Borsif. The shipwrecked crew find the island to be an idyllic paradise harboring many species of beast and fowl which roam about freely. The men proceed to trap and capture numerous animals. The animals protest their sudden state of subjugation and complain to the king that their human masters have perpetrated grave injustices against them. "By what right," demands Borsif, "do men justify their enslavement of animals?" A

Mohammedan replies that Scripture has clearly authorized man to have dominion over all fauna. "But is man, indeed, superior to the lower animals?" inquires the king.

Arguments testifying to the superiority of man over beast are put forth by the former and then refuted rather successfully by the latter. Man takes pride in his erect form, symmetry of limbs, and finely developed senses, but the animals are unimpressed, for they, too, feel equally well-endowed with physical traits necessary for survival. Men of differing faiths and nationalities extol the great contributions to civilization made by their respective groups. But the animals are quick to challenge the "greatness" of these contributions. Insects extol their own incomparable industriousness, superior activity, and sense perception. A jackal insists that the natural plumage and fur of bird and beast is far more colorful and attractive than any of man's artificial articles of clothing. Man boasts of his scientific advances in the field of medicine, but a parrot retorts that man's hedonistic existence and frenetic pace of living is the actual source of illness and disease in the first place! When man extols the uniqueness of his forms of religious worship and his rules of judicial equity, the animals point out that it is precisely man's lustful nature and cruel propensities that necessitate these vehicles of control in the first place. Religious institutions and judicial systems exist because of man's wickedness. Most fauna, in contrast, are so gentle and restrained as not to require such controls.

Even the lowly frog is the recipient of glowing words of praise. It is wise and precious and patient, full of praises, and sings steadily to its God throughout the day and night. It richly deserves to be honored by the Children of Israel because of two deeds of kindness done to them by it: one, when it fetched water in its mouth and spat it unto the fire at Ur Kasdim to extinguish it, thereby saving the life of young Abraham, who had been cast into the flames by Nimrod; the other occasion, when it helped facilitate the exodus from Egypt by assisting Moses in plaguing the Egyptians. The frog is extolled for its physical beauty as well: it has a lovely round head and gleaming eyes, and its two arms and two feet are spread wide, its manner of locomotion is a pleasing hopping-and-leaping pattern, and it is careful not to frighten human beings.

The volume concludes, however, with a clear statement testifying to the superiority of man over the beast. Man alone is capable of perfection of soul, man alone possesses the divine intelligence needed to draw himself closer to God, and man alone is subject to reward and punishment. Therefore man is justifed in asserting his dominance over all other forms of life.

But the king cautions man to treat his animal subjects fairly and not to abuse them. Indeed, some of the most eloqently moving passages in the volume are spoken by animals. Such diverse creatures as an ox, dog, fish, ass, lamb, and elephant relate heartrending tales of suffering and torture endured at the hands of their human oppressors. The best lines and most convincing arguments in this drama are given to the animals!

Their plaintive cry is that, whereas prior to man's advent they lived lives of peace and freedom, disturbing and threatening no one, they are now mistreated and tortured slaves at the hands of their human captors. However impressive the philosophical and theological arguments testifying to man's superiority over animals might be, far more moving and persuasive are *Iggeret Baalei Hayyim*'s descriptions of man's unjust treatment of his fellow living beings. As the cock laments:

> At midnight I rise to pray. . . .
> But the sleeping ones lay hold of me . . .
> They slaughter me and eat me.
> Have we not all one father?
> Has not one God created us all?

The injustices suffered by fowl and beast at the hands of man make them appropriate subjects in secular prose and poetry in medieval and modern times. Judah b. Solomon Al-Harisi (b. 1165) also describes the bitter complaints of an ill-treated rooster. In later Jewish literature we come across the horse as a symbol for Israel's pathetic plight, notably in the writings of Mendele Mocher Sefarim (Shalom Abramovitch, 1835–1917), and we read Shalom

Aleichem's (Shalom Rabinovitz, 1859–1916) sympathetic portrayal of the aged, toothless, emaciated, luckless Methuselah, and Saul Tchernichowsky's (1875–1943) eloquent plea for compassion for a suffering horse.

Shalom Aleichem's autobiographical tale, *A Rachmonis di Laibidicker* ("A Pity upon the Living"), depicts the soul-searching of a young boy attempting to cope with the inconsistency between his religious education and the reality of life around him. On the one hand, his rabbi taught him to believe that all living creatures are beloved by God and must therefore be treated with compassion. Yet, on the other hand, he is appalled at the spectacle of his friend's father slaughtering a chicken, a hungry cat being severely punished for stealing liver for itself, a dog being scalded in hot water, and similar incidents, and yet in the face of all these brutal injustices he is rebuked for shedding tears because "it is God's will, it is sinful to complain."

Animals are sympathetically portrayed in several of the Aesopian fables recounted and recast by Jacob Kranz, the *maggid* of Dubnow (1741–1804), and more notably in the works of the fabulist, Eliezer Steinbarg (1880–1932).

It is not difficult to identify with the creatures in Israel Zangwill's (1864–1926) "At the Zoo."

> Poor tropic creatures, penned in northern land,
> I, too, desire the sun and I am a slave.
> My heart is with you, and I understand,
> The lion turning in his living grave.

The following extracts from Mordecai ben Ammi's (1854–1932) "Sabbath in the Forest"[37] constitute a vivid portrayal of "animal rights" as seen through the eyes of an Eastern European rabbi.

Rabbi Abramtzi was a man full of compassion. . . . His compassion was for all living things. . . . He would not walk on the grass of the field lest he trample it down. He was careful not to tread on grasshoppers or crawling insects. If a dog came to the door of his house . . . he would instruct the members of his household to feed the animal. In winter he would scatter crumbs of bread and seed on the window sills. When the sparrows and other birds arrived and began to peck at the food, he would not remove his gaze from them and his face would light up with joy like that of a little child. . . .

He looked after his horses far better than his coachmen did. When travelling and the coach had to ascend an incline, he would climb down in order to lighten the load and more often than not he would push the cart from behind. On summer days he would compel his coachman to stop on the way and to turn aside to a field in order that the horses should rest and partake of the pure green grass. The rabbi loved these rest periods in the forest. While the horses were grazing . . . he would sit under a tree and interest himself in a book. At times he would pray in the field or the forest. This gave him great pleasure, for he used to say, "The field and the forest are the most beautiful and finest of the Houses of the Lord."

It happened once that the rabbi was on the road on a Friday. It would take another three hours to reach home.

Due to the rain the road was a mess. The wagon could only proceed with difficulty . . . the mud gripped the wheels and slowed down its progress. It was mid-day and they had not even completed half the journey. The horses were tired and fagged out. They had no energy to proceed further.

The *Tzaddik* told the driver to stop and to give fodder to the horses, so that they could regain their strength. This was done. Afterwards the journey was continued, but the going was heavy and the wagon sank up to the hubs of the wheels in the mud. In fact it was with the greatest difficulty that the horses maintained their balance in the swampy ground. The vapour of sweat enveloped their skin. Their knees trembled and at any moment they would have to rest. The coachman scolded and urged them on. He then raised his whip on the unfortunate creatures. The *Tzaddik* grabbed him by the elbow and cried out: "This is cruelty to animals, cruelty to animals." The coachman answered in fury: "What do you want me to do? Do you want us to celebrate the Sabbath here?"

"What of it?" replied the rabbi quietly. "It is better that we celebrate the Sabbath here than cause the death of these animals by suffering. Are they not the creatures of the Lord? See, how exhausted they are. They have not the energy to take one more step forward."

"But what of the Sabbath. How can Jews observe the Sabbath in the forest?" asked the coachman.

"My friend. It does not matter. The Sabbath Queen will come to us also here, for her glory fills the whole world, and particularly in those places where Jews yearn for her. The Lord will do what is good in His eyes. He will look after us, supply us with our wants and guard us against all evil."

But however feelingly the plight of fauna may be depicted in the preceding excerpts, and however sympathetic the folk-teller may have been to their plight, the animal was, nevertheless, *not* a popularly employed literary figure. As a matter of fact, the collections of the Israel Folktale Archives contain less than two percent animal fables![38] Apparently fauna were neither important enough nor familiar enough, perhaps, to urban Jewry to merit more frequent appearances in secular literature.

Halakhic Humaneness

As noted previously, the Talmud presents conflicting views as to whether or not *tzaar baalei hayyim* is a biblical ordinance. The consensus of opinion, however, was that it is biblically ordained, and all the principal post-talmudic codes of law reflect this conclusion.[39] Although it is true that they do not reflect an *excessive* concern for the well-being of animals, they surely do enjoin fair treatment and at times even lift halakhic restrictions for the sake of the welfare of animals.

The Sabbath and Festivals

The codes endorse the relaxation of Sabbath and festival laws in order to provide for the physical well-being of beasts. Therefore animals, like humans, are allowed to move about on the Sabbath wearing bandages and splints for their wounds, and cushions to keep away chills.[40] One is permitted to apply salve and oil to an animal's fresh, painful wounds on the Sabbath, and one may ask the assistance of a gentile in bleeding animals should venesection be necessary[41] or in milking them in order to relieve their discomfort.[42]

Although one should not actually deliver a cow's young on the Sabbath, one may assist in the delivery by holding on to the calf so that it will not fall to the earth, by blowing into its nostrils, and by placing the dam's teat in its mouth.[43] Furthermore, "If an animal rejected its young, it is permissible to sprinkle the water of its placenta on the latter and to place some salt into its mother's vaginal orifice so that she shall have compassion upon it (through being reminded of her birth-pangs), but one may not do so with an animal of the unclean species."[44]

One is permitted on the Sabbath to place an animal in cold water in order to cool it off as a treatment for congestion,[45] or to assist in raising it from a body of water into which it has fallen in order to ease its sufferings.[46] Although one is normally forbidden to remove a weight greater than fifteen *sain* (measures of grain), such a burden may be removed from an animal because of *tzaar baalei hayyim*.[47]

It is interesting to note that one is permitted to take an animal that has overgorged itself with food and race it to the point of exhaustion on the Sabbath in order to alleviate its pain from having overeaten.[48] In this respect the animal is the beneficiary of consideration denied to humans in a similar predicament, for such exercises are forbidden to men.[49] Likewise, one may cut a horse's hoof on a festival in order to ease its pain, even though the practice was to refrain from cutting human finger-or toe-nails on festivals.[50] A person who intentionally climbs up into a tree on the Sabbath should remain perched there until nightfall,[51] but one who climbs upon an animal must descend immediately because of *tzaar baalei hayyim*.[52]

By general consensus, a Jewish master was obligated to supply his domestic cattle and fowl with their provender on the Sabbath, as domesticated beasts are incapable of acquiring their own nourishment and are totally dependent upon their masters for sustenance.[53] Joseph b. Moses, a fifteenth-century Bavarian scholar, wrote that "it is necessary to give one's beast whatever it needs to eat even on Yom Kippur, for we must have compassion on the beasts, that heaven may have compassion on us."[54]

But this rule was limited to domesticated animals. Wild beasts, birds, not to mention fish, which existed in the wild and were totally independent of man for their sustenance, were not to be fed on the Sabbath. However, the testimony of Jacob b. Moses Molin (*MaHaRiL,* 1365–1427) describes the Jews of his time as enjoying feeding such animals:

> On festivals they strolled by brooks and streams and watched the fish disporting themselves in the water. They carried food with them which they threw into the streams, and derived a simple pleasure from the pastime, even though it was not strictly in accordance with Jewish ritual law.[55]

Miscellaneous Mitzvot

In a related issue, Jacob Emden was asked whether one has to provide a dog or cat with food prior to partaking of one's own meal. Presumably one should not be obligated to do so, as these are not, technically speaking, "domestic" animals. Emden replied that although dogs and cats clearly belong to the category of "wild" rather than "domestic" species, and we are not obligated to care for them to the extent that we are for the latter, we are, nevertheless, responsible for their well-being, as they perform labor on our behalf. Therefore, he concludes: "It is desirable that one who wishes to perform a righteous act should first feed the dog and cat before partaking of food himself."[56]

The prohibition against the muzzling of the "ox when he treadeth out corn"[57] was expanded to apply whether or not the working animal was actually the property of a Jew,[58] and came to include *all* species of animals, clean as well as unclean.[59] Abarbanel sees a relationship between the edict against muzzling and the passage "But in the seventh year thou shalt let it rest and lie fallow, that the poor of thy people may eat; and what they leave the beast of the field shall eat"[60] because animals, too, should be permitted to enjoy at all times (not merely during the Jubilee year) the produce which they have helped to harvest. Similarly, the prohibition against castration[61] was extended to apply to fowls as well as to beasts,[62] to unclean as well as to clean animals.[63]

Popular expositions of biblical and rabbinic legislation dealing with animals often emphasized *tzaar baalei hayyim* as *the* motivating factor behind such legislation.

For example, manuals for *shohtim* frequently cited Maimonides' emphasis upon the humane nature of *shehitah*,[64] paraphrasing it as follows:

> Why indeed is *shehitah* performed in the throat and not another part of the anatomy? Because the perpetration of cruelty to animals is forbidden in the Bible itself; and there is no death attendant with less pain than that which comes with being slaughtered at the throat, because then death comes most quickly.[65]

Saadiah Gaon, in discussing *shehitah,* centuries earlier, emphasizes that:

> Should their slaughtering, however, entail pain over and above that which is experienced in natural death, God would be fully aware of it, and He would, of course, in such event, compensate the beasts in accordance with the excess of pain.[66]

As we noted earlier, it was within a philosophic context that Saadiah and others argued that animals, although lacking in real intelligence, nevertheless do experience pain and are to be compensated by God for the excess pain which they are forced to endure.[67] But the question of the extent of the pain which animals experience is bound to have practical applications. It is significant that both David ben Solomon Ibn Abi Zimra *(RaDBaZ,* 1479-1573)[68] and Yair Hayyim Bacharach (1638–1702)[69] theorize that animals are rendered all the *more* sensitive to pain precisely because of their paucity of intellect! Whereas humans can use their superior intellect to better endure pain by accepting their sufferings "in love," or by rationally analyzing their predicament, animals are totally incapable of such reasoning. They merely suffer, period.

Needless to say, the traditional commentators are unanimous in their condemnation of *ever min hahai* as an act of unspeakable cruelty, to be abhorred by all humanity. Saadiah emphasizes that even a nonbeliever will be requited in the world to come for having performed three meritorous deeds: honoring one's parents, conducting one's business activities with integrity, and faithfully observing the commandment not to take a baby bird in its mother's presence, an act of compassion toward the animal.[70]

Abraham Ibn Ezra interprets the injunction "Thou shalt love thy neighbor as thyself" as implying that in the same way that one is obligated to manifest kindness to a fellow human who is *kamocha* ("as yourself"), so is one obligated to manifest kindness to those who are "not as yourself," i.e., the animals.[71] Rashi, in commenting upon the passage bidding the Israelite to permit his animals to also enjoy Sabbath rest, interprets *yanuah* ("rest") to mean: "Give it [the animal] some satisfaction [*noah*] by permitting it to pull up and eat grass from the ground as it pleases." Rashi here follows the *Mekhilta* in expanding the notion of rest to apply not merely to the cessation of physical labor but to the animal's achievement of a state of inner satisfaction and contentment.[72]

The injunction against plowing with an ox and an ass[73] is explained by Abraham Ibn Ezra and many others as being due to the fact that different species of animals possess varying capabilities. "God has compassion on all His creatures . . . for the strength of the ass is not equal to the strength of the ox." Jacob ben Asher (*Baal ha Turim*, 1270?-1340) sees a more subtle cause for the pain suffered by the poor ass. He attributes it to envy. For as the ox chews its cud and the ass does not, the latter will imagine the former to be constantly engaged in eating, and it will therefore feel frustrated and angry as it labors hungrily alongside the "chewing" ox. For Maimonides, any conjunction of diverse species presents a possible source of pain because "animals of different species do not copulate together unless by force."[74]

Even in cases where the principle of *tzaar baalei hayyim* was deemed inapplicable, as when it is in conflict with human need, it was nevertheless upheld. For example, Moses Isserles (1525 or 1530-1572) cites the ruling permitting one to inflict pain upon an animal for medical purposes but concludes that although one may theoretically pluck feathers from live geese, such practices are to be condemned because of cruelty to animals.[75] Similarly, Israel b. Pethahiah Isserlein (1390-1460) writes:

> To cut a bird's tongue so that it will be able to speak or to crop a dog's ears and tail so that its appearance will be enhanced does not constitute a violation of *tzaar baalei hayyim* so long as this is done for man's use and benefit. For all fauna were created solely for man's use. However, we refrain from commiting such acts. We do not wish to behave cruelly toward fauna because of possible retribution for having caused them pain.[76]

We read a critique of certain butchers who withhold food from cattle for a period of several days prior to the slaughter (in order to lessen the possibility of any lung adhesions which would render the animal's meat forbidden for consumption) on the grounds that it is forbidden to cause an animal pain merely for the sake of financial gain. Indeed, there is a twofold condemnation of those who deprive animals of their food in the belief that this will cause their meat to weigh more; not only is one guilty of violating *tzaar baalei hayyim*, one is also thereby guilty of cheating the purchaser.[77]

The rabbinic authorities of ensuing generations continued to consistently apply the principle of *tzaar baalei hayyim* to man-animal encounters. Now, theoretically, most authorities were surely in agreement with the notion that "fauna . . . have no purpose or role in existence other than constituting man's food supply,"[78] and accepted Moses Isserles' ruling that "*tzaar baalei hayyim* is not applicable when man's medical needs or his other needs are at stake."[79] But in practice, many respondents seem uncomfortable with the starkness of such statements and seek to restrict man's power of usership of fauna and to raise his sensitivity toward the beast by frequently invoking *tzaar baalei hayyim*.

For example, Samuel b. Moses Medina (1506-1589) follows

Rashi in attributing the inclusion of one's animals among the household members entitled to rest on the Sabbath to God's concern for *tzaar baalei hayyim*.[80] He calls our attention to the power of the rabbis of the Talmud to uproot certain biblical ordinances when they conflict with Sabbath observance (one does not sound the *shofar* or participate in the rituals of *etrog* and *lulab* on the Sabbath) and marvels that similar logic was not employed to prohibit aiding an animal on the Sabbath to emerge from a pit into which it had fallen. But the rabbis permit and even enjoin the assistance of an animal in such a predicament. Why? Because of the overriding importance of the biblical principle of *tzaar baalei hayyim*.

A similar perspective underlies the ruling of a Sephardic Chief Rabbi of Israel, Obadiah Yosef (b. 1920), permitting one, upon the Sabbath, to feed birds whatever specific food items are necessary for their sustenance,[81] and to move their cages from hot, sunny areas into the shade,[82] and the blanket statement that "it is permissible to violate *any* [emphasis added] laws of *muktzeh* because of *tzaar baalei hayyim*."[83]

One can cite numerous responsa in which the respondent deals with an animal's plight in the same terms with which he would treat a human being's predicament. For example, is one permitted to place a bird upon the eggs of a bird of another species in order to hatch them? Why should one not do so? Because the bird might suffer psychological agony upon observing chicks emerging from the eggs that are dissimilar in appearance to itself and whose patterns of locomotion and eating may vary extensively from its own.[84] May one poison animals which persist in ravaging one's fields? Now theoretically one should be permitted to protect one's property and financial interests by disposing of destructive beasts. But Shalom Mordecai b. Moses Shvadron (1835-1911) forbids, on the basis of *tzaar baalei hayyim*, the inflicting of such a painful and lingering death upon one of God's creatures.[85]

Other scholars deal with the permissibility of cutting off horses' hooves, seeing that the procedure is an extremely painful one,[86] and we encounter the interesting case of a goat about to be slaughtered whose peculiar horn formations preclude its being slaughtered according to the traditional procedure. Is one permitted to first cut off the animal's horns in order to facilitate *shehitah*, or would this inflict undue pain upon the creature and therefore constitute a violation of *tzaar baalei hayyim*?[87]

Even the concept of muzzling is extended beyond the limited scriptural context of a muzzled animal laboring in the fields. It is wrong to muzzle an animal, *in general*, argues Moses Sofer (*Hatam Sofer*, 1726-1839) even a beast not engaged in actual field labors, for animals, like humans, clearly experience hunger pangs when placed near food items.[88]

An interesting man-animal parallel centers about one's obligation to pay laborers in cash. Is an animal-laborer also entitled to cash remuneration, or can its master receive cash-value payment? The ruling is clear. A hired animal worker has the same rights as a hired human worker. It too should be entitled to its food immediately, and the payment should therefore be made to its master in cash![89]

Now, none of the aforementioned rabbinic respondents would deny to man the right of legitimate use of the animal kingdom for his needs. But they do raise, in this connection, some sensitive questions. What precisely is *legitimate* use? How does one determine what constitutes *use* and what constitutes *abuse*? And when is human *need* merely human *want* in disguise? The principle of *tzaar baalei hayyim* is frequently invoked as underlying such deliberations, whether or not the final verdict always lies with the animal.[90]

Hunting

Jews were decidedly *not* a part of the hunting culture of medieval Europe. This was due in part to the fact that they were excluded from the society of nobles who customarily engaged in hunting as a favorite sporting activity. More important, however, was the fact that Jewish tradition always looked askance at hunting for mere sport.

The rabbis of the Talmud interpreted the first verse in the Book of Psalms, "Happy is the man who has not walked in the counsel of the wicked," as referring to the "wicked" who hunt beasts with their hounds.[91] The *Piske Tosafot* appears to outlaw the sport of hunting on the grounds that the law forbids one from causing unnecessary pain to animals,[92] and Maimonides condemns hunters of fowl as violators of the precept against the wanton destruction of any of God's creations.[93] Isaac b. Moses of Vienna (ca. 1180-ca. 1250) forbade Jews to hunt,[94] and Meir b. Baruch of Rothenberg (ca. 1215-1293) proclaimed that "he who hunts game with dogs, as non-Jews do, will not participate in the joy of the Leviathan."[95] (Presumably, life in the hereafter will be denied him.)

Under what circumstances, then, is one permitted to take the life of an animal? The *Sefer haHinnukh* concludes that it is permissible to kill animals only for food, for reasons of health, or as part of the sacrificial rites. But to destroy an animal in the name of "sport" constitutes wanton destruction and is to be condemned as the spilling of blood.[96]

Ezekiel Landau addresses himself in greater detail to the question of the permissibility of hunting animals for sport. A wealthy coreligionist possesses a large estate which includes several villages and forests in which many wild animals stalk. The man asks whether it is permissible to hunt these animals for sport, or whether such actions would constitute a violation of the laws concerning cruelty to animals. Landau receives the inquiry through a mutual friend, Gomprecht Oppenheim, and gives his reply:

> Rabbi Israel Isserlein in his responsa has already considered this problem. He shows that only in the following instances will the rules of "cruelty to animals" not apply—viz, When an act is done for a material benefit to man, or when the victim is killed outright. . . .
>
> So much for the legal aspect of the problem. But I am surprised that you were moved to ask such a question. We find in the Torah the sport of hunting imputed to no one but to such fierce characters as Nimrod and Esau, never to any of the patriarchs or to their descendants. The customary blessing, "Thou shalt outlive," offered to one donning a new garment, is

according to a decision of Rabbi Weil omitted altogether in the case of a fur coat. Such a blessing might make it appear that the killing of animals is not only condoned but actually desirable, which is contrary to the verse in Psalms "And His tender mercies are over all His works."

It is true that Rabbi Moses Isserles, commentator upon Caro's code, the *Shulhan Arukh*, remarks that the reason given is weak. But the weakness lies only in the fact that putting on a fur coat does not necessarily imply that the owner directly caused the killing. The fur may be of animals who died a natural death. And Isserles agrees with the decision of Rabbi Weil. But I cannot comprehend how a Jew could even dream of killing animals merely for the pleasure of hunting, when he has no immediate need for the bodies of the creatures.

Some have tried to justify the hunting of wild animals on the ground that they are liable to injure man, basing their view on the dictum of Rabbi Eliezer: "Whoever is early in destroying them has done an act of merit." This, however, is a twofold mistake. First, because the final decision does not follow Rabbi Eliezer, and secondly, because as Resh Lakish explains, Rabbi Eliezer refers only to the animal which has already shown his danger to, and ferocity toward, man.

The view has also been advanced that this attitude toward beasts refers only to those who have an owner and are therefore under care and to some extent tamed. Where, however, there is no owner, it is considered to be in a ferocious state and liable to do harm; it is therefore permitted to kill them even on a Sabbath.

This is also erroneous, and does not touch our case. The above is true only when these wild animals are found in places inhabited by man, so that they are a menace to society. It is certainly no meritorious act to pursue them in their own haunts. It is rather a lustful occupation. There is a distinction made for one who derives his livelihood from hunting by selling the furs or skins, etc. The animal world is subordinated to man to provide for his needs. It makes no difference if we take the life of clean animals for food or kill unclean animals for their skins and furs. But when the act is not prompted by such a motive, it is downright cruelty.[97]

In a lesser-known responsum, an Italian rabbi, Samson Morpurgo (1681-1740), reacts with shock to the information that certain Jews are hunting down animals and birds in order to sell their dead bodies to non-Jews for food. He is incredulous that "the remnant of Israel, the holy seed, the children of Abraham, Isaac, and Jacob, those reputed to be compassionate, modest, and kind, could be guilty of such barbarities." For it has been established that the sole purpose for the elaborate requirements and restrictions pertaining to ritual slaughtering is to ensure that the animal's pain be minimal. How, then, can these hunters be justified in killing animals in such a cruel manner, i.e., by shooting them with hot lead?

> How can we behave so sadistically toward these lovely creatures fashioned by the Holy One, blessed be He, to inhabit His world? How can we justify killing these innocent animals in such a cruel manner? And should one retort; "What matters it to me if these fowl agonize unduly in their death throes? Will God choose to plead their cause and exact vengeance for their spilt blood?" I declare: "Open your eyes and behold how demanding our holy Torah is in the area of *tzaar baalei hayyim!*"

Morpurgo proceeds to cite the episode of Rabbi Judah and the calf as evidence that God *does*, indeed, bring retribution upon those who inflict pain upon innocent animals.

He dismisses as totally irrelevant the argument questioning whether fowl are truly capable of experiencing pain when they are killed, on the grounds that it is inherently evil to destroy a life. He cites Yedidya of Speyer's refusal to recite the blessing *shehehianu* when slaughtering an animal for the first time, because a living being has been destroyed, and Mordecai Jaffe's ruling that one ought not to recite the blessing when the death of a living creature has taken place. Morpurgo concurs that the slaughter of animals is, at times, justified on the grounds of legitimate human needs, but he questions whether one may legitimately kill merely for financial profit. Furthermore, there is a prohibition against earning one's livelihood by trafficking in forbidden foods. In addition, it is forbidden to waste one's time in such frivolous, nonconstructive, and inappropriate activities. Better that these hunters should

> lift up their eyes to the rock from whence they were hewn, to our father Jacob, of blessed memory, the simple man, the dweller in tents. Why choose to emulate the practices of his evil brother [Esau], the cunning hunter and man of the field? . . . they are guilty of cruelty in putting to death God's creatures for no reason. It is a doubled and redoubled duty upon man to engage in matters which contribute to civilization, and not in the destruction of creation for sport and entertainment.

Morpurgo concludes his impassioned responsum with an eloquent plea to fellow Jews to recognize that the blessing "by thy sword shalt thou exist" is not applicable to them, and to immediately set aside their hunting pursuits so that they will no longer cause pain to God's innocent creatures.[98]

Isaac Lampronti (1679-1756) includes in his encylopedic work on Jewish law a responsum in which he prohibits the hunting of animals or birds with weapons for the sole purpose of sport or entertainment. His objections are based primarily on the fact that this constitutes the "wanton destruction" of the world of nature, although he also observes that "since the gentiles and idolators are accustomed to indulge in hunting animals and birds with weapons for mere sport, the prohibition of 'ye shall not walk in their statutes' applies. Therefore a person who indulges in this sport is unworthy of the name of Jew."[99]

All authorities are in agreement that man is permitted to kill animals for his practical benefit: for food, for clothing, and certainly when they constitute a threat to his health and well-being. But as we have noted, to kill animals for financial profit is a questionable and shameful pursuit.[100] It is forbidden to kill or to purposely cause animals pain in the name of "sport." Needless to say, even when one is permitted to destroy animal life, the act must be done in as painless a manner as is possible.

There are probably no creatures that require more the protective Divine word against the presumption of man than the animals, which like man, have sensations and instincts, but whose body and powers are nevertheless subservient to man. In relation to them, man so easily forgets that injured animal muscle twitches just like human muscle, that the maltreated nerves of an animal sicken like human nerves, that the animal being is just as sensitive to cuts, blows and beatings as man. Thus man becomes the torturer of the animal soul, which has been subjected to him only for the fulfillment of humane and wise purposes; sometimes out of self-interest, at other times in order to satisfy a whim, sometimes out of thoughtlessness . . . yes, even for the satisfaction of crude satanic desire.[101]

Moses Isserles' comment in the *Shulhan Arukh,* cited by Ezekiel Landau in his responsum, reflects this sensitivity in the halakhic context of one's putting on a new article of clothing.

The customary greeting, "May it get old and may you have a new one," is not said to one attired in new shoes and new clothing which are made from the skins of animals. Because another animal must be killed before a new garment can be made (as it is written; "and His tender mercy is over all His works"), many people are scrupulous not to say it.[102]

Nevertheless, even mystical literature, not to mention halakhic literature, stops well short of placing "animal rights" high upon the agenda of moral priorities. A perusal of medieval Jewish ethical literature finds exhortations on behalf of the rights of animals to be few and far between. Is it reasonable to assume that all Jews treated their animals with such exceedingly great compassion that no sermons on the subject were ever needed? Hardly. It is more plausible to assume that the fair treatment of fauna was simply not perceived as being all that essential a factor in ethical living.

Hardly an echo of an exhortation on behalf of sensitivity to the beast is to be found in ethical literature such as Jonah Gerondi's (d. 1263) *Shaarei Teshubah,* Zerahya HaYevani's (d. 1263) *Sefer ha-*

Yashar, Israel Al-Nakawa's (d. 1391) *Menorat haMaor,* or Isaac Aboab of Toledo's (d. 1492) work of the same name, and only a few comments appear in the fifteenth-century *Orhot Tzaddikim,*[103] or in Moses Hayyim Luzzatto's (1707–1746) *Mesillat Yesharim.*[104]

It is significant that although the ethical wills and testaments of Eliezer b. Isaac of Worms, Judah Ibn Tibbon, Joseph Ibn Kaspi, Nachmanides, Asher b. Yehiel, Jacob b. Asher, and the kabbalists Abraham, Jacob, and Shabbetai Horowitz contain many moving pleas for ethical sensitivity and compassion, none of these includes animals among the rightful beneficiaries! Samson Raphael Hirsch, probably in the spirit of German romanticism, portrays Judaism as adumbrating "love of nature" as one of its principles. But he, too, fails to emphasize the rights of animals as part of nature.

Granted, the animal was to be treated fairly. It was not to be abused, and surely not to be tormented. But its treatment just did not rate the highest priority.

NON-JEWISH PERSPECTIVES

Christian Thought

The attitude of the Christian Church toward the animal kingdom was influenced by both Judaic and Greek thought. The latter, however, was neither uniform nor consistent. Some individuals, notably the followers of Pythagoras, espoused vegetarianism, possibly out of the belief that human souls transmigrated into the bodies of animals. But others, e.g., Aristotle, viewed animals as entities merely designed for the service of man.

> Plants exist for the sake of animals, and brute beasts for the sake of man, domestic animals for his use and food, wild ones for food and other accessories of life, such as clothing and various tools. Since nature makes nothing purposeless or in vain, it is undeniably true that she has made all animals for the sake of man.[1]

It was Aristotle's view that became normative in Christian thought.

The New Testament is bereft of any legislation or moral admonitions recommending compassion toward animals. Quite the contrary. Paul's comment on the biblical injunction forbidding the muzzling of an ox that treads out corn is an incredulous "Does God care for oxen?" Of course not, he replies. The purpose of the law is "altogether for our sakes."[2]

Jesus himself is portrayed as inducing two thousand swine to drown themselves in the sea. This event, along with the episode in which Jesus curses a fig tree, prompted St. Augustine to write:

> Christ himself shows that to refrain from the killing of animals and the destroying of plants is the height of superstition, for judging that there are no common rights between us and the beasts and trees, he sent the devil into a herd of swine and with a curse withered the tree on which he found no fruit.[3]

It is true that a few voices in early Christendom, such as Flavius Clemens (220 C.E.) and St. John Chrysostom (347–407), were raised against the eating of meat, but their arguments were based upon abstinence as a virtue and usually appear in the context of ecclesiastical sermonica condemning gluttony.

Thomas Aquinas (1225–1274), the dominant voice of pre-Reformation Christian philosophy, clearly reflects the Aristotelian position that the slaughtering of animals for food is legitimate.

> There is no sin in using a thing for the purpose for which it is. Now the order of things is such that the imperfect are for the perfect . . . things like plants, which merely have life, are all alike for animals, and all animals are for man. Wherefore it is not unlawful if men use the plants for the good of animals, and animals for the good of man, as the philosopher states.
>
> Now the most necessary use would seem to consist in the fact that animals use plants, and men use animals, for food, and this cannot be done unless these be deprived of life, wherefore it is lawful both to take life from plants for the use of animals, and from animals for the use of men. In fact this is in keeping with the commandment of God Himself.[4]

Aquinas has no place in his system for compassion for the beast as an end in itself, for "it matters not how man behaves toward animals, because God has subjugated all things to man's power."[5] Man's behavior toward animals is of importance only insofar as it may affect his conduct toward his human peers. This is the rationale advanced by Aquinas to explain the biblical legislation enjoining compassion for the beast. Echoing the thought of numerous Jewish philosophers, he writes: "How it is evident that if a man practices a pitiable affection for animals, he is all the more disposed to take pity on his fellowmen, wherefore it is written, 'The just regardeth the life of his beast.' "[6]

But in Aquinas's thought, man clearly has no obligations to the animal per se, a sentiment echoed centuries later when Pope Pius IX refused to sanction the establishment of a Society for the Prevention of Cruelty to Animals in Rome on the grounds that this would imply that humans have duties toward animals![7] Even St. Francis of Assisi, the venerated champion of "animal rights," nowhere advocated vegetarianism.[8]

The humanism of the Renaissance was precisely that, for the most part—a *human*ism, emphasizing the dignity and uniqueness of man, and only referring to the animal kingdom by way of unfortunate contrast with humankind. Descartes, in elaborating upon the Church doctrine declaring animals to be bereft of an immortal soul, denied them any true consciousness. He maintained that they are incapable of experiencing either pleasure or pain, for they are merely *automata,* i.e., machines.

Islam, too, exalted man's dominion over the beast. Although Islamic thinkers commented upon the accountability of the animal kingdom before God on a day of judgment, the earthly rights of animals are scarcely discussed. Animals are useful, and should, therefore, be treated in an appropriate manner, as befits a useful tool.[9]

It was in *secular* rather than religious circles that man's dominion over the animals was challenged, with individual voices clearly advocating vegetarianism.

Secular Thought

Some of these voices were already heard in antiquity. It is claimed that the Orphic poems of the eighth and seventh centuries B.C.E. contain traces of vegetarianism. Pythagoras (6th cent. B.C.E.), as has been noted, urged abstinence from flesh, possibly under the influence of Hindu metempsychosis. But humanitarian consideration for animals was not the principal motive in Pythagoras' thinking; he believed that vegetarianism would lead to greater peace among humans.

Siddhartha, or Sakya Muni, the founder of Buddhism (6th cent. B.C.E.) also taught abstinence from animal food, but from the perspective of the sacredness of all living beings: "There hath been slaughter for the sacrifice, and slaying for the meat, but henceforth none shall spill the blood of life, nor taste of flesh; seeing that knowledge grows and life is one, and mercy cometh to the merciful."[10]

Empedocles of Sicily (5th cent. B.C.E.), a poet who sang of a golden age when man and beast dwelt in peace, urged the abolition of the foul diet of blood and animal flesh, and Ovid (43 B.C.E.–18 C.E.) powerfully influenced by metempsychosis, sings beautifully in his *Metamorphoses*:

But how have you deserved to die, you sheep, you harmless breed brought into existence for the service of men—who carry nectar in your full udders—who give your wool as soft coverings for us—who assist us more by your life than by your death? Why have the oxen deserved this—beings without guile and without deceit—innocent, mild, born for the endurance of labour? Ungrateful, indeed, is man and unworthy of the boundless gifts of the harvest, who, after un-yoking him from the plough can slaughter the tiller of his fields—who can strike with the axe that neck worn bare with labour, through which he had so often turned up the hard ground, and which had afforded so many a harvest.

And is it not enough that such wickedness is committed by men. They have involved the gods themselves in this abomination, and they believe that a Deity in the heavens can rejoice in the slaughter of the laborious and useful ox. The spotless victim, excelling in the beauty of its form (for its very beauty is the cause of its destruction), decked out with garlands and with gold is placed before their altars, and, ignorant of the purport of the proceedings, it hears the prayers of the priest. It sees the fruits which it cultivated placed on its head between its horns, and, struck down, with its life blood it dyes the sacrificial knife, which it had perhaps already seen in the clear water. Immediately they inspect the nerves and fibres torn from the yet living being, and scrutinize, forsooth, the will of deity in them.

From whence such hunger in man after unnatural and unlawful foods? Do you dare, O mortal race, to continue to feed on flesh? Cease, I adjure you, and give heed to my admonitions. And when you present to your palates the limbs of slaughtered oxen, know and feel that you are feeding on the tillers of the ground.

. . . To what wicked habits does he accustom his palate, how does that impious man prepare himself for the shedding of human gore, who cuts the throat of a calf, turning a deaf ear to its piteous moans. Or, who has the heart to pierce the throat of a kid, that utters cries like those of a child, or, who can feed on the bird whom he had fed with his own hand?[11]

But perhaps the most eloquent exponent of vegetarianism in the ancient world was the biographer Plutarch (40 C.E.–120 C.E.). His essay *On Eating Flesh* poses the question of meat-eating as follows:

You ask me upon what grounds Pythagoras abstained, from feeding on the flesh of animals. I, for my part, wonder of what sort of feeling mind, or reason, that man was possessed who was the first to pollute his mouth with gore, and to allow his lips to touch the flesh of a murdered being: who spread his table with the mangled forms of dead bodies, and claimed as daily food and dainty dishes what but now were beings endowed with movement, with perception, and with voice? . . .

What struggle for existence, or what goading madness has incited you to imbrue your hands in blood—you who have, we repeat, a superabundance of all the necessities of existence? Why do you believe the earth as though she were unable to feed and nourish you? . . . Other carnivora you call savage and ferocious—lions and tigers and serpents—while yourselves pollute your hands with blood and come behind them in no species of barbarity. *And yet for them murder is the only means of sustenance; whereas to you it is a superfluous luxury.*

Plutarch proceeds to enumerate the cruel means by which animals are fattened up and tortured to death, condemning these practices as being both unnecessary and heartless. For, in his advocacy of vegetarianism, he argues that man is not carnivorous by nature, because the human body bears no resemblance to the bodies of carnivorous beasts. Furthermore, he believes flesh-eating to be injurious to one's intellect as well as dangerous to one's sense of morality. He theorizes: "Does it not seem admirable to foster habits of philanthropy? Who that is so kindly and gently disposed toward beings of another species would ever be inclined to do injury to his own kind?"

Plutarch's advocacy of vegetarianism is, in reality, an eloquent blending of ethical sensitivity and practical scientific observation. Not only is the eating of meat morally wrong, but it is also ultimately injurious to man himself. Finally, Plutarch argues in *On Intelligence* and *That The Lower Animals Reason* that, as the very titles of these works indicate, animals do possess intelligence and the power of reason, and are clearly designed to be far more than merely man's food supply.

However eloquent these voices of antiquity may have been, they were rare voices "calling in the wilderness" and failed to attract any substantial following. As a matter of fact, for a full millennium, between the fifth and fifteenth centuries, there is a conspicuous silence regarding "animal rights" and vegetarianism. Only the Cathari, a heretical sect persecuted by the medieval Roman Catholic Church, restricted their animal diet to fish and permitted themselves to kill only noxious beasts and reptiles. One of the Church's means for identifying these heretics consisted of putting them to the test by demanding that they eat the flesh of beast and fowl.[12]

Commencing in the fifteenth century, however, significant voices are raised in protest over the sufferings of the animal kingdom. Thomas More (1478–1535), author of *Utopia,* condemns hunting and envisions an ideal society which will "permit not their citizens to accustom themselves to the killing of beasts." Michel de Montaigne (1533–1593) writes that differences between man and animal are more a matter of degree than kind, for "we are neither above nor below the rest. 'All who are under the sky,' says the Jewish sage, 'experience a like law and fate!' " Pierre Gassendi (1592–1655) attempts to find a scientific justification for vegetarianism as the natural state of man. The horrors of the abbatoir are vividly and critically recounted by the physician Bernard de Mandeville (1670–1733), and other physicians, such as George Cheyne (1671–1743) and Abraham Cocchi (1695–1758) advocate, on medical grounds, radical dietetic reform in the form of vegetarianism.[13]

Alexander Pope (1680–1744) condemns hunting and the torture slaying of animals for food, and in the age of social criticism and liberalism, Jean Jacques Rousseau (1713–1778) extols vegetarianism, as he condemns his contemporaries for having departed from the authentic patterns of nature and natural living in adopting the barbarisms of civilization.

Now most of these thinkers were estranged from the teachings of the Church, and some of them even indict Christianity for its role in perpetuating injustices toward beasts. François Marie Arouet de Voltaire (1694–1778), for example, contrasts Hinduism's compassion and reverence for all life with Christianity's heartless subjugation of the animal kingdom. It is therefore interesting to note Voltaire, in his *Traité sur la Tolerance,* appealing to the Bible as the source for the sacred alliance between God and all living creatures, as he protests the shedding of their blood.

It may be inferred from these and other passages, what all antiquity has always thought, down to our own time, that animals have intelligence and knowledge. The deity does not make a pact with trees and with stones which have no feeling, but he makes it with animals whom he has endowed with feeling often more exquisite than ours, and with ideas necessarily attached to it. This is why he will not allow [men] the barbarity of feeding upon their blood, because, in reality, blood is the source of life, consequently of feeling. . . .

Of the seven precepts of the Noachians, admitted among the Jews, there is one which forbids to eat of the members of a living animal. This . . . prohibition proves that men have had the barbarous cruelty to mutilate living beings in order to devour their dismembered limbs, and that they suffered them to live in order to feed upon parts of the body in succession! . . . It must be agreed that it is barbarous to make them suffer. It, assuredly, is only custom which can diminish in us that natural horror of cutting the throat of an animal, whom we have fed up for butchery.[14]

The fact of the matter, however, is that several of the aforementioned "humanitarian" writers were guilty of not always practicing what they preached. In theory they eloquently endorsed the humane treatment of animals and advocated vegetarianism. But in practice they often failed to live up to their pronouncements. As Henry David Thoreau (1817–1862) later wrote in *Walden,* "*What ever my practice may be* [emphasis added], I have no doubt that it is a part of the destiny of the human race, in its gradual improvement, to leave off eating animals, as surely as the savage tribes left off eating each other, when they came in contact with the more civilized." Thoreau's convictions apparently did not affect his own practices, and Oliver Goldsmith (1728–1794) sarcastically commented about those who oppose cruelty to animals but who love to eat meat, "they pity and they eat the objects of their compassion."[15]

Many others advocated a nonflesh diet for practical rather than humanitarian reasons. Jean Baptiste Pressavin (1760–1830?) was convinced that it would prolong one's life span, Joseph Ritson (1761–1830) concurred, and argued that meat-eating is morally as well as physically injurious, for "the use of animal food disposes man to cruel and ferocious actions,"[16] while William Lambe (1765–1847) saw in a vegetable diet the most effective cure for countless maladies, and John Abernathy (1763–1831) used dietetics in treating cancer. Even Percy Bysshe Shelley (1792–1822), who deplores the butchery of animals and envisions in his *Queen Mab* a prophetic golden age in which vegetarianism will be the norm, insists that such a diet bestows great economic, social, and political benefits, not to mention the added gift of longevity.

Furthermore, not all who were vegetarians were consistent in their abstinence from meat. They were not *pure* or *true* vegetarians. Even Buddha approved of eating flesh which was "unseen, unheard and unsuspected"! In other words, one was permitted to consume the meat of an animal if one did not actually see or hear the beast being killed or suspect that the slaughter took place for one's benefit. Hindus may refuse to eat beef but do partake of the flesh of other animals. Other advocates of vegetarianism and "compassion for beasts," such as Arthur Schopenhauer (1788–1860) and Richard Wagner (1813–1883), were not always as compassionate when it came to judging their fellow-humans!

But basic to pure vegetarianism is the thesis that there is something terribly *wrong* in eating the flesh of any living being and a sensitive human should be repulsed by the very thought. As Gandhi (1869–1948) describes his own effort to eat a piece of meat,

> It began to grow on me that meat-eating was good, that it would make me strong and daring, and that, if the whole country took to meat-eating, the English could be overcome. . . . It was not a question of pleasing the palate, I did not know that it had a particularly good relish. . . . We went in search of a lonely spot by the river, and there I saw, for the first time in my life—meat. There was baker's bread also. I relished neither. The goat's meat was tough as leather. I simply could not eat it. I was sick and had to leave off eating. I had a very bad night afterwards. A horrible nightmare haunted me. Everytime I dropped off to sleep it would seem as though a live goat were bleating inside me, and I would jump up full of remorse.[17]

For some individuals, vegetarianism came to mean more than merely refraining from butchering and consuming the flesh of animals. The Jains, members of a religious offshoot of Hinduism, sweep the ground upon which they walk in an effort to remove any creeping or crawling insects so that they will not be crushed underfoot. They wear veils so as to minimize any chance of inadvertently inhaling tiny insects, and refrain from eating at night lest they consume some flying nocturnal insects along with their food. They even avoid consuming certain fruits out of fear that they might contain worms.[18] Others extend the notion of cruelty to animals to forbid the eating of eggs or the partaking of milk products because of the ruthless exploitation of hens and dairy animals.[19]

Lewis Gompertz (1784–1861), the distinguished British inventor, devoted his life to the betterment of the lot of the animal kingdom. The all-inclusive title of his magnum opus, *Moral Inquiries on the Situation of Man and of Brutes. On the Crime of Committing Cruelty on Brutes, and of Sacrificing Them to the Purposes of Man; with Further Reflections,* speaks for itself. Gompertz was the honorary secretary of the Society for the Prevention of Cruelty to Animals and later became the founder of the Animals' Friend Society.

He advocated extending to animals all rights and privileges appropriate to humans, and justified his policy by pointing to the basic similitude between man and beast. He argued that man can learn a great deal from his animal friends, and in a section reminiscent of the talmudic teachings on the subject, Gompertz describes how, from dogs and cats, "mankind may learn maternal, filial, conjugal, and in some cases, paternal affection," as well as candor![20] From certain species of fowl, one can also learn "real constancy in conjugal affections,"[21] and even porcupines can teach man the virtue of "strength of affection."[22]

Gompertz condemned the killing of animals for food as being contrary to the will of God, and disapproved of those who eat flesh killed by others, though he admits that their sin is not as great as that of the "killers." He also argued against the eating of eggs and drinking of milk on the grounds that this constitutes "stealing,"[23] and even disapproves of shearing a sheep of its wool, unless this be of benefit to the animal as well, or at least involve no discomfort on its part.[24] Gompertz put his inventive genius to good use by designing vehicles which could be pulled by working animals with great facility and ease.

Gompertz apparently blamed the Bible, at least in part, for certain tendencies of cruelty toward animals. He refers the reader to certain biblical passages for the benefit of "those who may wish for proof of the crime of cruelty to animals founded on Scriptural researches."[25] But his idyllic portrait of man's future role as the compassionate caretaker of all animals echoes the setting of the Garden of Eden.

> Man, then becoming truly religious, will glory in superintending the works of his Maker, which He has entrusted to him; as a faithful servant, he will then not deny to what he now calls the meanest reptile, his protection, and own it to be his brother, resembling himself in construction, and created with similar care by the Supreme Being.[26]

In Defense of Shehitah

We have attempted to demonstrate in preceding chapters how the principle of *tzaar baalei hayyim* came to dominate halakhic thinking vis-à-vis the animal and was reflected in a heightened sensitivity toward the animal's well-being. Yet it is a fact of history that religious Jewry has *not* been active in the "animal rights" cause or in the forefront of vegetarianism advocacy. Quite the contrary. It has often found itself on the defensive in having to justify the institution of ritual slaughter of animals against anti-*shehitah* movements.

The Royal Society for the Prevention of Cruelty to Animals brought suit against the London Jewish community in 1855, contending that the practice of *shehitah* was inhumane. The Russian Society for the Protection of Animals also investigated alleged brutalities associated with *shehitah*.

A number of nations actually banned *shehitah,* among them Switzerland in 1893, Norway and Bavaria in 1930, Sweden and Italy in 1937 and 1938 respectively. Such legislation may have been motivated by a sincere concern for "animal rights," but the factor of anti-Semitism should not be overlooked either. Nazi Germany also banned *shehitah* in 1933, and it was forbidden during World War II in countries under German occupation.

Now Jewish thinkers were obviously aware of the undeniable fact that animals being slaughtered experience pain, and even though they took pride in the fact that *shehitah* was a relatively painless procedure, nevertheless pain surely is involved.

Yehudah Assad agonizes over the fact that all *shehitah* constitutes a violation of the precept of *tzaar baalei hayyim*, for it is cruel to slaughter a living creature, and remarks that "on the Day of Judgment [Rosh haShanah], when all of us supplicate the Lord for mercy . . . 'He whose tender mercies are over all His works' . . . it is fitting for us to refrain from committing any act of cruelty, such as slaughtering living creatures,"[27] and several contemporary rabbinic authorities have advocated the amelioration of the animal's discomfiture prior to and during the act of *shehitah*. For example, the plight of baby milk-fed veal, segregated and confined in two-by-five pens, denied roughage in their diet and bedding in their stalls, has been decried by Moses Tendler, and some rabbis have recommended that cattle be conveyed to their slaughter erectly by means of ropes around their stomachs rather than be inhumanely suspended upside-down by their legs.[28] Actually this latter procedure of shackling and hoisting is not a mandated halakhic process at all, but rather stems from United States health regulations in the early part of the twentieth century which forbade the slaughter of animals upon the ground. The Rabbinical Council of America has recommended the use of special pens which would preclude the necessity of shackling and hoisting.

It is interesting to note that Dr. Isaac Dembo (1846–1906), a Leningrad Jewish physician who successfully defended the traditional Jewish manner of slaughtering against the Russian Society for the Protection of Animals by arguing that severing an animal's throat was more humane than the accepted secular manner of slaughtering, i.e. severing the cervical spinal cord, did criticize some of the procedures employed in conveying animals to their slaughter.[29]

Some critics of *shehitah* have advocated that the animal be stunned prior to slaughter in order to minimize any sensation of pain. But Jewish authorities have opposed stunning on the grounds that it causes damage to the animal's skull and brain and impedes the blood supply to the brain. Electrical stunning is also prohibited because the electric shock can cause disfigurement to the animal's musculature, not to mention hemorrhaging and the formation of blood clots.[30]

Proposals seeking to drug animals prior to their slaughter have also been rejected. One respondent argues that earlier generations of scholars were surely aware of the existence of procedures designed to minimize the pain of living beings about to be killed (potions were administered to numb criminals prior to their execution!),[31] yet none of them saw fit to advocate such procedures in the case of shehitah. Therefore, he concludes, such concerns need not occupy our attention.[32]

Moses Feinstein, in a responsum dated 1960, is asked to comment upon a government proposal to introduce gas into a confined pen so that the animal to be slaughtered would be rendered temporarily unconscious.[33] Although he agrees that this is theoretically permissible, Feinstein expresses concern as to the possibility of the animal suffering internal damage as a result of the gas and its attendant struggles, and also questions the advisability of performing a hasty shehitah under these circumstances.

To bring the issue up to date, Dr. I. M. Levinger, of the department of life sciences at Bar-Ilan University, participated in a study carried out at the Veterinary-Physiology Institute of Zurich University on the question of the compatibility of kosher slaughtering with present animal-protection laws. The study, augmented by subsequent investigation in Israel, resulted in the publication of "Medical Aspects of Shehita."[34]

While concurring that any method of slaughter is obviously cruelty to the animal, the researchers are convinced that "in comparison with other methods of slaughter, shehitah is at least as humane as any other method of slaughter."[35] This conclusion is based upon such evidence as the following:

After shehitah the central nervous system undergoes certain changes. Blood pressure as well as CSFP rapidly drop and produce shock reactions within the animal. Within 8–10 seconds, the centers for maintaining equilibrium lose their regulatory capacity. Corneal reflex disappears in small animals, though in large animals it takes 20–40 seconds before it disappears. Since it is known that the neo-encephalon is more oxygen sensitive than the phylogenetically older portions of the brain, it may be assumed that the functional ability of the cortex ceases within less than 10 seconds after *shehitah*. Since the animal does not move within 10 seconds, it may be concluded that the animal does not feel pain and that the movements of the animal are the result of reflexes in the spinal cord centers. The muscle contractions are uncoordinated and cannot be considered defense movements by the animal. They are rather reactions due to the firing of different centers in the nervous system and are the result of the anoxia in these centers.[36]

An animal is incapable of sensing approaching death and therefore it is unable to fear or suffer from the danger of death. It is likewise unable to recognize the instrument of slaughter as such. It may be stated with the utmost probability that an animal does not suffer physically or psychologically before, during, or after *shehitah*. The process of pain perception requires a given amount of time, but by that time the activity of the brain has been greatly impaired if not completely paralysed.[37]

The substance of such argumentation is truly beyond the scope of our study, and so we have alluded only briefly to the extensive literature which has developed in response to anti-*shehitah* legislation.

What is significant, however, is the fact that many Jewish religious authorities have been hesitant and somewhat resistant toward the further application of the principle of *tzaar baalei hayyim* to the area of *shehitah*. Why? Why the apparent resistance, at times, to even considering possible modifications designed to benefit the animal and ameliorate its sufferings?

Several answers suggest themselves. The act of *shehitah* is, after all, intimately associated with the sacrificial cult. It is divinely mandated. Can one, then, legitimately challenge God's commands and chosen procedures? Would it not be presumptuous of one to strive to be more pious than the Lord by questioning the "humaneness" of His traditional procedures? Religious sensitivities and sensibilities on this point can be a good deal stronger than those associated with *tzaar baalei hayyim*.

There is also an understandable wariness on the part of rabbinic leadership toward the *sources* of proposed modifications in the Jewish manner of slaughtering animals. In the aforementioned responsum of Rabbi Moses Feinstein, involving the permissibility of rendering an animal unconscious by means of gas prior to its slaughter, it is significant that the respondent (who personally refuses to partake of a meat dish by itself without bread on the grounds that this is gluttony) does not even dwell upon the factor of *tzaar baalei hayyim!* His principal concern is reflected in the concluding sentence of his responsum: "One should put forth every effort to achieve the annulment of this proposal which has been put forth by the enemies of Israel."[38] Indeed, the Jewish community has had good historic reason for being uneasy about outside interference in the realm of *shehitah*. Suggestions can easily become coercions, critiques can develop into prohibitions.

In any event, it is important to note that in modern times, Jewish religious authorities have occasionally been forced to adopt a defensive and apologetic position vis-à-vis ritual slaughtering procedures. But as a rule, this has been in response to *external* rather than *internal* agitation.

15

JEWISH VEGETARIANISM

Jewish religious thinkers were not unaware of the existence of vegetarianism. The twelveth-century biblical exegete Abraham Ibn Ezra commented that the ancient Egyptians refrained from eating flesh and reports that the people of India of his time abstain not only from meat-products but from milk as well, while yet others shun eggs because these are the products of living creatures.[1] But Ibn Ezra apparently sees nothing worth emulating in these practices.

Even the Karaite Aaron b. Eliezer, who taught that God's special providence extends to animals as well as to men, insists that it is perfectly legitimate for man to butcher animals for food, seeing that God has created the latter precisely for this purpose.

Tradition does record Isaac Luria's opposition to the eating of meat,[2] but history is curiously silent on the subject. As noted earlier, Luria's belief in the transmigration of souls seems, if anything, to have encouraged flesh-eating, at least under certain circumstances. Bahya Ibn Pakuda endorses a partial abstinence from food, but this would appear to stem from his conviction that such abstinence is beneficial to one's ethical and intellectual perfection. Bahya opposes gluttony in general, not meat-eating per se.

Others may have been sympathetic to vegetarianism, but their sympathies lay in the domain of theory, not practice, and were expressed in the context of scriptural commentary rather than public exhortation. For example, Don Isaac Abarbanel believed that eating meat would cause one to become callous and cruel. Why then did God permit it to Noah? Because, explains Abarbanel, when Noah emerged from the ark he found a desolate world of barren trees and dead plants. There was simply nothing for him to eat! Therefore, he was forced, out of necessity, to subsist upon the flesh of animals.[3] Abarbanel is content to conclude at this point, without raising the practical question of how one justifies the eating of meat *now*. Clearly it was not a burning moral issue to his mind.

Samson Raphael Hirsch theorizes that initially the earth was capable of sustaining all of life with its vegetation. However, the flood metamorphosed the world of nature, and so man must now partake of the flesh of animals, for meat is an indispensable element in the human diet.[4] This notion was significant in Hirsch's thinking, for he adds: "The Torah demands no vegetarianism, it has no aversion to the eating of meat, it even makes it a duty on *Yom-Tov*. If our physical condition were still the original one, the eating of meat would probably not be permitted to us, but now it is probably necessary."

Far more detailed expositions on the subject of vegetarianism are found in the writings of two fifteenth-century philosophers, Isaac b. Moses Arama and Joseph Albo, and the twentieth-century philosopher-mystic, Abraham Isaac haKohen Kook. These thinkers merit special consideration because they mirror so clearly the paradox inherent in a tradition which permits the slaughter of animals for food and at the same time affirms an ideal state of existence in the Garden of Eden, where man subsists totally on vegetation. In some respects these three espouse a moderate form of theoretical vegetarianism.

Isaac Arama

Isaac Arama's (ca. 1420–1494) discussions appear in his homiletical-philosophic commentary to the Pentateuch, *Akedat Yitzhak*.[5] He commences by extolling vegetarianism as the highest ideal. True, man was permitted in the epoch of Noah to eat the flesh of animals. But this was due to the fact that man is obviously superior to all beasts, and his level of spirituality is exalted far above theirs. A human who is boorish and ignorant, however, ought not to eat meat because he is on a level similar to that of the beast! At the other end of the human spectrum stand men of exceedingly great piety who similarly refrain from eating meat. They voluntarily abstain from flesh and limit their diet to vegetation because they wish to live in keeping with God's initial blueprint for mankind. Their level of spirituality is such that they are able to elevate themselves above crass bodily appetites.

Arama theorizes that God had hoped that the Israelites, once freed from Egyptian bondage, would willingly subsist on a diet of vegetation. Unfortunately, the people lusted after the fleshpots of Egypt and ate quail. Arama devotes a lengthy analysis to the *manna* eaten by the Israelites during their sojourn in the wilderness. This symbolizes for him the ideal relationship that ought to exist between man and his food. Ideally, people should not expend great time and energy in the pursuit of material sustenance, for God will surely provide all with their needs. Such will be the state of affairs in the messianic era, when mankind will enjoy fruits and vegetables from the Garden of Eden, the perfect food for perfected human beings.

Joseph Albo

Joseph Albo, in a fascinating biblical exegesis, addresses himself to two pertinent questions: Why was the eating of meat forbidden to Adam but permitted to Noah? Why was Noah permitted to eat any flesh of his choosing, while the Children of Israel were restricted in their meat-diet?

Albo states at the onset that it is wrong for man to kill animals. "In the killing of animals there is cruelty, rage, and the accustoming oneself to the bad habit of shedding innocent blood, but the eating of some animals produces, besides, coarseness, ugliness, and stupidity."[6] Therefore the Creator saw fit to deprive Adam of meat, permitting him, instead, the consumption of seed-bearing vegetables and fruits. But God differentiated between Adam and the animals insofar as the latter are permitted only green grass lacking in seed.

However, according to Albo, this distinction proved to be inadequate. Cain erroneously assumed that man and beast were on an equal plane, since both subsisted on a diet of vegetation, and deduced that man has no right to take the life of an animal. Cain believed that man's only superiority over the beast lay in his skillfulness in being able to till the soil and grow plants, and therefore he chose to bring to the Lord an offering from the fruit of the earth. But the Lord rejected his offering precisely because Cain was so far from grasping the truth of man's overwhelming superiority to the animal kingdom. Abel, on the other hand, was closer to the truth. He observed that man subdues animals and forces them to do his labors, and concluded that it is permissible for man to slaughter an animal upon an altar as an offering to God. However, Abel, too, failed to grasp the immense distinction between man and beast, and God therefore permitted him to die at Cain's hand.

Albo interprets God's rebuke to Cain in the following manner:

"Why art thou wroth? And why is thy countenance fallen? If thou doest well, shall it not be lifted up?" The meaning is: you are right, man is born a wild ass, and has no superiority over the animal in actuality when he comes into the world, but he has superiority potentially if he practices goodness and realizes his potentialities and recognizes the greatness of the Lord. If he does well, he will be lifted up above the animals.[7]

But Cain was incapable of understanding the message. Ironically, he murders his brother precisely because he could see no difference between man and beast, reasoning that "since God favors Abel and his present, it is clear that it is permitted to kill animals, and hence it is just as lawful to kill Abel as any other animal!"[8] Indeed, the deluge was visited upon the earth precisely because most people followed Cain's reasoning and saw no distinction between the oppression of animals and the oppression of men, "therefore they were corrupt and lived like animals."

Albo also interprets the act of Noah's bringing an animal offering to God after the flood as an indication that Noah, at last, grasps the truth of man's superiority over the beast. God understandably rejoices in his sacrifice and further emphasizes human superiority by permitting the killing of animals for food to Noah and his descendants, at the same time strongly forbidding the shedding of human blood, "giving as a reason that the spirit of man is not like the spirit of the animal, for in the image of God made he man, i.e., man has a rational form which is nobler than the spirit of the animal. For this reason it was necessary to permit all animals, without distinction, which He did, in order to eradicate the former opinion and wipe off its memory."

Why then the subsequent imposition of strict dietary laws upon the Israelites, severely limiting their choice of food? Albo responds with an interesting theory of "spiritual evolution and readiness."

He suggests that at this later date, there was no longer any doubt in people's minds as to man's preeminence over the animal. Therefore it was no longer necessary for God to insist on man's right (and even "duty") to eat *all* animals as an object lesson for this truth. God is now able to reveal His true intent to Israel, namely, that there is no law compelling man to eat of the flesh of animals. Quite the contrary!

> Even the animals that were permitted were merely a concession to human lust and desire, in the same way as the Israelites were permitted women taken in war. Thus the rabbis say, commenting on the verse "Because thy soul desireth to eat flesh." There is a moral lesson in this expression, namely, that one should not eat flesh unless he has an appetite for it. This shows clearly that the eating of flesh was permitted only because of necessity.[9]

To summarize Albo's position; it is necessary for man to view himself as being above the level of the animal. Otherwise he will sink to the level of beasts in moral and ethical behavior patterns. However, once man truly recognizes his elevated status and true spiritual essence, there is no longer any need for him to lord it over the animal kingdom, and surely no need for him to consume their flesh merely as a pedagogical device! For in reality, the killing of an animal is a cruel act and a dangerous habit for one to accustom himself to.

Abraham Isaac haKohen Kook

Kook comes the closest of these three to a position of true vegetarianism, both in theory and in practice. His writings embody a fusion of Jewish philosophy, popular Kabbalah, and Hasidic thought, with a heavy emphasis on mystical traditions. As mysticism often incorporates pantheistic elements, it is not surprising to find the animal kingdom endowed with a substantial measure of divinity in Kook's writings.

Kook's essays on vegetarianism and man's duties to the animal[10] reflect his portrait of man as a "spiritually evolving creature," with the emphasis on both "spiritual" and "evolving."

The free movement of the moral impulse to establish justice for animals generally and the claim of their rights from mankind are hidden in a natural psychic sensibility in the deeper layers of the Torah. In the ancient value system of humanity, while the spiritual illumination (which later found its bastion in Israel) was diffused among individuals without involvement in a national framework, before nations were differentiated into distinct speech forms, the moral sense had risen to a point of demanding justice for animals. "The first man had not been allowed to eat meat," as is implied in God's instruction to Adam: "I have given you every herb yielding seed which is on the face of all the earth, and every tree in which is the fruit of a tree yielding seed—it shall be to you for food." But when humanity, in the course of its development, suffered a setback and was unable to bear the great light of its illumination, its receptive capacity being impaired, it was withdrawn from the fellowship with other creatures, whom it excelled with firm spiritual superiority. Now it became necessary to confine the concern with justice and equity to mankind, so that divine fire, burning with a very dim light, might be able to warm the heart of man, which had cooled off as a result of the many pressures of life. The changes in thought and disposition, in the ways of particularized developments, required that moral duty be concentrated on the plane of humanity alone. But the thrust of the ideals in the course of their development will not always remain confined. Just as the democratic aspiration will reach outward through the general intellectual and moral perfection, "when man shall no longer teach his brother to know the Lord, for they will all know Me, small and great alike" (Jer. 31:34), so will the hidden yearning to act justly toward animals emerge at the proper time. What prepares the ground for this state is the commandments, those intended specifically for this area of concern.

To paraphrase Kook's theory; God has implanted within us deep feelings of kinship and compassion for all forms of life. Animals are "our friends," who, like us, emanate from God's creative powers, and the Torah bids us to behave compassionately toward all creatures. Therefore, vegetarianism is surely the ideal state for men. Unfortunately, the ancient philosophers rationalized away their compassionate feelings and instead condoned and even encouraged the mistreatment of animals. Because man sank to an exceedingly low level of spiritual sensitivity, it became necessary for the teachers of Israel to emphasize the relationship of man to his fellowman, *at the expense of man-animal relationships.* For it was essential that man be separated from the world of animals and be given a more elevated image of himself as a superior being. It is for this reason that the Torah distinguishes between man-man obligations and man-animal obligations, excusing man from some of the latter and even permitting him to butcher and eat of the flesh of fauna. This was deemed appropriate because it would have been incongruous and inconsistent for man to manifest ethical sensitivity toward beasts while, at the same time, persecuting his fellow human beings.

Moreover, argues Kook, man's spiritual growth is an agonizingly gradual and torturous process, and seeking to accelerate it could prove to be dangerous. In other words, were the Torah to suddenly deny man the right to eat meat, the result might conceivably be his eating the flesh of other human beings, for he might be incapable of controlling his lust for flesh!

When the animal lust for meat became overpowering, if the flesh of all living beings had been forbidden, then the moral destructiveness, which will always appear at such times, would not have differentiated between man and animal, beast and fowl and every creeping thing on the earth. The knife, the axe, the guillotine, the electric current, would have felled them all alike in order to satisfy the vulgar craving of so-called cultured humanity.

Scripture therefore permits man to eat meat, but it emphasizes that this is a reprehensible act, and the true meaning of the phrase "Because thy soul desireth to eat flesh" is, according to Kook, that when one's moral sensitivities vis-à-vis eating animals are as spiritually developed as those vis-à-vis consuming human flesh, one will undoubtably abhor the eating of animal flesh as much as one would abhor cannibalism! In the interim, however, one is permitted to eat meat, but only the flesh of certain animals slaughtered in accordance with the humane procedures of *shehitah*. One must cover the blood of certain animals to dramatize the sense of shame that prompts one to have to butcher innocent animals and consume their flesh. It is forbidden to eat *terefah,* for such an act places one in a league with those wild beasts which feed on small, helpless creatures; it would be as if man were sharing the "spoils" with them. Likewise, it is not permitted to eat *nebelah,* for such as act would show a total lack of compassion for the unfortunate animal, and a desire to gleefully benefit from its death.

Although Kook does not envision the ideal man-animal relationship as materializing until some future age, he exhorts his readers to put into practice acts of loving-kindness toward fauna. For example, a man should care for his old and weak working-animals long after their usefulness to him may have passed. Sheep-shearing and even milking a cow are, in reality, forms of robbery, and Kook cautions that such "gifts of nature" are not always ours for the taking.

Kook's central message is that man ought never to forget that meat-eating is but a temporary concession. The merciful God of Israel would never decree that man's survival should be eternally contingent upon his butchering animals. One day mankind will regain its true spiritual heights and recognize the deep kinship it shares with all of existence. Then the eating of meat will be abhored, and man and animal will coexist in peace.

In this connection, it is significant that Kook also envisioned the abolition of all animal sacrifices in the messianic era.

In the future the abundance of enlightenment will spread and penetrate even the animals. . . . The gift offerings of vegetation that will be brought as sacrifices will be as acceptable as the sacrifices of ancient days.[11]

Secular Jewish Vegetarianism

Lewis Gompertz, the distinguished nineteenth-century vegetarian and advocate of "animal rights," was a Jew but as was the case with most non-Jewish spokesmen for vegetarianism, "religion" was apparently not a factor in Gompertz's thinking, for his convictions also emerged from an essentially secular, humanistic world-outlook. One could argue that in the twentieth century as well, Jewish vegetarianism remains essentially secular rather than sacred in nature.

This is not to say that the vegetarian movement does not number distinguished rabbis among its ranks. In Israel, the Ashkenazi Chief Rabbi, Shlomo Goren (b. 1917) is a vegetarian, as are Rabbis David (the *nazir*) and Shear Yashuv Cohen. The Chief Rabbi of Ireland, David Rosen, is also a vegetarian, as are several young American-ordained rabbis. Rabbinic responsa have been authored declaring that one can fulfill the obligation to rejoice on the Sabbath and festivals *without* necessarily partaking of flesh, fowl, or fish at religious meals.[12]

But one has the impression that much resistance to vegetarianism remains among traditional Jews despite the example of the aforementioned rabbinic devotees. Rev. Chaim Zundel Maccoby (the Kamenitzer *maggid)* claimed that he was forced to emigrate from his native Poland in 1890 because his rabbinic colleagues "persecuted and hounded him on account of it,"[13] and one contemporary scholar has suggested (with some seriousness?) that rabbinic opposition to vegetarianism may be unconsciously motivated, stemming from the fear that abstinence from meat on the part of the general population would drastically minimize the need for rabbinic expertise in the area of *kashrut!*[14]

Be that as it may, there is little evidence that observant Jewry as a whole tends toward observing the regimen of a vegetarian diet.

However, evidence does point to a growing interest in, and sensitivity toward, vegetarianism on the part of general Jewish society, notably in the United States, England, and Israel, where membership in Jewish vegetarian societies is rapidly increasing. It is not difficult to draw inspiration from the statements of such Jewish literary giants as Shmuel Yosef Agnon (1888–1970) and Isaac Bashevis Singer (b. 1904). With an eloquence and passion not inferior to that of the aforementioned eloquent and impassioned non-Jewish devotees of vegetarianism, Singer declares:

> The longer I am a vegetarian, the more I feel how wrong it is to kill animals and eat them. I think that eating meat or fish is a denial of all ideals, even of all religions. How can we pray to God for mercy if we ourselves have no mercy? How can we speak of right and justice if we take an innocent creature and shed its blood? Every kind of killing seems to me savage and I find no justification for it.
>
> I believe that the religion of the future will be based on vegetarianism. As long as people will shed the blood of innocent creatures there can be no peace, no liberty, no harmony between people. Slaughter and justice cannot dwell together.
>
> Early in my life I came to the conclusion that there was no basic difference between man and animals. If a man has the heart to cut the throat of a chicken or a calf, there's no reason he should not be willing to cut the throat of a man.[15]

Agnon, upon being awarded the Nobel Prize for Literature, drew upon authentic Jewish mystical tradition when he expressed his gratitude to the world of fauna.

> Lest I slight any creature, I must also mention the domestic animals, the beasts and the birds from whom I have learned. Job

said long ago (35:11): "Who teacheth us more than the beasts of the earth, and maketh us wiser than the fowls of heaven?" Some of what I have learned from them I have written in my books, but I fear that I have not learned as much as I should have done, for when I hear a dog bark, or a bird twitter, or a cock crow, I do not know whether they are thanking me for all I have told of them or calling me to account.[16]

A thesis currently being put forth claims that "vegetarianism can draw much inspiration and support from the Hebrew Bible and from rabbinical thought."[17] One hesitates to endorse this view wholeheartedly. At first glance it seems a preposterous assertion, as both Scripture and Talmud maintain virtually total silence on the subject of vegetarianism. But some claim to be able to hear "the sounds of silence," or, at least, an echo of dreams of a future vegetarian ideal amidst past realities. Perhaps à la Agnon, an eclectic-selective reading of the Jewish tradition will eventually yield both inspiration and support to the vegetarianism movement.

CONCLUSION

It is understandable that the traditional Jewish attitude toward animals, although a positive one, is a "moderate" rather than an "excessive" concern. The Bible "demythologized" fauna and removed from the animal any role of cosmic significance, rendering it essentially a working "tool" in an agricultural society. The rabbinic era may have permitted a cautious and limited "remythologization," but this was held in check by halakhic restrictions, as well as the practical dictates of an agrarian culture which would militate against undue concern for beasts.

In the Middle Ages, the status of fauna was restricted by both philosophy and *halakhah,* the former exalting man's status far above that of the beast, the latter emphasizing interpersonal relationships at the expense of animal-person relations. Furthermore, both demography and sociology influenced the medieval scene to the detriment of the animal. The urban-dwelling Jew was driven from Western Europe during the Renaissance, precisely at the point when animals became popular as pets. It was not until the fifteenth and sixteenth centuries that European society, in conscious imitation of the nobility, proceeded to "adopt" animals as a social part of the family unit. But Jewish society could not afford the luxury of having animals as pets, as it was far removed from the life-patterns of the society of noblemen. Finally, at no time did the animal occupy an exalted place in Jewish religious symbolism, certainly nothing comparable to that of the lamb in Christian religious motifs. The animal was essentially a nonsymbolic creature.

Jewish vegetarianism, too, was greatly limited, for a simple and obvious reason. The Bible clearly permits, if not encourages, the butchering of animals for food, and the sacrificial cult mandates the slaughter of animals! It entails some degree of presumptuousness to refuse to partake of flesh on religious grounds when God Himself has sanctioned the act! Thus, those sympathetic to vege-

299

tarianism are limited in the extent to which they can justify their position. True, it can be argued that Scripture does not command the Israelite to eat meat, but rather permits this diet as a concession to lust. One can postulate the existence of an unfolding "spiritual evolutionary process" that will someday attain the pristine scriptural ideal of vegetarianism. But such ideas lack mass appeal and fail to wield authority.

Kabbalistic and Hasidic thought may have remythologized the animal in a pantheistic manner, but folklore and folk language served, paradoxically, to reaffirm the gap between man and beast. The folk language of Yiddish betrays this bias: such phrases as *zei a mentsch, behama, vilde chaya*, etc., are significant. Almost invariably, any comparison to an animal carried with it unflattering implications.

Man is to treat animals fairly and compassionately. He must exert benevolent stewardship over fauna, and he is limited as to the degree to which he may exploit the animal kingdom. But man's spiritual development entails a lonely climb to the summit. He must ascend far above the level of the animal and must leave the animal behind in his quest for ideal interpersonal relationships.

NOTES

Introduction

1. Isa. 34:15.
2. Deut. 14:5.
3. Ibid.
4. Isa. 13:22.
5. Esther 8:10, 14.
6. So it is identified by Moses Tendler.
7. Bill Clark, "Animals of the Bible—Living Links to Antiquity," *Biblical Archaeological Review* 7, no. 1 (January–February 1981): 35. The biblical verses cited are Isa. 35:6, Num. 24:8, and Deut. 32:11–12.
8. "Die vermeintliche Rechtlosigkeit der Tiere ist geradezu eine empoerende Roheit und Barberei des Okzidents, deren Quelle im Judentum liegt." Isak Unna, *Tierschutz im Judentum* (Frankfort-am-Main: J. Kaufmann Verlag, 1928), p. 6.
9. Samuel Dresner, *The Jewish Dietary Laws* (New York, 1959), pp. 24–27.

Chapter 1

1. Gen. 1:24.
2. Gen. 2:20.
3. Ps. 50:10.
4. Gen. 7:23.
5. Num. 3l:9.
6. Gen. 7:21, 37:20; Exod. 23:11.
7. Lev. 11:2.
8. Gen. 9:12.
9. Gen. 6:12, 13; 9:11, 17.
10. Gen. 6:17.
11. Gen. 7:22.
12. Gen. 1:20, 24; 9:10.
13. Gen. 9:2.
14. Gen. 1:24; 2:7, 19.
15. Gen. 1:27.
16. Compare the creation of Enkidu and Gilgamesh. Alexander Heidel, *The Gilgamesh Epic and Old Testament Parallels* (Chicago, 1946).
17. See commentary of Isaac Abarbanel to Gen. 1:26.
18. Gen. 1:26, 28.
19. Gen. 9:2.
20. Gen. 2:19.
21. Cf. Num. 32:38; II Kings 23:34, 24:17; IIChron. 36:4. See commentary of M. D. Cassuto to Gen. 2:10.
22. Gen. 1:5, 8, 10.
23. Job 18:3, Dan. 5:21.

24. Jon. 4:11.
25. Ps. 49:13, 21.
26. Ps. 8:7–9.
27. Exod. 22:8; Ezek. 38:12, 13; Job 24:2–4.
28. Gen. 12:16, 13:2; I Sam. 25:2; II Sam. 12:2; Job 1:3; Eccles. 2:7.
29. Gen. 21:28–30. See also II Kings 3:4.
30. Deut. 22:10, I Sam. 11:5, I Kings 19:19, Job 1:14, Amos 6:12.
31. Num. 7:3, II Sam. 6:6.
32. Deut. 25:4.
33. Deut. 22:10, Isa. 30:24.
34. I Sam. 16:20, Neh. 13:15.
35. Exod. 4:20, Num. 22:21, Josh. 15:18, II Sam. 17:23, II Kings 4:24.
36. Judg. 10:4, I Sam. 25:20. The ass was apparently a special animal, singled out from among the unclean species for redemptive ceremonies. See Exod. 13:13. Others, however, attribute its choice to the fact that it was the most common of all animals. See I. H. Weiss, *Dor Dor veDorshav,* pt.1, bk.2, chap. 6, p. 51.
37. Zech. 9:9.
38. Ezra 2:66–67, Neh. 7:68–69.
39. Gen. 12:16, 24:35, et al.
40. Lev. 13:47–48; Deut. 18:4; Prov. 27:23, 26, 31:13; Job 31:19–20; Ezek. 34:3.
41. Gen. 38:12, I Sam. 25:2, II Sam. 13:23.
42. Exod. 26:14.
43. Josh. 6:4.
44. Exod. 26:7, 36:14.
45. I Sam. 19:13, 16.
46. Gen. 21:14 , Josh. 9:4.
47. Zech. 13:4.
48. I Kings 19:13, II Kings 1:8.
49. J. B. Pritchard, *Ancient Near Eastern Texts Relating to the Old Testament,* 2d ed. (Princeton University Press, 1955), p. 151.
50. Exod. 25:4, 26:36, 28:5, 6, 15; Num. 15:38; Dan. 5:7; Ezek. 27:7, 16.
51. Gen. 24, 31:17.
52. Judg. 6:5, 8:21, 26; I Sam. 30:17; Isa. 21:7.
53. Gen. 37:25, Isa. 21:13, I Kings 10:2, II Kings 8:9, Isa. 30:6, 60:6.
54. Judg. 7:12; Job 1:3 , 42:12.
55. Gen. 41:43.
56. II Sam. 15:1.
57. II Kings 5:9.
58. II Kings 14:20.
59. II Chron. 23:15.
60. Neh. 3:28, Jer. 31:40.
61. I Kings 5:6; II Chron. 9:25 fixes the amount as 4,000.
62. I Kings 10:28–29.
63. In the "Myth of Ishtar," the horse is described as the "animal of battle." See Heidel, *Gilgamesh Epic* pp. 50–51. The idea developed here is that both the

horse and the lion suffer because of their strength and beauty, for these qualities are exploited by man, who traps them for his own selfish use.

64. Exod. 14:9; Judg. 5:22; I Kings 20:1; Jer. 4:13, 50:42; II Sam. 1:6.
65. Isa. 5:26–28.
66. I Kings 18:5 refers to Ahab's horses. I Kings 22:4, II Kings 3:7 refer to the war-horses of Jehoshaphat.
67. Deut. 17:16.
68. I Sam. 8:11.
69. Josh. 11:9.
70. II Sam. 8:4.
71. Zech. 9:9. In any event the ass is a more appropriate mount for a "poor man," as the Messiah is depicted as being.
72. Exod. 3:8 et al.
73. Deut. 32:14, Isa. 7:21–22.
74. Judg. 4:19.
75. Joel 4:18.
76. Prov. 30:33, I Sam. 17:18, Job 10:10.
77. Deut. 22:6.
78. Hul. 140a.
79. Nimrod (Gen. 10:9) and Esau (Gen. 25:27–28) were hunters.
80. Deut. 14:4–5.
81. Lev. 17:13.
82. See F. S. Bodenheimer, Animal and Man in Bible Lands (Leiden, 1960), pp. 87–92, for records of Assyrian royal hunters. Josephus records Herod's pleasure with the hunt (Wars I, 21:1).
83. Gen. 25:27.
84. Job 10:16, Jer. 16:16, Mic. 7:2.
85. Gen. 9:3.
86. Deut. 8:8.
87. Deut. 11:14.
88. Deut. 12:20.
89. Lev. 11:3–8, Deut. 14:4–8.
90. Deut. 14:21.
91. Lev. 17:15.
92. Gen. 9:4; Lev. 17:14–15; Deut. 12:16, 25 ; Lev. 7:23–25.
93. Gen. 32:33.
94. Exod. 23:19, 34:26; Deut. 14:21.
95. Lev. 11:9–12, Deut. 14:9–10.
96. Lev. 11:20–23, 29–38, 41–43; Deut. 14:19–20.
97. Lev. 11: 29–38, 41–45.
98. Lev. 11:13–19, Deut. 14:11–18.
99. Amos 6:4.
100. Gen. 27:9, 19; Judg. 6:19, 13:15; I Sam. 25:18; Isa. 22:13.
101. I Sam. 28:24.
102. Jer. 46:21.
103. Compare with a feast in Ugaritic literature. See M. D. Cassuto, HaElah Anat (Jerusalem, 1951), p. 63.

104. Gen. 18:7.
105. Gen. 27:3–4.
106. Deut. 32:14.
107. I Sam. 9:23–24.
108. I Sam. 25:18.
109. I Kings 1:19, 25.
110. Judg. 6:19.
111. Isa. 25:6.
112. Isa. 22:13.
113. Num. ll.5.
114. Zeph. 1:10; Neh. 3:3, 12:39; II Chron 33:14.
115. Neh. 13:16.
116. Jer. 16:16, Ezek. 47:10, Eccles. 9:12.
117. Isa. 19:8, Hab. 1:15, Ezek. 26:5.
118. Eccles. 9:12.
119. Job 40:31.
120. Isa. 19:8.
121. Ps. 124:7, Prov. 6:5, Jer. 5:26–27, Hos. 7:12, Amos 3:5.
122. Exod. 16:13.
123. I Kings 5:3.
124. Neh. 5:18.
125. Exod. 16:3, Num. 11:4.
126. See Ps. 78:24–32.
127. Amos 6:4.
128. Ezek. 24:3–5.
129. Prov. 23:20–21.
130. Mic. 3:2–3.
131. W. R. Smith, *Lectures on the Religion of the Semites,* 3d. ed. (New York: KTAV, 1969–70), pp. 319, 479–481.
132. Johannes Pedersen, *Israel: Its Life and Culture,* pt. IV (1956), pp. 330–334.
133. Roland de Vaux, *Ancient Israel,* 2:447–451.
134. Ibid., p. 451.
135. Ibid., p. 453.
136. I Sam. 15:9, II Sam. 6:13, I Kings 1:9, 19, 25.
137. Lev. 4:3, 14, 23, 28, 32. Num. 15:27, 28:15, 22–24, 30, 29:5, 11, 16, 19; Lev. 5:15–18, 19:21, 14:12; Num. 6:12.
138. Lev. 1:3–5, 10, 14.
139. Exod. 29:38–42, Num. 28:1–29, 29:2–38.
140. Lev. 3:1, 6, 12.
141. Lev. 7:16–17.
142. Lev. 7:16, Num. 15:3, Deut. 12:6.
143. Exod. 29:19–34, Lev. 8:22–32.
144. Gen. 4:4.
145. Gen. 8:10.
146. Gen. 22:13, 15:4 ff.
147. Ezra 3:2–7, 6:9–10, 17, 7:17, 8:35 , 10:19, Neh. 10:33–37.
148. *Taan.* 4:6, Josephus, *Wars* 6:94.
149. See I Kings 10:22, II Chron. 9:21.

150. Luckenbill, *Ancient Records of Assyria and Babylonia,* (New York, 1968), "Hunting Records of Tiglath-Pileser I," par. 247, p. 85; "Records of Tiglath-Pileser III," Par. 772, p. 276.

151. See commentary of Nachmanides to Lev. 1:9.

152. Exod. 7:18–21, 8:9, 10, 9:6, 10, 23, 12:29.

153. Deut. 2:35; Josh. 6:21, 8:27; I Sam. 15:3, 22:19, 30:20; Judg. 20:48.

154. Ps. 34:10–11.

Chapter 2

1. *Works of Philo Judaeus,* vol. 4, p. 3, vol. 3, p. 153.

2. W. R. Smith, "Animal Worship and Animal Tribes Among the Ancient Arabs and in the Old Testament," *Journal of Philosophy* 9 (1880): 75–100.

3. H. Frankfort and H. A. Frankfort, *The Intellectual Adventure of Ancient Man* (Chicago, 1946), p. 4.

4. J. G. Frazer, *The New Golden Bough,* ed. Theodor H. Gaster (New York, 1959), p. 467.

5. Samuel A. B. Mercer, "The Religion of Ancient Egypt," in *Forgotten Religions,* ed. Vergilius Ferm (New York, 1950), pp. 27–31. See also Bodenheimer, *Animal and Man in Bible Lands,* pp. 125–129.

6. John Gray, *Near Eastern Mythology,* p. 72.

7. Claude Levi-Strauss, *The Raw and the Cooked* (New York, 1969).

8. Henri Frankfort, *Kingship and the Gods* (Chicago, 1948), pp. 343–344.

9. Num. 26:17, 23, 26, 35.

10. J. Jacobs, *Studies in Biblical Archaeology* (1894), pp. 64–103.

11. For example, *Ayalon* (stag), *Arad* (wild ass), *En Gedi* (kid), *Eglon* (calf), *Beth Hoglah* (partridge), *Etam* (birds of prey).

12. Gen. 49, Deut. 33.

13. Deut. 4:17–18, the second commandment.

14. Ezek. 8:10.

15. Jacobs, *Studies in Biblical Archaeology,* pp. 64–103.

16. Isa. 65:4.

17. Isa. 66:17.

18. Isa. 66:3.

19. II Kings 23:11.

20. Deut. 32:17, Ps. 106:37, Isa. 34:14, 13:21.

21. Exod. 32:1.

22. Exod. 32:4.

23. I Kings 12:28.

24. Judg. 17–18; Hos. 9:15, 11:12; Amos 4:4 et seq.

25. Yehezkel Kaufmann, *Toledot haEmunah HaYisraelit* 8 vols. (Tel Aviv, 1937–56), 2:259–266.

26. It is significant that Jeroboam built the calves after his stay in Egypt, conceivably due to Egyptian influence. His primary intent was probably to draw people away from the city of Jerusalem, but possibly there were secondary benefits accruing to him from this manifestation of the symbols of Egyptian gods.

27. Num. 23:22, 24:8.

28. It was known as the Molten Sea or Bronze Sea (I Kings 7:24, II Chron. 4:2, II Kings 16:17, 25:13, I Chron. 18:8, Jer. 52:17) and was a giant cast-bronze vessel resting upon twelve oxen facing outward in four directions at right angles to one another. The Books of Kings do not give any purpose for the basin or significance for the oxen; II Chron. 4:6 relates that it was a washing basin for the priests.

29. I Kings 10:19, II Chron. 9:17–19.

30. Frazer-Gaster, *New Golden Bough*, p. 7.

31. E. O. James, *Myth and Ritual in the Ancient Near East* (New York, 1958), pp. 27–29.

32. For example, the transformation of Aaron's staff into a serpent. Exod. 4:2–4, 7:8–11.

33. Deut. 18:10–11; comp. II Kings 21:6, II Chron. 33:6.

34. Exod. 22:17, Lev. 20:6.

35. However, see the commentary of Yonathan b. Uziel to Gen. 30:27, and the commentary of Nachmanides to Deut. 18:9 concerning the art of divination by birds.

36. II Kings 13:14–19.

37. Hos. 4:12.

38. Gen. 44:5.

39. II Sam. 5:24.

40. Ezek. 21:26.

41. The Apocrypha does contain a few references to the use of animals in sorcery and in effecting magical cures. See Tob., chap. 3, 6:5 ff., 8:2–3, 11:10–11.

42. Pritchard, *Ancient Near Eastern Texts*, pp. 125–126. The Hittite version has the storm god Illuyankas locked in combat with the dragon Hupasya. The Sumerians told of Ninurta combating the monster Asag. The Ugaritic episode involved the gods in combat against several sea-monsters. See T. Gaster, *Myth, Legend and Culture in the Old Testament* (New York, 1969), pp. 575–577, 696.

43. Job 9:13, 26:12–13; Ps. 89:10; Isa. 51:9–10.

44. Job 3:8, Ps. 74:14, Isa. 27:1, Job 40:25–32.

45. Job 7:12, Ps. 74:13.

46. Gen. 1:21.

47. Ps. 104:26.

48. Ps. 148:7.

49. Cyrus H. Gordon, *Ugaritic Handbook* (1965), p. 178. Apparently two types of serpents or dragons assisted the evil god Mot, a twisting or writhing serpent and a straight serpent, either or both of which possessed seven heads.

50. Ps. Sol. II, Apoc. Esther 1:4 et seq., Test. Job. 12, Septuagint of Daniel.

51. Job 40:15–24.

52. En. 60:7–9, II Bar. 29:4, II Esd. 6:49–53. In rabbinic literature he is the *shor habor*, "the ox of the open field" (*Targ. Ps.* 50:10, *P.R.E.* 11), and together with Leviathan he will challenge God, only to suffer defeat (*B.B.* 74a, *Palestinian Targum* 9:26).

53. G. Contenau, *Everyday Life in Babylonia and Assyria* (1954), plate 23; J. Finegan, *Light From the Ancient Past* (1946), pp. 139–146; Y. Yadin, "Further Light on Biblical Hazor," *Biblical Archaeologist* 20 (May 1957): 43–44.

54. Gen. 3:1.

55. Gen. 3:14.
56. Num. 21:8–9.
57. II Kings 18:4.
58. See H. H. Rowley, "Zadok and Nehushtan," *Journal of Biblical Literature,* June 1939, pp. 113–141.
59. Lev. 16.
60. Lev. 16:21.
61. *Yoma* 6:6 supplies the account of how the animal was cast from a cliff.
62. The precise meaning of the phrase is open to question. The Septuagint renders it simply as "goat that departs." Most rabbinic exegeses and medieval commentaries view it as the place where the goat was sent (*Yoma* 67b, *Sifra-Ahere* 2:2 *Targum Lev.* 14:10). Other medieval authorities (Ibn Ezra, Nachmanides) interpret *azazel* as the name of the goat, while many modern scholars view it as the name of a desert demon (see Ibn Ezra and Nachmanides to Lev. 16:8).
63. Num. 19.
64. Comp. Isa. 1:18.
65. Deut. 21:1–9.
66. Num. 35:33.
67. See Gen. 4:11–12; II Sam. 1:21, 21:1; Ezek. 22:24.
68. The Talmud specifies that if the murder was committed in a manner in which the victim's blood was not shed (hanging, for example), the ritual is waived (*Sot.* 9:2; P.T., *Sot.* 9:2, 23c). Apparently it is essential that the victim's blood touch the earth. Furthermore, the area in which the heifer was killed was never to be cultivated.
69. *Sot.* 9:7, *Ket.* 37b.
70. Deut. 21:6–7.
71. Deut. 21:8.
72. Gen. 3:24.
73. Exod. 25:18–20, 37:7–9.
74. I Sam. 4:4, II Sam. 6:2, II Kings 19:15, Isa. 37:16, Pss. 80:2, 99:1.
75. Ezek. 1:5–28. See also chap. 10. Rabbenu Yosef Bekhor Shor, in his commentary to Gen. 3:24, identifies the cherubim with oxen and compares them to Ezekiel's vision of winged oxen.
76. I Kings 21:8, Isa. 29:11, Job 38:14.
77. Jer. 22:24, Hag. 2:23; see also Song of Songs 8:6.
78. However, some ancient Hebrew seals do depict animal forms. See John C. L. Gibson, *Textbook of Syrian Semitic Inscriptions,* vol. 1, chap. IV, pp. 59–70.
79. Gen. 40:1 ff., 41:1, 5.
80. I Sam. 17:46. See II Sam. 21:10; I Kings 14:11, 21:23 f.; II Kings 9:25 f., 34 ff., which describe the slain bodies of royalty being left to scavenging animals. It was customary for criminals to be denied burial. G. R. Driver and J. C. Miles, *The Babylonian Laws* (Oxford, 1952), 1:495–496.
81. Gen. 47:29 f., II Sam. 2:5 f., I Sam. 31:11 ff.
82. Gen. 23:3 ff., 25:9 f., 47:29 ff., 49:31 f.; I Kings 13:22.
83. Isa. 14:19, Jer. 8:1 f.
84. Y. Kaufmann, *The Religion of Israel* (Chicago, 1960), p. 103.
85. Lev. 22:25.
86. Lev. 21:6.

87. Lev. 1:17.
88. Ezek. 41:22, 44:16; Mal. 1:7.
89. Lev. 17:5, 7; Isa. 13:21, 34:14.

Chapter 3

1. Isa. 1:2, 50:1.
2. Jer. 2:2, Hos. chap. 2.
3. Isa. 2:4.
4. Isa. 41:21.
5. Jer. 20:11.
6. Jer. 15:7.
7. Isa. 5:2–7.
8. Isa. 1:25.
9. Jer. 31:4.
10. Isa. 28:26.
11. Jer. 30:17.
12. Jer. 8:13.
13. Jer. 5:24.
14. Isa. 42:16.
15. Jer. 14:8.
16. Ps. 23:1, Jer. 31:10.
17. Deut. 32:11.
18. Exod. 19:4.
19. Ps. 91:4.
20. Isa. 31:4, Hos. 5:14, 11:10.
21. Hos. 13:7.
22. Lam. 3:10.
23. Hos. 13:8. See also II Sam. 17:8 and Isa. 59:11.
24. Num. 24:8, 23:22.
25. Jer. 3:20.
26. Jer. 2:21.
27. Jer. 30:10.
28. Jer. 11:15.
29. Jer. 2:2.
30. Isa. 5:1-7.
31. Mic. 2:12.
32. Jer. 2:24.
33. Jer. 5:8.
34. Amos 4:1.
35. Ps. 74:19.
36. Jer. 31:18.
37. Isa. 41:14.
38. Judg. 14:14.
39. Deut. 1:44, Isa. 7:18, Ps. 118:12.
40. Song of Songs 4:1, 6:5.
41. I Kings 20:27.
42. Prov. 30:31.
43. Ezek. 34:17, Zech. 10:3, Dan. 8:5–8, Jer. 50:8, 51:40.

44. Job 6:5, 11:12, 24:5, 39:5; Jer. 14:6, 2:24; Hos. 8:9.
45. Jer. 50:11.
46. Hos. 4:16.
47. Jer. 46:20.
48. Isa. 13:22, Jer. 50:39, 51:37 describe Babylonia in this manner. Jerusalem (Jer. 9:10), Mount Zion (Lam. 5:18), and the cities of Judah are similarly depicted (Jer. 10:22).
49. Isa. 35:7.
50. Isa. 43:20.
51. I Sam. 15:22, Isa. 1:11, Mic. 6:7–8.
52. Eccles. 9:12, Hab. 1:14.
53. Jer. 16:16, Ezek. 47:10.
54. Ezek. 47:7–10.
55. Gen. 48:16.
56. Gen. 49:9.
57. Gen. 49:14.
58. Gen. 49:17.
59. Gen. 49:21.
60. Gen. 49:27.
61. Num. 23:24, 24:9.
62. II Sam. 1:23.
63. II Sam. 16:9.
64. II Kings 8:13.
65. See Job 30:1.
66. Ps. 59:7–14.
67. Isa. 56:11.
68. Isa. 56:10.
69. Prov. 26:11.
70. Exod. 22:30, I Kings 22:38.
71. II Kings 8:13. See also I Sam. 24:15, II Sam 3:8.
72. Deut. 23:19. See Nahum Slouschz, *Otzar HaKetubot HaPinkiot* (Tel Aviv, 1942), 3:80, 309. See *R.H.* 4a and Rashi to Deut. 12:31. It is surprising to find a biblical hero, Caleb b. Yefuneh, bearing this derogatory name. Perhaps the vocalization *kaleb*, reminiscent of *kadesh*, may indeed stem from the appellation of a male prostitute. Of course other biblical heroes also bear the names of unflattering animals: Oreb, Zeeb, Hamor, Nahash, Nachshon.
73. Isa. 41:14.
74. Ps. 22:7.
75. Job 25:6.
76. Prov. 11:22.
77. Isa. 65:4, 66:3, 17.
78. I Macc. 1:47.
79. Koran 2:168 (Fluegel ed., Leipzig, 1883).
80. Deut. 32:33.
81. Job 20:16.
82. I Kings 12:11, 14; II Chron. 10:11, 14.
83. Ezek. 2:6.
84. Interestingly, in the Babylonian account of the deluge, it is the raven, not

the dove, that disappears from sight, heralding the cessation of the flood. *Epic of Gilgamesh* XI, 145–154.
85. Song of Songs 5:2, 6:9.
86. Song of Songs 1:15, 4:1, 5:12.
87. Song of Songs 2:9, 17, 4:5, 7:4, 8:14.
88. Isa. 13:14. See also Prov. 6:5.
89. II Sam. 2:18, I Chron. 12:19.
90. Prov. 5:18–19.
91. II Sam. 22:34, Ps. 18:34, Hab. 3:19.
92. Job 39:1, Ps. 29:9.
93. As was alluded to in the introduction, a question of identification exists here. On the basis of passages ascribing to the *nesher* a bald head and the habit of scavenging carcasses, it has been identified by modern scholars as a griffin-vulture. R. Tam (*Tosafot* to *Hul.* 63a) doubted whether *nesher* really refers to an "eagle."
94. Prov. 23:5, Isa. 40:31.
95. Deut. 28:49, II Sam. 1:23, Jer. 4:13.
96. Job 9:26.
97. Deut. 28:49, Isa. 46:11, Hos. 8:1.
98. Job 39:27, Jer. 49:16.
99. Exod. 19:4, Deut. 32:11.
100. Deut. 32:11.
101. Ps. 22:13.
102. Ps. 68:31, Isa. 34:7, Jer. 50:27.
103. Deut. 33:17.
104. Judg. 6:5, Amos 7:1–2, Nah. 3:15, II Chron. 7:13.
105. Judg. 6:5, 7:12.
106. Judg. 6:5, 7:12; Jer. 46:23; Nah. 3:15–17.
107. Job 39:20.
108. Isa. 33:4, Amos 7:1.
109. Joel 2:1–11.
110. Num. 13:33, Isa. 40:22, Nah. 3:17, Ps. 109:23.
111. Hab. 1:8.
112. Jer. 5:6, Hos. 13:7.
113. Isa. 11:6.
114. Dan. 7:6.
115. Jer. 5:6.
116. Jer. 13:23.
117. II Sam. 17:10; Prov. 22:13, 26:13, 28:1, 30:30.
118. Judah (Gen. 49:9), Gad (Deut. 33:20), Dan (Deut. 33:22), Saul and Jonathan (II Sam. 1:23), King David (II Sam. 17:10), and the rulers of Judah (Ezek. 19:2–9).
119. I Kings 10:19, II Chron. 9:17–19.
120. Isa. 31:4, Hos. 5:14, 11:10.
121. Jer. 25:30, Joel 4:16, Amos 1:2, 3:8.
122. Num. 23:24, 24:9.
123. Isa. 5:29, Zeph. 3:3, Ps. 22:14.
124. Ps. 10:9, 34:11, 35:17.

125. Eccles. 10:8, Amos 5:19.
126. Ps. 58:6, Eccles. 10:11, Isa. 3:3.
127. Isa. 65:25, cf. Gen. 3:14.
128. Jer. 8:17. See also Deut. 32:33, Ps. 58:4–5, Isa. 14:29.
129. Gen. 49:17.
130. Num. 21:6–7, Deut. 32:24.
131. Job 39:19, Ps. 147:10.
132. Jer. 4:13, Hab. 1:8.
133. Isa. 63:13.
134. Isa. 5:28.
135. Job 39:20.
136. Jer. 47:3.
137. Jer. 8:16, 5:8.
138. Song of Songs 1:9.
139. Ps. 32:9.
140. Jer. 12:5.
141. Jer. 5:8.
142. Jer. 50:11.
143. Amos 6:12.
144. II Kings 2:11.
145. II Kings 6:17.
146. Zech. 1:8, 6:2, 3, 6.
147. Zech. 14:20.
148. II Macc. 3:25, 5:2–3, 10:29.
149. II Kings 23:11.
150. Ps. 20:8, 33:17; Isa. 31:1; Ezek. 17:15.
151. Zech. 9:9–10.
152. The Koran (Fluegel ed.), 67:19, marvels at God's miraculous feat in enabling birds to fly in the air.
153. Ps. 55:7, 74:19.
154. See *Jewish Encyclopedia,* 3:219, Frazer-Gaster, *New Golden Bough,* pp. 152, 215.
155. Ps. 11:1.
156. Hos. 11:11.
157. Prov. 27:8. Comp. Isa. 16:2.
158. Isa. 34:11, 15.
159. Job 30:29; Isa. 13:21, 34:13, 43:20; Jer. 50:39.
160. Job 39:17.
161. Lam. 4:3.
162. Ps. 22:13–14, 17, 21–22.
163. Ps. 118:12.
164. Joel 1:6, Isa. 5:29.
165. Jer. 8:16.
166. Hab. 1:8, Hos. 8:1.
167. Mic. 1:8; Jer. 10:22, 49:33, 51:37; Isa. 13:21–22, 34:14.
168. Mic. 1:8, Isa. 34:11, Ps. 102:7–8.
169. Zeph. 2:14, Isa. 34:11, Ps. 102:7–8.
170. Zeph. 2:14, Isa. 34:11.

171. Isa. 13:21–22.
172. Isa. 34:11.
173. Prov. 30:17.
174. Job 38:41.
175. Ps. 147:9. See also Luke 12:24, Matt. 6:26.
176. Isa. 11:6–9.
177. I Kings 5:12–13.
178. Prov. 23:4–5.
179. Prov. 6:6–8.
180. Prov. 30:25–29.
181. Job 38:39, 39:30, 40:15, 41:26.
182. Judg. 9:8–15, II Sam. 12:1–6, II Kings 14:9–10.
183. Ezek. 17:3–12, 19:2–9, 34:2–31.
184. Dan. 7:1–8, 24; cf. 8:3–8. See also En. 90:9 and II Esd. 11.
185. See Gaster, *Myth, Legend and Culture,* pp. 624–626, 635–636, 838, 876, for treatment of Ezek. 32:2–9 and Eccles. 10–12.

Chapter 4

1. *Nefesh,* Deut. 12:23.
2. Ps. 104:29–30.
3. Lev. 17:11.
4. Lev. 17:10, 3:17, 7:26; Deut. 15:23, 12:16, 23; I Sam. 14:32–34. Genesis 9:4 seems to prohibit even non-Jews from consuming the blood of animals. Maimonides (*M.N.* 3:46, 48) writes: "blood and fat belong to God and must be brought upon the altar [*Targum Yer.* to Lev. 3:17]; they are divine property . . . therefore the blood of any animal, even when it is unfit for the altar, must be poured out as water."
5. Exod. 12:23, the blood of the paschal lamb.
6. Lev. 7:23.
7. Frazer-Gaster, *New Golden Bough,* pp. 218–219.
8. Exod. 29:13, 22; Lev. 3:9, 7:3, 8:25, 9:19.
9. Lev. 17:3–4.
10. Lev. 17:13–14.
11. Lev. 11:47, 14:4, 20:25; Deut. 14:11–20.
12. Lev. 22:20–25.
13. Lev. 3:17, 7:26, 17:10–14; Deut. 12:15–16, 20–24.
14. Gen. 9:3–4.
15. Lev. 17:11.
16. Exod. 21:37.
17. I Sam. 14:32–35.
18. I Sam. 20:29.
19. See *Hul.* 16b–17a. A. M. Haberman, ed., *Kitve R. Abraham Epstein,* 1:27–28.
20. Deut. 12:12, 18, 19.
21. Deut. 12:6–7, 11–12, 15–19, 26; I Sam. 1:3–4.
22. See Gen. 14:18–20, 26:30; Josh. 9:14.
23. Deut. 12:7.

24. Exod. 22:30, Deut. 14:3–21, Lev. 11:43, 20–24.
25. Frankfort, *Kingship and the Gods,* pp. 9–10, figs. 11–12.
26. Gen. 1:29.
27. Gen. 9:3.
28. M. D. Cassuto, *MeNoah ad Avraham* (Jerusalem, 1953), p. 86.
29. Deut. 12:20.
30. Hos. 2:20, 23–25.
31. Isa. 65:25, comp. Isa. 11:6–9. Most of the prophetic utterances concerning the messianic era refer to nations rather than individuals. Isaiah 65, however, refers to individuals within the nation; hence the curse upon Adam, Eve, and the serpent is mentioned. The snake's subsisting upon a diet of dust is, of course, not a pro-vegetarian statement but merely an allusion to the curse placed upon it by God.
32. Hos. 2:20.
33. Joel. 4:18.
34. Amos 9:14.
35. Hos. 2:24.
36. Ezek. 47:6–12.
37. Frazer-Gaster, *New Golden Bough,* p. 655.
38. Ezek. 38:19–20.
39. Isa. 53:7. In the Koran, a hamstrung she-camel, unable to graze or drink, is effectively used as a symbol for suffering and compassion (Fluegel ed., 7:71–79, 11:61–68, 26:141–159, 27:45–53).
40. Prov. 5:18–19, Song of Songs 2:9, 17, 4:5, 7:4, 8:14.
41. Prov. 27:8.
42. Eccles. 3:19, 20, 21. See also Job 10:9, 34:15; Ps. 104:29, 146:4.
43. Gen. 1:20–25.
44. Job 7:16.
45. Job 7:7.
46. Job 7:9.
47. Job 20:8.
48. Job 8:9, 14:2. See also I Chron. 29:15, Ps. 39:6, 102:12, 109:23, 144:4; Eccles. 6:12, 8:13.
49. Ps. 103:15, Isa. 40:6.
50. Ps. 102:12, 103:15; Isa. 40:6–7.
51. Gen. 6:17.
52. Gen. 1:24.
53. Gen. 6:12, Ps. 145:21, Isa. 40:5–7.
54. Gen. 6:17, 7:15, 21, 8:17, etc.; Ps. 136:25.
55. Gen. 9:4, 40:19; II Kings 9:36; Mic. 3:2–3; Dan. 7:5.
56. Job 34:15, Ps. 78:39, II Chron. 32:8, Isa. 31:3.
57. Ps. 147:9.
58. Ps. 145:16.
59. Ps. 36:7.
60. Ps. 104:14.
61. Job 12:10.
62. Jon. 3:6–8.
63. Gen. 9:8–10.

64. Gen. 3:14–15.
65. Exod. 19:13.
66. Exod. 21:28–32.
67. Gen. 9:5.
68. Exod. 22:18, Lev. 20:15–16.
69. Compare Deut. 22:25–27, where the maiden is not punished. *Sanh.* 55a cites Raba's statement that "the Torah ordained that the animal be destroyed because it, too, derived pleasure from sin."
70. T. Gaster, *Myth, Legend and Culture in the Old Testament,* pp. 243–250.
71. Plato, *Laws* IX, 873D–874A.
72. Gaster, *Myth, Legend and Culture,* p. 250.
73. Exod. 9:6, 10, 25.
74. Exod. 11:5, 12:29.
75. Gen. 6:12.
76. Gen. 6:7.
77. Gen. 6:5–6 records that God observed man's wickedness to be great, with no mention of animals as offenders.
78. Jer. 21:6.
79. I Kings 17:2–7.
80. I Kings 13:24, 26.
81. II Kings 17:24–28.
82. Ezek. 39:17–20.
83. See also Ezek. 14:15–21 and Jer. 15:3.
84. II Kings 2:24. See commentary of S. D. Luzzatto to Isa. 37:36, where he quotes Buchart's account of Herodotus' description of mice being sent to aid Egypt in her battle against Sennacherib's attacking forces. Comp. I Sam. 6:4, where the Philistines employ golden mice. Of particular interest is *Targum Uziel* to Deut. 21:7–8, where swarms of creatures emanate from the body of the *eglah arufah* and proceed to the locale of the murderer. Jastrow renders *moranim* as "worms," but "ants" would seem a more accurate identification.
85. Isa. 1:3.
86. Jer. 8:7.
87. I Kings 5:13.
88. Prov. 30:18–19.
89. Job 12:7–8.
90. See Gaster, *Myth, Legend and Culture,* pp. 309, 310, 401, 402. Job 36:33 is interpreted as attributing to cattle a special sagacity for weather prediction.
91. Num. 22:25 et seq.
92. Ps. 104:20–21.
93. Ps. 104:27–28.
94. Ps. 145:9.
95. Ps. 145:15.
96. *Shab.* 107b.
97. Jer. 49:19.
98. Song of Songs 4:8.
99. Isa. 30:6.
100. Ps. 104:17–18.
101. Job 39:6.

102. Isa. 34:11–17.
103. Occasionally pagan gods are concerned with justice. Shamash was the Babylonian god of justice.
104. Exod. 20:10, 23:12; Deut. 5:14.
105. Lev. 25:6–7.
106. Lev. 22:23–24.
107. Gen. 9:3.
108. Gen. 9:4.
109. Deut. 25:9.
110. Deut. 23:25–26. Interestingly, Paul (I Cor. 9:9, II Tim. 5:8) cites this ruling as illustrative of the fact that a laborer is entitled to his wages. Other cultures had no restraints about muzzling diverse species together. See Claude R. Conder, *Tentwork in Palestine,* 2:258, 260.
111. *B.K.* 54b.
112. Quoted in J. H. Hertz, ed., *Pentateuch and Haftorahs* (London, 1938), p. 854. In Carthage, mill workers were muzzled during their labors.
113. Deut. 22:6–7.
114. *Encyclopaedia Britannica* (1955 ed.), 3:636.
115. Lev. 22:28.
116. Exod. 23:19, 34:26; Deut. 14:21.
117. Deut. 22:10.
118. Deut. 22:1, comp. Exod. 23:4–5.
119. Deut. 22:4.
120. Exod. 23:4–5.
121. Num. 22:28, 30.
122. Prov. 29:7.
123. Prov. 31:9.
124. Prov. 21:26.
125. Prov. 12:10.
126. Prov. 10:3, 13:25, 27:7. See also Ps. 107:9, 18, and Isa. 56:11.
127. Humphrey Primatt, *Dissertation on the Duty of Mercy and Sin of Cruelty to Brute Beasts* (London, 1776), p. 208.
128. Jon. 4:11.
129. Moses, Exod. 3:1; David, I Sam. 16:11, 17:15, II Sam. 7:8.
130. Ps. 78:70–72. Babylonian kings were called "shepherds"; see Luckenbill, *Ancient Records of Assyria and Babylonia,* 2:128, etc.
131. Ps. 23:2, Isa. 40:11.
132. I Sam. 17:34–36.
133. Job 1:14 et seq.
134. Ezek. 34:4.
135. Isa. 40:11.
136. II Sam. 12:3.
137. Gen. 33:13–14.
138. Isa. 53:7, Jer. 11:19, Num. 27:17.
139. Isa. 53:7.
140. Ps. 23:1–4. See also Ps. 68:11, 78:52, 80:2.
141. Isa. 40:11.
142. Jer. 23:3–4. See also Jer. 31:10, 17:16.

143. Ezek. 34.

144. William E. H. Lecky, *History of European Morals* (1869), 3d ed., 2:162.

Chapter 5

1. Exod. 23:4, Deut. 22:1.
2. Exod. 23:5, Deut. 22:4.
3. Prov. 14:4.
4. Gen. 9:4.
5. Lev. 7:15, Deut. 12:12, 18, 19.
6. Dan. 10:3.
7. Only later, in the *Testament of the Twelve Patriarchs,* are Reuben and Judah pictured as abstaining from meat as part of a pattern of self-denial of pleasure.
8. Ps. 24:1, 50:10, 12.
9. Ps. 50:10–12.
10. Exod. 20:13, Deut. 5:17; comp. Gen. 4:10.
11. Deut. 20:19–20.
12. Gen. 1:29.
13. Gen. 9:3.
14. Gen. 4:4, II Kings 3:27, Mic. 6:7.
15. Exod. 13:11–16, 34:19–20, Lev. 27:26–27, Num. 18:15–17.
16. Num. 3:12.
17. Exod. 22:28–29, 23:19, 34:26.
18. Lev. 23:10, Num. 18:12–14, 15:20–21, Deut. 18:4; comp. Neh. 10:37.
19. Lev. 19:23–25.
20. Deut. 14:22 et seq. See also Num. 15:17–21, 18:12–13, Deut. 26:1–11, Exod. 34:22, Lev. 23:15–22, Num. 28:26. Deut. 16:9–12 describes the annual redemptive ceremony at the festival of Shavuot.
21. Lev. 23:9–14.
22. Exod. 23:10–11, Lev. 25:1–7, 18–22, Deut. 15:1–11.
23. Cyrus H. Gordon, *Ugaritic Literature* (Rome, 1949), p. 5, theorizes that the reason why the land was to lie fallow in the Sabbatical year is because "the ending of one cycle without a harvest was believed to bring on a seven-year cycle of plenty."
24. G. Dalman, *Arbeit* 3 (1933):183–185. M. Noth, *Exodus* (1959), pp. 153–154, *Leviticus* (1959), pp. 157–169.
25. Lev. 25:23.
26. Lev. 27:30–33. See II Chron. 31:5–6.
27. Deut. 12:16, 14:22, et seq.
28. Num. 18:21 et seq. For later references to different forms of tithing, see Amos 4:4, Mal. 3:8–10, Neh. 10:37 et seq., II Chron. 31:6–12.
29. Gen. 14:20, 28:22.
30. Lev. 27:32.
31. Deut. 14:22 ff. and 26:2 ff.
32. I Sam. 22:10, II Kings 11:10.
33. Num. 3:13. See also Exod. 13:15.
34. Deut. 28:1–14.
35. Deut. 28:15–24.

36. M. Douglas, *Purity and Danger* (London: Routledge & Kegan Paul, 1976), p. 35.

37. Lev. 18:22–23, 20:13, 15, 16.

38. Lev. 19:19. See commentary of Nachmanides ad loc.

39. Deut. 22:11.

40. Deut. 22:10.

41. See M., *Kil* 8:2, 4. See Nachmanides to Lev. 19:19 on the subject of "purity" for flora and fauna, and the prohibition against the intermingling of species.

42. Although we have not seen fit to devote attention to "hygienic" reasons as a possible rationale for scriptural injunctions concerning animals, we note, in passing, that one author proposes such a reason even for the prohibition against muzzling a threshing ox! "Some chemical may be produced by the ox, as a result of being muzzled, which would be excreted into the grain making it more subject to disease microorganisms." Elihu A. Schatz, *Proof of the Accuracy of the Bible*, p. 650.

43. Exod. 23:19, 34:26; Deut. 14:21.

44. W. R. Smith, *The Religion of the Semites* (1927), p. 221. "The heathenistic practice of boiling a kid in its mother's milk is found as a milk charm in one of the ancient tablets recently discovered at Ras Shamra in Syria and dated as early as the 15th century, B.C. *(Syria* XIV, 1933, 130, comp. also commentary *Ibid.* p. 140). Sir James Frazer *(Folklore in the Old Testament,* III, 110 ff.) points out similar practices among savage tribes and semi-civilized peoples. Max Radin *(American Journal of Semitic Languages,* XL 1923–24, 209 ff.) endeavored to trace this custom to the Orphic-Dionysiac ceremonial in anicent Greece where, as it now appears, it had been borrowed from Syria." Joseph Reider, *Deuteronomy with Commentary* (Philadelphia, 1948), see note 535 to Deut. 14:21. See also M. D. Cassuto, *HaElah Anat* (Jerusalem, 1953), p. 40. Later research, however, seems to cast doubt as to whether the unearthed tablet indeed speaks of boiling a kid in this manner.

45. Similarly, Philo does not claim to see *only* compassion as a factor in these prohibitions. For him, an "unnatural" act is a wrong act, ipso facto, and the seething of a kid in its mother's milk and harnessing together an ox and an ass are placed in a similar category with the prohibitions against wearing wool and linen together and sowing diverse seeds in a field. Philo, *De Specialibus Legibus.*

46. Lev. 22:24.

47. B.T., *Shab.* 110b–111a.

48. *Sanh.* 56b.

49. Lev. 22:28.

50. S. R. Driver, *A Critical and Exegetical Commentary on Deuteronomy,* p. 251, quoting Fenton, *Early Hebrew Life,* p. 48.

51. Lev. 11:10–12.

52. Lev. 11:20–26.

53. Lev. 11:27.

54. Lev. 11:41–44.

55. Lev. 11:29 et seq.

56. I Kings 8:46, comp. Eccles. 7:20.

57. Ps. 7:9–10, 18:25.

58. Isa. 28:17, 60:21, Jer. 23:5–7, Hos. 10:12, Zech. 8:8.
59. Deut. 25:1, Exod. 23:7, II Sam. 15:4, Isa. 5:23.
60. Isa. 5:23, Hos. 10:13, Amos 5:12.
61. Amos 5:21–27, Hos. 6:6, Mic. 6:6–8, Isa. 1:11–17, Jer. 6:20, 7:21–22.
62. Isa. 1:15.
63. Amos 5:24, Mic. 6:8, Isa. 1:16–17, Jer. 7:23.
64. I Sam. 13:21.
65. Gen. 24:14.
66. Zulma Steele, *Angel in a Top Hat* (New York, 1942), p. 169.
67. William E. H. Lecky, *History of European Morals,* 3d ed., 1:288.
68. I Sam. 11:7.
69. Lev. 24:18, 21. See also Exod. 21:33–34, 22:6–14.
70. Eccles. 3:18–21.
71. Ps. 8:4–8.
72. Joel 1:18–20.
73. Joel 2:22.
74. Harry A. Wolfson, *The Philosophy of the Church Fathers,* 3d ed. (Cambridge, 1970), 1: 289.
75. William A. Irvin, "The Hebrews," in H. Frankfort and H. A. Frankfort, *The Intellectual Adventure of Ancient Man* (Chicago, 1946).

Chapter 6

1. L. Ginzberg, *The Legends of the Jews,* 7 vols. (Philadelphia, 1909–1956) 5:43, n. 127.
2. En. 60:7–10, Apoc. Bar. 29:4, II Esd. 4:49–53.
3. *B.B.* 74b, *Gen. R.* 7:4.
4. Ginzberg, *Legends,* 5:45, n. 127.
5. *B.B.* 74b.
6. *Pesikta de Rav Kahana* 6, *Num. R.* 21:18.
7. *B.B.* 74a.
8. *Pesikta de Rav Kahana,* supplementary 2:4.
9. *B.B.* 74b–75a.
10. *B.B.* 75a.
11. *B.B.* 74a–75b, *Lev. R.* 13:3, 22:10.
12. *Lev. R.* 13:3.
13. Ps. 74:14. See Ginzberg, *Legends,* 5:43, n. 127.
14. *B.B.* 75a.
15. *Targum Yerushalmi,* Gen. 1:21; *B.B.* 74b.
16. *Lev. R.* 22:10.
17. *Lev. R.* 22:10, *Pesikta Rabbati* 16:4.
18. *Targum Yerushalmi,* Num. 9:6; *B.B.* 75a.
19. See Ginzberg, *Legends,* 5:47, 48, n. 134, 139.
20. *Targum* to Ps. 50:11, *B.B.* 73b.
21. *Gen. R.* 19:4, *Lev. R.* 22:10.
22. *Lev. R.* 22:10.
23. *B.B.* 73a–74b.

24. *Gen. R.* 19:5, *Tanhuma,* intro, 155. Other references cited in Ginzberg, *Legends,* 5:95, n. 67.
25. *Midrash Tehillim* 22:28, 91:1; *B.B.* 73b.
26. *M.H.G.* I, 87.
27. *P.R.E.* 31.
28. *Erub.* 18b.
29. *P.R.E.* 31.
30. *Shab.* 28b, P.T. *Shab.* 2, 4d.
31. *Tanhuma, Ki Tissa* 19:24.
32. *Mekhilta, WaYassa* 1:44b.
33. *Eccles. R.* 2:25.
34. *Nid.* 24a.
35. See *Rashi* to *Pes.* 54a, *Maimonides* to Abot 5:6, Ginzberg, *Legends,* 5:53, n. 165, 6:299, n. 82.
36. *Avot* 5:6, *Pes.* 54a.
37. Tos., *Sot.* 15:1; *Sot.* 48b; P.T., *Sot.* 9:20d.
38. Ibid.
39. *Sifrei, Shemini* 5; *Hull.* 127a.
40. *Shab.* 107b.
41. *Hag.* 27a.
42. P.T., *Shab.* 1:3b, *B.K.* 16a.
43. *Sanh.* 67b, 65b; P.T., *Sanh.* 7:19, 25d.
44. Tos., *Atikata* 5:19; *Rimze Haftarot, Naso*; Ginzberg, *Legends,* 6:206, n. 111.
45. *Sifra, Shemini* 6.
46. *Kil.* 8:5; P.T., *Kil.* 8:4–5, 31c; introduction to *Midrash Tanhuma.*
47. Tos. *Bekh.* 1:11; *Bekh.* 8a.
48. *Sifra, Shemini* 3.
49. Ginzberg, *Legends,* 5:50, n. 150.
50. Loew, *Flora* 4, p. 348.
51. *Erub.* 18a, *Gen. R.* 14:10.
52. *Gen. R.* 23:6.
53. *Tanhuma* and *Midrash Avkir* to Gen. 5:29.
54. *Gen. R.* 23:6, *Sanh.* 109a, Ginzberg, *Legends,* 5:152, n. 55.
55. *Gen. R.* 23:6–7, Sherira Gaon, as quoted by David Kimhi to Gen. 6:4.
56. Ginzberg, *Legends,* 5:203–204, n. 88.
57. See ibid., 6:423–424, n. 104.
58. *Arak.* 19b.
59. *Taan.* 21b.
60. *Gen. R.* 84:19.
61. Exod. 22:17, Lev. 20:17, Deut. 18:9 ff., I Sam. 15:23, Isa. 3:2–3, 47:8–15, Jer. 10:2–3.
62. M., *Sanh.* 7:7.
63. M., *Shab.* 6:10; *Shab.* 67a. See S. Lieberman's observations in *Tosefot Rishonim,* I, 126–127.
64. *Avot* 2:7, *Erub.* 64b, *Git.* 45a, *Sot.* 22a–b.
65. P.T., *Shab.* 6:8c.
66. Saul Lieberman, *Hellenism in Jewish Palestine* (New York, 1950), p. 72.

67. *Sifra, Kedoshim* 6; *Sifrei, Deut.* 17; *Sanh.* 65b.
68. *Git.* 45a.
69. *Sanh.* 93a, *Ber.* 57a.
70. *Sanh.* 65b.
71. *B.K.* 60b.
72. H. W. Longfellow, *Golden Legend VIII*, "The Village School."
73. *Shab.* 77b.
74. *Ket.* 50a.
75. *Shab.* 109b, 77b; *Yoma* 83b–84a.
76. *Shab.* 110b.
77. *Sanh.* 108b, 63b; *Hag.* 27a.
78. *Git.* 68b–69a.
79. *Shab.* 67a.
80. *A.Z.* 28b.
81. Tos., *B.K.* 8:12.
82. *Ber.* 6a.
83. *Git.* 69a.
84. Ibid.
85. J. Preuss, *Biblical and Talmudic Medicine,* trans. F. Rosner (New York, 1978), p. 306.
86. *Git.* 68b.
87. Tos., *Shab.* 8:8.
88. *Shab.* 67a.
89. *A.Z.* 28b.
90. Preuss, *Biblical and Talmudic Medicine,* p. 433.
91. *Song of Songs R.* 2:3.
92. *A.Z.* 28a.
93. Preuss, *Biblical and Talmudic Medicine,* p. 168.
94. *Avot* 5:6.
95. *Ber.* 6a.
96. *Pes.* 111b.
97. *Midrash Tehillim* 91:3, *Pes.* 111b.
98. *B.K.* 21a.
99. *Pes.* 111b–112a.
100. *Kid.* 29b.
101. *Ber.* 6a.
102. *Pes.* 112b.
103. *Sanh.* 107a.
104. *Sanh.* 95a, *Gen. R.* 59:11.
105. *Sifrei, Deut.* 43 (Finkelstein ed., 1939), p. 97.
106. P.T., *A.Z.* III, 6:43a; *A.Z.* 48a.
107. P.T., *A.Z.* 5:4, 44b; *Hul.* 6a; *Sanh.* 63b.
108. Tos., *Hul.* 2:18; *Mekhilta, Yitro* IV.
109. Tos., *A.Z.* 2:1, 5:10; P.T., *A.Z.* 3:6, 43a; *A.Z.,* 22b, 54a, passim; *Bekhorot* 41a, 42a, 57a.
110. See, for example, M., *Zeb.* 8:1, 9:3, 14:2, and M. *Tem.* 6:1.
111. *Sanh.* 63b.
112. *Shab.* 67b.

113. *Num. R.* 20:4.
114. *M., R.H.* 3:8, *R.H.* 29a, Wisd. of Sol. 16:5–13.
115. II Kings 18:4, *Ber.* 10b.

Chapter 7

1. *M., Nid.* 6:9.
2. Ibid.
3. *Hul.* 59a.
4. Ibid.
5. *M., Hul.* 12:2, *Hul.* 138b.
6. *Yeb.* 121a–b.
7. *B.B.* 73b.
8. *Hul.* 58b.
9. *Shab.* 77b.
10. *Lev. R.* 13.
11. *P. R. E.* 20, *A.Z.* 30b.
12. P.T., *Shab.* 7, 10.
13. *B.K.* 18b.
14. Tem. 31a, *Shab.* 109b, *Git.* 69b, *Ber.* 36a.
15. P.T., *Kil.* 1:6, 27a.
16. *Bekh.* 7b–8a.
17. Prov. 5:19.
18. *Ket.* 77b.
19. *Git.* 69b.
20. P.T., *Ter.* 8:4, 5d.
21. *Hul.* 94a.
22. *M., Ter.* 8:6.
23. *Pes.* 112b.
24. *Yoma* 83b.
25. M. *Yoma* 8:6. But others disagreed. See P.T. *Yoma* 8:5.
26. F. Rosner, *Medicine in the Bible and Talmud* (New York, 1977), p. 50.
27. *Hul.* 27b, *Eccles. R.* 7:23, 3.
28. *Cratylus* 393c, ed. Wohlrab (Leipzig, 1887, 1), p. 19, Quoted by Preuss, *Biblical and Talmudic Medicine,* p. 415.
29. Tos., *Bekh.* 1:9. See also *Sanh.* 58a.
30. *M., Nid.* 3:2; *Nid.* 23a; Tos., *Nid.* 4:6.
31. *Bekh.* 8a, Tos., *Bekh.* 1:5.
32. A. Kohut, *Arukh haShalem* (New York: Pardes, 1955), 3:72–73. These passages have been the source of fascinating interpretations by later authorities. Rashi describes these creatures as being half-human and half-fish, referring to them in Old French as *syrene,* i.e., "mermaids." Variant textual readings accepted by many commentators read: "Dolphins are fruitful and multiply *from* human beings." i.e., humans are able to impregnate them! See Rosner, pp. 221–222.
33. *Hul.* 127a, *Sanh.* 91a, *Sifra* 52b.
34. Ovid, *Metamorphoses* I, 423 et seq.; Pliny, *Natural History* IX, 84, 179.
35. F. S. Bodenheimer, *Animal and Man in Bible Lands,* p. 47.
36. *Historia Animalium* 5:26. Cited by Bodenheimer, p. 72.

37. *Historiae Naturalis* 10:67:86, 11:53:116. Cited by Bodenheimer, p. 68.
38. *Sanh.* 108b.
39. *Historia Animalium* 5:47.
40. *Historiae Naturalis* 29, 4:29.
41. *Shab.* 77b.
42. Bodenheimer, *Animal and Man in Bible Lands,* p. 42.
43. J. Trachtenberg, *Jewish Magic and Superstition* (New York, 1939), p. 11.
44. See H. W. F. Saggs, *The Greatness That Was Babylon,* pp. 308–312, for detailed lists of "animal omina."
45. *De divinatione* 1:15, 1:39:85. Cited by Bodenheimer, pp. 53, 57.
46. Bodenheimer, p. 81.
47. *Hag.* 15a, *Hul.* 95b, etc.
48. *B.B.* 12b.
49. Sifra, *Ked.* 6.
50. *Encyclopaedia Judaica,* 4:118.
51. *Shab.* 67a.
52. *Tanna d'Be Eliyahu* 1.
53. Trachtenberg, *Jewish Magic and Superstition,* p. 203.
54. See Preuss, *Biblical-Talmudical Medicine,* pp. 436–437.
55. Lieberman, *Hellenism in Jewish Palestine,* p. 72.
56. Ps. 49:2.
57. Ps. 39:7, P.T., *Shab.* 14:1, 14c.
58. Ginzberg, *Legends,* 5:60 n. 191.
59. *Shab.* 77b.
60. *Git.* 56b, *Gen. R.* 10:7, *Lev. R.* 22:3, etc.
61. *Ber.* 56b.
62. See Ginzberg, *Legends,* 5:43–44, n. 125, for a discussion concerning allegorizations of the messianic banquet.
63. *Ber.* 17a.
64. *Hul.* 59b.
65. See Samuel Edels (*MaHarSha*) ad loc., and Yom Tob b. Abraham Ishbili (*Ritba*).
66. *B.B.* 74a.
67. See, for example, Yom Tob Ishbili and Samuel Edels ad loc., and the ingenious interpretations of Meir Leibush (*Malbim*) (commentary to Gen. 2:19).
68. See *RashBam* to *Pes.* 112b.
69. Ps. 104:26, Job 40:29, *A.Z.* 3b.
70. See *Hul.* 67b and *MaHarSha* ad loc.; P.T., *Shab.* 9:7; *Lev. R.* 22:10.
71. *Lev. R.* 22:4.
72. *Hul.* 57b.
73. Ibid.
74. *Deut. R.* 5:3.
75. *M.K.* 6b.
76. *Yeb.* 76a.
77. *Sanh.* 5b.
78. *A.Z.* 31b.
79. *Hul.* 51a.
80. I. L. Katzenelson, *HaTalmud veHakhmat haRefuah* (Berlin, 1928), pp. 7–8.

81. *Hul.* 113a.
82. Preuss, *Biblical and Talmudic Medicine*, pp. 131–132.
83. *Hul.* 57b. See Preuss, p. 211.
84. *Hul.* 48b, 49a, 50a–b, 52b.
85. See *Hul.* 76a, for example. See Aristotle, *Historia Animalium* 2:1, cited by Preuss, p. 56.
86. *Bek.* 39a.
87. See *Jewish Encyclopedia*, 1:222–224.
88. P.T., *A.Z.* 3:3, 42d; 4:1, 43d.
89. P.T., *A.Z.* 3:1, 42c.
90. Lieberman, *Hellenism in Jewish Palestine*, p. 128.
91. See M., *Hul.* 2:9; *Hul.* 41b.

Chapter 8

1. *Ber.* 43b.
2. *Hul.* 63b.
3. *Pes.* 112b.
4. *Hul.* 58b.
5. P.T., *B.B.* 8:7; *Kid.* 44a.
6. *B.K.* 92b.
7. *Exod. R.* 31:9.
8. *B.K.* 92b.
9. *Ber.* 32a, *Sanh.* 102a.
10. *Deut. R.* 1:5.
11. *Sanh.* 29b.
12. *Tanhuma, Pekudei* 4.
13. *Ket.* 107b.
14. *Sanh.* 52a.
15. *Gen. R.* 45:7.
16. *Ket.* 72a.
17. *Erub.* 86a.
18. *B.K.* 92b.
19. *Sanh.* 105a.
20. *Pes.* 112a.
21. *Ber.* 61a.
22. *Taan.* 5a.
23. *Eccles. R.* I:2.
24. *Pes.* 113a.
25. M., *Kin.* 3:6.
26. *Sanh.* 37a, *Abot* 4:20. Comp. P.T. *Sanh.* 4:8.
27. *B.K.* 117a, *B.M.* 84b.
28. P.T., *Shev.* 9:4.
29. *Meg.* 16b.
30. *Shab.* 112b, etc.
31. *Shab.* 53a.
32. *B.K.* 92b. In the more interesting variation cited earlier, "If two people say you have donkey's ears, get yourself a halter" *(Gen. R.* 45:7).
33. P.T., *Sanh.* 6:23b.

34. M., *Sof.* 16:7.
35. *Suk.* 23a, *B.B.* 134a, *Sof.* 16:6.
36. *Sanh.* 38b–39a, *Sot.* 49a.
37. *Eccles. R.* 1:3, *Lev. R.* 28:2–3.
38. See *Jewish Encyclopedia,* 5:324.
39. *Taan.* 8a. See Rashi, ibid.
40. *Sanh.* 20b.
41. I Kings 5:13.
42. *Shir HaShirim R.* 1:1, *Tan B.* IV, 112, *Targum Sheni* 1:2, 5. See Ginzberg *Legends* 6:289, n. 38.
43. Gen. 3:15.
44. *Midrash Tanhuma,* ed. S. Buber, *Mavo,* p. 79; *Maaseh Buch,* no. 144; P.T., *Kid.* 4:11, 66c.
45. Ginzberg, *Legends,* 6:286, n. 31.
46. *Git.* 68b; *Midrash Tehillim* 78:12; Ginzberg, *Legends,* 4:166–168, 6:290.
47. Ginzberg, *Legends,* 6:298, n. 79.
48. Ibid., 6:288, n. 34.
49. *Alphabet of Ben Sira* 25a, 34a.
50. Ibid., 25a, 25b; Ginzberg, *Legends,* I:54, n. 172.
51. *Alphabet of Ben Sira* 25a–26b, 34b; Ginzberg, *Legends,* 5:54, n. 172.
52. *II Alphabet of Ben Sira* 24:25, Ginzberg, *Legends,* 5:56, n. 180.
53. *II Alphabet of Ben Sira* 26b.
54. *Sanh.* 106a.
55. *Alphabet of Ben Sira* 29; *Midrash Tanhuma* (Buber), *Mavo,* 79b; Ginzberg, *Legends,* 5:187, n. 51.
56. *Gen. R.* 19:1, *Midrash Tehillim* 58:300.
57. *II Alphabet of Ben Sira* 27a–28b, 36a. See also *Midrash HaGadol II* (ed. Schechter. Cambridge, 1902), p. 45; *Midrash Sechel (Tob)* to Exod. 29; *Yalkut* I, 182; Ginzberg, *Legends,* 5:56–60, nn. 187–190.
58. See Rashi to *Sanh.* 38b–39a.
59. Tos., *A.Z.* 6:469. Comp. *Deut. R.* (Lieberman ed.), p. 63, n. 1.
60. *B.K.* 79b, 83a.
61. *B.K.* 83a.
62. Ibid.
63. *Yoma* 83b–84a, P.T., *Yoma* 8:5.
64. *Gen. R.* 22:6, *Yalkut Shimoni, Tehillim* 89.
65. *Hor.* 13a.
66. *Gen. R.* 22:12.
67. P.T., *Ter.* 8:46a; *Pesikta* 10, 79b.
68. P.T., *Ter.* 8:3; *Gen. R.* 54:1.
69. B. M. Levin, *Otzar haGeonim,* 6, pt. 2, on *Succah* (1934, pp. 31–32).
70. *Gen. R.* 64:10.
71. *A.Z.* 54b.
72. *Ber.* 61b.
73. *Eccles. R.* 12:9.
74. *Esther R.* 3:1.
75. *Esther R.* 3:2.
76. *Eccles. R.* 5:14.

77. Ps. 37:20.
78. *Esther R.* 7:2.
79. *Esther R.* 7:10.
80. *Sifre* 157 to Num. 31:2.
81. *Sanh.* 105a.
82. See D. Daube's analysis in *Ancient Hebrew Fables* (Oxford, University Press, 1973), pp. 26–29.
83. Amos 5:18.
84. *Sanh.* 98b.
85. H. Strack and P. Billerbeck, *Kommentar zum Neuen Testament aus Talmud und Midrasch* (1928), 4:854; W. Bacher, *Die Agada der Palaestinischen Amoräer* (1899), 3:344.
86. Job 35:11.
87. *Erub.* 100b.
88. *Shebet Musar,* 22, 70b, 73c, 98a.
89. Prov. 6:6.
90. *Deut. R.* 5:2.
91. Ibid.
92. *Lam. R.* I:51.
93. *Num. R.* 20:14–15.
94. Ps. 74:19, 68:14.
95. *Cant.* 1:15.
96. *Cant. R.* 1:15, 2:14, 4:12; *Ber.* 53b.
97. P.T., *M.K.* 3, 82b; P.T., *Yeb.* 15, 15c; *Midrash Tehillim* 11:102; *Sanh.* 91a.
98. Quoted from an unknown *midrash* by Rashi and Kimhi on II Kings 25:4, Jer. 39:4.
99. *Yalkut* 2:214; *P.R.* 14, 13a.
100. *Tanhuma, Tezaveh* 10; Ginzberg, *Legends,* 6:19, n. 110.
101. *Sifre Z.* 96, Midr. *Tehillim,* 93:414. See Septuagint on I Sam. 5:6 et seq. and Josephus, *Antiquities* VI, 1:1.
102. *Ber.* 54b. Other traditions credit the hoopoe and raven for having perforated the mountain. See Ginzberg, *Legends,* 6:120, n. 695.
103. *Tanhuma B.* 5:6, *Sot.* 36a, *Num. R.* 18:22.
104. *Taan.* 22a.
105. *Song of Songs R.* 24:4.
106. Ginzberg, *Legends,* 6:432, n. 6, 436, n. 16.
107. *Erub.* 54b.
108. *Sanh.* 95a.
109. *Midrash Tehillim* 22:195, 91:395, 92:408.
110. Gaster, *Exempla,* no. 336.
111. *Eccles. R.* 2:25, *Patshegen ha-Khetav, Targum Sheni,* Esther 1:2.
112. *Gen. R.* 22:8, *P.R.E.* 21.
113. *Ruth R.* 3:2.
114. Ginzberg, *Legends,* 6:272, n. 127.
115. *Shalshelet haKabbalah* 19a, quoted by Ginzberg, *Legends,* 4:261.
116. *P.R.E.* 23; *Targum Yerushalmi,* Gen. 5:20; *Gen. R.* 32:8; *Zeb.* 116a. According to some versions there were 366 species of fowl and 366 reptilian species which chose to voluntarily enter.

117. *Zeb.* 116a, *Gen. R.* 32:8.
118. Num. 21:4–7.
119. *Num. R.* 19:22.
120. *Ned.* 41a, *Gen. R.* 10:7.
121. *Lev. R.* 22:3, *Num. R.* 18:22.
122. *Gen. R.* 10:7, *Lev. R.* 22:4.
123. *Gen. R.* 10:7, *Eccles R.* 5:8 f., par. 5.
124. *Zohar, Yitro* 68b.
125. *Lev. R.* 22:3.
126. *II Alphabet of Ben Sira* 24b, *Targum Yonatan,* Ps. 57:3.
127. Preface to *Perek Shira, Yalkut on Psalms* (end), *Zohar* III, 222b, 232b.
128. *Hul.* 64b.
129. See Ginzberg, *Legends,* 5:61, n. 194; E. M. Beit-Arie, *Perek Shira* (critical ed., Jerusalem, 1966), 2 vols.
130. *Jewish Encyclopedia,* 11:294–295.
131. S. Baer, *Avodat Yisrael,* pp. 546–552.
132. Ps. 148:7.
133. Ps. 29:3.
134. Prov. 6:9.
135. Song of Songs 2:14.
136. Ps. 84:4.
137. Ps. 59:17.
138. Jer. 22:13.
139. Isa. 33:3, *Sanh.* 95b. The word *hayyot* might also refer to the celestial beings of Ezekiel's mystic visions.
140. *Hul.* 7a–7b, *Gen. R.* 60:8, P. T. *Dem.* I, 21d.
141. *Avot de Rabbi Natan,* p. 38.
142. *Taan.* 24a.
143. *Pesiqta Rabbati,* 14 (ed. Friedman), 56b–57a.
144. *Tanhuma Masse* 4, *Num. R.* 23:9.
145. *Ps. Philo* 53–54, 55:2–9.
146. *Gen. R.* 54:4, *A. Z.* 24b.
147. *Tanhuma, Wa-era* 12; *Pes.* 53b.
148. *Gen. R.* 22:12.
149. Exod. 11:7.
150. *Yalkut* to Exod. 187. See Aptowitzer, "The Rewarding and Punishing of Animals and Inanimate Objects," *Hebrew Union College Annual* 3 (1926), p. 131, n. 29.
151. Exod. 13:13, 34:20; *Bekh.* 5b: *Mekilta de Rabbi Ishmael,* tractate *Amalek,* vol. II, pp. 138 f.
152. *Gen. R.* 22:8; *Tanhuma, Bereshit* 9.
153. *Tanhuma, Bereshit* 9; *P.R.E.* 21; *Gen. R.* 22:8; *Midrash haGadol,* Gen. 4:16. See Ginzberg, *Legends,* 5:142–143, n. 31.
154. *Midrash Tehillim (Shocher Tov),* Buber ed., Ps. 28, p. 229.
155. *Midrash Samuel* 12:4; *Midrash haGadol,* Gen. 3:4; *Gen. R.* 19:5.
156. *Sanh.* 108a–b, *Gen. R.* 28:8.
157. *Tanhuma, Noah* 5. See Recanati to Deut 22:6.
158. *Sanh.* 108b.

159. *M. K.* 17a.
160. *Mekhilta* to Exod. 15.
161. *Gen. R.* 28:6.
162. Exod. 21:28–32.
163. M., *Sanh.* 1:4; *Sanh.* 15a–b; Tos., *Sanh.* 3:1.
164. M., *B.K.* 4:6; Tos., *B.K.* 4:5; *B.K.* 41b, 43a–b, 44a–45a.
165. M., *Sanh.* 1:4; *Mekilta de R. Ishmael,* tractate *Shirata,* chap. II, p. 21.
166. *Ed.* 6:1, *Ber.* 27a, P. T., *Erub.* 10:26.
167. Exod. 22:18, Lev. 18:23, 20:15–16.
168. Deut. 27:21.
169. *Gen. R.* 26:5.
170. *Sanh.* 105a.
171. *R. H.* 4a.
172. *Kid.* 4:14.
173. *A.Z.* 22b.
174. M., *A.Z.* 2:1.
175. *A.Z.* 22b.
176. P.T., *Sanh.* 6:23b.
177. *Yeb.* 59b, *Derekh Eretz* I, 55d.
178. Aptowitzer, pp. 137–138. See Plato, *Laws* IX, 873D–874A.
179. Daniel R. Mannix, *The History of Torture* (London, 1970), cited by Aaron M. Schreiber, *Jewish Law and Decision Making: A Study Through Time* (Temple University Press), p. 261.

Chapter 9

1. *Ber.* 4b.
2. *A.Z.* 3b, *Shab.* 107b.
3. *Pes.* 118a, *Seder Eliyahu Rabbah* XV (Friedman ed.), p. 70.
4. Ps. 147:9.
5. *Lev. R.* 19:1, *P.R.E.* 21 (Friedlander ed.), pp. 156–157, *Midrash Samuel* 5:57.
6. *Makeri* (vol. I, p. 113), quoting from *P.R.E.* Cited by Ginzburg, *Legends,* 5:56, n. 181.
7. *Shab.* 155b.
8. *Shimoni* to Ps. 104, par. 862, pp. 951 f.
9. *B.B.* 73b, Ginzberg, *Legends,* 5:49–50, n. 144, 5:181, n. 34.
10. *Shab.* 77b.
11. *Exod. R.* 1:16, *Sot.* 11b.
12. *Kid.* 82b.
13. *Midrash Tehillim* on Ps. 117:1.
14. *Shimoni* to Numbers, *Balak,* pp. 528–529, par. 765.
15. Gen. 8:1, *Tanhuma* on Noah 9.
16. *Lev. R.* 37:1; *Gen. R.* 33:1; P.T., *B. M.* 2, 8c; *Tamid* 32b; *Midrash Tanhuma* (Buber ed.), *Emor* 9.
17. *Taan.* 16a; A. Jellinek, *Bet HaMidrash, Midrash Jonah,* 2d ed., 1:102.
18. See *Ketab Tamim* 61, in Blumenfeld, *Otzar Nehmad,* and R. Bahya to *Ki-Tetze.*
19. Prov. 11:30.

20. *Gen. R., Noah* 31:14.

21. *Jerusalem Targum* to Gen. 14:18 identifies him with Noah's oldest son, Shem. See also *Midrash Tehillim* to Ps. 37:1, p. 252.

22. *Midrash Tehillim* to Ps. 37:1, p. 252. Comp. *Sanh.* 108b.

23. *Tanhuma, Noah* 3.

24. Gen. 37:14.

25. Num. 20:2–4; *Yelamdenu* to *Yalkut* I, 763; *Mekilta Amalek* 6, 52a; *Ned.* 81a.

26. *Gen. R.* 20:8,

27. *Ps. Philo* 52, 53:1 seq. Possibly the reading "bird's nest" is an inaccurate one and the priests are actually being condemned for their mishandling of the "bird-sacrifices" brought by women as a purification offering after childbirth. See Ginzberg, *Legends,* 6:226–227, n. 40.

28. Deut. 11:15.

29. *Yasher Wa-Yesheb* 85a–85b. Ginzberg suspects this story to be Arabic in origin, "since in genuinely Jewish legends animals do not talk." Ginzberg, *Legends,* 5:332, n. 66.

30. *Tehillim,* 105:452, 114:470.

31. *Exod. R.* 31:7.

32. *Tehillim* 78:357, *Song of Songs R.* 2:2–3.

33. *Exod.* 23:4–5, Deut. 22:1–4. See *B.M.* 30b–33a. *Shab.* 128b.

34. Deut. 22:10.

35. Deut. 25:4.

36. Deut. 22:6.

37. *Num. R.* 10:1, 17:5.

38. Lev. 22:28.

39. Ibid.

40. Prov. 12:10.

41. *Lev. R.* 27:11, ed. Margulies, pp. 644 f.

42. *Hul.* 82b. The passage in the Torah clearly refers to the *male* animal and its progeny (see *Targum Yonatan* ad loc.), but the certainty of maternity and uncertainty of paternity led to its practical interpretation in terms of the *female* and its calf.

43. Lev. 22:27, Exod. 22:29.

44. *Deut. R.* 1.

45. *Works of Philo Judaeus* (Yange trans.), 3:440–442.

46. Deut. 22:6.

47. *Deut. R.* 6:1.

48. *Works of Philo Judaeus,* 3:446.

49. *B.K.* 54b; M., *B.K.* 5:7; Rashi to Deut. 25:4, 22:10.

50. Exod. 23:5.

51. *B.M.* 32b.

52. *B.M.* 31a–32a.

53. Deut. 23:25–26, *B.M.* 87b.

54. Deut. 24:14–15.

55. Deut. 25:4.

56. Num. 18:3 ff., 18:8 ff., 18:25 ff.

57. *Ter.* 9:3; comp. *B.M.* 90a.

58. *M.T., Mishpatim, Hilkhot Sekhirot* 13:3; *B.M.* 90b.

59. Deut. 11:15.
60. *Git.* 62a, *Ber.* 40a.
61. *Git.* 62a.
62. *Midrash HaGadol to Genesis* (ed. Margulies), par. 747; Ginzberg, *Legends,* 5:348, n. 221.
63. P.T. *Ket.* 4:8, 29a; P.T., *Yeb.* 15:3, 14d.
64. *Shab.* 110b–111a, *Hag.* 14b.
65. *Sanh.* 56b; Tos., *A.Z.* 8:6; *B.M.* 90b.
66. Tos., *Mak.* 5:6.
67. *Hag.* 14b.
68. *Hul.* 7b.
69. *B.M.* 90a–90b.
70. M., *Hag.* 1:8.
71. *Yoma* 84b; Tos., *Shab.* 16:16; *Mekhilta de Rabbi Yismael to* Exod. 31:14; *Ket.* 5a.
72. *Shab.* 128b, *B.M.* 32b.
73. *Shab.* 128b.
74. *Shab.* 128a–128b.
75. Ibid.
76. M., *Shab.* 16:2.
77. M., *Shab.* 5:2; *Shab.* 53a.
78. *Shab.* 53b.
79. *Shab.* 122a, 95a; M., *Shab.* 16:8.
80. M. *Shab.* 24:1.
81. *Shab.* 153a.
82. *Gen. R.* 28:6.
83. Ginzberg, *Legends,* 3:49.
84. Deut. 12:20.
85. *Hul.* 101b–102b derives it from Deut. 12:23, *Sanh.* 56a–b from Gen. 9:4, *Targum Onkelos* from Exod. 23:30. See also Tos., *A.Z.* 8:4–6.
86. *Sanh.* 56a.
87. M., *Betz.,* 3:2; M., *Shab.* 1:6.
88. M., *Shev.* 7:4.
89. *Shab.* 106b.
90. M., *M. K.* 1:4; M., *Ed.* 2:5.
91. *Wars* 1, 429; *Antiquities* 15:244, 16:313.
92. *Hul.* 60b. *Mekhilta* to Exod. 16:21 describes non-Jewish hunters, but curiously *Targum Pseudo-Jonathan* depicts Jewish hunters.
93. Ps. 1:1.
94. *A.Z.* 18b.
95. *Lev. R.* 22:7; *Sifrei, Deut.* 75; *Hul.* 16b–17a. Rabbi Ishmael's view is disputed by Rabbi Akiba. See also Ginzberg, *Legends,* 6:95, n. 519, on meat-eating in the wilderness.
96. *Zeb.* 120a.
97. So *Ps. Jerome* to I Sam. 14:34 is interpreted by Ginzberg (*Legends,* 6:232, n. 58).
98. *Targum Yerushalmi* to Lev. 3:17.
99. Deut. 12:21.

100. *Bekh.* 5b.
101. *Hul.* 67a–67b.
102. *Hul.* 59b.
103. *Bekh.* 7b.
104. *Hul.* 92b,111a,117a; M.T., *Maakhalot Asurot* 6:3, 4.
105. *Hul.* 115a–115b.
106. *Works of Philo Judaeus,* 3:445.
107. *Deut.* 12:21.
108. *Hul.* 28a. *Lev.* 1:5, 11, 3:2, 8, 13, employs the phrase *shahat* in connection with sacrifices.
109. *Hul.* 27a.
110. *Ket.* 37b, *Sanh.* 52b. *Sanh.* 45a states that all the sages are in agreement with Rabbi Nahman. Rashi on *Ket.* 37b explains the phrase "easy death" as being "with a blade on the side of the neck where the vital organs are in order that he should die more quickly."
111. *Hul.* 10a, 17b, 18a.
112. *M.N.* 3:48.
113. I. Ewen, *Fun Rebe's Hauf* (New York, 1922), p. 113. Cited in Louis I. Newman, *The Hasidic Anthology,* 4:6, p. 14.
114. *Gen.* 2:20, 23.
115. See *Yeb.* 63a. *MaHarSha* to *Yeb.* 63b; Rashi to *Gen.* 2:21–23; *Sifte Hahamim* to *Gen.* 2:23; Nachmanides and *Or HeHayyim* to *Gen.* 2:20.
116. *B.M.* 85a; *P. T. Kil.* 9:4; *Gen R.* 33:3; *Yalkut Shimoni* to *Ps.* 145.
117. *Tos. B.K.* 9:30; *Sifrei, Deut.* 96.

Chapter 10

1. Isak Unna, *Tiershutz im Judentum* (Frankfort-am-Main, 1928), 6:14 ff., as cited by Noah J. Cohen, *Tsaar Baale Hayim* (Washington, D.C.: Catholic University of America Press, 1959), pp. 4–5.
2. *Gen. R.* 16 end; *Tanhuma, Shemini* 8; *Sanh.* 59b.
3. *Midrash Agada* 58.
4. *Midrash Tehillim* to *Ps.* 146.
5. See E. E. Urbach, *Y. Baer Jubilee Volume* (1960), pp. 48–68.
6. *P.T., Kid.* 4:12, 66d.
7. *Pes.* 109a.
8. *Shab.* 118b, 119a.
9. *Shab.* 119a.
10. *Betza* 16a.
11. *Gen. R.* 72:4.
12. *Shab.* 119a.
13. *Gen. R.* 11:4.
14. *Taan.* 24a.
15. *Sifrei* to *Ekev* 11:11.
16. *Ket.* 67b. In some locales meat was apparently a daily menu item.
17. *Hul.* 84a.
18. *Tanhuma, Pinhas* 18; *Pesikta de Rav Kahana* 195b (Buber ed.).
19. *Pes.* 114a.
20. Ibid.

21. Prov. 27:27.
22. *Hul.* 84a.
23. Deut. 21:18–21.
24. M., *Sanh.* 8:2.
25. Prov. 23:20–21.
26. *Hul.* 84a.
27. Tos., *Sot.* 15:10.
28. *Pes.* 42a.
29. Tos., *Zab.* 2:5.
30. *Ber.* 57b.
31. *Ber.* 44b.
32. *Shab.* 129a.
33. P.T., *Ber.* 2:5c.
34. *Ned.* 54b, *A.Z.* 29a.
35. *Ket.* 60–61a.
36. Ibid.
37. *Git.* 67b.
38. P.T., *Peah* 8:21a.
39. P.T., *B.K.* 8:6b.
40. *Ket.* 59b.
41. *Hul.* 49a.
42. *A.Z.* 29a, *Ket.* 60b, Rashi to *Ned.* 54b.
43. *Sanh.* 98a, *Ber.* 40a. Apparently some felt that meat-eating could prove injurious to the convalescent. See *Ber.* 57b.
44. *Git.* 69b.
45. *Ber.* 40a.
46. *Shab.* 129a.
47. *B.K.* 71b–72a.
48. *Yoma* 75b.
49. Exod. 16:8.
50. Lev. 11:46–47.
51. *Pes.* 49b.
52. *Aristeas* 142–7.
53. *Spec.* 4:118.
54. *Tehillim* 146:535.
55. *Gen. R.* 44:1.
56. *Tanhuma B., Shemini* 15b.
57. Such indeed is the argument advanced by Eldad HaDani. See *Kitve R. Abraham Epstein* (Haberman ed., Jerusalem, 1950), 1:26–27.
58. *Hul.* 27b, based on Num. 11:23.
59. *Shab.* 18a; P.T. *Shab.* 13:5, 14a; *Git.* 60b–61a; *M.K.* 11a; *Kid.* 72a; *B.M.* 12b.
60. *Hul.* 74a–b.
61. *Sanh.* 59b.
62. *Hul.* 33a.
63. *Midrash Maaser Sheni* 5:15; Tos., *Sot.* 13:10. See Isaac Hirsch Weiss, *Dor Dor veDorshav*, pt. II, pp. 26–27, and Saul Lieberman, *Hellenism in Jewish Palestine*, pp. 141, 142, 158–159.

64. *Midrash Tehillim*, XXII (Buber ed.), p. 196.
65. *Gen. R.* 86:2.
66. P.T., *Betza* 2:7, 62b.
67. Tos., *B.M.* 3, end 379 (Lieberman ed.).
68. Jos. 11:6, *A.Z.* 13a.
69. *A.Z.* 11a.
70. *Hul.* 7b. See also *B.M.* 31a.
71. *Ber.* 33b.
72. *B.M.* 30a.
73. *Sanh.* 18b, *Sifre* to Deut. 22:1, 115a, par. 272
74. Exod. 23:4.
75. *Works of Philo Judaeus* 3:439.
76. *Targum* to Exod. 23:5.
77. *B.M.* 32b.
78. *B.M.* 2:26.
79. *Shab.* 128b.
80. *Shab.* 155a.
81. *Shab.* 128b.
82. *Ps.* 136:25–26. See *Pes.* 118a. *Seder Eliyahu Rabbah* (Friedman ed.), p. 70.
83. M., *Shab.* 24:3.
84. *Taan.* 20b.
85. M., *Kil.* 8:6.
86. Deut. 22:6–7.
87. Exod. 20:12.
88. *Deut. R.* 6:2; *Tanhuma* to *Ekev*, p. 103b, par. 2; *Tanhuma* to *Tetzeh*, p. 115a, par. 2; *Hul.* 142a.
89. *Deut R.* 6:2; *Pesikta Rabbati*, chap. 23, p. 121b; *Tanhuma* to *Ekev*, 3. See also P.T., *Kid.* 1:7, 61b; P.T., *Peah* 1:1, 15d.
90. *Avot* 2:1.
91. M., *Hul*, 12:5. See Rashi to Deut. 22:7.
92. *Deut. R.*, *Ki Tezte* 6:5.
93. P.T. *Hag.* 2:1, 77a; *Ruth R.* 6:4. See also *Kid.* 39b.
94. M., *Meg.* 4:9.
95. M., *Ber.* 5:3.
96. See Ephraim E. Urbach, *The Sages: Their Concepts and Beliefs* (Jerusalem, 1971), p. 852, n. 53.
97. M., *Ber.* 9:5.
98. P.T., *Ber.* 5:3; P.T., *Meg.* 4:10.
99. Ibid.
100. *Meg.* 25a, *Ber.* 33b.
101. See Rashi ad loc.
102. Urbach, *The Sages*, p. 55.
103. *Sanh.* 21b.
104. See *Lev. R.* 27:11, where it is taught in the name of Rabbi Levi that both Deut. 72:6–7 and Lev. 22:28 are motivated by reasons of compassion. See also *Deut. R.* 6:1.
105. R. T. Herford, *Christianity in Talmud and Midrash* (London, 1903), pp. 202 ff.

106. S. D. Luzzatto, *Yesodei HaTorah* (Jerusalem, 1947), p. 35, n. 6.
107. M. Kadushin, *Worship and Ethics* (Evanston, Ill.: Northwestern University Press, 1964), p. 297, n. 72.
108. *Erub.* 100b.
109. See S. Lieberman, "How Much Greek in Jewish Palestine," in *Biblical and Other Studies* ed. A. Altman (Cambridge, Mass., 1963), pp. 128–129.
110. *Tanhuma, Masse* 6.
111. See Urbach, *The Sages,* pp. 323–324.
112. *Pesiqta Rabbati* XIV (ed. Friedman), p. 57a.
113. *Git.* 7a.
114. *Sifre, Deut.* 307, p. 344.
115. *B.B.* 16a.–16b.
116. *Sifra, Shemini,* sec. 5, 52b. See *Hul.*127a.
117. *Shab.*77b; P.T., *Ber.* 9:3,13c.
118. See Plutarch, *De Stoicorum Repugnantiis* 21, 31, quoted by Urbach, *The Sages,* p.778, n. 84.
119. *Gen. R.* 10:7.
120. *Alphabet of Rabbi Akiba* 59. See Rashi to Gen. l:27.
121. *A.R.N.* 31, 91–92. See Ginzberg, *Legends,* 5:64, n. 4.
122. *Gen. R.* 1:4, *Sanh.* 98b, *Ber.* 6b, *Hul.* 89a.
123. *Midrash Eccles.* 3:18, *Sifrei, Deut.* 306
124. *Gen. R.* 8:1. See Ginzberg, *Legends,* 5:74, n. 17.
125. Numerous references, See Ginzberg, *Legends,* 5:75–78, n. 20.
126. *Gen. R.* 12:8, *Lev. R.* 9.
127. *Gen. R.* 8:11, *Hag.* 16a.
128. *Gen. R.* 12:8, 14:3–4, *Hag.* 16a. Comp. Philo, *De Fortitud.* 3.
129. *Sifre, Haazinu* 306, pp. 340–341.
130. Although, according to one sage, the fact that animals wound, bite, and kick is indicative that they *do* possess an evil impulse. See *Gen. R.* 14:4, *Ber.* 61a.
131. *Tanhuma,* manuscript (intro. 152, 154). See Ginzberg, *Legends,* 5:65, n. 6.
132. See Akiba's observation in *Gen. R.* 21:5.
133. Jacob Neusner, *The Glory of God Is Intelligence,* p.9.
134. *Hag.* 13b.
135. *Eccles. R.* 10:19, l–20:1, 32:1–2.
136. Lev. 20:15–16.
137. *Sanh.* 54a.
138. IV Ezra 7:66, Slavonic Enoch 58:5. See Aptowitzer, p. 140.
139. *Alphabet of Rabbi Akiba, Beth haMidrash* III, p. 38; *Seder Eliyahu Zuta,* chap. 24.
140. *Sanh.* 54a; *Sifra , Ked.* 11:3; *Lev. R.* 27:3.
141. Exod. 12:29.
142. *Mekhilta* 38, *Pesiqta de R. Kahana* 7:65. See Kasher, *Torah Shelema,* 12:32.
143. Ginzberg, *Legends,* 5:180, n. 32. See Rashi to Gen. 6:7.
144. *Sanh.* 108a.
145. *Gen. R.* 8:3–9, *Sanh.* 38a.
146. *Eccles. R.* 6:11.
147. *Eccles. R.* 3:18.
148. Tos., *Sanh.* 8:7–8; *Sanh.* 38a; P.T., *Sanh.* 4; *Lev. R.* 14:1.

149. *Yoma* 22b; *Eccles R.* VII, 6:1 to VIII 17:1; *Midrash Shmuel* 18:2 (Buber ed., p. 99); *P. R. E.* 44:49–54. See also *Tehillim* 52:284, where Saul argues that even among animals one is forbidden to put to death both parents and young in a single day.

150. *Gen. R.* 22:9; *Tanh. Mattot* 7 (p. 95b, par. 7).

Chapter 11

1. Leo Strauss, *Liberalism: Ancient and Modern* (1968), p. 162; *Persecution and the Art of Writing* (1952), pp. 78–94.

2. In his *Guide*, Maimonides would appear to be addressing himself to an intellectually elite audience, focusing on what he considers to be the reasons underlying biblical legislation. A few of his theories appeared sufficiently radical as to cast doubt in the minds of some as to the true authorship of the book. Jacob Emden, *Siddur Hallon Shebii*, comments that "the book *Moreh Nebukhim* is not the work of art of the great scholar, *RamBam*, may his memory be a source of blessing; rather it comes from someone who wished to strangle himself and hung himself upon a mighty tree." No evidence at all exists, however, to support any claim of non-Maimonidean authorship for the *Moreh Nebukhim*.

3. *M.T., Nezikim, Hilkhot Rozeach uShmirat Nefesh*, chap. 13.

4. *Kesef Mishna*, ad loc.

5. *Derish uPerisha, S.A., H.M.* 272.

6. Commentary of Elijah of Vilna to *S.A., H.M.* 272:16. The same reasoning is applicable to par. 14 of Maimonides' chapter.

7. *B.M.* 32b.

8. *M.T., Ahavah, Hilkhot Tefillah* 9:7.

9. M., *Ber.* 5:3; M., *Meg.* 4:9.

10. *M.N.* 3:48, pp. 599–600.

11. *Sefer haMitzvot*, 361 negative; *M.T., Kedushah. Hilkhot Issurei Biah* 16:10.

12. *M.T., Zemanim, Hilkhot Shabbat* 11:8.

13. *M.T., Zemanim, Hilkhot Shabbat* 26:16.

14. Ibid., 21:9–10.

15. Ibid., 25:26.

16. *M.T., Zemanim, Hilkhot Yom-Tov* 2:4.

17. Ibid 4:16.

18. *M.T., Mishpatim, Hilkhot Shehirot* 13:3.

19. *M.T., Kinyan, Hilkhot Avadim* 9:8.

20. *Yakar Tiferet, Hilkhot Shluhim veShutafim, Hilkhot Avadim* 9:5.

21. *M.T., Zemanim, Hilkhot Yom-Tov* 4:16.

22. *M.T., Kedushah, Hilkhot Shehitah* 13:8.

23. *M.T., Zemanim, Hilkhot Shabbat* 21:35–36.

24. *Hul.* 102a; *M.T., Kedushah, Hilkhot Maakhalot Asurot* 5:1.

25. *M.T., Kedushah, Hilkhot Maakhalot Asurot* 5:2.

26. Ibid 5:3–4.

27. *M.T., Kedushah, Hilkhot Shehitah* 1:2.

28. *M.N.* 3:17. See also *Letter to the Jews of Marseilles*, where Maimonides emphasizes that "we have rational proofs that the vicissitudes that befall men are different from those that occur to animals."

29. *M.N.* 3:18.

30. *M.N.* 3:26.
31. *M.N.* 3:48.
32. Ibid.
33. *M.N.* 3:17.
34. *M.N.* 3:48.
35. *Emunot veDeot*, end of chap. 3.
36. *Teshubot HaGeonim,* Harkavy ed., no. 375, p. 191.
37. See *M.N.* 3:17. According to Moshe Zucker, Aptowitzer misunderstood Maimonides because of Ibn Tibbon's translation of *taavitz* ("compensation") as *gemul* ("reward"), and was thus misled into thinking that Maimonides denied to animals any reward or punishment in the hereafter.
38. Gershom Scholem in *Encyclopaedia Judaica,* 13:1282.
39. M. H. Luzzatto; *Derekh HaShem* and *Ma'amar haIkkarim* (Feldheim, Jerusalem and New York. 1978), p. 385.
40. *Keter Malhut.*
41. *Milhamot Adonoi,* IV, chaps. 1–7.
42. *Or Adonoi,* bk.II, sec. 2.
43. *Hegyon ha-Nefesh,* pp. 5b–8a (ed. Freiman, Leipzig, 1860).
44. Saadiah Gaon, *Emunot veDeot,* treatise III, chap. 2:117 *(The Book of Beliefs and Opinions,* trans. S. Rosenblatt, p. 144).
45. *Sefer haYashar* (Trans. Seymour Cohen, New York, 1973), xi–xv.
46. Commentary to the Pentateuch, Gen. 3:1.
47. For discussions relating to man's *uniqueness,* see A. Tkhursch, *Tiferet HaAdam* (Jerusalem: Mosad HaRav Kook, 1951), and E. Urbach, *The Sages: Their Concepts and Beliefs* (Jerusalem: Magnes Press, 1971), pp. 189–226.
48. Gen. 2:7.
49. *Book of Beliefs and Opinions,* introduction to fourth treatise.
50. *Kuzari* 1:31–43.
51. M., *Kil.* 8:5. See P.T., *Kil.* 8:4.
52. See Maimonides, *Commentary to the Mishnah* (Jerusalem: Mosad HaRav Kook, 1963), 1:214.
53. See *Eruv.* 31b. Some interpret this statement to mean that one can train an ape *using* seventy different languages, but most likely Meiri is referring to the ape's capacity to comprehend different languages. See. M. Kasher, *Torah Shlemah,* 2:251.
54. *M.T., Hilkhot Yesodei HaTorah* 4:8; *M.N.* 3:48.
55. *M.N.* 1:1–2.
56. See Commentary of Abraham Ibn Ezra to Gen. 3:1 and Num. 22:28.
57. *Commentary to the Torah,* (Tel Aviv: Dvir, 1965), pp. 480–481.
58. *Ikkarim,* p. 5.
59. Ibid., p.19.
60. Ibid., p. 39.
61. Ibid., p. 110.
62. *Shab.* 107b.
63. *Sefer HaHinnukh,* Mitzvah 545, comp. Mitzvah 169.
64. *Sefer HaHinnukh,* Mitzvah 294.
65. Gen. 6:7.
66. *Abot de Rabbi Natan,* chap. 31; *Zohar,* II, p. 76a–b.

67. Cordovero, *Shiur Komah*, p. 113. Quoted by G. Scholem in *Kabbalah* (New York, 1974), p.383.

68. See Georges Vajda, "Le probleme de la Souffrance Gratuite selon Yusuf Al-Basir," *Revue des études Juives* (Rome: Historia Judaica, 1972), pp. 317–321.

69. *Etz Hayyim*, chaps. 82–89.

70. Commentary to Deut. 22:6.

71. On Deut. 22:7.

72. Mitzvah 294, 545.

73. Chap. III.

74. S. R. Hirsch, *Horeb*, II (London: Soncino Press, 1962).

75. Lev. 17:13.

76. *Sheelot YaAVeTZ*, pt. 1, 17:110.

77. Mitzvah 596.

78. Commentary of Nachmanides to Deut. 22:6.

79. *M.N.*, 3:28.

80. Mitzvah 451.

81. *M.T.*, *Hilkhot Issurei Mizbeach* 3. See also *M.N.* 3:46.

82. Mitzvah 293.

83. *A.Z.* 13a.

84. *Nimukei Yosef* to B.M. 82.

85. See *Tosafot* to *B.M.* 32b, *A.Z.* 11a.

86. See *Binyan Zion, Otzar HaPoskim, Eben HaEzer* 5:14; Abraham Hafutah, "BeDin Tzaar Baalei Hayyim L'zarchei Refuah," *Noam* 4 (1961); Natan Zevi Friedman; "Nisyonim Maadiim Shel Gufot Baalei Hayyim," *Noam* 5.

87. *Otzar haPoskim, E. H.* 5:14.

88. *Noda B'Yehudah, Tinyana, Y.D.* 10.

89. *Hul.* 7b.

90. *TaZ, Y.D.* 117:4.

91. Commentary of Samson of Sens to *Kil.* 8:5.

92. J. Trachtenberg, *Jewish Magic and Superstition* (New York, 1979), pp. 182, 302, n. 2.

93. H. J. Zimmels, *Minhat Bikkurim* (Vienna, 1926), pp. 1–9.

94. Trachtenberg, *Jewish Magic and Superstition*, p. 38.

95. *Sefer Hasidim* (ed. J. Wistinetski, Frankfort a.M., 1924), no. 1466.

96. M. Gaster, *Ma'aseh Book*, 2 vols. (1934), 2:576 ff.

97. David de Pomis, *Zemah David* (Venice, 1587), p. 73, quoted by Trachtenberg, 278.

98. Moses Taku, *Otzar Nehmad*, III, p. 97.

99. Trachtenberg, *Jewish Magic and Superstition*, pp. 130, 295 n. 24.

100. Cited in ibid., p. 43.

101. *Sefer Hasidim* (Wist. ed.), no. 140; *Sefer Hasidim* (ed. Margolis, Jerusalem, 1957), nos. 1145, 1146.

102. *Sefer Hasidim* (Wist. ed)., no. 764.

103. *Pithe Teshuvah* to *S.A., Y.D.* 179:4.

104. *Sefer Hasidim* (Mar. ed.), no. 1146.

105. *Responsa* (Lemberg, 1811), pt. 1, no. 395, p. 47a.

106. *S.A., O.H.* 605.

107. Trachtenberg, *Jewish Magic and Superstition*, p. 128.

108. *Sefer Hasidim* (Mar. ed.), no. 477.
109. *Sefer Hasidim* (Wist. ed), no. 377. See *Pes.* 110a and *RaSHBaM* ad loc.
110. *Git.* 56b, *Gen. R.* 10:7, *Lev. R.* 22:3.
111. *Meor Einayim* (Cassel ed., Vilna, 1866), p. 214.
112. Quoted by B. Levin, "Zur Charakteristik und Biographie des R. Scherira Gaon," *Jahrbuch der juedisch-literarischen Gesellschaft* 8 (1910): 335.
113. *Likkutei Maharil* (Amsterdam, 1730), p. 90. See Trachtenberg, *Jewish Magic and Superstition*, pp. 196, 304, n. 7.
114. *Y.D.* 336:1.
115. See Yair Hayyim Bacharach, *Havoth Yair*, no. 234.
116. *Hatam Sofer, Y.D.* 101.
117. Paraphrased by I. Zinberg, *A History of Jewish Literature*, trans. B. Martin (Cleveland and London, 1972), 1:204–205.
118. *Kalila v'Dimna* I, no. 14, pp. 265–270.
119. Cited by Zinberg, *History of Jewish Literature*, 1:200.
120. Ibid., 1:201.
121. Ibid., 7:265.
122. *Kalila v'Dimna* I, no. 5, pp. 106–111.
123. *Mishle Shualim*, no. 26 (trans. in M. J. Bin-Gorion, *Mimekor Yisrael*, [Indiana University Press, 1976],4:1312–1313).
124. *Ben haMelekh vehaNazir* xxi, pp. 65–67 (Mantua,1557), trans. in *Mimekor Yisrael*, 4:1285–1287.
125. L. Ginzberg, ed., "Haggadot Ketuot," in *HaGoren* IX, 41–42, no. 3. (trans. in *Mimekor Yisrael*, 4:1284–1285).
126. *Avot* 5:23.
127. Isa. 31:5.

Chapter 12

1. *History* 2:123.
2. See *Emunot veDeot*, treatise 6, chap. 8.
3. Ibid, chap. 7.
4. *Emunah Ramah*, treatise 1, chap. 7.
5. *Or Adonai* 4:7.
6. *Ikkarim*, treatise 4, chap. 29.
7. Israel Abrahams, *Jewish Life in the Middle Ages* (Philadelphia, 1896), p. 152, n. 3.
8. G. Scholem, *Kabbalah* (New York, 1974), pp. 312–315.
9. Hayyim Vital, *Sefer Shaar haGilgulim* (Jerusalem, 1963), vol. II, chap. 22, pp. 58, 60.
10. Ibid., p. 59.
11. Ibid., pp. 63, 59. According to the Talmud, children of such unions die at a young age.
12. *Shivhe he-Ari* 5.
13. Vital Calabrese, *Sefer haGilgulim* (ed. Warsaw), p. 125.
14. Hayyim Vital, *Shibhe Hayyim Vital* (ed. Lemberg), p. 16.
15. *Shivhe he-Ari* 5, *Sefer ha-Maassiyot*, no. 81.
16. Vital, *Sefer Shaar haGilgulim*, p.63.
17. See *Mimekor Yisrael*, 2:844–845.

18. *Kav haYashar*, no. 34, p. 71; *Sefer haMaassiyot*, no. 95.
19. *Sefer Shaar haGilgulim* (Frankfort), p. 69.
20. Isaac Luria, *Sefer haKavanot*, p. 62b.
21. *Tomar Deborah*, chap. 3.
22. Ps. 29:9.
23. Moses Cordovero, *Pardes Rimonim*, gate 24:10, as cited by Elie Munk, *The Call of the Torah*, trans. E. S. Maser (Jerusalem and New York: Feldheim, 1980), 1:203–204.
24. *Sefer Shaar haGilgulim*, p. 61.
25. See *haggahot* to Vital, *Shaar haMitzvot*, p. 101.
26. Cited by A. Shoshan, *Baalei Hayyim BeSifrut Yisrael*, p. 157.
27. Nahman of Tcherin, *Sefer Nahat haShulhan* (Jerusalem, 1977), pp. 87–91.
28. Gen. 9:3.
29. Dan. 10:2–3, *Tur*, *O.H.* 551.
30. See *Beit Joseph* to *Tur*, *O.H.* 551.
31. *Siddur Beit Tefillah, Nusah Sefarad* (Vilna, 1900), p. 161.
32. *S.A., Y.D.* 341a. See Commentary of Shabbetai haKohen, *Pithe Teshubah*, ad loc.
33. Ps. 27:4, *Responsa Ginat Veradim*, pt. I, 2:15.

Chapter 13

1. *Sefer Hasidim* (Mar. ed.), par. 669.
2. *Sefer Hasidim* (Wist. ed.) par. 138.
3. Ibid., pars. 142, 145.
4. Ibid., par. 44.
5. Henry J. Van Lennep, *Bible Lands and Customs*, 1:217.
6. *Sefer Hasidim* (Mar. ed.), par. 589.
7. Ibid., par. 665.
8. Ibid., par. 665; *Sefer Hasidim* (Wist. ed.), par. 137.
9. *Sefer Hasidim* (Wist. ed.), par. 1955.
10. Cited by Solomon Schechter, *Studies in Judaism*, Second Series (Philadelphia, 1908), pp. 174–175.
11. *Tomar Deborah*, chap. 3.
12. Jacob Emden, *Sheelot YaAVeTZ* (Altona, 1739), I, p. 110.
13. *Kav haYashar*, no. 7, p. 11; *Sefer Zekhirah* 103.
14. *Toledot Yaakob Yosef*, p. 25.
15. *Tanya*, chap. XLII.
16. A. Shoshan, *Anuu Vaalei Hayyim*, p. 206.
17. *Shivhei haBesht: In Praise of the Baal Shem Tov* (trans. Mintz), p. 245.
18. *Likutei Muharam M'braslav: Rabbi Nahman's Wisdom*, p. 306.
19. *Magid Sihot*, p. 48.
20. Shneur Zalman, *S.A., H.M.*, vol. 6, *Hilkhot Ovre Derakhim u'tzaar Baalei Hayyim*, sec. 8, p. 48.
21. Yisroel Yaakov Klapholz, *Tales of the Baal Shem Tov* (1974), 2:14.
22. Martin Buber, *Or Ganuz* (1958), p. 227.
23. Shoshan, *Baalei Hayyim BeSifrut Yisrael*, p. 328.
24. Z. M. Rabinovicz, *HaYehudi HaKadosh* (Piotrkov, 1932), p. 19, quoted by Louis I. Newman, *Maggidim and Hasidim: Their Wisdom* (New York, 1962), p. 8.

25. *Baalei Hayyim BeSifrut Yisrael*, p. 328.
26. *Shivhei haBesht*, p. 115.
27. J. Mintz, *Legends of the Hasidim*, pp. 300–301.
28. Ibid., pp. 306–307.
29. *Shivhei haBesht*, pp. 26–28; *Sippurei Anshei Shem*, no. 5, p. 4.
30. *Shivhei haBesht*, pp. 133-134, 258–259.
31. Ibid., pp. 142–144.
32. Mintz, *Legends of the Hasidim*, pp. 257—258.
33. S. Y. Agnon, *Yomim Noraim*, p. 297.
34. *Baalei Hayyim BeSifrut Yisrael*, p. 71.
35. Ibid., p. 327.
36. See summary of A. M. Haberman in *Iggeret Baalie Hayyim* (Jerusalem, 1949), p. 167.
37. Cited in Joe Green, *The Jewish Vegetarian Tradition* (Johannesburg, 1969).
38. *Encyclopaedia Judaica*, 6:1131.
39. See Joseph Karo, *Kesef Mishna*, *Hilkhot Rozeach* 18:9; Moses Isserles, *S.A.*, *H.M.* 272:9.
40. *S.A.*, *O.H.* 305:8, 10.
41. *S.A.*, *O.H.* 332:2, 332:4.
42. *S.A.*, *O.H.* 305:20. See *Asheri* to *B.M.* 2:29.
43. Some difference of opinion exists as to whether these concessions are applicable only on the festivals or on the Sabbath as well. See *Turim* to *O.H.* 332 and Karo ad loc.
44. *S.A.*, *O.H.* 523:4. Based on *Shab.* 128b.
45. *S.A.*, *O.H.* 332:4.
46. *S.A.*, *O.H.* 305:19.
47. *Magen Avraham* to *O.H.* 266:9; Israel Mordecai b. Zeeb Joseph, *Sefer Shulhan haShabbat*, p. 220, par. 2.
48. *S.A.*, *O.H.* 332:3.
49. *S.A.*, *O.H.* 228:42.
50. *S.A.*, *O.H.* 532:1, gloss. See also *S.A.*, *O.H.* 536:1–3; *M.T.*, *Shebitat Yom-Tob* 8:15.
51. *Magen Avraham* to *O.H.* 305:18.
52. *O.H.* 305:18; *Sefer Shulhan haShabbat*, p. 220, par. 1. There is a difference of opinion in the Talmud as to whether one may ride an animal on the Sabbath. See *Shab.* 94a, *Sanh.* 46a, P.T., *Betza* 5:2, 63a. *S.A.*, *O.H.* 524:1 prohibits riding an animal even on a festival, and some authorities forbid one to even support himself against an animal on the Sabbath. See *S.A.*, *O.H.* 305:1, *Kitzur S.A.* 87:2.
53. *Shab.* 155b, *O.H.* 324:11, *Kitzur S.A.* 87:18.
54. Agnon, *Yomim Noraim*, p. 278, cites the *Leket Yosher.*
55. Cited by Abrahams, *Jewish Life in the Middle Ages*, p. 373.
56. *Sheelot YaAVeTZ*, 1, 17.
57. Deut. 25:4.
58. *B.M.* 90a; *M.T.*, *Mishpatim*, *Hilkhot Sehirot* 13:3; *S.A.*, *H.M.* 338:5.
59. *S.A.*, *H.M.* 338:2–3; *Kitzur S.A.* 18:1.
60. Exod. 23:11.
61. Lev. 22:24.

340 o Animal Life in Jewish Tradition

62. M.T., Kedushah, Hilkhot Issurei Biah 16:10.
63. See Rashi to Lev. 22:24.
64. M.N. 3:48.
65. Quoted by Benjamin Winternitz in his commentary to the *Shehitot uBedikot* of Jacob Weil, and cited in Jeremiah J. Berman's *Shehita* (New York, 1941), p. 443.
66. *Emunot veDeot* 175.
67. Ibid., 181.
68. *Responsa*, pt. 1, no. 728.
69. *Havoth Yair* 191.
70. *Emunot veDeot*, treatise V, 113.
71. Lev. 19:18.
72. Exod. 23:12.
73. Deut. 22:10.
74. M.N. 3:49, p. 609.
75. S.A., E.H. 5:14; S.A., O.H. 59:36. See Beth Hillel, ibid.
76. *Terumot haDeshen, Responsa Peaskim uKetavim*, pt. II, par. 105:1.
77. *Otzar ha Poskim, E.H.* 5:14.
78. *Responsa Ginat Veradim*, pt. I, 2:16.
79. S.A., E.H. 5:36.
80. *Responsa MaHaRaSHDaM O.H.* 2:1.
81. *Responsa Yabeah Omer*, pt. I, O.H. 30:8.
82. Ibid., O.H. 26:4.
83. *Responsa Har Zevi*, pt. I, O.H. 205:3, 8.
84. *Responsa of Menahem Azariah de Fano* 102:2.
85. *Responsa MaHaRSHaM*, pt. IV, no. 140:1.
86. *Responsa Noda B'Yehudah, Kamma, Y.D.* 83:2.
87. *Responsa Rav Poalim*, pt. I, Y.D. 83:2.
88. Pt. V, H.M. 185:13.
89. *Responsa of David Hayyim Joseph Azulai*, pt. III, no. 458:2.
90. See, for example, *Responsa Binyan Zion* 108:4, *Responsa MaHaRSHaM*, pt. V, no. 52:8.
91. A.Z. 18b.
92. To A.Z. 11a.
93. M.T., Hilkhot Melakhim 6.
94. Or Zarua, II, 17, p. 37b.
95. Responsa, no. 27.
96. Mitzvah 186.
97. *Nodah B'Yehudah, Y.D.*, no. 10.
98. *Shemesh Zedaka* (Venice, 1743), no. 18.
99. *Pahad Yitzhak, Zeidah*.
100. See, for example, *Nimukei Yosef* to B.M., end of chap. 2.
101. Hirsch, *Horeb*, 2:292.
102. S.A., O.H. 223:6. See also *Piske Maharig* and *Teshuva M'Ahavah*, pt. 1, no. 53.
103. See chaps. 7–8.
104. See chap. 19.

Chapter 14

1. Aristotle, *Politics* (Everyman's Library ed.), p. 16.
2. I Cor. 9:9–10.
3. St. Augustine, *The Catholic and Manichaean Ways of Life* (Boston: Catholic University Press, 1966), p. 102.
4. Thomas Aquinas, *Summa Theologica* II, Q. 64, art. 1.
5. Ibid., III, Q 102, art. 6.
6. Ibid.
7. Peter Singer, *Animal Liberation*, pp. 213–214.
8. *St. Francis of Assisi: His Life and Writings as Recorded by His Contemporaries* (London, 1959), p. 145.
9. G. H. Bousquet, "Des Animaux et de leur traitement selon le Judaisme le Christianisme et l'Islam," *Studia Islamica* (Paris: La Rose, 1958), pp. 31– 48.
10. *The Light of Asia*, quoted in Howard Williams, *The Ethics of Diet* (Manchester of London, 1907), p. 12.
11. Ovid, *Metamorphoses* XV, 73–142.
12. H. C. Lea, *A History of the Inquisition of the Middle Ages*, 3 vols. (1889), 1:97.
13. *The Ethics of Diet*, pp. 113–122, 128–150.
14. Voltaire, *Traité sur la Tolerance*.
15. Oliver Goldsmith, *The Citizen of the World*, in *Collected Works*, ed. A. Friedman (Oxford, 1966), 2:60.
16. Joseph Ritson, *An Essay on Abstinence from Animal Food as a Moral Duty*, pp. 57,86,102,124,146.
17. M. K. Gandhi, *Diet and Diet Reform* (1949), pp. 3–4.
18. F. Simoons, *Eat Not This Flesh* (Madison, Wis., 1961), p. 10.
19. See Singer, *Animal Liberation*, pp. 96–166.
20. Lewis Gompertz, *Moral Inquiries on the Situation of Man and of Brutes. On the Crime of Committing Cruelty on Brutes, and of Sacrificing Them to the Purposes of Man; with Further Reflections* (London, 1824), p. 20.
21. Ibid., p. 21.
22. Ibid., p. 22.
23. Ibid., pp. 79–80.
24. Ibid., p. 94.
25. Ibid., p. 13.
26. Ibid., p. 31.
27. *Responsa Yehudah Yaaleh*, pt. 1, sec. 164:3.
28. *Responsa Har Zevi*, Y.D. 11:1.
29. See Isaak Dembo, "HaChana LeShehita," *HaMelitz* (1892), and idem, *Jewish Manner of Slaughter* (London, 1894).
30. See I. Lewin, M. L. Munk, and J. J. Berman, *Religious Freedom: The Right to Practice Shehitah* (New York, 1946), pp. 179 ff., and in particular Yehiel Yaakov Weinberg, *Sheelot uTeshubot Seridei Eish*, 1: 1–172, 3, sec. 90, for a definitive study of the issue. Salomon Sassoon, *A Critical Study of Electrical Stunning and the Jewish Method of Slaughter* (Letchworth, 1955), concludes that stunning an animal is a clear violation of Jewish law. However, Federbusch, *Binetivot haTalmud*, pp., 209 ff., sees no impropriety in the act of stunning.

31. *Sanh.* 43a.
32. *Responsa Minhat Yitzhak,* pt. II, sec. 27:4.
33. Moses Feinstein, *Iggrot Moshe, Y.D.,* pt. II, no. 18 (New York, 1973).
34. It appears in *Shehita,* pt. II of *"Edut Ne'emana": Religious and Historical Research on the Jewish Method of Slaughter,* ed. Michael L. Munk and Eli Munk (Jerusalem, 1976).
35. Ibid., p. 198.
36. Ibid., p. 165.
37. Ibid., p. 185.
38. *Iggrot Moshe, Y.D.,* pt. II, no. 18.

Chapter 15
1. Commentary to Gen. 46:34, Exod. 8:22, 19:9.
2. See Testament of Moses HeHasid in Israel Abrahams, ed., *Hebrew Ethical Wills,* 2 vols. (Philadelphia, 1926), 2:289.
3. Abarbanel to Isa. 11:7 and Gen. 9:3.
4. Gen. 1:29, 9:3.
5. Pt. 3, chap. 41 (Poland).
6. *Sefer haIkkarim,* trans. Isaac Husik (1930), vol. III, chap. 15, pp. 129–130.
7. Ibid., p. 133.
8. Ibid.
9. Ibid, p. 137.
10. "Afikim baNegeb," in *HaPeles* (Berlin), 1903–4; "Talele Orot," in *Takhkemoni* (Berne), 1910.
11. *Olat Rayah* (Jerusalem: Mosad HaRav Kook, 1949) 2:292, quoted in *Abraham Isaac Kook,* trans. by Ben Zion Bokser (New York: Paulist Press, 1978), p. 23.
12. See *Responsa Sdei Chemed,* vol. 6; *Yakhel Shlomo* to *S.A., O.H.* 529:2, *Kerem Shlomo* to *S.A., Y.D.* 1; *Responsa of Moshe Halevi Steinberg,* no. 1 (cited by Richard Schwartz, *Judaism and Vegetarianism* [New York, 1982], p. 148, n. 3).
13. See Louis I. Rabinowitz, "Rabbinics vs. Vegetarianism," *Jewish Vegetarian* 45 (Summer 1978): 34.
14. Ibid. Cited in Louis Berman, *Vegetarianism and the Jewish Tradition* (New York, 1982), p. 37.
15. Philip Pick, "Agnon, Teller of Tales," in *The Tree of Life* (New York, 1977), p. 56.
16. "When Keeping Kosher Isn't Enough," *New York Times,* Sept. 14, 1977, p. 64 (cited by Schwartz, pp. 125–126).
17. Zalman Schachter, introduction to Berman, *Vegetarianism and the Jewish Tradition,* p. xiii.

BIBLIOGRAPHY

1. General

Abrahams, Israel. *Hebrew Ethical Wills.* 2 vols. Philadelphia, 1926, 1948.
———. *Jewish Life in the Middle Ages.* New York and Philadelphia, 1958.
Altmann, A., ed. *Biblical and Other Studies.* Cambridge, Mass., 1963.
Baron, Salo W. *A Social and Religious History of the Jews.* 17 vols. New York, 1952–1980.
Berman, Jeremiah J. *Shehita: A Study in the Cultural and Social Life of the Jewish People.* New York, 1941.
Berman, Louis A. *Vegetarianism and the Jewish Tradition.* New York, 1983.
Bin-Gorion, M. J. *Mimekor Yisrael* (Eng. trans.). 4 vols. Bloomington, Ind., 1976.
Bodenheimer, F. S. *Animal and Man in Bible Lands.* Leiden, 1960.
Bousquet, G. H. "Des Animaux et de leur traitement selon le Judaisme le Christianisme et l'Islam." *Studia Islamica,* Paris, 1958.
Carson, Gerald. *Man, Beasts, Gods: A History of Cruelty and Kindness to Animals.* New York, 1972.
Clark, Bill. "Animals of the Bible: Living links to Antiquity." *Biblical Archeological Review* 7, no. 1 (January–February 1981).
Cohen, Noah J. *Tsaar Baale Hayim.* Washington, D.C., 1959.
Contenau, G. *Everyday Life in Babylonia and Assyria.* London, 1954.
Daube, David. *Ancient Hebrew Fables.* Oxford, 1973.
De Vaux, Roland. *Ancient Israel.* 2 vols. New York, 1965.
Dembo, Isaak Alexandrovich. *The Jewish Method of Slaughter.* London, 1894.
Diole, Philippe. *The Errant Ark: Man's Relationship With Animals.* New York, 1974.
Dov Baer b. Samuel. *In Praise of the Baal Shem Tov: The Earliest Collection of Legends about the Founder of Hasidism.* Trans. Dan Ben-Amos and Jerome R. Mintz. Bloomington, Ind., 1970.
Douglas, Mary. *Purity and Danger.* London, 1976.
Dresner, Samuel, and Seymour Siegel. *The Jewish Dietary Laws.* New York, 1959.
Driver, G. R., and J. C. Miles. *The Babylonian Laws.* Oxford, 1952.
Encyclopaedia Britannica. 24 vols. Chicago, 1955.
Encyclopaedia Judaica. 16 vols. Jerusalem, 1972.
Feliks, Jehuda. *The Animal World of the Bible.* Tel Aviv, 1962.
Fletcher, Joseph F. *Morals and Medicine.* Princeton, 1954.
Fluegel, Gustavus, ed. *Corani, Textus Arabicus.* Leipzig, 1883.
Frankfort, Henri. *Kingship and the Gods.* Chicago, 1948.

————, and H. A. Frankfort. *The Intellectual Adventure of Ancient Man.* Chicago, 1946.

Frazer, James G. *The New Golden Bough.* Ed. Theodor H. Gaster. New York, 1959.

Friedlander, Michael. *The Jewish Religion.* New York, 1946.

Gandhi, M. K. *Diet and Diet Reform.* Ahmedabad, 1949.

Gaster, Moses. *The Exempla of the Rabbis.* New York, 1968.

————, ed. *Ma'aseh Book.* 2 vols. Philadelphia, 1934.

Gaster, Theodor. *Myth, Legend and Culture in the Old Testament.* New York, 1969.

Ginzberg, Louis. *The Legends of the Jews.* 7 vols. Philadelphia, 1909–28.

Godlovitch, Stanley, Rosalind Godlovitch, and John Harris. *Animals, Men and Morals: An Enquiry into the Maltreatment of Non-Humans.* London and New York, 1972.

Goldsmith, Oliver. *Citizen of the World* in *Collected Works,* ed. A. Friedman, Oxford, 1966.

Gompertz, Lewis. *Moral Inquiries on the Situation of Man and of Brutes on the Crime of Committing Cruelty on Brutes, and of Sacrificing Them to the Purpose of Man's with Further Reflections.* London, 1824.

Gordon, Cyrus H. *Ugaritic Literature.* Rome, 1949.

Gray, John. *Near Eastern Mythology.* Hamlyn, 1969.

Green, Joe. *The Jewish Vegetarian Tradition.* Johannesburg, 1969.

Guttmann, Julius. *Philosophies of Judaism.* New York, 1964.

Hastings, James, ed. *Encyclopedia of Religion and Ethics.* 13 vols. New York, 1912.

Heidel, Alexander. *The Gilgamesh Epic and Old Testament Parallels.* Chicago, 1946.

Hertz, Joseph Herman, ed. *The Pentateuch and Haftorahs.* London, 1938.

Hirsch, Samson Raphael. *Horeb: A Philosophy of Jewish Laws and Observances.* London, 1962.

Horowitz, George. *The Spirit of Jewish Law.* New York, 1953.

Husik, Isaac. *A History of Medieval Jewish Philosophy.* New York, 1958.

Jacobs, J. *Studies in Biblical Archaeology.* London, 1894.

James. E. O. *Myth and Ritual in the Ancient Near East.* New York, 1958.

Jakobovits, Immanuel. *Jewish Medical Ethics.* New York, 1959.

James, William. *The Varieties of Religious Experience.* London, 1952.

Jewish Encyclopedia. 12 vols. New York and London, 1901–12.

Kadushin, Max. *Worship and Ethics.* Evanston, Ill., 1964.

Kaufmann, Yehezkel. *The Religion of Israel.* Trans. M. Greenberg. Chicago, 1960.

Klapholz, Yisrael Yaakov. *Tales of the Baal Shem Tov.* 2 vols. Jerusalem, 1974.

Lea, H. C. *History of the Inquisition.* 4 vols. New York, 1907.

Lecky, William E. H. *History of European Morals from Augustus to Charlemagne.* London, 1911.

Levi-Strauss, Claude. *The Raw and the Cooked.* New York, 1969.

Lewin, B. M. "Zur Chamleristik und Biographie des R. Scherira Gaon." *Jahrbuch der juedisch-literarischen Gesellschaft* 7 (1910).

Lewin, Isaac, Michael L. Munk, and Jeremiah J. Berman. *Religious Freedom: The Right to Practice Shehita.* New York, 1946.

Lieberman, Saul. *Hellenism in Jewish Palestine.* New York, 1950.

———. "How Much Greek in Jewish Palestine?" In *Biblical and Other Studies,* ed. A. Altmann. Cambridge, Mass. 1963.

Luckenbill, Daniel D. *Ancient Records of Assyria and Babylonia.* New York. 1968.

Mercer, Samuel A. B. "The Religion of Ancient Egypt." In *Forgotten Religions,* ed. Vergilius Ferm. New York, 1950.

Mintz, Jerome R. *Legends of the Hasidim: An Introduction to Hasidic Culture and Oral Tradition in the New World.* Chicago and London, 1968.

Morris, Richard Knowles, and Michael Fox, eds. *The Fifth Day: Animal Rights and Human Ethics.* Washington, D.C., 1978.

Munk, Elie. *The Call of the Torah.* Trans. E. S. Maser. Jerusalem and New York, 1980.

Munk, Michael L., and Elie Munk, eds. *Edut Ne'emana: Religious and Historical Research on the Jewish Method of Slaughter.* Jerusalem, 1976.

Nahman of Nemirov. *Rabbi Nahman's Wisdom.* Trans. Aryeh Kaplan. New York, 1973.

Newman, Louis I. *The Hasidic Anthology: Tales and Teachings of the Hasidim.* New York, 1944.

———. *Maggidim and Hasidim: Their Wisdom.* New York, 1962.

Noth, Martin. *Exodus.* New York, 1962.

———. *Leviticus.* New York, 1977.

Noy, Dov, ed. *Folktales of Israel.* Chicago, 1963.

Pearl, C. *The Medieval Jewish Mind.* London, 1971.

Pedersen, Johannes. *Israel: Its Life and Culture.* Oxford, 1926.

Pliny. *Natural History.* New York, 1909.

Preuss, Julius. *Biblical and Talmudic Medicine.* Trans. Fred Rosner. New York and London, 1978.

Primatt, Humphrey. *Dissertation on the Duty of Mercy and Sin of Cruelty to Brute Beasts.* London, 1776

Pritchard, J. *Ancient Near Eastern Texts Relating to the Old Testament.* 2d ed. Princeton, 1958.

Plutarch. "On Flesh Eating," "On Intelligence," and "That the Lower Animals Reason." In *Moralia.* 15 vols. Cambridge, Mass., 1936.

Regan, Tom, and Peter Singer. *Animal Rights and Human Obligations.* Englewood Cliffs, 1976.

Reider, Joseph. *Deuteronomy with Commentary.* Philadelphia, 1948.

Reines, A. J. "Maimonides' Concept of Providence and Theodicy." *Hebrew Union College Annual* 43 (1977).

Ritson, Joseph. *An Essay on Abstinence from Animal Food as a Moral Duty.* London, 1802.

Rosner, Fred. *Medicine in the Bible and the Talmud.* New York, 1977.

———. *Modern Medicine and Jewish Law.* New York, 1972.

346 ○ Animal Life in Jewish Tradition

Rowley, H. H. "Zadok and Nehushtan." *Journal of Biblical Literature,* 1939.

Russell, Bertrand. *A History of Western Philosophy.* New York, 1945.

Saggs, H. W. F. *The Greatness That Was Babylon.* New York, 1962.

Sassoon, Salomon. *A Critical Study of Electrical Stunning and the Jewish Method of Slaughter.* Letchworth, 1955.

Schatz, Elihu A. *Proof of the Accuracy of the Bible.* New York, 1973.

Schechter, Solomon. *Studies in Judaism.* Second Series. Philadelphia, 1908.

Scholem, Gershom. *Jewish Gnosticism, Merkabah Mysticism, and Talmudic Tradition.* New York, 1960.

———. *Kabbalah.* New York, 1974.

———. *Major Trends in Jewish Mysticism.* New York, 1941.

———. *On the Kabbalah and Its Symbolism.* New York, 1969.

Simoons, Frederick J. *Eat Not This Flesh: Food Avoidances in the Old World.* Madison, Wis., 1967.

Singer, Peter. *Animal Liberation: A New Ethic for our Treatment of Animals.* New York, 1975.

Smith, William Robertson. "Animal Worship and Animal Tribes Among the Ancient Arabs and in the Old Testament." *Journal of Philosophy* 9 (1880).

———. *Lectures on the Religion of the Semites.* 3d ed. New York, 1969–70.

St. Augustine. *The Catholic and Manichaean Way of Life.* Boston, 1966.

St. Francis of Assisi: *His Life and Writings as Recorded by his Contemporaries.* London, 1959.

Stein, S. "The Dietary Laws in Rabbinic and Patristic Literature." *Studia Patristica,* vol. 64.

Strack and Billerback. *Kommentar zum Neuen Testament aus Talmud und Midrash,* 1928.

Strauss, Leo. *Persecution and the Art of Writing.* Glencoe, 1952.

Thoreau, David. *Walden.* Garden City, New York, 1970.

Trachtenberg, Joshua. *Jewish Magic and Superstition.* New York, 1979.

Twersky, Isadore. *Introduction to the Code of Maimonides.* New Haven and London, 1980.

Unna, Isak. *Tierschutz im Judentum.* Frankfort-a-Main, 1928.

Vajda, Georges. "Le Probleme de la Souffrance Gratuite selon Yusuf Al-Basir" in *Revue des études Juives. Historica judaica.* Rome, 1972.

Waxman, Meyer. *A History of Jewish Literature.* 4 vols. New York, 1948.

Williams, Howard. *The Ethics of Diet.* Manchester, London, 1907.

Wolfson, Harry A. *Studies in the History of Philosophy and Religion,* ed. I. Twersky and G. Williams. 2 vols. Cambridge, Mass. 1973–76.

———. *The Philosophy of the Church Fathers.* 3rd. ed. Cambridge, 1970.

Yadin, Yigal. "Further Light on Biblical Hazor." *Biblical Archaeology* XX, May, 1957.

Zinberg, Israel. *A History of Jewish Literature,* trans. from Yiddish by Bernard Martin. Cleveland and London, 1972.

Zimmels, H. J. *Magicians, Theologians and Doctors.* London, 1952.

2. Hebrew Sources

"Afikim baNegeb." Abraham Isaac HaKohen Kook. In *HaPeles* (Berlin) 1903–4.
Akedat Yitzhak. Isaac Arama. Jerusalem, 1960.
Alphabet of Ben Sira. Ed. M. Steinschneider. Berlin, 1858.
Anu uVaalei Hayyim. Aryeh Shoshan. Tel Aviv, 1963.
Arbaáh Turim. Jacob ben Asher. Warsaw, 1860–69.
Arukh haShalem. A. Kohut. New York, 1955.
Arukh haShulhan. Yehiel Michal Halevi Epstein. 8 vols. New York, n.d.
Avot de Rabbi Natan. Ed. S. Schechter. New York, 1945.
Ateret Zekenim. Isaac Abravanel. Jerusalem, 1967.
Baalei Hayyim B'Sifrut Yisrael, Bein Yehudi L'Vehemto. Aryeh Shoshan. Rehovot, 1971.
"BeDin Tzaar Baalei Hayyim l'zarchei Refuah." *Noam* 4 (1961).
Ben haMelekh veHanazir. Abraham Ibn Hasdai. Amsterdam, 1766. Trans. in M. J. Bin-Gorion, *Mimekor Yisrael*. Bloomington, Ind., 1976.
Beit haMidrash. Ed. A. Jellinek. 2 vols. Jerusalem, 1967.
Beit Joseph. Joseph Karo. In standard editions of *Arbaa'h Turim*.
B'eur haGra. Elijah of Vilna. In standard editions of *Shulhan Arukh*.
Binetivot haTalmud. Simon Federbusch. Jerusalem, 1956/57.
Cuzari. Yehudah Halevi. Hebrew trans. by Judah Ibn Tibbon, ed. A. Zifroni. Tel Aviv, 1948. English trans. by H. Hirschfield. New York, 1946.
Darkhei Moshe. Moses Isserles. In standard editions of *Arbaáh Turim*.
Derekh haShem. Moses Hayyim Luzzatto. Jerusalem and New York, 1978. English trans. by A. Kaplan. *The Way of God*. Jerusalem and New York, 1978.
Derisha uPerisha. Joshua Falk Cohen. In standard editions of *Shulhan Arukh*.
Dor Dor veDorshav. Issac Hirsch Weiss. New York and Berlin, 1884.
Emunot veDeot. Saadiah ben Joseph Gaon. Josefov, 1885. English trans. by Samuel Rosenblatt. *The Book of Beliefs and Opinions*. New Haven, 1948.
Encyclopedia Miqrait. 7 vols. Jerusalem, 1950–.
Encyclopedia Talmudit. 15 vols. Jerusalem, 1947–.
"Hachana LeShehita." Isaak Alexandrovich Dembo. *Hamelitz*, 1892.
Ha-Elah Anat. M. D. Cassuto. Jerusalem, 1951.
Ha-Emunah ha-Ramah. Abraham Ibn Daud. Jerusalem, 1966.
Haggahot veHiddushei Dinim (Mappah). Moses Isserles. In standard editions of *Shulhan Arukh*.
HaHai beArtsot ha-Mikrah. F. S. Bodenheimer. 2 vols. 1951, 1956.
HaMashal be-Sifrut ha-Agada; Tipusim uMotivim. Dov Noy. Jerusalem, 1960.
HaMishpat haIvri. Menahem Elon. 3 vols. Jerusalem, 1973.
HaTalmud veHokhmat haRefuah. I. L. Katzenelson. Berlin, 1928.
Hatam Sofer, Moses (Schreiber) Sofer. 7 parts, 5 vols. Jerusalem, 1969/70, 1971/72.
HaYehudi haKadosh. Z. M. Rabinovicz. Piotrkow, 1932.
Hazal. Ephraim E. Urbach. Jerusalem, 1969. English trans. *The Sages: Their Concepts and Beliefs*. 2 vols. Jerusalem, 1971.

Hegyon ha-Nefesh. Abraham bar Hiyya. Ed. Freimann, Leipzig, 1860. English trans., G. Wigoder, London, 1969.

HeHai B'Mishna. Jerusalem: Institute for Mishna Research, 1972.

Hiddushei Halakhot va-Aggadot. Samuel Edels (Maharsha). In standard editions of *Talmud Bavli.*

Hiddushim. Yom Tov ben Abraham Ishbili (Ritba). *Talmud Bavli,* Warsaw, 1902.

Hobot HaLebabot. Bahya ibn Pakuda. Ed. A. Zifroni. Jerusalem, 1928.

Iggeret Baale Hayyim. Trans. Kalonymos ben Kalonymos. Ed. Habermann. Jerusalem, 1949.

Kalila veDimna. Ed. J. Derenbourgue. Paris, 1881.

Kav haYashar. Zevi Hirsch Kaidanover. Frankfurt am Main, 1903.

Keli Yakar. Solomon Efraim Lunchitz. In standard rabbinic editions of Pentateuch.

Kesef Mishna. Joseph Karo. In standard editions of *Mishneh Torah.*

Keter Malhut. Solomon Ibn Gabirol. Sephardic prayerbook.

Kitve R. Abraham Epstein. Abraham Epstein. Ed. A. M. Haberman. Jerusalem, 1950.

Kitzur Shulhan Arukh. Solomon Ganzfried. Jerusalem, 1954.

Kol Bo. New York, 1945/46.

Kol Yaakov. Jacob Kranz. Warsaw, 1869/70.

Likkutei Maharil. Jacob ben Moses Halevi Mollin. Amsterdam, 1730.

Ma'amar haIkkarim. Moses Hayyim Luzzatto. Jerusalem and New York, 1978.

Maarchei Lev. Judah Leib Zirelsohn. Kishinev, 1932.

Maaseh Buch. Trans. Moses Gaster. 2 vols. Philadelphia, 1934.

Magen Abraham. Abraham Gumbiner. In standard editions of *Shulhan Arukh.*

Mekhilta de Rabbi Ishmuel. Ed. J. Lauterbach. 3 vols. Philadelphia, 1933.

MeNoah ad Avraham. M. D. Cassuto. Jerusalem, 1959. English trans., *From Adam to Noah,* Jerusalem, 1953.

Menorat haMaor. Isaac Aboab. Ed. J. Fries. Jerusalem, 1961.

Menorat haMaor. Israel Al-Nakawa. Ed. H. Enelow. 4 vols. New York, 1929–32.

Meor Einayim. Azariah de Rossi. Ed. Cassel. Vilna, 1866.

Meshalim Vegam Sipurim. Jacob Kranz. Tel Aviv, 1956/57.

Mesholim. Eliezer Steinbarg. Tev Aviv, 1956.

Mesillat Yesharim. Moses Hayyim Luzzatto. Ed. M. Kaplan, Philadelphia, 1948.

Midrash haGadol. Ed. Margaliot. Jerusalem, 1947.

Midrash haGadol: Bereshit. Ed. S. Schechter, Cambridge, 1902.

Midrash haGadol: Shemot. Ed. D. Hoffman, Berlin, 1913.

Midrash Lekah Tov. Ed. S. Buber, Vilna, 1884.

Midrash Megillat Esther. In A. Jellinek, *Beit ha-Midrash.* 2 vols. Jerusalem, 1967.

Midrash Otiyot de Rabbi Akiba, I, II. In A. Jellinek, *Beit ha-Midrash.* 2 vols. Jerusalem, 1967.

Midrash Pesikta Rabbati. Ed. M. Friedmann. Vienna, 1880. English trans. William G. Braude. 2 vols. New Haven, 1968.

Midrash Rabbah. Vilna: Romm, 1921.

Midrash Rabbah: Bereshit Rabbah. Ed. J. Theodor and H. Albeck. 3 vols. Jerusalem, 1965.
Midrash Rabbah: Vayikra Rabbah. Ed. M. Margulies. Jerusalem, 1972.
Midrash Rabbah. English trans. H. Freedman and M. Simon. 10 vols. London, 1939.
Midrash Sechel Tob. Ed. S. Buber. Berlin, 1900.
Midrash Shmuel. Ed. S. Buber. Cracow, 1893.
Midrash Soher Tob. In A. Jellinek, *Beit ha-Midrash.* 2 vols., Jerusalem, 1967.
Midrash Tanhuma. Ed. S. Buber. 2 vols. Jerusalem, 1963–64.
Midrash Tehillim. Ed. S. Buber. Jerusalem, 1965/66. English trans. by William Braude. *The Midrash on Psalms.* 2 vols. New Haven, 1959.
Midrash Temurah. In A. Jellinek, *Beit ha-Midrash.* 2 vols. Jerusalem, 1967.
Milhamot haShem. Levi ben Gershon. Leipzig, 1866.
Minhat Bikkurim. H. J. Zimmels. Vienna, 1926.
Mishlei Shualim. Berekhia ha-Nakdon. Ed. A. M. Habermann. Jerusalem and Tel Aviv, 1946.
Mishnah. 12 vols. New York, 1963.
Mishnah Berurah. Israel Meir haKohen. 6 vols. New York, n.d.
Mishneh Torah. Moses Maimonides. Vilna: Rosencrantz, 1900.
Mordecai. Mordecai ben Hillel. In standard editions of *Talmud Bavli.*
Moreh Nebukhim. Moses Maimonides. Warsaw, 1872. English trans. by S. Pines. *The Guide of the Perplexed.* Chicago, 1963.
Nahalat Abot. Isaac Abravanel. New York, 1953.
Nimuke Yosef. Joseph Habib. Standard editions of *Alfasi.*
"Nisyonim Madaiim shel Gufot Baalei Hayyim." Zevi Natan Friedman. *Noam,* vol. 5.
Noda B'Yehudah. Ezekiel Landau. 2 vols. Jerusalem, 1960.
Or Adonoi. Don Hasdai Crescas. Vienna, 1860.
Or heHayyim. Hayyim ben Moses Ibn Ittar. In standard rabbinic editions of Pentateuch.
Orhot Hayyim. Aaron haKohen of Lunel. Berlin, 1898–1902.
Orhot Tzaddikim. Vilna, 1913.
Otzar Dinim uMinhagim. Judah David Eisenstein. New York, 1917.
Otzar haGeonim. Benjamin M. Levin. 13 vols. Haifa, 1928–43.
Otzar haKetubot haPinkiot. Nahum Slouschz. Tel Aviv, 1942.
Otzar haPoskim. 9 vols. Jerusalem, 1962–65.
Pardes Rimonim. Moses b. Jacob Cordovero. Munkács, 1906.
Perek Shira. Ed. E. M. Beit-Arie. 2 vols. Jerusalem, 1966.
Perush Ibn Ezra. Abraham Ibn Ezra. In standard rabbinic editions of Pentateuch.
Perush al haTorah. Samuel David Luzzatto. Tel Aviv: Dvir, 1965.
Perush haTorah. Bahya ben Asher. Ed. C. Chavel. Jerusalem, 1968.
Perush haTorah. Moses b. Nahman (Nachmanides). Ed. C. Chavel. Jerusalem, 1966/67.
Perush haTorah. Isaac Abravanel. Warsaw, 1862.

Perush al Neviim uKetubim. Isaac Abravanel. Tel Aviv, 1959/60.

Perush al haMishnah. Moses Maimonides. Jerusalem, 1963.

Perush RaDBaZ. David ibn Abi Zimra. In standard editions of *Mishneh Torah.*

Perush Rashi. Rabbenu Shlomo Yitzhaki. In standard rabbinic editions of Pentateuch and standard editions of *Talmud Bavli.*

Pesakim uKetavim. Israel b. Petahiah Isserlein. In *Terumot haDeshen.* Tel Aviv, n.d.

Pesikta de-Rab Kahana. Ed. S. Buber. Lyck, 1868. English trans. by William G. Braude and Israel J. Kapstein. (Philadelphia, 1975).

Pesiqta Rabbati. Ed. M. Friedmann. Vienna, 1880. English trans. by William G. Braude. 2 vols. New Haven, 1968.

Pirke deRabbi Eliezer. Jerusalem, 1969/70. English trans. by Gerald Friedlander. London, 1916.

Piske Maharig. Yehudah Gershon Ashkenazi. Kolomayya, 1903.

Pnei Yehoshua. Joshua of Cracow. Lemberg, 1860.

"Rahamim." Zalman Schneour. In *Shirim* (Tel-Aviv), 1958/59.

RaSHBaM. Samuel ben Meir. In standard editions of *Talmud Bavli.*

Rimze haHaftarot. Eliezer of Worms. Warsaw, 1875.

Sefer haBehemot. Shalom Jacob Abramowitz (Mendele). In vol. 1 of *Alleh Verk fun Mendele Mocher Sefarim* (Cracow, 1911).

Sefer haHinnukh. Aaron haLevi of Barcelona. Ed. Chavel. Jerusalem, 1952.

Sefer haIkkarim. Joseph Albo. English trans. by Isaac Husik. 4 vols. Philadelphia, 1930.

Sefer haIttur. Isaac ben Abba Mari. New York, 1955.

Sefer haMa'asiyot. M. Ben Yehezkel. Rev. ed. 6 vols. Tel Aviv, 1960.

Sefer haManhig. Abraham haYarhi. Ed. I. Refael. 2 vols. Jerusalem, 1978.

Sefer haMaor. Zerahiah haLevi. Ed. Ehrenreich. Jerusalem, 1967.

Sefer haMitzvot. Moses Maimonides. Jerusalem, 1952/53.

Sefer haOlam haKatan. Joseph ibn Zaddik. Ed. S. Horowitz. Breslau, 1903.

Sefer haRokeach. Eliezer ben Judah of Worms. Ed. B. Schneerson. Jerusalem, 1966.

Sefer Hasidim. Ed. R. Margulies. Jerusalem, 1957.

Sefer Hasidim. Ed. J. Wistinetzki. Frankfort a.M. 1924.

Sefer haYashar. Jacob b. Meir Tam. Ed. Schlesinger. Jerusalem, 1959.

Sefer haYashar (Midrashim). Warsaw, 1889.

Sefer Nahat haShulhan. Nahman of Tcherin, Jerusalem, 1977.

Sefer Recanati: Piske Halakhot. Menahem Recanati. Sedilkow, 1836.

Sefer Shaar haGilgulim. Hayyim Vital Calabrese. Tel Aviv, 1962/63.

Sefer Yesod Olam. Isaac Israeli. Ed. B. Goldberg. 2 vols. Berlin, 1848–51.

Shaarei Teshubah. Judah heHasid Gerondi. Jerusalem, 1961.

Sheelot YaAVeTZ. Jacob Emden. New York, 1961.

Sheelot uTeshubot Havoth Yair. Yair Hayyim Bacharach. Frankfurt amMain, 1899.

Sheelot uTeshubot Hayyim Sha'al. Hayyim Joseph David Azulai. Lemberg, 1886.

Sheelot uTeshubot Maharsham. Shalom Mordecai Schwadron. 6 vols. Warsaw, 1902–46.

Sheelot uTeshubot Seredei Eish. Yehiel Yaakob Weinberg. Jerusalem, 1961–69.
Sheelot uTeshubot Yabeah Omer. Obadiah Yosef. Jerusalem, 1938.
Sheelot uTeshubot Shemesh Zedakah. Samson Morpurgo. Venice, 1743.
Shivhei haBesht. Dov Baer b. Samuel. Lemberg, 1908.
Shulhan Arukh. Joseph Karo. 10 vols. Vilna, 1874/75.
Shulhan Arukh. Shneur Zalman of Liadi. 4 vols. New York, 1970/71.
Siddur Avodat Yisrael. S. Baer. Tel Aviv, 1957.
Siddur Beit Tefillah. Nusach Sefarad. Vilna, 1900.
Siddur Beit Yaakob. Jacob Israel b. Zeb Emden. Zhitomir, 1880.
Sifra (Torat Kohanim). Ed. I. H. Weiss. New York, 1947.
Sifrei. Ed. Finkelstein. New York, 1939.
Sifrei Zutta. Ed. S. Horowitz. Breslau, 1917.
Sifte Hahamim. In standard rabbinic editions of Pentateuch.
Sifte Kohen. Shabbetai haKohen. In standard editions of *Shulhan Arukh.*
"Simha Lev Dakka." Saul Tchernichowsky. In *Kitve Shaul Tchernichowsky,* 8 vols. Vilna, 1929–.
Sipurei Baalei Hayyim beEdot Yisrael. Dov Noy. Haifa, 1976.
"Talele Orot." Abraham Isaac haKohen Kook. In *Takhkemoni,* Berne, 1910.
Talmud Bavli. 20 vols. Vilna, 1895.
Talmud Yerushalmi. 7 vols. Vilna, 1921–22.
Tanna d'vei Eliyahu. (Seder Eliyahu Rabbah veSeder Eliyahu Zuta). Ed. M. Friedman, Vienna, 1902.
Teshuba meAhavah. Eleazer Fleckeles. Prague, 1809.
Teshubot haGeonim. Abraham Elijah Harkavy. Jerusalem, 1966.
Tiferet haAdam. A. Tkhursch. Jerusalem, 1951.
Toledot haEmunah haYisraelit. Yehezkel Kaufmann. 4 vols. Jerusalem, 1955.
Tomar Deborah. Moses b. Jacob Cordovero. Petah Tikva, 1953.
Torah Shlemah. Menahem M. Kasher. 27 vols. New York, Jerusalem, 1938–82.
Tosefet Rishonim. Saul Lieberman. 4 vols. Jerusalem, 1937–39.
Tosefta. Vilna, 1911.
Tosefta Atikata. Ed. Hayyim H. Hurwitz. Cracow, 1889.
Tosefta kiFeshuta. Ed. Saul Lieberman. 13 vols. New York, 1955–73.
Turei Zahab. David b. Samuel Halevi. In standard editions of *Shulhan Arukh.*
Yakar Tiferet. David ibn Abi Zimra (RaDBaZ). Ed. S. B. Werner. Jerusalem, 1945.
Yalkut haMakhiri. Makhir b. Abba Mari. Berlin, 1893.
Yalkut Reuveni. Comp. Reuven Hoeshke. Hamburg, 1712.
Yalkut Shimoni. Comp. Shimon Ashkenazi. 2 vols. New York, 1944.
Yesodei haTorah. Samuel David Luzzatto. Jerusalem, 1947.
Yitzhak Baer Jubilee Volume. New York, 1960.
Zohar. Ed. R. Margoliot. 5 vols. Jerusalem, 1960. English trans. by H. Sperling and Maurice Simon. Soncino, 1970.
Zohar Hadash (Midrash haNeelam). Amsterdam, 1701.

INDEX